To Maureen,
for all your love
for the Paso fino horses.

Diego B.- July 24/2007

SCIENCE AND ART OF THE PASO FINO HORSE

By DIEGO BRAVO

ISBN: 1-4276-0609-9

The photographs in this book were taken/provided by Mildred Arent, Ada Barandica C., Bravo Equine Enterprises, Judy Brick Freedman, Olga García, Alba Regina López "AlGalope," Ulises Muñoz, Beth Nabors, Presidential press secretary of Colombia, Chery Prill Photo, Lynda Sanders, Jesús A. Soto, Ticker Time Paso Fino Farm, Tina Tripoli, Robin Varney, Larry Williams Photography, WNC Photography, and Darlene Wohlart.

The drawings on pages 236, 328 and 329 were originally by Cristian Cipriani for the book "*Caballo Colombiano Ciencia y Arte*" (written by Diego Bravo). The other drawings are by the author. All drawings for this book were ´finished´ by Cecilia Bravo.

Book designer Elkin A. Muñoz
Cover designer Laura M. Vélez

Disclaimer: Information in this book is accurate and complete to the best of my knowledge. However, recommendations made by the author are not guaranteed, since working with animals is both a science and an art. The author and Bravo Equine Enterprises disclaim any liability resulting from the use of information presented in this book.

PFHA and ***CONFEPASO*** rules referred to in this book have been updated through September 2006.

Printed in Medellín, Colombia (S.A.)
First Edition: March 2007

To my mother Cecilia and my father Mario,
who introduced me to the world of horses at the age of three,
and always taught me how to give my best to everything I do.

To my sisters Cecilia and Liliana
and brothers Fabio and Hernán,
who always encouraged and supported me
in all the projects I started.

To my beloved wife Olga,
who helped me throughout the process
of making this "dream book" come true.

To all my students with whom
I have had the opportunity to grow
over the past fifteen years.

A LITTLE ABOUT THE AUTHOR

I was born in Medellín, Colombia (South America) into a family of seven. As I remember, we always had a farm where we spent our weekends and vacations. I loved to go there, ride our Paso horses together as a family, and take care of them. From a very young age, I decided to stay in the world of horses - breeding, riding, and taking care of these graceful animals. Later as I entered *Universidad Nacional de Colombia* (in Medellín), horses became not only my passion, but also my profession.

Life guided me through most aspects of the fascinating world of horses, and also through the fulfilling experience of becoming a teacher. After some years of working professionally with horses during the day and teaching different courses at night in my beloved high school, *Colegio Calasanz - Medellín*, the son of one of my students asked me to teach him *everything* I knew about horses. I taught him how to ride, feed, tack, and take care of horses. This awoke in me an interest in sharing my knowledge about horses with others. Some notes that I wrote for him, and for others after him, became articles that were published in various horse magazines, and then they became four books, one for each semester of the school year. I used these books to teach students in the second Paso riding school that I founded.

Teaching all I knew about horses turned into a new way to ´live´ my passion for horses. This eventually took me to *Universidad de Antioquia* and *Universidad Nacional de Colombia* to teach "Producción Equina" (equine husbandry). In 2001, I published the book, "*Caballo Colombiano Ciencia y Arte*" for my students at the Universities and the riding school, plus many Spanish-speaking Paso horse enthusiasts in Colombia and other countries, such as Ecuador, Puerto Rico, and Venezuela.

In 2003, I moved to the United States with my wife, Olga, for me to start a Paso riding school (*Ocala's School of Equestrian Art*) in Ocala, Florida. Shortly after I arrived, I began writing a second book, this time in English, in order to share this information with as many people as possible. English is a new language for me, and of course the culture in America is different. But, both the language and the culture have provided me with a fascinating experience that has allowed me to grow personally and professionally.

This book is meant to be a "reference book" for all Paso Fino enthusiasts - to be read many times in the whole, and in part when the reader requires more in depth information on a particular aspect of the Paso Fino horse. Although each reader may have his or her own areas of interest, I recommend that the reader start at the beginning and read through all the chapters. In this way, when questions arise, the reader will immediately know where to locate the information that is required.

My wish is that you enjoy this book and that it enhances your interest in learning even more about this magnificent breed of horses.

Diego B.

CONTENTS

CHAPTER 1

IMPORTANCE OF THE HORSE THROUGHOUT TIME

A CHANGING FACTOR OF HISTORY

Since prehistoric time, the horse has played a very important role in human life. Based on archeological research, it has been determined that equines initially were hunted 23,000 years B.C. by ancient cultures, which used the meat as food and the skin as clothing and shelter. After thousands of years of hunting, horses were domesticated and became an important factor in history.

Dogs were probably the first domesticated mammal species. Later, other mammal species, such as cats, cattle, and sheep, were domesticated by nomadic and semi-sedentary tribes of the Old World, before horses were domesticated. However, no domesticated animal has had as great an influence on human civilization as the horse, due to the following reasons:

- Once horses began to be used as a means of transportation, people were able to travel long distances on land faster than ever before, and with much less effort. This allowed man tc conquer new wildernesses.
- Trade rapidly increased because horses provided fast transport of goods from the area of production to the trading centers.
- The cultures that had the largest and best trained armies with horses (used for both pulling wagons/chariots with warriors and for riding in the battlefield) dominated other cultures and expanded their empires.

After a time, the horse became extremely important not only as a means of transportation and in war, but also as a working tool (e.g., drafting, cattle herding) and as a means of communication (e.g., the great empires in history had riders on horses that transported messages quickly). In addition, equestrian sports developed and grew in popularity.

DOMESTICATION OF THE HORSE

It is not easy to determine the exact time when horses began to be domesticated or the place where it occurred. Most researchers agree that domestication could have started in different areas of the Old World, such as the Middle East (between the Black Sea and the Persian Gulf) and Central Asia, at the end of the Neolithic age (about 4,000 - 4,500 years B.C.). The initial purpose for herding horses was to use the meat as a protein source, the skin as clothing and shelter, and the manure as combustion for bonfires.

About 3,500 years B.C., domesticated horses were kept in many areas of the Old World by different cultures (from Spain and Morocco to China), not only to obtain food (milk, blood, and meat) and goods (clothing and shelter), but also for carrying, pulling, and moving loads. Later, the horse was used for riding. Since that time, the horse has become one of the most important underpinnings of different civilizations and has transformed lifestyles.

From the time the horse was domesticated until today, several changes occurred that resulted in better control of the horse. The first tack used on the horse was a piece of cord or line wrapped around its neck and extended, as a rope, for one or more people to hold. Soon after, a second wrap was added around the horse's muzzle for better control. The most vigorous horses required a third wrap of cord in their mouths for control, which was later replaced by bits made of hard materials, such as bone, horn, and wood (See Chapter 14: "The bit – magic or science?"). Bits made of metal were designed as soon as humans learned how to use different metals (e.g., copper, bronze, iron) between 1,200 and 700 years B.C.

Once the mechanical advantage of wheels was discovered, wheels began to be used with horses. Carts and heavy wagons with four wheels, and chariots with two wheels, were pulled by horses to transport goods and warriors. This provided efficiency in transportation and military power.

It is not known exactly when and where horses began to be shod. However, it is known that metal horseshoes were applied to the horse's hooves during both the Greek and Roman empires. At the beginning, the metal horseshoes were tied to the hooves with cords (not with nails), like sandals. Later they were nailed, as is done today. Horseshoes gave comfort to the horse's hooves for traveling long distances on abrasive surfaces, which allowed the cavalries of those empires to become faster and more powerful.

INSPIRATION OF ARTISTS

Since the time when man hunted equines to eat, the horse has been the inspiration of artists in many cultures. Probably the first artistic manifestations that were inspired by horses were several drawings found in Spanish and French caves from about 13,000 years B.C. They depict horses running alone and others being hunted by man.

After that, most human civilizations have displayed images of the horse in many different ways:

- Horses have been carved and painted on vases, plates, jars, etc., either for decoration or daily use, and on everyday useful tools (e.g., maces and knives).

- Carpets and furniture, such as chairs, tables, beds, and lamps, have been decorated with equine images.

- Artists from many cultures have immortalized the horse with drawings, paintings, sculptures, and carvings.
- Earrings, bracelets, pendants, rings, and other ornaments have been made in the shape of horses.
- The horse has been engraved on coins and printed on bills and stamps.
- Horses have been painted and embroidered on clothes and all kinds of accessories.
- Kings, emperors, and other celebrities have had their portraits painted while riding on horses.

The horse has influenced literature since at least the eighth century B.C., either as the main character or the main companion in literary adventures. Many novels, historical books, science fiction books, children's books, and cartoons have included the horse. In addition, many scientific and technical books have been written about horses.

The horse is an important companion in hundreds of movies and TV series, causing many children and adults to dream of owning these beautiful creatures. Who can forget, for example, the adventures of Roy Rogers and his palomino, Trigger; the Lone Ranger and his white horse, Silver; or Zorro and his black horse, Tornado?

The horse is the main character in movies and TV series, such as *The Black Stallion, Black Beauty, Fury, My Friend Flicka, National Velvet,* and *Sea Biscuit*. Also, horses have always played a crucial role in Westerns throughout movie history.

Today, worldwide, horse lovers wear T-shirts and caps with painted, printed or embroidered horse images. They also collect posters, photographs, calendars, and all kinds of horse memorabilia. In addition, the use of horse photos as computer screensavers becomes more popular every day.

THE HORSE IN MYTHOLOGY

The horse was so important in certain cultures that they made it part of their beliefs, cults, and religions. For instance, Greek mythology included horses pulling the carriages of their gods, Apollo, Helios, and Ares.

Different ancient civilizations used to bury sacrificed horses in the tombs of their warriors, tribal chiefs, emperors, and kings. Others used to sacrifice horses to their gods. Several civilizations adorned their temples with images of horses (sculptures, paintings, and carvings on rock or wooden façades).

CULTURE

Some cultures in the past were closely associated with horses. Who could imagine, for example, cultures like the Mongols, Barbs, Arabs, Greeks, and Romans without horses? Could the Christian crusades or Napoleon's infantry be imagined without horses? Many of these cultures developed important horsemanship techniques and produced several breeds of horses.

After horses were brought to the New World (the Americas) at the end of the fifteenth century, they spread to every corner of the continents. Several subcultures, very well-known for their horsemanship skills and the horse breeds that they produced, flourished. Some examples are the "Gauchos" from the Argentine "pampa" (prairie), the "Llaneros" from West Venezuela and East Colombia, the "Vaqueros" from the cattle farms in other areas of Colombia, the "Charros" from Mexico, and the Native Americans and the "Cowboys" from many places in the United States,.

Paso Fino horses are actually part of the culture in many Latin-American countries. In Colombia and Puerto Rico, Paso Finos are not only a very important means of transportation and work in the countryside, but also a sport and hobby that hundreds of thousands of people enjoy as horse breeders, riders (in horse shows, equitation competitions, or weekend trail rides), trainers, technicians, aficionados, or enthusiasts.

Medellín (the second largest Colombian city) celebrates "La Feria de las Flores" (the Flower Fair) from the last days of July through the first week of August every year. One of its central events is the "Cabalgata Feria de las Flores" (The Flower Fair Horse Parade), in which several thousand horses (mainly Paso Fino and the three Colombian diagonal Paso horse breeds) with their riders, participate in a huge parade along some of the city's main avenues. This event was awarded the *Guinness World Record* as "The Largest Horse Parade" on July 31st 1999, having 7,895 horses with their riders. The same event was awarded a new *Guinness World Record* on July 29th 2006, having 8,233 horses with their riders.

During the same fair weeks, the "Exposición Equina Grado A de Medellín," one of the most important Paso horse shows in Colombia, also takes place every year. Both events are like a party for Paso horse lovers, not only from Colombia, but for the many tourists from other countries. Likewise, most cities and little towns in Colombia have horse shows/parades within the annual celebration, "Fiestas Patronales" (a religious fair in remembrance of a Saint), or the annual civic fair.

THE HORSE INDUSTRY

In many countries, the horse industry greatly impacts the economy. The American horse industry, with over nine million horses of different breeds, is one of the strongest in the world. In Colombia, the country with the largest Paso Fino population in the world, there are over 2.5 million horses, including Paso Fino horses, the three Colombian diagonal Paso horse breeds, sport horse breeds, draft horse breeds, and work horses.

Although the impact of the equine industry in Colombia has not been formally estimated, it plays an important role, due to a combination of historic, geographic, and economic factors. Of prime importance is that the ancestral passion for horses began when the Spanish conquistadors used horses to colonize the Colombian territory. Geographic reasons for breeding horses are obvious in a country where much of the population lives in the mountainous areas and where horses and mules are still reliable means of transportation and work.

In addition, high quality Paso horses (Paso Fino, Pure Trocha, Trocha and Collected Galope, and Collected Trote and Galope) are highly prized not only for the internal market, but also for exportation to all the Americas and Europe.

Mr. Alvaro Uribe Vélez, President of Colombia since 2002, riding a Paso Fino horse. Note the cup of coffee held in his right hand, while the horse is in gait. Photo courtesy of the Presidential press secretary of Colombia.

EMPLOYEES IN THE PASO FINO HORSE INDUSTRY

Besides owners/breeders, the Paso Fino horse industry generates hundreds of thousands of jobs worldwide, either directly or indirectly involved with horses. Some of the main professions directly related to the horses are as follows:

- The **groom** takes care of the horse by feeding, maintaining clean waterers, cleaning the stall, brushing the horse's coat, etc. The groom must be patient and observant in order to understand the individual particularities and needs of each animal. A responsible groom knows each horse so well that it is very apparent when one behaves in a different way or seems sick. For example, the groom should check whether each one of the horses is eating and drinking water, that there is a normal amount of manure in the stall, with a normal texture and color, and whether the horse is acting normally or is depressed, anxious, or shows any injury or pain.
- The **trainer** develops the horse's skills and potential. Any Paso Fino horse may be beautiful, well-gaited, graceful, etc., but, before being trained, a horse is like a diamond before it is properly cut. The horse trainer is best described as the "horse's teacher," who prepares the animal to reach its potential (see Chapter 15: "Horse psychology and training").
- The **farrier** is in charge of trimming and shoeing the horse's hooves regularly in order to keep them healthy, with proper angles and shapes, and to assure that the legs are well-balanced (see Chapter 7: "Hoof trimming and shoeing").
- The **equine veterinarian** is a Doctor of Veterinary Medicine who is dedicated to studying and working with the equine species. A veterinarian works in several areas, such as disease prevention, attending to sick horses, applying reproductive technology, and adjusting the horse's environment. Veterinarians specialize in such areas as dentistry, reproduction, surgery, internal medicine, pathology, and exercise physiology.
- The horse **farm manager** is in charge of planning, organizing, administrating, and evaluating all the processes related to horses and personnel who work on the farm. Thus, the manager must understand all aspects of the horse business. The manager may also be responsible for hiring the other professionals who are needed on the farm (see Chapter 11: "Managing equine information").

Many other professionals, indirectly related to horses, play a role in the horse industry:

- Producing all kinds of horse supplies such as tack, horseshoes and nails, shoeing tools, medicines, feed and nutritional supplements, grooming implements, farm tools and equipment, fertilizers, insecticides, bedding material, fencing, etc.
- Manufacturing items for the rider, such as clothes, boots, helmets, hats, and chaps.
- Marketing and selling the many horse supplies.
- Staffing veterinary laboratories and horse hospitals.
- Researching horses and teaching at universities.
- Transporting horses or supplies.
- Building horse facilities (barns, fences, round pens, etc.).
- Directing horse associations.
- Judging all kinds of equestrian sports.
- Running riding schools.
- Marketing horses.
- Publishing horse magazines, books, and calendars.
- Painting, sculpting, and photographing horses.

In summary, horses have been important to humans for thousands of years and have had a major impact on human history. Today, horses still play an important role in recreation, sport, and work, and will no doubt continue to do so for many more years to come.

CHAPTER 2

EVOLUTIONARY HIGHLIGHTS OF TODAY'S HORSE

ZOOLOGICAL CLASSIFICATION

Special characteristics of the horse may be better understood by briefly studying the horses' zoological classification. All domestic horse breeds are of the same Species, ***Equus caballus***. Horses (domestic and wild), zebras, and asses (donkeys) of today are Genus ***Equus***.

Family ***Equidae*** includes not only today's Species of Genus ***Equus***, but also their ancestors. ***Equidae*** are described as mono-gastric (non-ruminant) with a large cecum (the first portion of the large intestine), 36 to 40 well-distinguishable teeth (incisors, canines, premolars, and molars), a cylindrical body with a medium-long neck that permits the mouth to reach the grass, and one toe per foot covered by a hoof.

Equidae are included in Sub-Order ***Perissodactyla***; they have an odd number of toes on their feet (one or three toes per foot) and each toe is covered by a hard, keratinized structure (hoof). ***Perissodactyla*** are part of Order ***Ungulata***, described as herbivores with big, flat premolars and molars adequate for chewing roughage, and long legs ending in hooves.

All ***Ungulata*** are included in Sub-Class ***Eutheria***, that develop placenta for the fetus during pregnancy, Class ***Mammalia***, that lactate their offspring after birth, and Super-Class ***Tetrapoda***, that have four legs for locomotion.

Class ***Tetrapoda*** are included in Sub-Phylum ***Vertebrata***, described as animals with a spinal column, and Phylum ***Chordata***, with a bilateral symmetry and a central nerve cord.

Chordata are part of Sub-Kingdom ***Eumetazoa*** (all animals except sponges) and Kingdom ***Animalia*** (all animals).

The following chart summarizes the zoological classification of the horse:

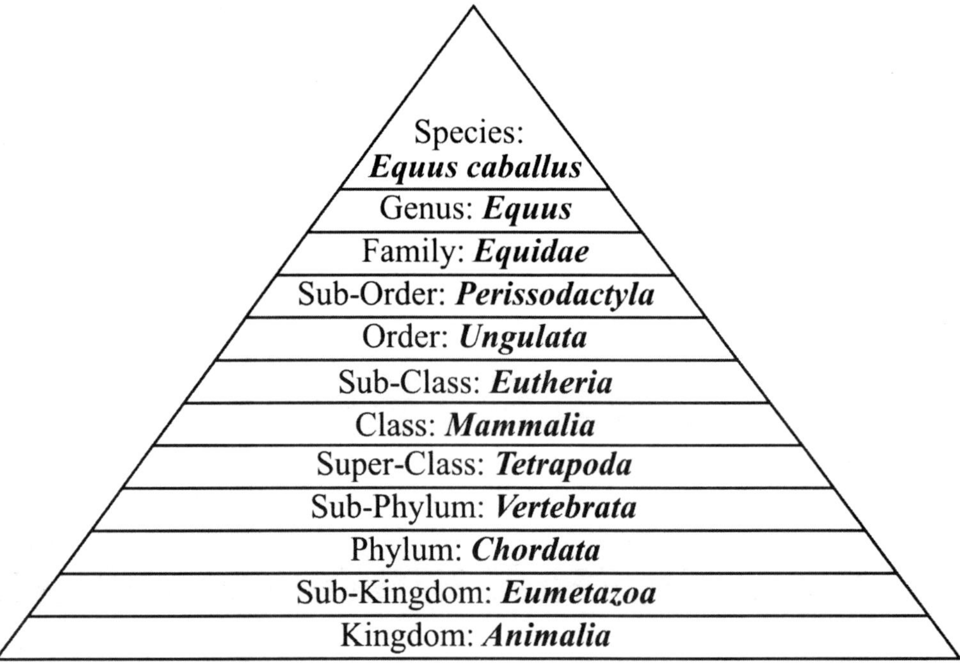

EVOLUTION OF THE HORSE

Domestic horses, like most plant and animal species of today, have had many evolutionary changes that are widely substantiated through scientific research of fossils. Horses began to evolve during "the Age of Mammals" (also known as Cenozoic Age).

The horse's evolution began approximately 60 million years ago (Eocene Epoch) from the ancient ***Eohippus***, whose size is commonly compared to that of a fox (about 12 to 16 inches in height and 14 to 25 lbs.). The front feet ended in four toes, and the hind feet in three toes, all slightly inclined toward the front. Although the toes did not have nails, they had little digital pads that were in contact with the ground, plus a bigger pad behind the toes. ***Eohippus*** lived in areas around rivers and in forests and jungles, where it ate the tender leaves of plants that it could reach from the ground; thus, its teeth were small. Although it was prey for predators, this species survived 20 million years by having a camouflaged coat that was brown with darker bands, so it could blend with plants, soil, and shade.

From ***Eohippus***, many species evolved in different directions until Genus ***Equus*** appeared. The most recognized species are described below:

Mesohippus replaced ***Eohhippus*** 25 - 40 million years ago (Oligocene Epoch). Its main evolutionary changes included: increased size (approximately 22 inches in height), each foot ending in three toes that supported its body weight evenly, and teeth that became slightly larger (like a pig's teeth), in order to eat leaves from a wider variety of plants on the forest floor.

After several climatic changes, about 10 - 25 million years ago (Miocene Epoch), large areas of jungle turned into prairies covered by different kinds of grasses and bushes. As the habitat changed, ***Merychippus*** evolved. This new species increased in size (to about 35 inches in height) and had longer legs to run faster; thus, its neck was longer to reach plants (grass) on the ground. Its feet ended in three toes, but the central one was longer than the other two and supported its weight. Its coat turned to brown with yellowish areas for camouflage in the tall grasses. Its teeth became bigger and flatter to cut and chew grasses and other kinds of plants on the prairie.

Pliohippus existed about two to six million years ago (Pliocene Epoch). The main changes included increased size (to about 42 inches in height, similar to a pony), longer and thicker legs, a neck that continued to get longer, and feet ending in only one toe, covered by a hoof (like a modern horse).

Several species of Family ***Equidae*** appeared about two million years ago (Pleistocene Epoch), living in prairies and steppes of North America, Asia, Europe, and Africa. These species, that were between 40 and 58 inches in height, were the origin of all species of Genus ***Equus*** (horses, zebras, asses, and tarpans). The legs and neck of this Family became longer. Coats of the different species had a wide variety of colors including white, beige, yellow, and brown, with or without dark brown/black bands, tails, and manes. Because their diets were based primarily on grasses, their incisor teeth became "nipper" shaped in order to cut the grass. The premolars/molars became bigger and flatter for properly chewing fibrous roughage.

Note: The severe climatic conditions in North America during the Ice Age, about 10,000 years ago, dramatically diminished areas with grass, causing ***Equidae*** to become extinct on the American continent.

The current domestic horse breeds (***Equus caballus***), with 64 chromosomes, are the result of crossing, at minimum, three horse-type species of Family ***Equidae***:

- The "Nordic" horse-type from Northwest Europe: This subspecies had the thickest body and leg bones and the biggest hooves and head. Additionally, because the horse used to live in very cold areas, the coat became very thick. Abundant, long hair appeared on the fetlocks, which may also have covered the hooves. This is the origin of today's "draft" horse breeds.

- The "Arab" horse-type from the Middle East: This subspecies had the most refined conformation with thin leg bones, high tail, and concave (known as "dished") face. It was light and a very fast runner. This is the origin of the Arabian horse.

- The "Barb" horse-type from Southern Asia and Northern Africa: This subspecies was a little less refined than the "Arab" type, but still light and fast. It was very resistant to heat and unfavorable conditions. This produced the Barb horse breed. Many specimens of this breed were taken to Spain by the North African warriors (Moors) during the several invasions from the eighth to fifteenth centuries. Later, the Barb horse became the foundation of most horse breeds on the American Continent.

Other ***Equidae*** species from Central Europe, Western and Central Asia, the Middle East, and Northern Africa later produced asses; others from Eastern Asia produced Przewalski horses (tarpans); and others from Africa developed zebras (see descriptions under "Other equine species").

SIGNIFICANCE OF EVOLUTION FOR TODAY'S HORSE

- The horse's height and weight increased tremendously, in direct proportion to the abundance of plants available to eat and the need to escape from predators, when the horse changed from living in the forest to the open space of the prairie. Thus, leg bones became longer, stronger, and thicker. Additionally, toes per foot decreased from four to one and were protected by a hoof in order to run faster. That is why today's horse needs to run by itself everyday, either in a pasture or paddock, to be physically and mentally healthy.

- While the legs became longer during each evolutionary stage, the horse's neck also needed to become longer so that its lips and incisors could reach plants on the ground.

- Front teeth (incisors) became nipper-shaped in order to cut selected blades of grass. Back teeth (premolars and molars) became harder, flatter, and bigger in order to chew the fibrous grass properly. Although the horse is a non-ruminant animal, its digestive system is well adapted to process nutrients from fibrous plants (grass) in the same way as ruminants (such as cows), except that the horse's digestive system is less efficient. Therefore, no matter the breed, horses must eat a substantial amount of roughage every day to fulfill their needs.

OTHER EQUINE SPECIES

Besides horses, Genus ***Equus*** includes other species:

- A donkey, ***Equus asinus***, also known as a burro or ass, is an equine species known for its longer ears, strength, and resistance to adverse conditions. Although a donkey has 62 chromosomes, two chromosomes less than a horse, these two equine species (donkey and horse) are crossed to produce strong hybrids for work.

  A "mule" is the result of breeding a jack (male donkey) and a mare (female horse). A "hinny" is obtained from breeding a stallion (male horse) and a jennet (female donkey). Although both gender hybrids have normal sexual behavior, they are considered sterile; therefore, male mules and hinnies should be gelded. Rarely, female mules may conceive and foal a normal offspring.

  Note: Breeding Paso Fino mules for show, trail riding, and work is very popular in Colombia.

- The three subspecies of zebras, ***Equus zebra*** (known as "mountain" zebra), ***Equus grevyi*** (known as "Grevy's zebra"), and ***Equus burchelli*** (known as "common" or "plain" zebra), live wild in different areas of the African continent. However, some zebras are housed in zoos and farms, and they reproduce there. The three subspecies differ from each other by their size, black and white stripe pattern, and their ear size and shape. Additionally, they have a different number of chromosomes (32, 44, and 46 respectively).

- The "Przewalski" horse, ***Equus Przewalskii***, also called "tarpan," is from Eastern Asia. Few animals of this horse subspecies with 66 chromosomes still exist in Mongolia and zoos. Its head is big in proportion to the body, and its looks are very primitive. It has a dark, short mane, not abundant dark tail, yellowish coat, and dark dorsal stripe.

ORIGINS OF THE PASO FINO HORSES

As explained above, all ***Equidae*** were extinct from the Americas about 10,000 years ago. The first horses to come back to the American continent were the approximately 25 animals brought by Christopher Columbus on his second trip. These horses landed at the end of 1493 on "Dominica" island, today the Dominican Republic. These were of the Barb breed, apparently multi-gaited (trot and/or pace and/or gallop) because of the previous interbreeding and natural selection in North Africa and the Iberian Peninsula. These first 25 horses, and others brought on future trips, produced offspring that, during the first two decades of the sixteenth century, were spread throughout the areas where Spaniards expanded their territory in the New World: islands such as Puerto Rico, Cuba, and Jamaica; Mexico (in Central America); and Colombia and Peru (in South America).

Fantasma de Aristocratica (Vigilante de Casta x Aparecida de MED), a beautiful Paso Fino colt at 17 months of age. Owner Mildred Arent, Criadero Aristocratica, Ocala, FL. Photo by Olga García.

It is important to note that, because there were no horses in the Americas when the Conquistadors arrived, most natives assumed that such a splendid duo of horse and rider were actual gods; thus, horses played a very important role in Spanish colonization efforts. Horses gave the Spaniards a significant military advantage by allowing them to conquer the different tribes that, in most cases, outnumbered them. In addition, horses gave the Conquistadors the necessary mobility to colonize the vast territories of the South American Andes. These brave horses needed to be relatively small, very athletic and full of energy to be able to perform, and even survive long journeys.

Within the last five centuries, these horses have evolved into the Paso Fino horses and many other breeds, such as the Peruvian Paso, the three Colombian diagonal Paso horse breeds, and the Argentinean Criollo, among others. This evolution occurred as part of a complex process that included the following:

- Natural selection caused by living and working in a completely different topography, as well as a new climate and different types of grasses
- Several crosses with some Iberian horse breeds, such as the Andalusian, Lusitano, and the already extinct Spanish Jennet
- Human selection and training

The great Paso Fino breed, with an evenly alternated movement among the four hooves, emerged over 200 years ago after repeatedly crossing the pacing group of horses of the Barb breed (two-beat, laterally-gaited horses) with some of the Iberian horse breeds (Andalusian, Lusitano, and Spanish Jennet), and being selected for working and traveling many hours daily over mountainous terrains while maintaining a smooth gait. The two most well-known groups of Paso Fino horses were developed in Colombia and Puerto Rico. Other smaller, important groups were developed in Cuba and the Dominican Republic.

One of the most recent important influences of the Iberian horse breeds on Colombian horses is Danesa, who was born in 1950. This mare was the product of crossing a Colombian Paso Fino mare, named Diana, with a Lusitano stallion owned by the female horseback bullfighter, Conchita Cintrón. Danesa, who performed Trote and Galope, was bred with different Colombian stallions (who performed Paso Fino, Trocha, Trote and Galope, or Trocha and Galope), and produced at least ten outstanding quality offspring of different gaits, most of which were multi-champions in Colombian horse shows. Those were Dalila, Danes, Dante, Don Danilo (who was able to perform Paso Fino, Trote, Trocha, and Galope gaits), Fantasía, Pacheco, Reliquia, Rosalinda, Tango, and Tormento. Their offspring are now part of the Colombian horse bloodlines.

The first Paso Fino horses introduced in the United States (in 1950) came from Puerto Rico. Later, more Paso Finos came from Colombia, Venezuela, and the Dominican Republic. Since then, the population of the Paso Fino horse breed has been growing steadily in the States.

Currently, the Paso Fino sport is very important in the countries with horse associations/federations affiliated with *CONFEPASO* (*Confederación Internacional de Caballos de Paso*, which may be translated into English as *International Confederation of Paso Horse Breeders*): Aruba, Canada, Colombia, Curacao, Dominican Republic, Germany, Panama, Puerto Rico, Switzerland, United States, and Venezuela. Paso Finos are also becoming more important in Ecuador, Spain, and the United Kingdom.

Note: The *Paso Fino Horse Association, Inc.*, which is affiliated with *CONFEPASO,* promotes and regulates Paso Fino horses in the United States.

CHAPTER 3

THE HORSE INSIDE AND OUT

In this chapter, the horse is described with an emphasis on the integumentary, skeletal, and nervous systems. The **INTEGUMENTARY** system (or **COVERING** system) is formed by the **hair**, **skin**, **sweat glands**, **sebaceous glands**, and **hooves**. The functions of this system are to cover the body and to keep the horse isolated and protected from the outside environment.

The **SKELETAL** system is made up of **bones**, **cartilage**, and **joints**. The functions of this system are very diverse, such as providing the bony framework of the horse to protect the vital organs (brain, heart, liver, lungs), allowing locomotion (legs), forming blood cells (inside the long bones), and storing minerals (such as calcium).

The **NERVOUS** system is formed by the **brain**, **spinal cord,** and all the **nerves**, including those connected to the **five specialized sensory organs** (vision, hearing, smell, taste, and touch). The functions of this system are perceiving changes in the horse's metabolism and recovering balance, perceiving changes in the environment by means of the sensory organs (for example, dangerous conditions), finding food and water, and leading to movement.

OVERVIEW OF THE HORSE

Knowing the parts of the horse, as well as the internal framework, assures a better understanding of the horse's biology and therefore its care.

- **HEAD**: When viewed from the side, the horse's head has the shape of a big hammer. The head size should be in proportion to the horse's body. In contrast to the rest of the horse's skeleton, the cranial cavity is formed by several small, semi-flat bones that contain and protect the horse's brain.

Each one of the two small **ears** is erect and shaped like half of an empty cone with the point at the top; the wide bottom joins the top of the head. Each ear may be rotated toward the front, the side, or the back, allowing the horse to locate the direction of the origin of a sound. Movements of the ears are also used by horses to communicate with other horses, as part of a complex body language. The ears are covered by skin and hair of the same kind and color as the coat. The hardest structure of the ears is cartilage.

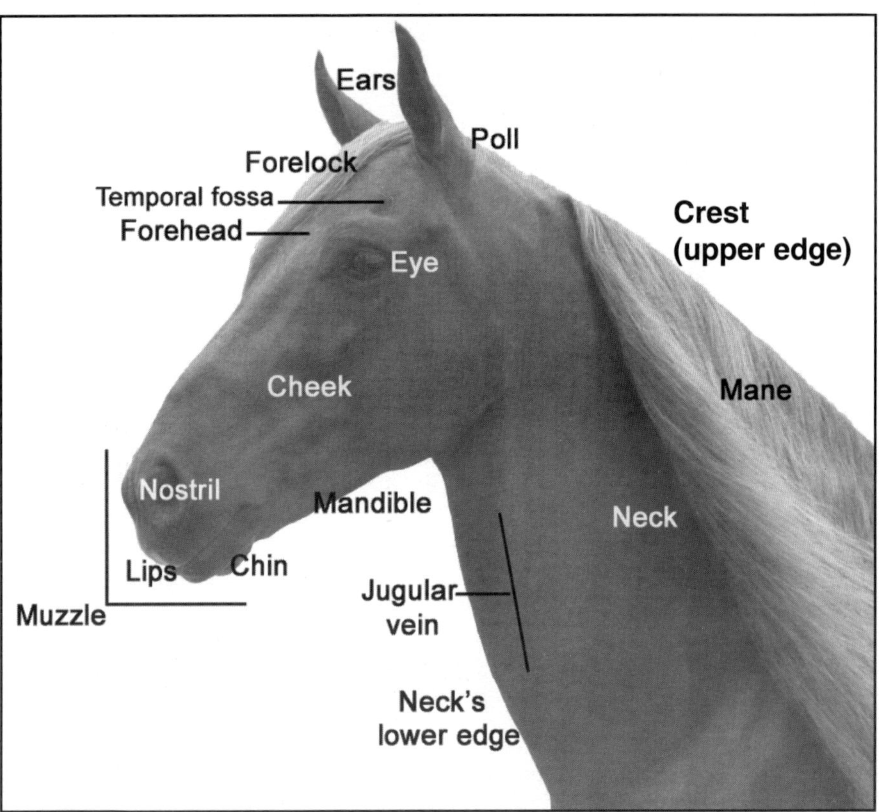

The top edge of the **forehead** is defined by the ears, and its lower edge is defined by the eyes. If a horse has a large, flat forehead, this is considered by some to be a sign of intelligence because it appears to provide more room for the brain.

The horse's two big **eyes** are located on each side of the head, just at the corners of the lower edge of the forehead. Each eye occupies one **orbital cavity**. The strategic placement of the eyes allows the horse to have a binocular field of vision of about 65 degrees toward the front. In addition, each eye has a large monocular field of vision, toward the sides, almost reaching behind the head. 2 inches above each eye, there is a small oval groove called the "**temporal fossa**."

The horse's **face** (front profile and cheeks) is located below the eyes. The face is only supported by the nasal and the maxillary bones, covered by very thin muscles and skin. When the horse suffers "big head disease" due to an excess of phosphorus in its diet for an extended period of time, the maxillary bones become weak and rounded out toward the **cheeks** (see Chapter 10: "Health basics"). The **muzzle** is the bottom of the head, formed by the nostrils, upper and lower lips, and the chin.

The **nostrils** are two oval holes located below the face at the front lower corners of the muzzle. Although a horse's nostrils will dilate during exercise, large nostrils are better than small ones because they are the primary entry way of fresh air to the respiratory system.

The **lips**, upper and lower, have great mobility, pressure ability, and sense of touch (comparable to a person's hand). They allow the horse to select food before introducing it to the mouth. When a horse is not eating, its lower lip should be closed firmly against the upper one. The point where the upper and lower lips join at each side is called the "corner of the mouth." The **chin** is the fleshy and rounded prominence located behind/below the lower lip.

The horse's **teeth** have different functions in the mouth. They are located in the sockets of the maxillary and mandible bones, supported firmly by the gums. The function of the **incisors**, located at the front of the mouth and covered by the lips, is to cut grass from the pasture and to bite while fighting. **Premolars** and **molars**, located above the corners of the mouth, chew food. **Canines** are located in the interdental spaces between the incisors and premolars in males over four years old; however, canines have no purpose for the modern horse.

The **tongue** is a relatively big muscular organ in the horse, the function of which is to taste food and to carry it from the front part of the mouth to the premolars and the molars located in the back for chewing. The tongue also aids in swallowing.

Chewing food is accomplished by the movement of the **mandible** (or lower jaw), both upper ends of which join with the temporal bones. The masseter muscles, and other facial muscles, produce the chewing motion. The mandible has two branches (bones) starting above each side of the masseteric region, which are projected downward, and are fused at the chin area. These two bones of the mandible may fracture above the chin area if the horse pulls forcefully while tied with a halter or jaquima that has a poorly designed bosal-barbada, which becomes tighter as the horse pulls.

- **NECK**: The horse's head is connected to the trunk by means of the neck. One of the main functions of the neck is to lower the horse's head until the horse's lips and incisors are able to reach the grass on the ground. Additionally, the horse uses its neck and head together to provide optimal balance during locomotion. Regions of the neck include the poll, crest (upper edge), lower edge, sides of the neck, and jugular groove.

The **poll** unites the head with the neck, just behind the ears. The joint between the occipital bone (rear of head) and the atlas (first vertebrae) allows the head to move up and down. The joint between the atlas and the axis (second vertebrae) allows the head to move from side to side. In addition to the atlas and axis, the neck has five other cervical vertebrae, which allow the neck to move in different directions.

More than 20 pairs of muscles control neck movements. This abundance of muscles provides a good location for intramuscular injections in both sides of the neck. With age, the neck's **crest** of some horses starts to fall to one side (known as "fallen crest"), which is increased/anticipated when horses have been fed in feeders placed above the ground level for several years. Hypothyroidism may also result in a big crest that falls to one side as the horse ages.

Numerous long hairs, called the **mane**, grow in the neck's crest. When the mane is well taken care of, it may become long and abundant, giving the horse great beauty. The **forelock** is the part of the mane that grows between the ears and hangs down to cover the horse's forehead and face.

The **jugular vein**, located under the jugular groove on both sides of the neck, is the site for injecting intravenous drugs and taking blood samples for clinical exams. Subcutaneous injections are given between the skin and flesh of the neck. The skin of the neck is also one of the best places to verify whether a horse is dehydrated. If the skin returns slowly to its original position after being pinched and released (known as the "skin pinch test"), this is a very distinguishable sign of dehydration (see Chapter 10: "Health basics").

- **TRUNK**: The sections of this largest part of the horse's body include the withers, back, shoulders, thorax, chest, loin, ventral edge, girth area, abdomen, inguinal region, and flanks.

"Mercurio de Lusitania" (Zodíaco de Lusitania x Dorotea de Lusitania), owned by Janis Paushter, D and J Buckley Farm, Ocala, FL.

The **withers** are located at the point where the back joins the neck. They also may be defined as the highest point where the back joins the crest. Withers are formed by the upper edges of the third, fourth, and fifth thoracic vertebrae. Due to the fact that the withers are often the highest point of the horse's trunk, when the horse stands balanced, the withers are used to determine its height.

The **back** starts at the withers and projects backward to the loin. The back is the upper line of the barrel, where the saddle should be placed and the rider should sit. The back is supported by the withers, the other 13 thoracic vertebrae behind the withers, and some muscles. Ideally, the back behind the withers should be as straight as possible and very firm. Conversely, a significant downward curvature called "sway back appearance" or "lordosis" is not desirable because it weakens the horse.

The **shoulders**, or **scapulas**, project down from the withers to the corners of the chest on both sides of the horse. Each scapula may be felt under the skin by touching its flat surface.

The **thorax** is the cage that protects many internal organs. The thoracic vertebrae (on the top of the barrel) are attached to the upper ends of the ribs on both sides of the horse. The lower ends of the 18 pairs of ribs join directly or indirectly (by means of cartilage) to the sternum, a bone at the bottom of the thorax. The ribs should be thick and rounded to provide resistance; additionally, they are arched and long to provide deepness to the barrel and room for the vital organs. In the spaces between the ribs, there are bands of intercostal muscles that allow a slight expansion of the thorax for breathing and for movement.

The **chest** is the frontal region of the barrel that is located below the neck. The upper corners of the chest, on both sides, end at the points of the shoulders. The lower edge of the chest ends at the sternum. Keeping in mind that the horse is an athlete, a wide and deep chest provides more room for the organs of the circulatory and the respiratory systems, which has many advantages during exercise.

The **loin** is located behind the back and is supported by six lumbar vertebrae. Although it is not attached to the ribs, the loin is joined firmly to the back and to the hips by strong muscles. The horse should not be sensitive to pressure on the loin; in most cases, this discomfort is caused by an ill -fitting saddle. In more serious circumstances, it may be a sign of kidney problems.

The **ventral** (lower) **edge** of the barrel is formed by the girth area and the abdomen. Because the sternum provides a firm structure at the girth, it is the area to position the saddle's cinch. The **girth area** starts just behind the elbows and projects backward to the rear end of the sternum, ending in line with the abdomen.

The front of the **abdomen** ends at both the rear of the sternum and at the lower end of the rear ribs. The sides of the abdomen end at the bottom of both flanks, and the rear of the abdomen ends at the front of the inguinal region. Some horses have a big rounded abdomen, while others have a very small one. In the Paso Fino breed, the size of the abdomen should be intermediate. However, in the same horse, the size of the abdomen may vary depending on the amount and kind of food contained in the intestine; for example, a horse has a bigger abdomen when it is kept in a pasture full- time than when it is fed in a stall or corral with hay and grain on a regular schedule.

The **inguinal region** is located behind the rear of the abdomen and between the thighs. The penis and testicles (in the male) and the udder (in the mare) are located in the inguinal region.

The **flanks** are located below both sides of the loin, descending toward the abdomen, just behind the rear ribs. Flanks have no bones in their structure.

- **HIPS**: The hips are located behind the loin, in front of the tail, and above the hind legs. The bone structure of the hip is formed by the "sacrum" and the pelvic girdle (ilium, ischium, and pubis). Hips have a big muscle mass around the bones, making them a good place to give intramuscular injections.

  The two **hip bones**, or **tuber coxaes**, are the hardest points on each side of the hips. These bones are located behind the upper edge of each flank. The **tuber ischiies**, or **buttock bones**, are at the back end of the hips, located on both sides below the root of the tail.

  The **croup** is the upper, narrow band on top of the hips. The bone structure of the croup is formed by the five sacral vertebrae that are fused into only one bone, called the "sacrum." Although the croup should be slightly inclined, a croup with too great a downward incline is less beautiful and presents more risk for a mare when foaling. The perineum is the narrow band between the anus and the scrotum in the male, and between the vulva and the udder in the female.

- **TAIL**: The tail is located behind the sacrum and projects downward. The tail is formed by the coccygeal vertebrae, many tendons (that provide great mobility), veins, arterioles, nerves, and skin. Many long hairs (known as the "tail's skirt"), similar to those of the mane, grow out of the lateral and the upper surfaces of the tail, which give the horse beauty and grace.

  The tail serves several important functions. The horse may use it to swat flies and as a fan to comfort a friendly neighbor. It also helps the horse maintain proper balance when running and is a very effective cover that protects the anus and the vulva.

- **LEGS**: The horse is a quadruped, which allows it to reach high speeds when running. The two front legs, or forelegs, sustain from 55% to 60% of the body weight, and their main function is for support. The two rear legs, or hind legs, sustain the remaining 40% to 45% of the body weight. The other function of the hind legs is propulsion.

  The bones, ligaments, muscles, and tendons of the legs are very strong to allow the horse to walk, run, jump, carry, and pull. Each joint is embraced by ligaments to keep the joint secure. The muscles and the tendons of the legs pull the bones above and below the joints to cause movement. Each leg ends in a single "toe" protected by the **hoof**, which consists of material similar to human fingernails (see Chapter 7: "Hoof trimming and shoeing").

  - **Forelegs**: From bottom to top, the foreleg is described as follows: The hoof covers the third phalanx (also known as "coffin bone"), the navicular bone (or distal sesamoid), and the very lower end of the second phalanx. The upper end of the third phalanx joins with the lower end of the second phalanx at the coffin joint.

    The upper end of the second phalanx joins the lower end of the first phalanx at the pastern joint. The **pastern** is the lower end of the leg above the hoof, which includes the first phalanx, located on top, and most of the second phalanx, located at the bottom. The pastern is inclined forward in the same direction and approximately the same degree as the scapula of the horse.

The upper end of the first phalanx joins the lower end of the **cannon bone**, at the fetlock joint. In addition, the two proximal sesamoid bones are located at the back and the bottom of the cannon bone. The **ergot** is a callous, cone-shaped structure at the rear of the fetlock, made of the same material as the hooves, but slightly softer. The long coat hairs on the skin around the ergot are called "**feathers**;" they allow the sweat, coming down from the body, to drain. When the feathering is cut for aesthetic reasons, the sweat drains through the rear of the pastern and may irritate the skin of some horses.

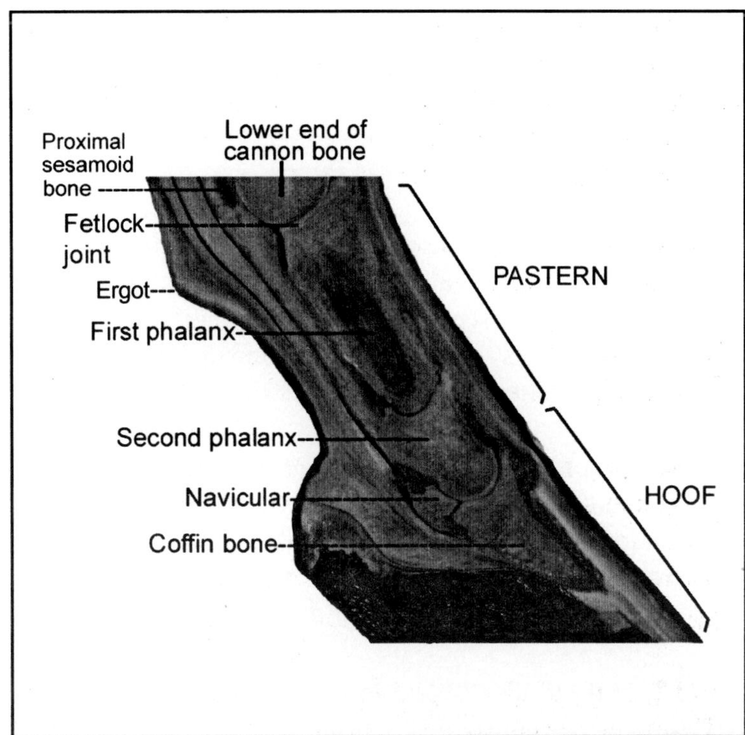

The cannon bone projects straight up from the fetlock joint, and has two small splint bones attached to it on each side. The upper end of the cannon bone joins the lower articulating surface of the **carpus joint** or "false knee" (also known as "horse's knee"). The carpus is a joint formed by two rows of four small bones. The upper articulating surface of the carpus joins the lower end of the **forearm**. The forearm projects straight up.

The **chestnut** is a 1 to 2 inch long, oval-shaped, callous structure made of similar material as the ergot. The chestnut of the foreleg is located on the inside surface of the forearm, 2 to 3 inches above the carpus joint.

The forearm's bones are called the "radius" (the longest bone) and the "ulna" (a small bone that is joined to the top end of the radius, and is also known as the "point of elbow" or "olecranon process"). When the horse is viewed from the side, the "point of elbow" is easy to identify as the point where the foreleg joins the lower edge of the trunk.

The upper end of the forearm joins the lower end of the **arm** at the **elbow joint**. The arm projects up forward and joins the **shoulder**. The arm's only bone is the humerus.

- **Hind legs**: From bottom to top, the hind leg is described as follows. The hoof, pastern, fetlock joint, and cannon bone are similar as the foreleg, and have the same internal structures.

  The hind cannon bone projects straight up from the fetlock joint, and has two small splint bones attached to it on each side. The upper end of the hind cannon bone joins the lower articulating surface of the **tarsus** or hock. The hock is a joint formed by seven small bones. The chestnut of the hind leg is located on the inside surface of the tarsus at its bottom. It is usually slightly smaller than the chestnut of the foreleg.

The hock joins the lower end of the **gaskin**. The tibia (the longest bone) and the small fibula (a bone that is joined to the tibia on one side) are the bones that make up the gaskin. The gaskin projects up and forward to the **stifle joint**. The **patella** is a small bone at the front of the stifle joint. The **thigh** has only one bone, called the femur. The lower end of the femur joins the stifle joint. The thigh projects diagonally up and backwards to the **hip joint**.

- **SKIN**: It is formed by the **epidermis** (the most external layer) and the **dermis** (under the epidermis). The skin covers the entire body and is excellent protection from outside agents. The skin has nerve endings that make up part of the sense of touch. Additionally, the skin has a blood supply (capillaries), hair follicles, glands (sebaceous and sweat glands), and muscle fibers in some areas. Even though the horse's skin is very strong, it often takes a long time to heal after being wounded or burned.

  When the horse's internal temperature gets high, the warmer blood is taken through veins that are close to the body's skin and the sweat glands release sweat on the surface of the body. Through the evaporation of sweat, the blood cools down. Therefore, a ′web′ of veins around the neck and shoulder are easy to see under the skin after several minutes of physical activity; this is a sign of good thermoregulation, which keeps the horse more comfortable during exercise.

- **COAT**: One of the primary functions of the coat is to provide protection from cold and hot weather. Thousands of small hairs cover the entire skin, except on the nostrils, lips, anus, genital organs, udder, inside the thighs, perineum, and underneath the tail. The colors of the coat, mane, and tail are defined by genetic inheritance (see Chapter 5: "Colors of Paso Fino horses").

  Where each hair grows, there is also a small **sebaceous gland** that secretes a kind of oil that protects the hairs and provides luster to the coat. The condition of the coat indicates the general condition of the horse and is a good indication that the horse lives in a favorable environment. When the coat is in optimal condition, the hairs are very small, shiny, and silky.

HORSE'S PERCEPTION OF THE ENVIRONMENT

The five specialized sensory organs allow the horse to be in contact with the environment:

- **VISION**: Compared to man, the horse has less visual acuity. Although a horse cannot identify many details from a distance, it is able to identify movement; this helps protect the horse from a sudden predator attack. Additionally, when objects are closer than 2 feet away from its eyes, the horse's ability to identify details of these images is reduced.

  The horse has developed several ways to compensate for these disadvantages:

  - Looking forward with both eyes at the same time, the horse's binocular field of vision is around 65 degrees. Binocular vision allows the horse to estimate the distance from an object, which is very important for "judging" obstacles when running.

    In order to experience the importance of binocular vision, the reader may try the following exercise: 1) close one eye; 2) move one hand away from the face and raise the forefinger; and 3) touch the already raised forefinger with the forefinger of the other hand. Since binocular vision helps calculate the three dimensions, the exercise may not be accomplished on the first attempt because the distance may not be calculated properly by using only one eye.

- By using each one of the eyes separately, the horse sees the environment on both sides of its body. The entire space that one eye may see is known as the monocular field of vision. If the horse has its head and neck straight forward, it only needs to turn one eye slightly backward in order to see almost the entire space at that side, up to its hip bone.

- The horse may see relatively well in low light at night due to the large size of its pupils.

The horse is able to distinguish most colors. However, some colors may produce adverse reactions in horses. When facilities/devices (such as doors, buckets, waterers) are red or orange, they may cause anxiousness in the horse and the horse may tend to bite at them. When big objects are black or dark blue, they may cause fear. In contrast, green and light blue help the horse to relax. Further, some horses are afraid of bright objects and puddles on the ground.

Vision problems may make many horses spook from objects in their path, which, subsequently, result in them being dangerous to ride. The most common vision problems in horses are myopia (difficulty seeing objects far away), hypermetropia (difficulty seeing close objects), double image vision, and inverted image vision.

- **HEARING**: The horse has great audible acuity. When compared to a human, a horse perceives sounds of higher frequency from a greater distance. Additionally, the horse has another advantage over humans by being able to rotate each ear in nearly all possible directions to locate precisely the origin of a sound. Therefore, this sense helps the horse stay safe from danger in the environment and meet with other horses by following their whinny (the sound used by horses to communicate with others).

- **SMELL**: This sense in the horse is more acute than it is in humans. A horse recognizes other horses by their fragrance. For example, a stallion identifies the mares of his herd through smell and vice-versa. The horse identifies new smells, especially strong ones, which may cause the horse to become very alert and/or curious. Additionally, a horse recognizes a person by his/her fragrance.

  Horses use the sense of smell to find food, too. Because the ′smell sense′ is closely related to the ′taste sense,′ the horse uses the smell sense to help choose the most palatable food, such as certain plants in the pasture. Additionally, when a concentrate or a supplement is changed or added to the diet, the horse may reject it just after smelling it, even before tasting it.

  Sense of smell also has great importance for the stallion; he uses this sense to test the urine of the mare in order to verify that she is in heat (estrus). The stallion also uses smell to determine if a pile of manure or a spot of urine belongs to a member of his group. To activate the special smell receptors, the stallion raises his upper lip very close to the material being tested; afterwards, he exposes the inside lip to fresh air. This is known as the "Flehmen reflex"

- **TASTE**: This sense is developed similarly as in humans. The horse is able to identify diverse flavors: salt, sweet, bitter, and sour. This sense of taste helps the horse to choose preferable blades of grass and reject the dusty or contaminated ones. A horse is able to identify a change in the flavor of water when it is transported to a different place, and may refuse to drink. Because horses seem to prefer sweet flavors, many concentrates, supplements, and veterinary products purposely are sweetened.

- **TOUCH**: The organ of this sense is the horse's entire skin. There are receptive cells distributed all over the body of the horse that perceive changes in the environment (e.g., temperature). Additionally, when the horse is bitten by an insect, the skin usually detects it, and the horse will then remove the insect by swishing its tail, scratching with its lips or teeth, or twitching the skin by means of the muscle fibers located in the dermis of the trunk. Riders may benefit from this skin sensitivity by squeezing their legs in order to "push" the horse.

  Due to the position of the horse's eyes, the horse cannot see what is close to its lips. To compensate for this limitation when eating, the horse has many receptive cells all over its muzzle that give it a well-developed sense of touch. These allow the horse to choose exactly the food it prefers to eat, assisted by the smell and the taste senses. The reader may view this ability by watching the horse's lips when the animal is grazing. Even in darkness, the muzzle's sense of touch enables the horse to reject objects different than those it wants. The long tactile hairs of the muzzle and around the eyes also have receptive cells, which are an important part of the sense of touch. Unfortunately, it is common practice for these tactile hairs to be cut on show horses for aesthetic reasons.

TEETH OF THE HORSE

The different teeth of the horse (incisors, canines, premolars, and molars) are designed and located for a wide range of functions:

- **INCISORS**: These 12 teeth are located at the front of the mouth: six teeth on the maxillary bone (top) and six teeth on the mandible bone (bottom). The upper teeth should coincide perfectly with the lower ones, similar to a pair of nippers, because their function is to cut grass from the pasture.

  The horse develops two series of incisors during its life. The first series, called temporary incisors or milk incisors, is developed within the first six to nine months of life. The second series, called permanent incisors, replaces the first series by groups of four teeth starting at the age of two and a half years and finishing at four and a half years of age.

- **CANINES**: These four pointed, permanent teeth appear in all males after four years of age. Each one is located far behind every corner incisor on both sides of the upper and the lower jaws. The two lower canines are located more forward than the two upper canines; therefore, they never make contact, nor do they have any known function.

  A few mares develop small (infantile) canines, generally only the lower pair. Some people associate the presence of canines in mares with reproductive problems; however, experience shows that these mares are absolutely normal, and their ability to reproduce is similar to others.

- **PREMOLARS**: There are generally 12 premolars that are used for chewing food. In groups of three, they grow on both sides of the upper and the lower jaws.

  Like the incisors, the horse develops two sets of premolars during its life. The temporary premolars or milk premolars are replaced by the permanent premolars in groups of four teeth, starting at the age of two and a half years and finishing at four and a half years of age.

  Between six and twenty-four months of age, some horses, males and females, may develop a fourth permanent premolar in front of every upper first premolar; those two teeth are called "Wolf teeth." They have no function for the modern horse and, due to the fact that they are pointed, they may be extracted by an equine dentist or a veterinarian.

  When planning to extract Wolf teeth from a Paso Fino horse, it is necessary to evaluate if they are really a problem. In general, when a Wolf tooth joins the premolar next to it, this does not present a real problem for the mouthpiece of thc bit, and the tooth may be floated as the other premolars. Conversely, when the Wolf teeth have a space between the premolars, they must be extracted because they may interfere with the bit's mouthpiece, and the horse may develop undesirable vices.

- **MOLARS**: These 12 permanent teeth are located immediately behind the premolars by groups of three on both sides of the upper and lower jaws. They are slightly bigger than the premolars and their function is also for chewing food. Molar teeth eruption starts at one year and ends at four years of age.

  A horse's teeth grow continuously throughout life, so that the teeth continue to be functional after being worn down from cutting grass and/or chewing food. Due to this continuous growth and wear, and because the horse's upper jaw is wider than the mandible, sharp points may occur on the premolars and molars. Sharp points on the upper premolars and molars may hurt the cheeks, and sharp points on the lower premolars and molars may hurt the tongue while the horse is chewing.

  Additionally, when upper sharp points are present, they may hurt the horse's cheeks due to the pressure caused by the training jaquima when the horse's neck is being flexed. This situation often upsets the horse and may lead to behavior problems. Therefore, an equine dentist or a veterinarian should examine the horse's mouth once or twice a year to float sharp points.

In summary, the total number of teeth in an adult horse may vary as follows:

- Male (stallion or gelding):
  - Regularly: 12 incisors, 4 canines, 12 premolars, 12 molars = 40 teeth
  - Probably: 2 additional Wolf teeth = 42 teeth
- Female (mare):
  - Regularly: 12 incisors, 12 premolars, 12 molars = 36 teeth
  - Probably: 2 additional Wolf teeth and/or 2 lower canines = 38 or 40 teeth

DETERMINING THE AGE OF A HORSE

There is no better way to know the age of a horse than knowing the date of birth; however, observing the horse's physical condition, as well as its teeth, helps to estimate its age as described below:

- Low height and incomplete development are signs that the horse is still young.
- Young horses normally have a more rounded face. When the horse becomes older, the face is flatter and more angular. In addition, after 15 years of age, the upper edge of the joint between the two bones (branches) of the mandible (above the chin) becomes thinner, and almost sharp when touched.
- Hard, dry skin is a sign of age; however, soft skin is not always a sign of youth.
- Grey/white color on the horse's coat over black skin may also indicate the horse's age. For example, most grey horses are dark (almost black) when they are young (from one to four years old); they become gradually grey, and then white, with age.
- Watching and evaluating the eruption, growth, replacement, wear, and marks of the incisor teeth is another way to calculate the horse's age.

Paso Fino breeders used to say that a horse over ten years is considered "old." However, a 14 year-old horse is perfectly able to work, show, and reproduce. The usefulness of a horse begins to decline after 17 years. The average life span of a well-managed horse is 25 years, but horses may live until 30 or longer.

HOW TEETH HELP TO REVEAL A HORSE'S AGE

By observing and evaluating the incisors, it is possible to estimate a horse's age fairly accurately until the horse is 11 years old. After that, estimates become less exact because there are some factors that cause significant individual differences among horses, such as tooth hardness, the kind of food offered (grass in the pasture or hay in the stall), type of soil, and vices (such as cribbing and chewing wood).

In order to use the incisor teeth to estimate age, it is important to know the difference between temporary and permanent ones. The temporary incisors are narrower, thinner, smaller, and whiter than permanent incisors. The more wrinkled surface of the permanent incisors tends to accumulate different substances that make the teeth darker, with areas colored from beige to yellow, or brown.

The incisors of adult horses gradually incline forward with age. In a young horse, the incisors grow almost straight up and down. As the horse matures, however, these same teeth flatten and grow more in an outward direction from both jaws, as shown in the following pictures:

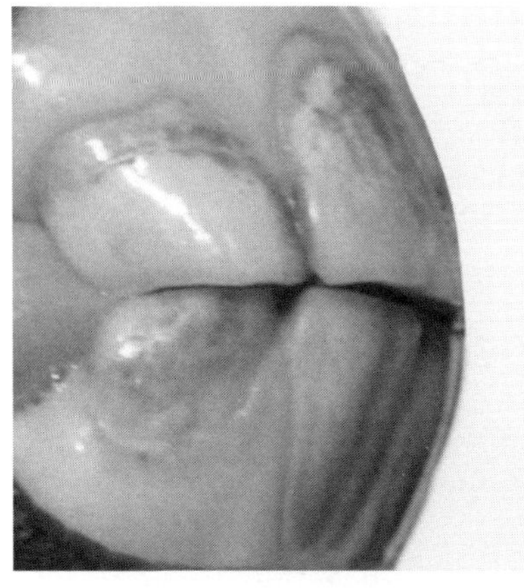

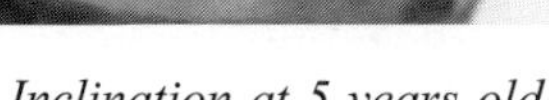

Inclination at 5 years old

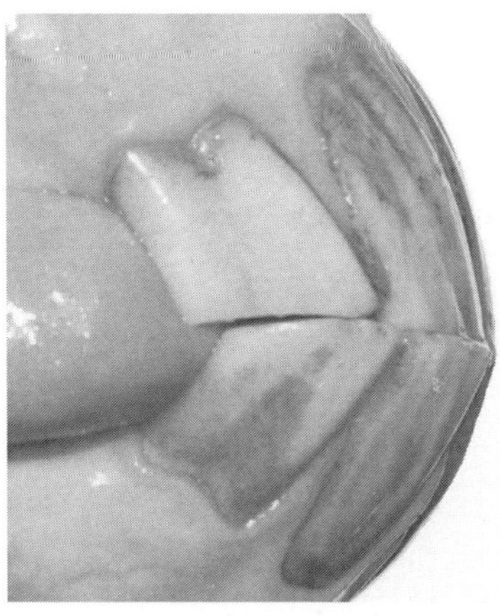

Inclination at 10 years old

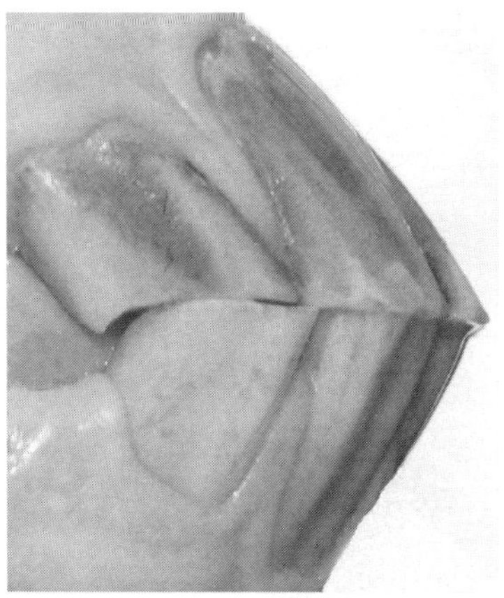

Inclination at 16 years old

According to their position, the 12 incisors have different names:

- Central or first incisors: two in the upper jaw and two in the lower jaw, located at the center of the mouth (in the middle of the other incisors).
- Intermediate or second incisors: two in the upper jaw and two in the lower jaw, each located on both sides of the central incisors.
- Corner or third incisors: two in the upper jaw and two in the lower jaw, each located on both sides of the intermediate incisors.

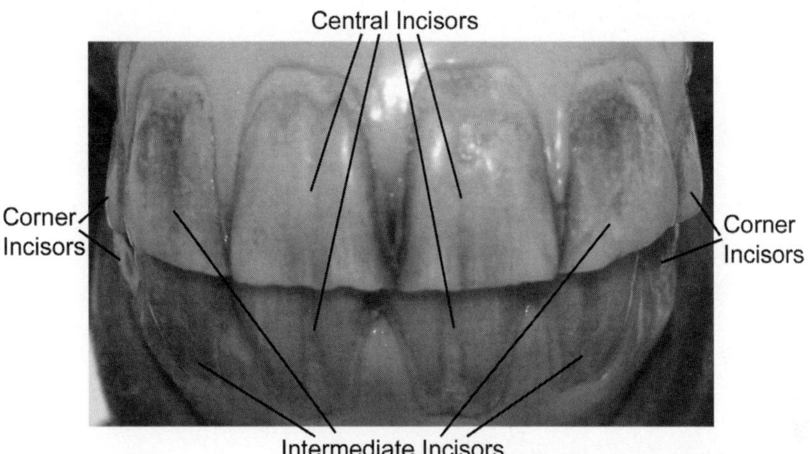

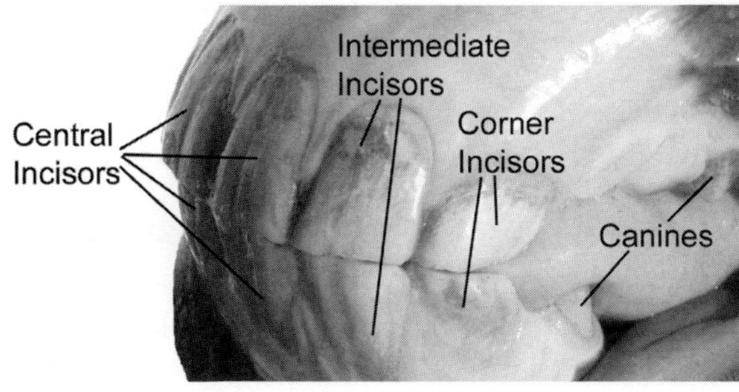

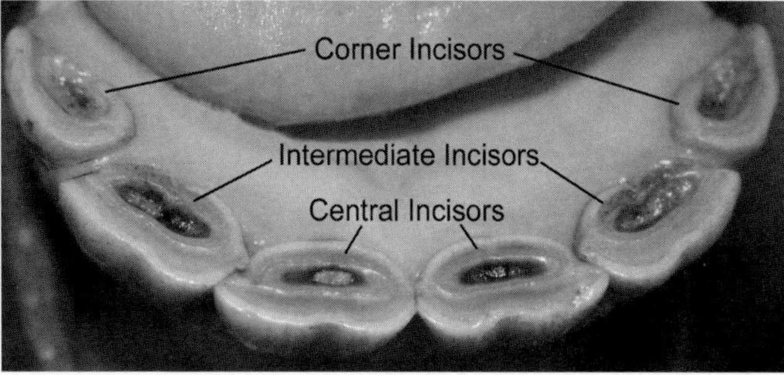

The following table lists information which helps to estimate the age of a horse from birth to 23 years old, based on changes in the teeth:

HORSE AGE	***TEETH CHANGES***
0 – 21 days	The 12 temporary premolars and the four temporary central incisors erupt
1 ½ – 4 months	The four temporary intermediate incisors erupt
6 – 9 months	The four temporary corner incisors erupt
12 -15 months	The chewing surfaces of the four temporary central incisors appear worn The four first molars erupt
18 – 20 months	The chewing surfaces of the four temporary intermediate incisors appear worn
24 months	The chewing surfaces of the four temporary corner incisors appear worn The four second molars erupt
29 months	The gums around the temporary central incisors look inflamed and are sensitive and red in color
30 months	The four temporary central incisors are shed; the permanent central incisors appear at the gum line The four first temporary premolars are shed and replaced by permanent ones
36 months (3 years)	The chewing surfaces of the upper and lower permanent central incisors begin to touch and wear down
41 months	The gums around the temporary intermediate incisors look inflamed and are sensitive and red in color
42 months	The four temporary intermediate incisors are shed; the permanent intermediate incisors appear at the gum line The four second temporary premolars are shed and replaced by the permanent ones
48 months (4 years)	The chewing surfaces of the upper and lower permanent intermediate incisors begin to touch and wear down The four third molars erupt The four canines start erupting in males
53 months	The gums around the temporary corner incisors look slightly inflamed and are sensitive and red in color
54 months	The four temporary corner incisors are shed; the permanent corner incisors appear at the gum line The four third temporary premolars are shed and replaced by the permanent ones
60 months (5 years)	The chewing surfaces of the upper and lower permanent corner incisors begin to touch and wear down ***Note***: At this time, the horse has a full set of permanent teeth
6 years	The brown cups of the lower permanent central incisor chewing surfaces disappear and the shape of these surfaces becomes oval
7 years	The brown cups of the lower permanent intermediate incisor chewing surfaces disappear and the shape of these surfaces becomes oval A small hook appears on the rear lower edge of the upper permanent corner incisors
8 years	The brown cups of the lower permanent corner incisor chewing surfaces disappear and the shape of these surfaces becomes oval The small hook on the rear lower edge of the upper permanent corner incisors disappears
9 years	The brown cups of the upper permanent central incisor chewing surfaces disappear and the shape of these surfaces becomes oval The shape of the lower permanent central incisor chewing surfaces becomes rounded and a dental star appears ***Note***: The dental star is a dark yellow/light brown mark on the incisor's chewing surface, shaped as a short line (about 1/8 of an inch long), located next and parallel to the outside surface

HORSE AGE	*TEETH CHANGES*
10 years	The brown cups of the upper permanent intermediate incisor chewing surfaces disappear and the shape of these surfaces becomes oval The shape of the lower permanent intermediate incisor chewing surfaces becomes rounded and a dental star appears The beginning of the "Galvayne's groove" appears on the upper edge of the upper permanent corner incisors ***Note***: The Galvayne's groove starts to appear on the outside surface of the upper permanent corner incisors, gradually covers the entire upper corner tooth, and later disappears as explained below
11 years	The brown cups of the upper permanent corner incisor chewing surfaces disappear and the shape of these surfaces becomes oval The shape of the lower permanent corner incisor chewing surfaces becomes rounded and a dental star appears
13 years	The Galvayne's groove covers half of the permanent corner incisors from the upper edge
15 years	The shape of the upper permanent central incisor chewing surfaces becomes rounded and a dental star appears The shape of the lower permanent central incisor chewing surfaces becomes triangular A hook appears on the rear lower edge of the upper permanent corner incisors
16 years	The shape of the upper permanent intermediate incisor chewing surfaces becomes rounded and a dental star appears The shape of the lower permanent intermediate incisor chewing surfaces becomes triangular The Galvayne's groove covers the entire upper permanent corner incisors
17 years	The shape of the upper permanent corner incisor chewing surfaces becomes rounded and a dental star appears The shape of the lower permanent corner incisor chewing surfaces becomes triangular The Galvayne's groove of the upper permanent corner incisors starts to disappear from the upper edge
18 years	The shape of the upper permanent central incisor chewing surfaces becomes triangular The shape of the lower permanent central incisor chewing surfaces becomes biangular (like a horizontal number eight)
19 years	The shape of the upper permanent intermediate incisor chewing surfaces becomes triangular The shape of the lower permanent intermediate incisor chewing surfaces becomes biangular The Galvayne's groove disappears from half of the upper permanent corner incisors
20 years	The shape of the upper permanent corner incisor chewing surfaces becomes triangular The shape of the lower permanent corner incisor chewing surfaces becomes biangular
21 years	The shape of the upper permanent central incisor chewing surfaces becomes biangular The Galvayne's groove disappears from the upper permanent corner incisors
22 years	The shape of the upper permanent intermediate incisor chewing surfaces becomes biangular
23 years	The shape of the upper permanent corner incisor chewing surfaces becomes biangular

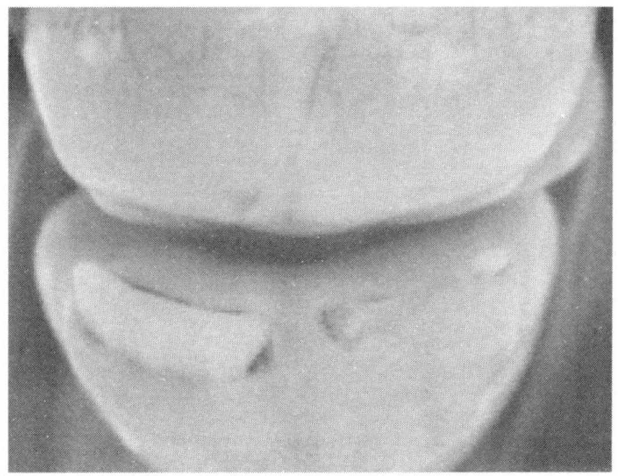

Baby teeth (at 2 days old): Temporary central incisors are erupting.

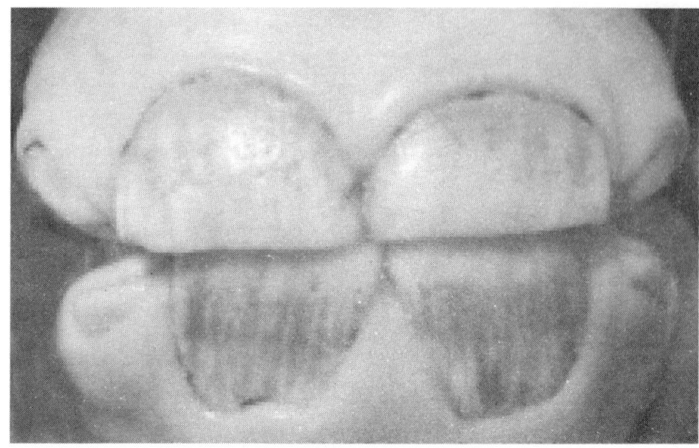

At 2 months old: Temporary intermediate incisors are erupting.

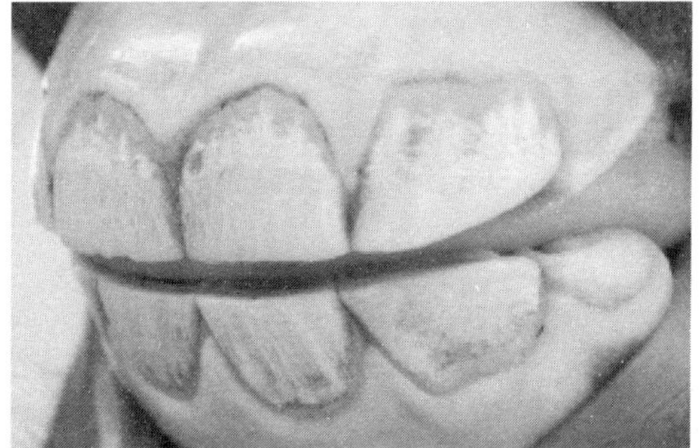

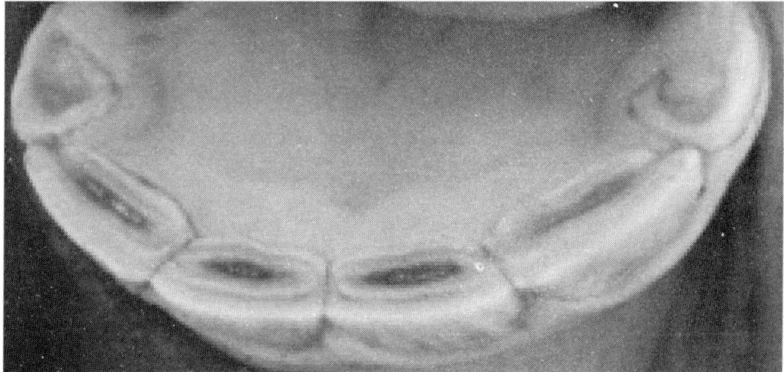

Yearling's teeth: The four temporary corner incisors have erupted and the chewing surfaces of the four temporary central incisors are worn.

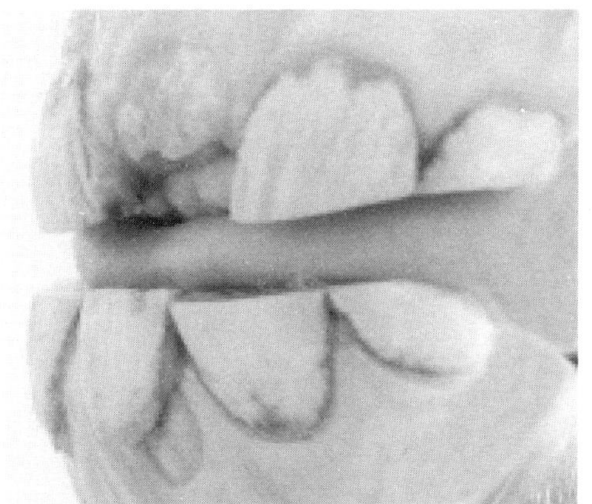

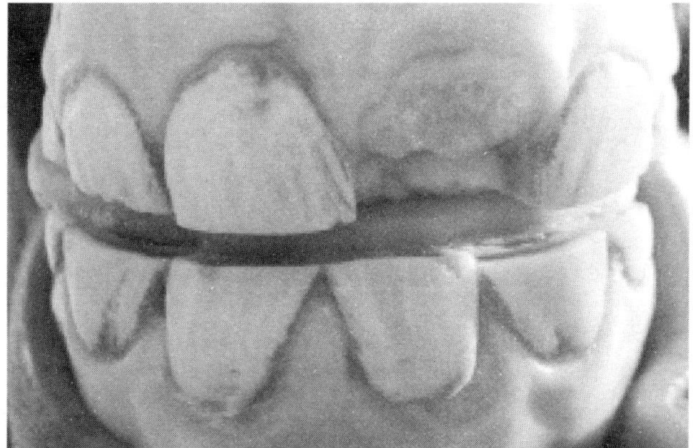

At 30 months old: One upper temporary central incisor has already shed and the permanent incisor is erupting. The lower temporary central incisor is ready to be shed.

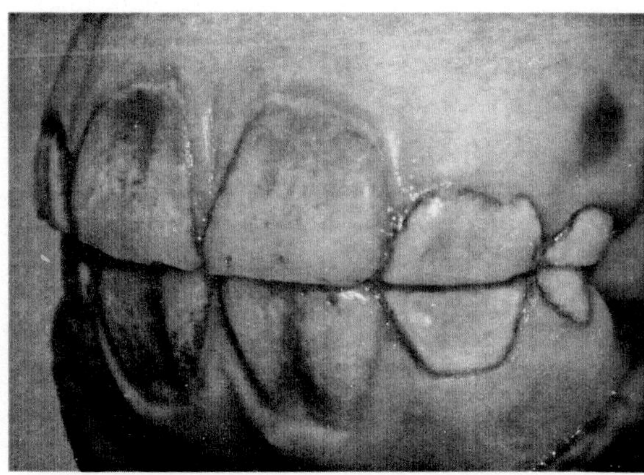

At 36 months old: Permanent central incisors are larger and darker than temporary incisors. The chewing surfaces of the permanent central incisors are already touching and wearing down.

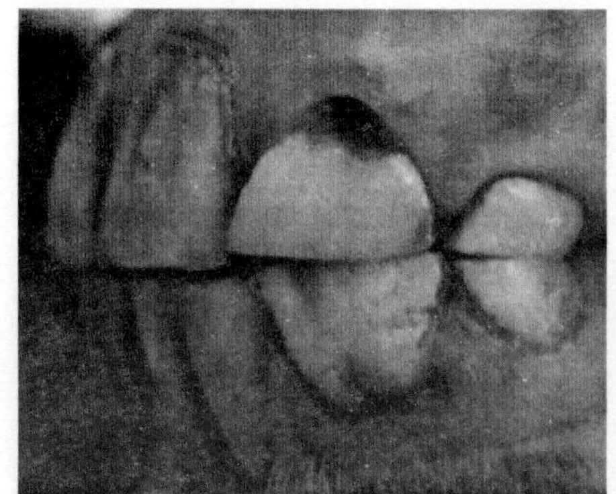

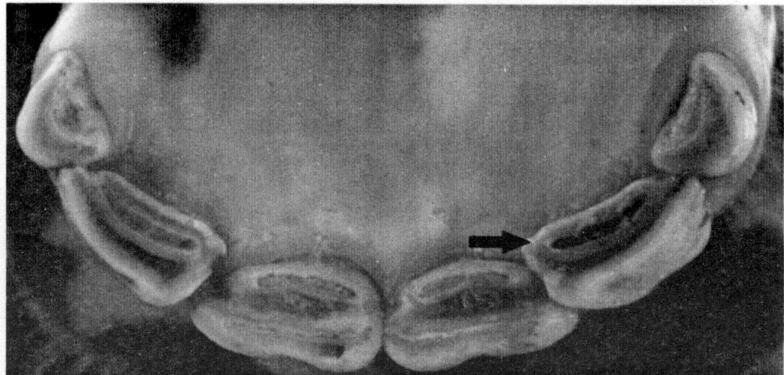

At 42 months old: The horse is ready to shed a lower temporary intermediate incisor.

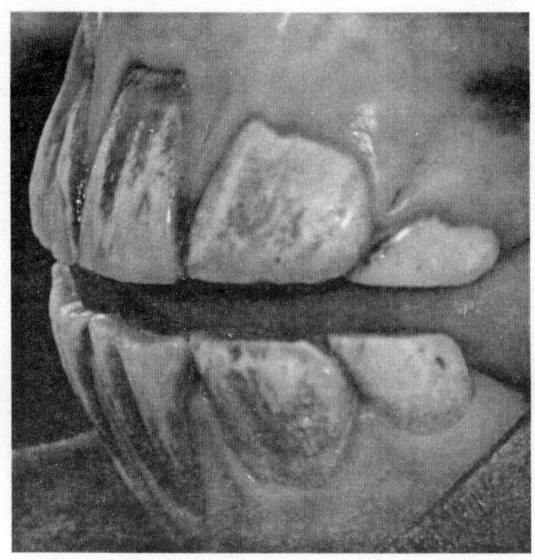

At 48 months old: Permanent central and intermediate incisors are larger and darker than temporary corner incisors. The chewing surfaces of the permanent central and intermediate incisors are already touching and wearing down.

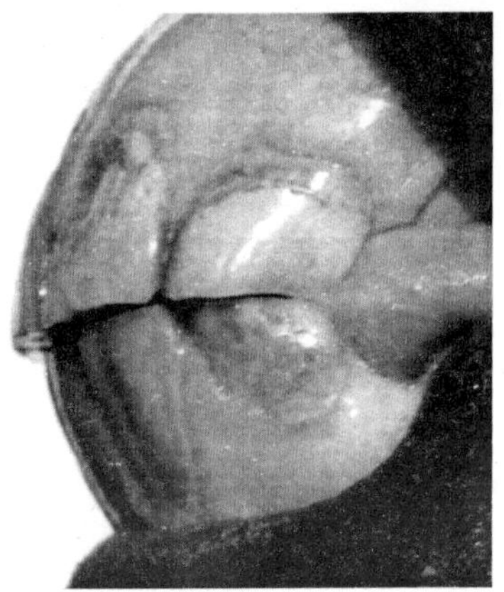
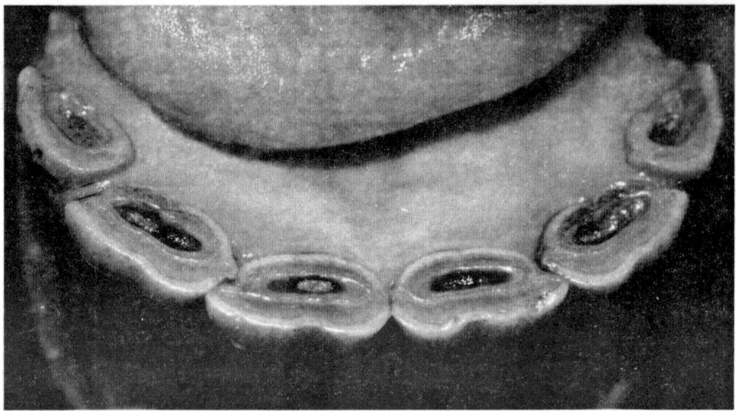

At 60 months old: All permanent incisors are touching their opposites and the chewing surfaces are wearing down.

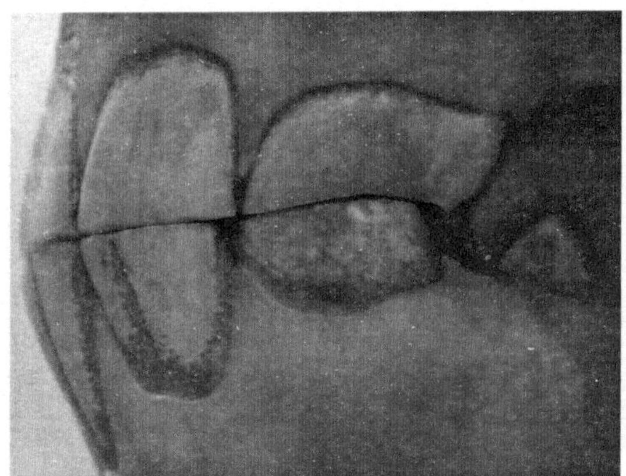
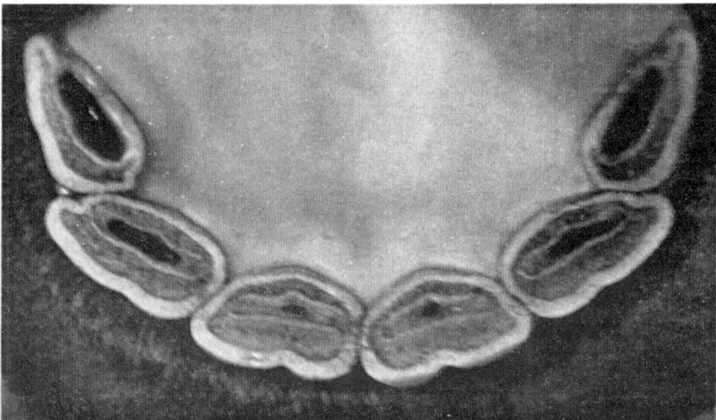

At 6 long years old: A small hook is starting to appear on the rear lower edge of the upper permanent corner incisor. Brown cups of the lower central incisors have disappeared and the brown cups of the lower intermediate incisors are starting to disappear.

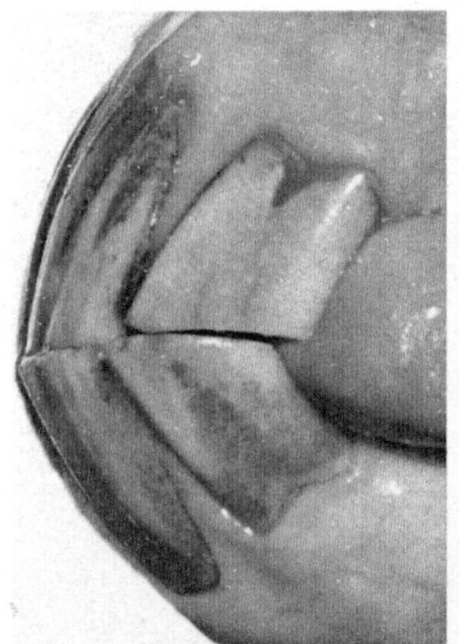
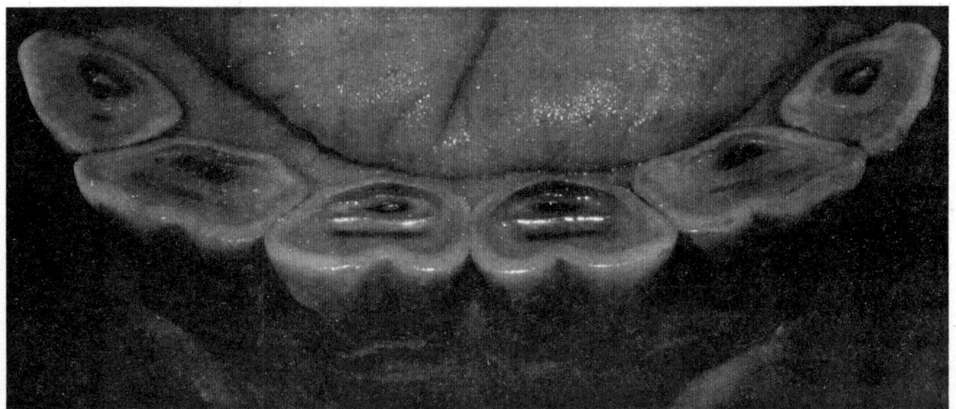

At 10 years old: The Galvayne's groove is starting to appear from above on the outside surfaces of the upper permanent corner incisors. The brown cups of all lower permanent incisors have disappeared from the chewing surfaces. The shape of the chewing surfaces of the lower permanent central incisors and the lower permanent intermediate incisors are rounded and have the dental star.

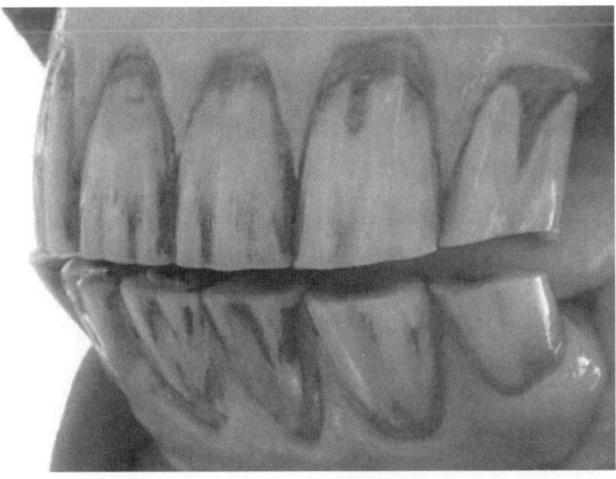

At 13 years old: The Galvayne's groove is seen on half of the upper permanent corner incisors.

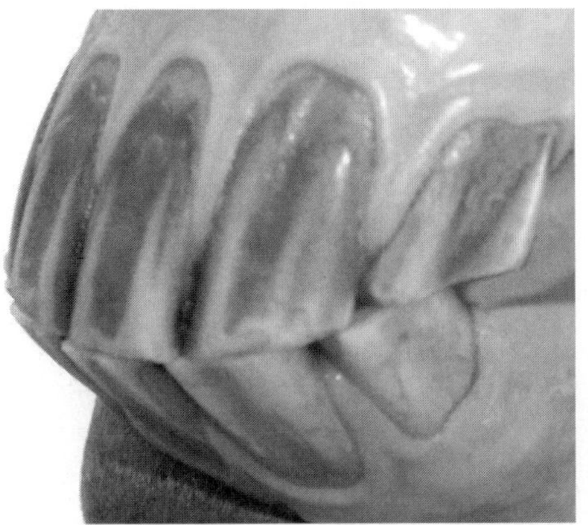

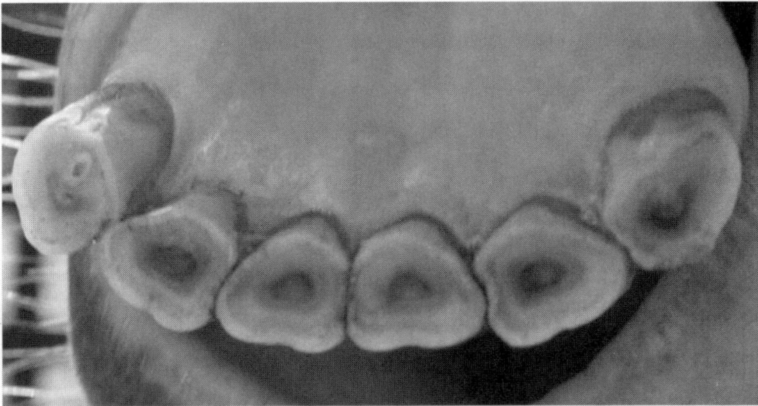

At 16 years old: The Galvayne's groove has covered the upper permanent corner incisors. The chewing surfaces of the lower permanent central incisors have a triangular shape, and the chewing surfaces of the lower intermediate incisors are turning triangular, also.

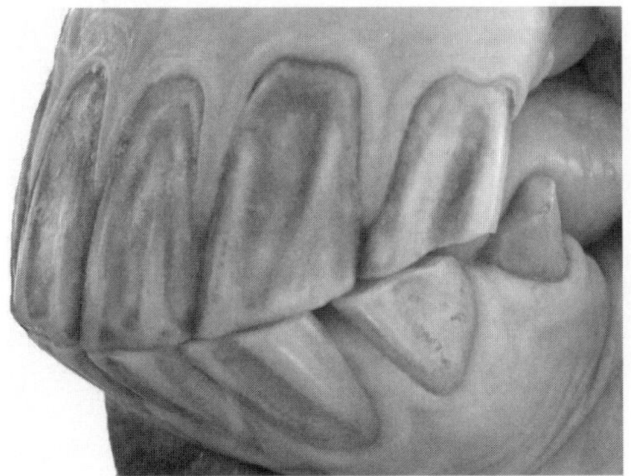

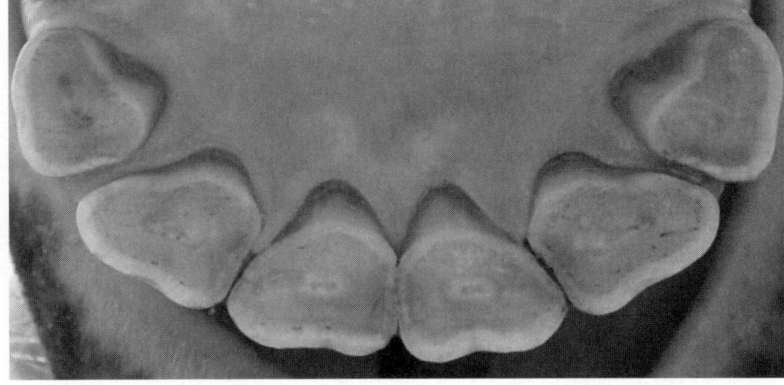

17 to 18 years old: The Galvayne's groove has disappeared a third of the way from the top of the permanent upper corner incisors. The chewing surfaces of the lower permanent central incisors are starting to have a biangular shape. The chewing surfaces of the lower permanent corner incisors have a triangular shape.

Note: A horse shedding teeth (e.g., at about 30 months and 42 months of age) may tend to lose weight for a few weeks, due to discomfort in chewing.

CHAPTER 4

UNIQUE CHARACTERISTICS OF THE PASO FINO HORSE

The most important characteristic of Paso Fino horses is their smooth gait, explained below in "The Paso Fino gait." Although Paso Fino horses come originally from Latin American countries, such as Colombia, Cuba, the Dominican Republic, and Puerto Rico, their popularity has been increasing in many other countries over the last five decades. Paso Fino horses may also be found in other countries in South America (Ecuador and Venezuela), Central America (Costa Rica and Panama), the Caribbean (Aruba and Curaçao), Canada, the United States, Europe (Germany, Spain, Switzerland, Czech Republic, and United Kingdom), and recently in several Arab countries. Nevertheless, Paso Finos deserve to gain an even higher status for their amazing characteristics and uniqueness, and to become better known worldwide as the smoothest of all riding horses.

Because of their many outstanding characteristics (smooth gait, beauty, elegance, brio, intelligence, etc.), Paso Fino horses raise a variety of positive emotions in people who own and/or work with them, or just see a Paso Fino for the first time. People express those emotions in very different ways: "The Paso Fino horse gives the smoothest and most exciting ride." "The Paso Fino is the sweetest and smartest horse breed in existence." "The Paso Fino is pure power under control." "The Paso Fino is the Rolls Royce of horses." "Once you ride a Paso Fino, you want to ride many more times. It's addictive."

CLASSIFICATION OF THE PASO FINO WITHIN HORSE BREEDS

A breed is a group of domestic animals of the same species that share some unique phenotypic characteristics, which are transmitted genetically for generations. For our purposes, the horse breeds are classified into four groups: miniatures, ponies, light horses, and heavy horses.

Most horse breeds from all over the world have associations of breeders that have permanent registries. They provide information related to ancestry, color, foaling date, standards, etc., to preserve the pureness of the animals. Paso Fino horses in the United States are registered by the *Paso Fino Horse Association, Inc.*

(PFHA), which has over 48,500 registered horses, over 8,500 members, and 24 Regional affiliated groups. Additionally, the *PFHA* promotes the Paso Fino horse throughout the States, sets rules and sanctions for the shows being held by the Regional groups during the year, and holds a National Championship in September of every year.

Outside the United States, Paso Fino horses are registered in other associations/federations that are affiliated with *CONFEPASO (Confederación Internacional de Caballos de Paso)*. For instance, *FEDEQUINAS* (*Federación Colombiana de Asociaciones Equinas*), the federation of horse associations in Colombia, and affiliated with *CONFEPASO*, has over 61,500 registered Paso Fino horses. Additionally, *FEDEQUINAS* has over 80,000 Colombian diagonal Paso registered horses (Collected Trote and Galope, Pure Trocha, and Trocha and Collected Galope). *FEDEQUINAS* (whose office is in Bogotá) has 25 affiliated associations from different areas of the country.

In many books, horse breeds are classified solely by the horse's height at the withers. However, height is not the only classification criteria for grouping horses. The most common confusion occurs between ponies and light horses, which are usually classified as follows: ponies less than 14 hands in height and light horses 14 hands in height or more. Others set the limit at 14 hands, 2 inches.

Note: 1 hand equals 4 inches; 1 inch equals 2.54 cm.; 1 hand equals 10.16 cm.

Grouping a horse is based on four parameters of the adult specimen: height, weight, conformation, and common use. This classification system is shown in the table below:

GROUP	HEIGHT	WEIGHT	CONFORMATION	COMMON USE
MINIATURES	Less than 9 hands, 2 inches (96.5 cm.) **Note**: There is another category for miniatures that are 8 hands, 2 inches (86.4 cm.) in height and under	Less than 420 lbs. (189 kg.)	Small to intermediate size head Either wide, short body or narrow, intermediately long body in proportion to their size	Companion Drafting small carriages
PONIES	From 9 hands, 2 inches (96.5 cm.) to under 13 hands, 2 inches (137 cm.)	From 420 lbs. (189 kg.) to under 666 lbs. (300 kg.)	Intermediate to big head Either wide (thick), short body or narrow, intermediately long body in proportion to their size	Companion Ridden by children Drafting small carriages Pack animals
LIGHT HORSES	From 13 hands, 2 inches (137 cm.) to 18 hands (182 cm.)	From 666 lbs. (300 kg.) to 1,666 lbs. (750 kg.)	Moderately small and refined head Slightly narrow and intermediately long body in proportion to their size Thin and aerodynamic leg bones	All equestrian sports under saddle Racing Traveling Cattle herding Drafting intermediate size carriages
HEAVY (DRAFT) HORSES	More than 15 hands and 3 inches (160 cm.)	More than 1,333 lbs. (600 kg.)	Big head and wide, with short to moderately long body in proportion to their size Thick leg bones and big hooves Feathers (long hairs under ergot and pastern) cover the hooves in most breeds	Drafting large carriages Equestrian sports (e.g., dressage and vaulting) Pack animals

Certainly, Paso Finos are small horses when they are compared with draft horses and some light horse breeds, such as Thoroughbreds, Quarter Horses, Andalusians, and Hanoverians. However, according to the Paso Fino standard and the four parameters shown in the table above, this breed may easily be classified in the group of light horses.

Additionally, horse breeds are developed based on either of the two situations described below or as a combination of both:

- **Geographic isolation**: Horses that live for many generations in an isolated region adapt some of their characteristics to the habitat (climatic conditions, geography, availability of feed, etc.); thus, natural selection encourages only the best adapted specimens to survive and produce the next generations. Inbreeding commonly is present and facilitates favorable changes for better adaptation to the environment.

- **Controlled selection**: According to particular needs or desires, breeders are able to redirect natural selection in a group of horses by selecting and breeding only the specimens from which improved offspring are expected (even if the foundation stock initially comes from different breeds). After the offspring are born and raised, only the specimens with the proper characteristics (phenotype) will be reproduced, and the same will happen with the following generations. In addition, inbreeding may be used to maintain some favorable characteristics of the group (see Chapter 8: "Reproduction").

PASO FINO STANDARDS

- **HEIGHT**: The average height of adult Paso Fino horses (at five years of age or older) is around 14 hands (142 cm.). However, the minimum height for adult Paso Fino mares (at five years of age or older) being shown in *CONFEPASO* sanctioned shows is 136 cm. (13 hands, 1 and 9/16 inches) and for adult Paso Fino males, either stallions or geldings, is 138 cm. (13 hands, 2 and 5/16 inches) *(Reglamento de Competencias de Caballos de Paso - CONFEPASO, Chapter 4, Article 7, Section 3 "Alzadas Mínimas," Subsection B).*

  Paso Fino breeders and associations/federations worldwide must maintain the average height of the breed and keep it from being reduced. Any height reduction may cause the Paso Fino breed to be classified as a pony. Conversely, Paso Finos of both genders may reach heights over 15 hands (152.4 cm). These horses may perform a smooth gait but rarely reach the great, quick cadence of the modern Classic Finos.

- **WEIGHT**: The average weight of adult Paso Finos is 870 lbs. (391.5 kg.), but weight may range from 720 lbs. (324 kg.) to 1,120 lbs. (504 kg.).

- **CONFORMATION**: The head of a Paso Fino is moderately small, but proportional to the horse's size. The head bones are smoothly assembled and mainly covered with skin; this gives a refined appearance to the head. Permanently alert ears, elegantly shaped at the tips, and short (ideally up to 5 inches long), are preferred. A wide forehead provides a good distance between the two big, shiny, and expressive eyes. The forehead either may be flat or slightly convex.

In Paso Finos, a straight face profile is more desirable than a concave face profile (also called "dished" face) or a convex face profile (also called "Roman nose"). The muzzle has large nostrils (about 2 ¼ inches high and 1 ¼ inches wide at rest, at a minimum) and strong, flexible, and refined lips.

The neck should be arched at the crest, intermediately long, moderately to very muscled, especially on the sides, and flexible. The neck of the Paso Fino is projected upward from the withers, which makes the withers be moderately high and look smoothly fused with the neck. This neck position gives elegance to the Paso Fino horse. The ideal shape of the neck is like a "swan" (crest is longer than the lower edge). The neck may be regular or "even" (similar length of crest and lower edge). Nevertheless, a "deer" (or "ewe") neck (crest is shorter than the lower edge) is not desirable. The Paso Fino's abundant, thick mane and tail have many long hairs, either straight or slightly curly, that lend an air of grace to the horse.

The withers and upper point of the croup should be level. The back must be muscular, firm, and almost straight. A back with an upper line that is very concave (sway-back appearance) is not desirable.

A horse is considered sway-backed, and, therefore, cannot be shown in *CONFEPASO* sanctioned shows, when its back has any point deeper than 8 cm. (about 3 3/16 inches). This is in reference to a straight line drawn between the withers and the highest point of the lumbar-sacral joint (the upper point of the croup). Mares older than five years, however, are accepted with up to a 12 cm. (4 ¾ inches) deep point in their backs in reference to the same straight line *(Reglamento de Competencias de Caballos de Paso - CONFEPASO, Chapter 4, Article 7, Section 11).*

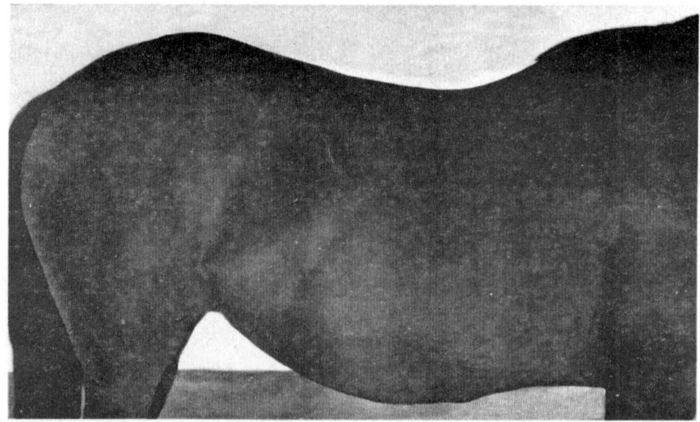

Horse with sway-back appearance

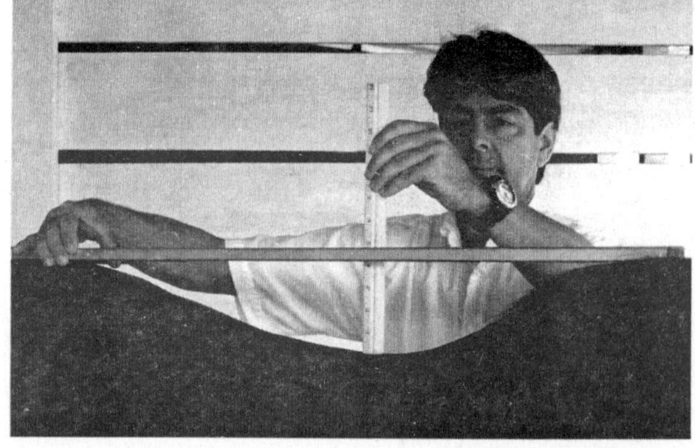

Proper way to measure sway-backed horses

The top of the shoulders (or scapulas) is smoothly attached to the withers and the bottom of the shoulders to the chest. The shoulders are inclined downward about 55-56 degrees over the ground level. The chest is moderately wide and deep to provide good respiratory capacity.

Paso Fino horses have deep barrels (thorax) and arched ribs to provide room enough for the internal organs. The loins should be wide, flat, and moderately muscular. The hips should be of medium length, wide, rounded, and well-proportioned. The croup neither should be flat nor inclined downward to a great degree. Additionally, mares with a croup that is inclined downward to a great degree may have problems with foaling.

Paso Fino legs are not very long. The upper halves of the forearms, entire thighs, and upper halves of the gaskins are intermediately muscular. The leg bones below the forearms and gaskins are thin to provide an aerodynamic design for the gait. The joints (carpus, hock, and fetlock) are very noticeable and look firm while the horse both stands and performs the gait. In addition, because the skin of the legs is very fine, the tendons are very distinct from the bones. The hooves are relatively small, but proportional to the horse's size and bone width.

For smoothness, the Paso Fino horse should keep the croup steady while performing the gait. This occurs when the hind legs have elasticity (especially at the hocks) to propel the body forward. The tail's root should be smoothly kept between the rounded buttocks and projected backward and down from the end of the croup.

- **COMMON USES**: Although, initially, Paso Fino horses may look like small and weak animals with a very delicate gait, actually they are just the opposite. Paso Finos are very strong and powerful horses with the ability to develop an amazing endurance. This ability comes from the origins of the breed. Initially, they were not developed for esthetic purposes, but to provide smooth rides during long daily work hours (from eight to ten hours a day).

  Currently, Paso Fino horses are used for many purposes:

  - **Work and as a means of transportation**: In their countries of origin, Paso Finos are still used for work and as a means of transportation. They work herding cattle, taking cowboys throughout large farms, carrying heavy loads of products to and from the countryside, pulling carts to transport milk cans (in the countryside) and building/remodeling debris (in the cities). Some people who live in the countryside still travel to small towns on Paso Fino horses for shopping, studying, and working.

Left, Paso Fino horse working on a street in Caldas, Antioquia (Colombia). Right, Paso Fino horses pulling carts with building/remodeling debris in Medellín (Colombia). Photos by Mildred Arent.

  - **Trail riding**: Due to their smooth gait and endurance, Paso Finos are a good choice for people who like to go on trail rides.
  - **Endurance competition**: Because of their ancestral heritage, natural selection over centuries, athletic conformation, and gait, Paso Finos are competitive in endurance contests with other horse breeds.

- **Therapeutic horseback riding**: Although trotters are more commonly used as therapy horses, Paso Finos are recommended for those patients with back/spine problems, weak neck muscles, lack of equilibrium, etc.

- **Cutting and team penning**: Paso Finos are well-suited to do these sports because they have inherited their ancestor's ability to work with cattle.

- **Carriage driving**: Paso Finos are able to work pulling carts with heavy loads, as well as pulling carriages for pleasure or show purposes.

- **Show**: Diverse competition categories are offered in *Paso Fino Horse Association* sanctioned shows in the United States. The categories are Classic Fino, Paso Performance, Paso Pleasure, Bellas Formas (Conformation), Paso Versatility, Paso Western Pleasure, and Paso Trail *(PFHA – Constitution and Rule Book, Chapter Three, Sections II, III, IV, V, VI - Subsections A, B, and C).* The same competition categories are offered in *CONFEPASO* sanctioned shows (e.g., biannual Paso Horse World Cup). However, the name given to the Classic Fino category classes is "Paso Fino" *(Reglamento de Competencias de Caballos de Paso - CONFEPASO, Chapter 3, Article 1).* A brief explanation of these categories is found on page 43. These categories have a wide range of classes according to the horse's age and gender. In addition, the Equitation category has different classes according to the riders' ages (see Chapter 16: "Equitation - not just sitting pretty").

  The rules of the *Paso Fino Horse Association* also include other show categories: Paso Costume, Paso Fino Country Pleasure, and Paso Pleasure Driving *(PFHA – Constitution and Rule Book, Chapter Three, Section VI, Subsections D, E, and F).* Additionally, some categories such as Classic Fino, Paso Performance, and Paso Pleasure have different classes according to the riders' status: youth, amateur owner, and professional.

- **Drill Team**: A team of Paso Fino horses and their riders who perform well-synchronized maneuvers (a choreography) that riders and viewers may enjoy.

"Paso Elegante - Drill Team" performing at the Horse Park in Ocala, FL (2006), coached by the author. Photo by Olga García.

- **Company**: Some enthusiasts own Paso Fino horses as pets or for company due to the gentleness, beauty, and easy manners of most specimens of this breed.

Above, Sarah Freedman at four years of age, longeing "Pincel del Juncal," a Paso Fino gelding. This shows the great temperament of the Paso Fino breed.
Photo courtesy of Allen and Judy Brick Freedman – Charlotte Valley Farms, Anthony, FL. Photo by Judy Brick Freedman.

Right, Jorge Suárez, Jr. at five years of age, riding "Altanero," a Classic Fino gelding, during the 6th ***CONFEPASO*** *Youth Mundial held in Kissimmee, FL (2006). Jorge represented the US team and was awarded the Bronze medal.*
Photo courtesy of Jorge and Michelle Suárez. Photo donated by WNC Photography.

OTHER CHARACTERISTICS OF THE PASO FINO HORSE

The Paso Fino breed has a great variety of colors, described in Chapter 5: "Colors of Paso Fino horses." For showing, the *Paso Fino Horse Association* accepts horses with all coat, skin, and eye colors, with or without white markings *(PFHA – Constitution and Rule Book, Chapter Two, Section IV, Subsection B).* On the other hand, *CONFEPASO* only accepts solid colors (black, seal bay, bay, buckskin, dun, blue dun, chestnut, palomino, and chestnut with flaxen mane and tail), grey/white, flea-bitten, and roan colors. Horses with white markings (over these colors) may have some restrictions in competition under *CONFEPASO* rules (see Chapter 5: "Colors of Paso Fino horses").

In addition to their amazing gait, Paso Finos are creatures of great grace and beauty. They are also horses with a wonderful temperament. Paso Finos are generally smart, have a liking for people, and, ideally, they are full of brio. The term, "brio" (in Spanish), is an outstanding characteristic not easily translatable to English. Brio may be defined as "spirited," "full of energy," "lion-hearted," and always ready to work, even to death, if that were necessary. Conversely, brio has nothing to do with being "crazy" or out of control.

When a Paso Fino horse is in gait, either under saddle or not, the tail should be extended back firmly, arched down, and display a beautiful skirt (the long hairs of the tail) hanging down. Holding the tail in this manner looks elegant and displays the pride of the Paso Fino breed. In addition, although Paso Fino horses have the same natural mobility of their tails as other horse breeds, Paso Finos should not swish their tails when gaiting; even if there are flies or other insects bothering them. This rule has its origin in the fact that a Paso horse swishing its tail on the narrow mountain paths, with a lot of mud during the rainy season, was clearly a nuisance for the rider and other riders behind or at its side.

Swishing the tail, when gaiting under saddle, is considered a vice that may arise from a bad attitude or fear. However, swishing the tail in a horse that does not have this vice may be caused by discomfort (due to several external factors) or pain, and therefore is a clear sign that something is wrong. The next step is finding the cause of the discomfort or pain and correcting it.

In *CONFEPASO* sanctioned shows, a horse performing the gait should not swish its tail. If the horse swishes its tail from one to five times, the horse will be penalized; if the horse swishes six or more times, the horse will be excused *(Reglamento de Competencias de Caballos de Paso - CONFEPASO, Chapter 4, Article 8, Section H, Subsection 8 and Article 9, Section A).*

THE PASO FINO GAIT

A Paso Fino horse is born with the natural ability to perform the gait. This means that the Paso Fino gait is neither an artificial gait created by the rider nor a gait that takes years of training. Therefore, young riders and new riders easily are able to ride Paso Finos and maintain a smooth gait.

Although the Paso Fino gait is natural, these horses require training like any other breed of horse. However, training is not oriented to changing the gait, but rather allowing the horse to learn all of the rider's commands and achieving a balanced gait with perfect symmetry, while carrying extra weight on its back. In addition, during the training process, the Paso Fino horse gradually develops the muscles to perform its gait in a collected manner, with the hind legs properly underneath the abdomen.

When a horse is in gait, each hoof performs the whole movement (from the time when the hoof leaves the ground until it hits the ground again) in two phases: elevation and advance. Each phase reaches a maximum level (maximum elevation and support). These phases and maximum levels are described below:

- **Elevation**: The first phase in which the hoof is raised from the ground.
- **Maximum elevation**: The hoof stops ascending because it reaches its highest elevation.
- **Advance**: The second phase when the hoof is going down from the maximum height and goes forward.
- **Support**: The hoof reaches the ground to support the body weight.

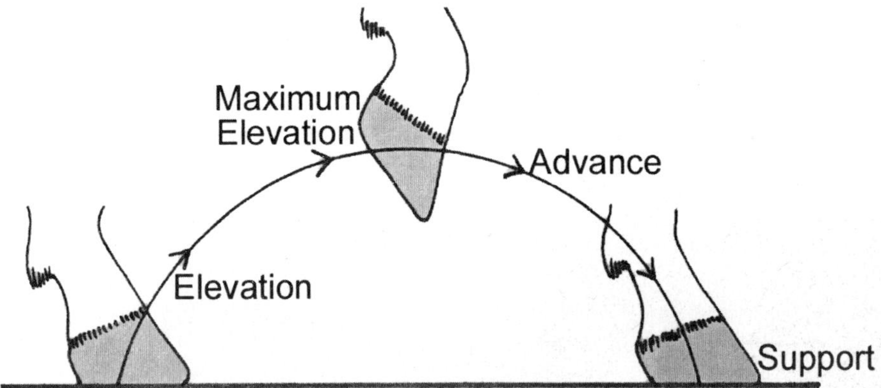

"Paso Fino" may be translated from Spanish to English as "Fine Step," due to the smoothness, elegance, and well-coordinated movement of the four hooves. In Paso Fino, each hoof moves independently from the other three hooves in a perfect succession, which translates into a rhythm of four by four. Thus, four independent quick beats (sounds) are heard when the four hooves hit the ground during every cycle, one sound for each hoof. The evenly alternated movement among the four hooves makes the Paso Fino an isochronic gait.

Note: In gaits, a cycle is completed when the horse moves each one of the four hooves one time. A gait, then, is a succession of similar cycles.

The maximum smoothness of a Paso Fino depends on how perfectly the horse performs the gait, using an equally alternated sequence of its four hooves, as follows: 1) a hind leg; 2) the same side foreleg; 3) the other hind leg; 4) the last foreleg. For instructional purposes, the sounds produced for this sequence of four beats are like "TA - CA – TA – CA," respectively.

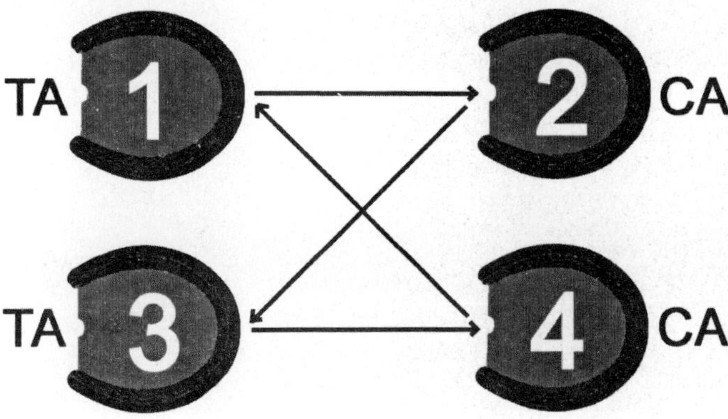

While the four hooves are moved in this sequence within every cycle, the horse supports its weight in eight different stages (see photographs on pages 54 and 55): two lateral supports (same side legs being on the ground); two diagonal supports (opposite front and hind legs being on the ground); two supports with one front leg and both hind legs being on the ground; and two supports with both front legs and one hind leg being on the ground.

The symmetry of the Paso Fino gait is seen when each hoof reaches the same distance within a step as the other hooves, and when the front hooves move evenly (with similar elevation and advance to each other), and so do the hind hooves.

As an acoustic aid for the rider, judges (when the horse is being shown), and enthusiasts, Paso Fino horses are ridden over a sounding board made of wood. This helps the individual hear the clearness of the evenly alternated gait (rhythm) and its consistency. Thus, if a rider and a Paso Fino horse are compared to a musician and a musical instrument, the rider may play the music of the gait on a sounding board and give commands to "tune" the horse in order to adjust the symmetry, rhythm, and cadence of the "music" (the Paso Fino gait).

*Mr. Lee Vulgaris, a student of Ocala's School of Equestrian Art, is shown passing over the sounding board on his Classic Fino mare, "Creación de La Luisa" (Patrimonio del Ocho x Inquietud de La J). Creación had just been awarded US 2006 **PFHA** National Champion Amateur Owner Classic Fino mare. Creación was trained at United Paso Fino Show Horses. Photo courtesy of Lee and Margaret Vulgaris. Photo by Larry Williams Photography.*

MOTIONS OF THE PASO FINO GAIT

The Paso Fino gait is performed in three characteristic motions: Classic Fino (also known as "Fino-Fino"), Paso Corto (pronounced /quor-to/), and Paso Largo (pronounced /lahr-goh/). These motions depend on three factors:

- The **cadence** of the gait: the quickness of the hooves being moved. Or, similarly, the quickness of the rhythm.
- The **extension of the steps**: The distance reached by each hoof within a step.
- The resultant **forward speed** of the horse.

The three motions of the Paso Fino gait, and the factors involved, are shown in the following table:

MOTION OF PASO FINO	*CADENCE*	*EXTENSION OF EACH STEP*	*FORWARD SPEED*	*EFFORT REQUIRED*
CLASSIC FINO	Extremely quick (570-700 beats per minute)	Very short	Very slow	The most demanding motion of the Paso Fino gait
PASO CORTO	Less quick than Classic Fino (450 beats per minute, at a minimum)	Intermediate between Classic Fino and Paso Largo	Intermediate between Classic Fino and Paso Largo	The least demanding motion of Paso Fino
PASO LARGO	As quick as Paso Corto or slightly quicker	The longest of the Paso Fino motions	The fastest of the Paso Fino motions	Requires more effort than Paso Corto and slightly less than Classic Fino

The three motions of the Paso Fino must be performed with rhythm, symmetry, energy and steadiness of steps, collection, elegance, and consistency. Consistency is the ability of a horse to maintain the rhythm, cadence, extension of steps, and, therefore, the forward speed of any motion of the Paso Fino gait for a long time, as asked by the rider. Only horses full of brio are able to perform Classic Fino.

PASO FINO SHOW CATEGORIES

The show categories offered by the *Paso Fino Horse Association (PFHA)* and *CONFEPASO* are explained briefly:

- **Classic Fino**: In *PFHA* shows, the Classic Fino horse is evaluated for the execution and naturalness of its Classic Fino gait, in terms of an animated cadence (quickness of its footfall), rhythm and consistency, collection, smoothness, and symmetry (75%). Other qualities evaluated are conformation, appearance, and way of going (15%), and manners (10%). When in movement (around the ring, on the sounding board, or executing any figure), the horse only performs the Classic Fino gait. Missing the Classic Fino gait or mixing gaits, any lack of consistency or smoothness, fighting the bit, swishing the tail, and/or flattening the ears (which shows aggression) is penalized *(PFHA – Constitution and Rule Book, Chapter Three, Section III, Subsection A)*.

In *CONFEPASO* shows, Classic Fino horses also perform only the Classic Fino gait (called "Paso Fino," in the rules), including an individual presentation consisting of a figure eight, backing up (not in gait), serpentine, and passing over the sounding board *(Reglamento de Competencias de Caballos de Paso - CONFEPASO, Chapter 5, Article 3, Sections B to G)*. Horses are judged for rhythm, cadence, and smoothness of their gait (24 points), brio and temperament (8 points), rear legs (6 points), front legs (6 points), and hip steadiness (6 points), all of which total is 50 points = 50%. They are also judged for training, responsiveness to the reins, and head-neck set (8 points), consistency of the gait (8 points) and harmony of the gait (8 points), all of which total is 24 points = 24%. Other qualities judged are phenotype (conformation) of the head, neck, chest, rib cage, back, croup, and height for the Paso Fino breed (14 points), leg balance (8 points), color (2 points), and tail (2 points), all of which total is 26 points = 26%. Total 100 points = 100% *(Reglamento de Competencias de Caballos de Paso - CONFEPASO, Chapter 5, Article 3, Section J)*.

See the representative standard of Classic Fino stallion *MARCAPASOS* on page 46 and the representative standard of Classic Fino mare *REINA DE LA ESTANCIA* on page 47.

- **Paso Performance**: In *PFHA* sanctioned shows, the Paso Performance horse is judged performing consistent, smooth, and brilliant collected Paso Corto (30%), collected Paso Largo (30%), and an animated, brilliant Walk (10%), as each motion is requested. The evaluation of gaits is based on the motions described above, as well as the transitions. Other qualities evaluated are conformation, appearance, and way of going (20%), and manners *(10%) (PFHA – Constitution and Rule Book, Chapter Three, Section IV, Subsection A)*.

  In *CONFEPASO* sanctioned shows, the Paso Performance horse is judged performing consistent, smooth, and brilliant collected Paso Corto (30%), collected Paso Largo (30%), and an animated, brilliant Walk (15%), as each motion is requested. Conformation, appearance, and way of going (15%), and manners *(10%)* are also evaluated *(Reglamento de Competencias de Caballos de Paso - CONFEPASO, Chapter 5, Article 4)*.

  See the representative standard of Paso Performance stallion *RIVAL DE LA ESTANCIA* on page 48 and the representative standard of Paso Performance mare *MARAQUITA LA ROSA TRES* on page 49.

- **Paso Pleasure**: In *PFHA* sanctioned shows, the Paso Pleasure horse is judged performing Paso Corto (25%), Paso Largo (25%), and Flat Walk (10%), as each motion is requested. The evaluation of gaits is based on motions and transitions. Conformation, manners, attitude, and way of going are also judged (40%) *(PFHA – Constitution and Rule Book, Chapter Three, Section V, Subsection A)*.

  In *CONFEPASO* sanctioned shows, the Paso Pleasure horse is judged performing Paso Corto (30%), Paso Largo (30%), and Flat Walk (10%), as each motion is requested. The evaluation of gaits is based on motions and transitions. Conformation, manners, attitude, and way of going (20%), and backing up (10%) are also judged *(Reglamento de Competencias de Caballos de Paso - CONFEPASO, Chapter 5, Article 6)*.

  See the representative standard of Paso Pleasure gelding *MAHATMA GANDHI DE CVF* on page 50 and the representative standard of Paso Pleasure mare *ESENCIA DE UNITED* on page 51.

- **Bellas Formas (Conformation)**: In *PFHA* sanctioned shows, the Bella Forma horse is shown bareback, without any rider, and led with one or two long reins that are held by one or two 'drivers' who walk behind. The horse is primarily evaluated for conformation (60%), and quality and naturalness of Classic Fino or Paso Corto gait (30%). Appearance, grooming, and manners are also judged (10%) *(PFHA – Constitution and Rule Book, Chapter Three, Section II, Subsection A)*.

  In *CONFEPASO* sanctioned shows, the Bella Forma horse is presented in the same way and primarily evaluated for conformation (60%), and quality and naturalness of Classic Fino or Paso Corto gait (40%) *(Reglamento de Competencias de Caballos de Paso - CONFEPASO, Chapter 5, Article 2, Section 3)*.

- **Paso Versatility**: In *PFHA* sanctioned shows, the Paso Versatility horse is judged performing collected Paso Corto (20%), collected Paso Largo (20%), Canter (10%), and Walk (10%). The evaluation of gaits is based on the four motions. Manners (understood as good behavior) and some exercises (figure eight, backing up, and jumping over an obstacle at a Canter) are also evaluated (40%). Canter is a three - beat gait that starts with a hind leg and ends with the opposite foreleg, which is also the lead leg for turns *(PFHA – Constitution and Rule Book, Chapter Three, Section VI, Subsection A, 1)*.

  In *CONFEPASO* sanctioned shows, the Paso Versatility horse is judged in the same way: Collected Paso Corto (20%), collected Paso Largo (20%), Canter (10%), and Walk (10%). Manners and some exercises (figure eight, backing up, and jumping over an obstacle at a Canter) are also evaluated (40%) *(Reglamento de Competencias de Caballos de Paso - CONFEPASO, Chapter 5, Article 5)*.

- **Paso Western Pleasure**: In *PFHA* sanctioned shows, the Paso Western Pleasure horse is judged performing Paso Corto (35%), Lope (a smoother and less elevated Canter) (evaluated as 30%), and Flat Walk (10%). It should look like the horse is capable of working with cows, while maintaining the pride and elegance of a Paso Fino. Manners, attitude, and way of going are also evaluated (25%) *(PFHA – Constitution and Rule Book, Chapter Three, Section VI, Subsection B, 1)*.

  In *CONFEPASO* sanctioned shows, the Paso Western Pleasure horse is judged performing Paso Corto (35%), Lope (30%), and Flat Walk (10%). Manners, attitude, and way of going are evaluated (15%), as well as backing up straight (10%) *(Reglamento de Competencias de Caballos de Paso - CONFEPASO, Chapter 5, Article 7)*.

- **Paso Trail**: In *PFHA* sanctioned shows, the contestant duo competing in this class completes a designed course of six to eight obstacles that horse and rider commonly face on a trail ride. Some of the obstacles include operating a gate, carrying an object, crossing a bridge, riding through water, backing up through obstacles, side passing, etc. Although the evaluation is 100% based on the obstacle work, the horse must perform Paso Corto, Paso Largo, Flat Walk, and Lope or Canter, depending on what is necessary to complete the obstacles *(PFHA – Constitution and Rule Book, Chapter Three, Section VI, Subsection C, 1)*. In *CONFEPASO* sanctioned shows, this class is judged in the same way (*Reglamento de Competencias de Caballos de Paso -CONFEPASO, Chapter 5, Article 8*

Note: Before showing a Paso Fino horse in any of these categories, either in a *PFHA* or a *CONFEPASO* sanctioned show, it is highly recommended that the corresponding rules be read so that the rider is fully aware of the judging procedures, causes for penalization or exclusion, proper tack, rider's attire, etc.

REPRESENTATIVE STANDARD OF CLASSIC FINO STALLION

MARCAPASOS

* *Multi-champion Classic Fino stallion/colt in Colombia, Puerto Rico, and the United States.*

** *One of the most important Classic Fino stallions of today, sire of multi-champion Classic Fino horses in numerous countries.*

Registration number: 35,587 (PFHA)
Foaling date: 02/16/1997 (Colombia)
Color: Dark bay
Sire: Rescate Del Ocho (Resorte III x Tempestad II)
Dam: Daleska (Resorte IV x Hidalga)
Breeder: Orozco Family
Owner: Rubén Sierra
Farm: Hacienda La Sierra, Summerfield, FL
Rider: Janine Suárez (during the 6th CONFEPASO Youth Equitation World Championship)
Courtesy of Rubén Sierra
Photo by Cheri Prill Photo

REPRESENTATIVE STANDARD OF CLASSIC FINO MARE

REINA DE LA ESTANCIA

Multi-champion Classic Fino mare/filly, including

* ***PFHA** sanctioned shows: US 2005 National Champion 4 yr.old filly, 2006 The Spectrum International (Kissimmee, FL) Champion (1st place) mare and Grand Champion mare/filly.*

** *Other shows: 2005 Paso Fino Grand Prix (Miami, FL) Champion (1st place) 4 yr.old filly and Reserve Grand Champion mare/filly, 2006 Paso Fino Grand Prix (Miami, FL - Feb.) Reserve Champion (2nd place) mare and Reserve Grand Champion mare/filly.*

Registration number: 38,524 (PFHA)
Foaling date: 10/01/2001
Color: Chestnut
Sire: Mensaje del Ocho (Nevado x Colombia de Resorte III)
Dam: Pretenciosa de la Estancia (Cosmos x Reina de Santa Cruz)
Breeder: Criadero La Estancia
Owners: Edgar and Alei Ortiz
Farm: United Paso Fino Show Horses, Summerfield, FL
Rider: Alei Ortiz
Courtesy of United Paso Fino Show Horses
Photo by WNC Photography

REPRESENTATIVE STANDARD OF PASO PERFORMANCE STALLION

RIVAL DE LA ESTANCIA

Multi-champion Paso Performance stallion/colt, including

* ***PFHA*** *sanctioned shows: 2003 The American Classic (Tunica, MS) Champion (1st place) 3 yr.old colt, 2004 El Carnaval de Marzo (Ocala, FL) Reserve Grand Champion stallion/colt, 2004 The American Classic (Tunica, MS) Champion (1st place) 4 yr.old colt and Grand Champion stallion/colt, 2004 The Magnolia Classic (Hattiesburg, MS) Am./Owner Champion (1st place) 4 yr.old colt and Am./Owner Grand Champion stallion/colt, 2005 The Magnolia Classic (Hattiesburg, MS) Champion (1st place) stallion and Reserve Grand Champion stallion/colt, 2006 The Spectrum International (Kissimmee, FL) Am./Owner Reserve Grand Champion stallion/colt, 2006 Magnolia Classic (Hattiesburg, MS) Am./Owner Champion (1st place) stallion and Am./Owner Grand Champion stallion/colt.*

Registration number: 40,015 (PFHA)
Foaling date: 01/07/2000
Color: Chestnut
Sire: Capuchino de Los Terremotos (Capuchino x Soraya de los Terremotos)
Dam: Fabiola de Tanama (Piloto de Resorte Cuarto x Guanina de Amoretto)
Breeder: Criadero La Estancia
Owners: Dale and Mary Younce
Farm: Brio Farm, Magnolia Springs, AL
Rider: Julio Pérez
Courtesy of Dale and Mary Younce
Photo by Bravo Equine Enterprises

REPRESENTATIVE STANDARD OF PASO PERFORMANCE MARE

MARAQUITA LA ROSA TRES

Multi-champion Paso Performance mare, including

* ***PFHA** sanctioned shows: 2004 The Spectrum International (Kissimmee, FL) Champion (1st place) Am./Owner mare and Grand Champion Am./Owner mare/filly, US 2004 Grand National Champion Am./Owner mare/filly, 2005 The Spectrum International (Kissimmee, FL) Champion (1st place) Am./Owner mare and Grand Champion Am./Owner mare/filly, US 2005 National Champion Am./Owner mare and Grand National Champion Am./Owner mare/filly, US 2005 National Champion mare and Grand National Champion mare/filly, 2006 The Spectrum International (Kissimmee, FL) Champion (1st place) mare and Grand Champion mare/filly, 2006 Grand National Champion Am./ Owner mare/filly.*

** *Other shows: 2005 Paso Fino Grand Prix (Miami, FL) Champion (1st place) mare and Grand Champion mare/filly, 2006 Paso Fino Grand Prix (Miami, FL - Feb.) Champion (1st place) mare and Grand Champion mare/filly.*

Registration number: 33,194 (PFHA)
Foaling date: 02/24/1998
Color: Bay
Sire: Simbolo de Besilu (Monarca de Besilu x Capuchina de Besilu)
Dam: La Maraca (Independiente x Altanera)
Breeder: Criadero La Rosa
Owner: Davis Love, III
Farm: Sinclair Farms, Sea Island, GA
Rider: Alexia Love
Courtesy of Davis Love, III
Photo by Larry Williams Photography

REPRESENTATIVE STANDARD OF PASO PLEASURE GELDING

MAHATMA GANDHI DE CVF

* *US 2005 **PFHA** National Champion Am/Owner 3 yr.old colt.*
Registration number: 39,465 (PFHA)
Foaling date: 03/03/2002
Color: Bay
Sire: Gandhi de La Vitrina (Privilegio de La Vitrina x Gaitana de La Vitrina)
Dam: Calendula del Juncal (Contragolpe de Conquista x Suprema del Juncal)
Breeder: Charlotte Valley Farms
Owner: Julio and Martha Anzola
Ocala, FL
Rider: Martha Anzola
Courtesy of Julio and Martha Anzola
Photo by Bravo Equine Enterprises

REPRESENTATIVE STANDARD OF PASO PLEASURE MARE

ESENCIA DE UNITED

Multi-champion Paso Pleasure mare, including

* ***PFHA** sanctioned shows: 2006 The Spectrum International (Kissimmee, FL) Grand Champion mare/filly, US 2006 2nd place National Champion mare and Grand National Champion mare/filly.*

** *Other shows: 2006 Paso Fino Grand Prix (Miami, FL - Feb.) Champion mare.*

Registration number: 43,130 (PFHA)
Foaling date: 02/15/2001
Color: Dark bay
Sire: Insólito de La Luisa (Patrimonio del Ocho x Gambeta de Lusitania)
Dam: Gabriela de Amadeus (Amadeus de Resorte Cuarto x Negra Línea La Mística)
Breeder: United Paso Fino Show Horses
Owner: Michael Hingle, Slidell, LA
Rider: Alei Ortiz
Courtesy of Michael Hingle
Photo by Larry Williams Photography

Note: The "representative standard" horses of the Paso Fino breed were selected by the author for their outstanding characteristics, including gait, conformation, bloodlines, genetic value, and show records.

THE PASO FINO: A LATERAL GAIT

After several centuries, the Paso Fino horse breed was developed from laterally-gaited horses (pacers) of the Barb breed brought to the Americas by the Conquistadors. The most pronounced lateral gait a horse may perform is the "pace" or "amble," in which the two hooves of the same side (foreleg and hind leg) move simultaneously. Therefore, the four hooves only make two beats. On a pacing (or ambler) horse, the rider's hips are shaken back and forth.

Because of their uncomfortable gait, pacing horses are unpopular in the Paso Fino world. In Colombia, however, they have not disappeared completely, mainly because some mule enthusiasts cross "pace" mares with "jacks" (male donkeys) in order to produce smoothly-gaited mules for show, pleasure, and work.

Although a horse performing Paso Fino gait moves each hoof independently from the other three hooves in a perfect succession, Paso Fino is considered a lateral gait because the mechanics of propulsion/support have a lateral sequence: A hind leg (that propels the horse forward) always moves before the front leg of the same side. And this occurs equally on both sides. This natural way a Paso Fino horse moves its legs can be seen from the time the horse first walks. Thus, the Paso Fino gait also may be described as a horse "walking very quickly."

Because the Paso Fino horse moves each hoof evenly alternated with the others (isochronic gait), in both walk and gait, the rider's body is carried smoothly without any back and forth, or up and down, movement. The smoothness of a Paso Fino horse may be demonstrated by having the rider hold a cup of water or coffee in one hand; the liquid remains steady while the animal is in gait (see the illustration on page 5).

When a properly gaited Paso Fino is photographed, in some of the pictures the horse appears to have a lateral pair of hooves on the ground; in others, the horse appears to have a diagonal pair of hooves on the ground; and in others, the horse appears to have three legs on the ground. Thus, it is essential to view a video of a horse performing Paso Fino in slow motion (or image by image) to identify properly the eight-stage sequence. This sequence is shown on pages 54 and 55.

It is easiest to hear the four-beat gait of the Paso Fino when the horse and rider are going over a sounding board. In fact, during Paso competitions, often a microphone is used so the judges and audience may hear distinctly the rhythm of the horse's legs, while performing any Paso Fino motion (Classic Fino, Paso Corto, or Paso Largo)

Other laterally-gaited horse breeds from the Americas are the Peruvian Paso (developed in Peru initially for work and transportation), the Missouri Fox Trotter (a pleasure/trail horse), the Rocky Mountain (a pleasure horse), and the Tennessee Walking Horse (developed for endurance).

FUTURE OF THE PASO FINO BREED

The main distinguishable phenotypic characteristic of the Paso Fino breed is the smooth, isochronic, four-beat gait, that has been passed down for many generations, as well as brio, beauty, and elegance. However, the breed continues to evolve and improve, as seen by the new, amazing and improved quality of horses that appear every year, especially in the Classic Fino, Paso Performance, and Paso Pleasure show divisions.

Likewise, there is a notable improvement in the quality of horses in other show divisions, such as Bellas Formas (Conformation), Paso Versatility, Paso Western Pleasure, and Paso Fino Country Pleasure. More youth riders (who will keep the Paso Fino breed moving forward) are involved in showing every year, not only in the typical classes of Youth, Equitation and Horsemanship, but also in the Amateur Owner classes (Classic Fino, Paso Performance, and Paso Pleasure). Nevertheless, although many people enjoy showing Paso Finos, due to their versatility, this unique breed of horses has a wide spectrum of other attributes.

As with any other horse, Paso Fino horses are "prey of predators," and, therefore, they are able to canter (three-beat gait) and gallop (four-beat gait) when they need to escape from a sudden predator's attack. Due to this natural ability to run, in the countries where Paso Finos were developed (such as Colombia and Puerto Rico), the horses work herding cattle; sometimes walking, sometimes performing Paso Fino, and sometimes cantering/galloping. Their canter/gallop may not be as smooth as their Paso Fino gait, but it does make a difference when going faster is required. Cantering/galloping to chase cows certainly does not ruin their natural Paso Fino gait.

Thus, trail riders, cutting and team penning competitors, and endurance riders can take advantage of the Paso Fino's ability to canter/gallop. This does not mean that all Paso Fino horses should canter/gallop. Show horses in Classic Fino, Paso Performance, Paso Pleasure, Bellas Formas (Conformation), and Paso Fino Country Pleasure divisions do not need to canter/gallop. They specialize in performing the motions of the Paso Fino gait.

Spreading the word about this unique breed can occur in many ways. Television, the internet, books, magazines, all-breed shows, videos, lectures, clinics, etc., can introduce the general public to the Paso Fino breed. All of us who love Paso Finos should play a role in communicating information about the breed as a tribute to all the great things that these horses have given to us. This will enlarge the market of potential Paso Fino enthusiasts, who also may help this breed to continue to spread throughout the world.

Note: For more information about the ***Paso Fino Horse Association, Inc.***, visit the web site at *www.PFHA.org.*

EIGHT-STAGE SEQUENCE OF THE PASO FINO GAIT *(on both pages)*

1. *Three legs on the ground. Only left fore leg up.*

2. *Support on a diagonal pair of legs. Right hind leg up (in elevation) and left fore leg up (in advance).*

5. *Three legs on the ground. Only right fore leg up.*

6. *Support on a diagonal pair of legs. Left hind leg up (in elevation) and right fore leg up (in advance).*

3. *Three legs on the ground. Only right hind leg up.*

4. *Support on a lateral pair of legs. Right hind leg up (in advance) and right fore leg up (in elevation).*

7. *Three legs on the ground.* Only left hind leg up.

8. *Support on a lateral pair of legs. Left hind leg up (in advance) and* left fore leg up (in elevation).

Above, Mrs. Debbie Kolody, a student of Ocala's School of Equestrian Art, riding "Sucesor de Expresso" (Expresso del Lago x Jibarita de la Victoria), owned by Mildred Arent, Criadero Aristocratica, Ocala, FL.

CHAPTER 5

COLORS OF PASO FINO HORSES

This chapter describes the coat, mane, tail colors, and the white markings of Paso Fino horses. It also provides an overview of skin pigments and color inheritance. In addition, the last pages include information regarding special care of the coat, mane, and tail.

PIGMENTS OF THE HORSE

Melanin is the main pigment of dark skin; this pigment may be black- or red/yellow-colored. Conversely, white spots (white markings) have underlying pink skin with no presence of melanin.

Grey and white Paso Fino horses have dark skin, indicating the presence of melanin. They are born with dark coats (except where white markings are present) and the coat turns grey, and then white, as they mature. The phenomenon is similar to the grey hairs that appear as people age; the original dark hair suffers gradual loss of color.

Some horses have special white patches that appear as "chains" of small patches where the hair is white, but the underlying skin is dark. Those are not considered white markings, but "flecks" or "marble markings." They may appear on the back and/or the croup, but they are not common.

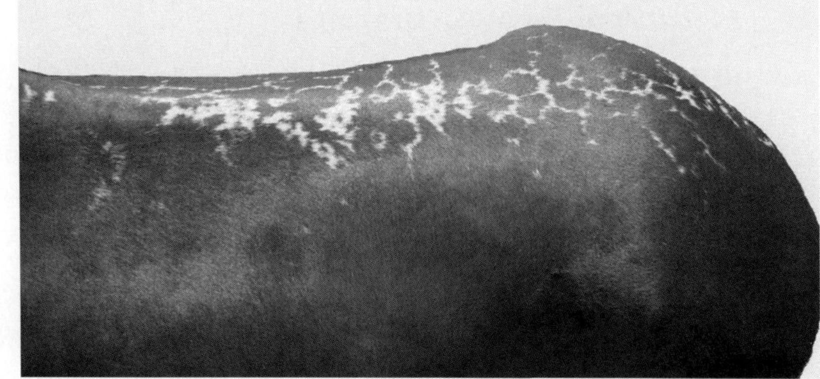

Some horses have a dark, thin stripe (black or brown) along the back, from the withers to the tail, known as a "dorsal stripe." Although less common, some horses with dorsal stripes have several dark, thin stripes, horizontally oriented, on the forearms' back area and the gaskins' front area. These stripes on the legs are known as "leg barring".

COLOR OF THE HORSE

A mix of two different kinds of melanin determines the color of a horse's hair: black is called "eumelanin" and red/yellow is called "pheomelanin." The white hair (either from white markings or grey/white horses) does not have any of these pigments.

This chapter will discuss the horse's color in relation to the following:

- Coat: Hair that covers the head, neck, trunk, hip, arms, forearms, thighs, and gaskins.

- Mane and tail: Long hair that grows on the crest (called "mane") and the tail.

- Bottom of the legs: Hair that covers the leg from the hoof to the carpus (on the foreleg) and to the hock (on the hind leg).

In the Paso Fino breed, colors may be classified into five groups:

1. **BLACK FACTOR**: This includes solid colors with the presence of black on the mane, tail, and bottom of the legs. Several colors are represented in this group:

    - **BLACK**: Hair on the three regions mentioned above (coat, mane/tail, and bottom of the legs) is black with no presence of brown hair. See photo on page 61.

    - **SEAL BAY** or **SEAL BROWN**: The majority of hair on the coat is black, but there is the presence of a small amount of brown hair on the muzzle, around the eyes, behind the elbows, and on the flanks. Hair on the mane, tail, and bottom of the legs is black. When a seal bay horse is wet or sweaty, its coat looks black. See photo on page 61.

    - **BAY**: All coat hair is brown. The mane, tail, and bottom of the legs are black. Due to the variety of bays (from light to dark,) they are classified as "dark bay," "red bay," and "light bay." Some bay horses have a dorsal stripe. See photos on page 62.

    - **BUCKSKIN**: Coat hair is yellow, cream, or golden. The mane, tail, and bottom of the legs are black. Buckskin horses with a black or dark brown dorsal stripe along the back and croup and, sometimes, leg barring, are called "dun buckskin." However, the term "**Dun**" is more commonly used for horses whose coats are yellow-red, and have a dark dorsal stripe and, sometimes, leg barring. See photos on page 63.

    - **BLUE DUN** or **GRULLA**: Coat hair has a smoky color, which looks like a dilution of brown and grey, as the color of a mouse. The mane, tail, and bottom of the legs are black, and there is the presence of a dorsal stripe and leg barring. See photo on page 64.

2. **RED/YELLOW FACTOR**: This includes solid brown/yellow colors with no presence of black hair.

   - **CHESTNUT**: Hair on the three regions (coat, mane/tail, and bottom of the legs) is brown. There are a variety of chestnut shades: A dark chestnut is commonly called "liver chestnut" and a chestnut with reddish brown hair is called "red chestnut." A "light chestnut" is also known as a "sorrel." If the horse's coat is light brown with a dark brown dorsal stripe (sometimes with dark brown leg barring on the forearms and gaskins), it may be called "dun chestnut." See photos on pages 64 and 65.

   - **PALOMINO**: Coat hair and bottom of the legs are yellowish or golden. The mane and tail are lighter, such as beige or silver. See photo on page 66.

   - **CHESTNUT WITH FLAXEN MANE AND TAIL**: Coat hair and bottom of the legs are brown (like any chestnut), but the mane and tail are lighter, such as beige, white or silver. Some horses may have a mane that is lighter than the tail, and vice-versa. See photo on page 66.

Note: The colors above are known as "solid colors."

3. **GREY AND ROAN FACTORS**: These horses are born solid-colored, but all hair, or a portion, becomes white as they mature. The underlying skin, however, remains black.

   - **GREY**: The foal is solid-colored during the first months. At two to five months of age, grey hairs gradually appear on the head. Because more dark hairs continue to lose melanin during every shedding, the coat looks like a mixture of the initial dark color and grey. The mane and tail also gradually turn grey. Grey horses usually are born black, seal bay, or dark bay, but they may also be born chestnut or buckskin. When a grey horse, that was born chestnut, starts turning grey, it is known as "rose-grey" or "grey over chestnut." When a grey horse, that was born buckskin, starts turning grey, it is known as "grey over buckskin."

     When approximately half of the hair is white, white and grey dapples may appear on the neck, trunk, and hips. After a time, most grey horses turn completely "**White**." However, because white Paso Fino horses come from a ´greying´ process, some of them keep some dark hair mainly on the mane, tail, carpus, and/or hock. See photos on pages 67 and 68.

   - **ROAN**: Roan horses are born solid-colored. Although roan horses are not actually grey, after a time, some grey and white hair appear mixed with dark hair, except on the head, mane, tail, and legs, which keep their dark color.

     If a roan horse is born bay, it is called "bay roan" or "three-hair roan" because it has black hair (mane, tail, and bottom of the legs) and brown hair mixed with white hair (body). When a roan horse is born chestnut, it is called "red roan." See photo on page 68.

     In roan horses, the number of white hairs does not increase abundantly with age, except if the horse has both genes: grey and roan. When both genes are present, the horse becomes grey. Instead of becoming completely white with age, the body retains many dark points (black or brown), making it look like it is being infested by hundreds of flies or has been bitten by hundreds of fleas. Thus, this color is called "**Flea-bitten**." See photo on page 69.

4. **PAINT** (or **PINTO) FACTOR**: Paso Fino horses with large asymmetrical, white areas on the coat, mane, tail, and legs are popular in the United States. The foals are born with white areas (white hair on pink skin) over a basic color. The white areas keep their basic shape while the horse grows.

   Depending on the basic color of the horse, the pinto patterns may be classified as follows:

   - **CHESTNUT PINTO**: The dark areas are brown, so the basic color is chestnut. See photo on page 69.

   - **BLACK PINTO**: The dark areas are black, so the basic color is either black or seal bay. See photo on page 70.

   - **BAY PINTO**: The dark areas on the coat are brown and the dark areas on the mane, tail, and bottom of the legs are black. Therefore, the basic color is bay. Since the horse has brown and black-colored areas and white areas, this type of pinto is known as "Tri-color Pinto." See photo on page 70.

   - **PALOMINO PINTO**: The darkest areas are beige, yellow, or golden. Thus, the basic color is palomino.

   - **WHITE ON PINTO**: The foal is born with dark and white areas all over its body. Moreover, because the horse also has the grey gene that masks the dark effects, the colored areas turn grey and then white with age, making the horse look completely white. Its skin, however, retains pink and dark areas, depending on the initial color. See photo on page 71.

   Pinto horses in the Paso Fino breed have white areas located on their back and legs, and the head is colored with white markings. In addition, the edges of the white areas are very well-defined. This distribution of dark and white areas is known as a "**tobiano**" pattern.

   Note: "Appaloosa" refers to a spotted horse pattern that is not present in the Paso Fino breed.

5. **FALSE ALBINO FACTOR**: The number of Paso Fino horses with this factor has been reduced because of a history of genetic selection in the countries where the breed was developed.

   - **CREMELLO**: When the foal is born, it has creamy, almost white hair over the entire body (coat, mane, tail, and bottom of the legs) that is kept all its life. White markings on the head or legs, when present, are clearly lighter than the coat. The skin is pink and the eyes are blue or grey. See photo on page 71.

   - **PERLINO**: When the foal is born, it has pearly-white coat hair that is kept all of its life and a white mane and tail, that may be slightly darker. White markings on the head or legs are not differentiated from the coat. The skin is pink and the eyes are blue.

MANDATO DE LA LUISA

** Number one 'bred to' stallion in 2004 and 2005 in the USA.*
Registration number: 36,745 (PFHA)
Foaling date: 08/12/1999 (Colombia)
Sire: Patrimonio del Ocho
Dam: La Calma del Ocho
Breeder: Criadero La Luisa
Owners: Edgar and Alei Ortiz
Farm: United Paso Fino Show Horses
Summerfield, FL
Courtesy of United Paso Fino Show Horses
Photo by Darlene Wohlart

Color: ***BLACK***

NEGRA ROSA

Registration number: 22,328 (PFHA)
Foaling date: 06/01/1993
Sire: Capuchino
Dam: Laguna
Owner: Richard Thompson
Farm: Thompson Trails Farm
Reddick, FL
Courtesy of Richard Thompson
Photo by Bravo Equine Enterprises

Color: ***SEAL BAY***

CAMELOT'S KNIGHT DE VEZ

* 2006 **PFHA** Hi-point Paso Country Pleasure of the year. US 2006 **PFHA** National Champion Paso Country Pleasure.

Registration number: 29,490 (PFHA)
Foaling date: 06/18/1997
Sire: Corals John Henry de Vez
Dam: Melodita de Vez
Breeder: Barbara Preiss
Owner: Jerry and Deborah Jacobs
Farm: Ticker Time Paso Fino Farms
Auburn, IN and Clermont, FL
Courtesy of Jerry and Deborah Jacobs
Photo provided by Ticker Time Paso Fino Farms

Color: **DARK BAY**

EL DOLLAR DEL JUNCAL

Registration number: 33,184 (PFHA)
Foaling date: 05/27/1999
Sire: Capiro Thirteen
Dam: La Consigna del Juncal
Breeder: El Juncal
Owner: Richard Thompson
Farm: Thompson Trails Farm
Reddick, FL
Courtesy of Richard Thompson
Photo by Bravo Equine Enterprises

Color: **RED BAY**

DULCE ELEGANCIA

* *Multi- champion Classic Fino mare, including 1995* ***CONFEPASO*** *World Cup 1st place Classic Fino mare, and US 1996* ***PFHA*** *National Champion Classic Fino mare.*

Registration number: 17,789 (PFHA)
Foaling date: 10/03/1990
Sire: Plebeyo Dos
Dam: Fantasia La Joya
Breeder: Codelia (Dee) Torcise
Owner: Hacienda Los Angeles
Farm: Hacienda Los Angeles
Anthony, FL
Courtesy of Jorge and Angela Redondo
Photo by Bravo Equine Enterprises

Color: **BUCKSKIN**

RESPLANDOR CUARTO DE CVF

Registration number: 44,006 (PFHA)
Foaling date: 02/09/2004
Sire: Resplandor Tres
Dam: Plegaria de La Palmera
Breeder: Charlotte Valley Farms
Owner: Allen and Judy Brick Freedman
Farm: Charlotte Valley Farms
Anthony, FL
Courtesy of Allen and Judy Brick Freedman
Photo by Bravo Equine Enterprises

Color: **DUN**

JUGUETON DE FANTASY

* *2006 **PFHA** Spectrum International (Kissimmee, FL) Champion (1st place) Paso Pleasure gelding, US 2006 **PFHA** 3rd place National Champion Paso Performance geldings for Gold.*

Registration number: 39,803 (PFHA)
Foaling date: 02/26/2000
Sire: JLM'S Jaranero
Dam: Cielito Lindo del Conde
Breeder: Fantasy Paso Finos
Owner: Katreena Haley
City: Gainesville, GA
Courtesy of Katreena Haley
Photo by Bravo Equine Enterprises

Color: ***BLUE DUN (GRULLA)***

LA SUPREMA DE MENSAJE

Registration number: 36,301 (PFHA)
Foaling date: 06/02/2002
Sire: Mensaje del Ocho
Dam: La Candelaria
Owner: Katreena Haley
City: Gainesville, GA
Courtesy of Katreena Haley
Photo by Bravo Equine Enterprises

Color: ***LIVER CHESTNUT***

CANDELOSO DE CASTA
Registration number: 12,760 (PFHA)
Foaling date: 04/05/1988
Sire: Castellano
Dam: Condela
Breeder: Los Arrieros de Casta
Owner: Rebecca V. Anderson
Farm: Criadero Hidalgo, LLC
Jay, FL
Courtesy of Criadero Hidalgo, LLC
Photo by Bravo Equine Enterprises

Color: **RED CHESTNUT**

PRECIOSA DE SANTA CRUZ
Registration number: 11,612 (PFHA)
Foaling date: 01/15/1986
Sire: Kopeki
Dam: Pretenciosa de Kofresi
Owner: Diana Venegas
Farm: Royal Eagle Farm
Belleair, FL
Courtesy of Diana Venegas
Photo by Bravo Equine Enterprises

Color: **DUN CHESTNUT**

COQUETA DE ARISTOCRATICA

Registration number: 26,885 (PFHA)
Foaling date: 01/03/1996
Sire: Oro de Piloto
Dam: La Aristocratica de Casta
Breeder: Criadero Aristocratica
Owner: Rebecca V. Anderson
Farm: Criadero Hidalgo, LLC
Jay, FL
Courtesy of Criadero Hidalgo, LLC
Photo by Bravo Equine Enterprises

Color: ***PALOMINO***

PICAFLOR DE LA SIERRA

* *2006* ***PFHA*** *PasO-lympics (Conyers, GA) Champion (1st place) Classic Fino 3 yr.old Classic Fino colt, 2006* ***PFHA*** *Paso Fino Gold Cup (Las Vegas, NV) Champion (1st place) 3 yr.old Classic Fino colt and Grand Champion Classic Fino stallion/colt.*

Registration number: 46,260 (PFHA)
Foaling date: 07/01/2003
Sire: Marcapasos
Dam: Shakira de La Tierra
Breeder: Rubén Sierra
Owner: Vicente Rodríguez
Farm: Hacienda Culminante
Ocala, FL
Courtesy of Vicente Rodríguez
Photo by Cheri Prill Photo

Color: ***CHESTNUT WITH FLAXEN MANE AND TAIL***

LA GALA DE CVF

Registration number: 41,509 (PFHA)
Foaling date: 05/14/2003
Sire: Prometido de Selecta
Dam: Veronica de la Victoria
Breeder: Charlotte Valley Farms
Owner: Allen and Judy Brick Freedman
Farm: Charlotte Valley Farms
Anthony, FL
Courtesy of Allen and Judy Brick Freedman
Photo by Bravo Equine Enterprises

Color: **GREY**

(with more dark hair than white hair)

CALYPSO EL CLASSICO

* *2002* ***PFHA*** *May Day Show (Ocala, FL) Champion (1st place) Pleasure 3 yr.old colt/gelding, 2003* ***PFHA*** *May Day Show (Ocala, Fl) Champion (1st place) Pleasure 4 yr.old colt/gelding.*

Registration number: 33,066 (PFHA)
Foaling date: 06/05/1999
Sire: El Classico de Plebeyo
Dam: Salsa Mora
Breeder: Paramount Farm
Owner: Kay Reeves
Farm: Rosa Salvaje
Troy, AL
Courtesy of Kay Reeves
Photo by Bravo Equine Enterprises

Color: **GREY**

(with half of the hair white and dapples)

GAVIOTA DE BESILU

** US 1998 **PFHA** National Champion Classic Fino 3 yr.old filly, 2003 **PFHA** Fall Magnolia Classic (Hattiesburg, MS) Champion (1st place) Classic Fino mare and Grand Champion Classic Fino mare/filly.*

Registration number: 26,255 (PFHA)
Foaling date: 02/15/1995
Sire: Profeta de Besilu
Dam: La Gaviota
Breeder: Besilu Collection
Owner: Allen and Judy Brick Freedman
Farm: Charlotte Valley Farms
Anthony, FL
Courtesy of Allen and Judy Brick Freedman
Photo by Darlene Wohlart

Color: ***WHITE***

ESCOLLO DE ISABEL

** US 2006 **PFHA** 2nd place National Champion Am./Owner Paso Pleasure gelding and Grand National Champion Am./Owner Paso Pleasure gelding.*

Registration number: 39,883 (PFHA)
Foaling date: 12/20/1998
Sire: Profeta de Besilu
Dam: Esterlina IV
Owner: Kertrin Kohler
Farm: El Río del Zorro
Osteen, FL
Courtesy of Kertrin Kohler
Photo by Bravo Equine Enterprises

Color: ***RED ROAN***

F.G.'s MI CORAZON

Registration number: 30,413 (PFHA)
Foaling date: 05/13/1997
Sire: Bochica Tres
Dam: Los Paseantes Solo Tu
Breeder: Beth Knowlton
Owner: Jerry Jacobs
Farm: Ticker Time Paso Fino Farms
Auburn, IN and Clermont, FL
Courtesy of Jerry Jacobs
Photo provided by Ticker Time Paso Fino Farms

Color: ***FLEA-BITTEN***

LIBERTAD DE ARISTOCRATICA

Registration number: 41,174 (PFHA)
Foaling date: 05/27/2002
Sire: Durango
Dam: Mariposa Elegante
Breeder: Criadero Aristocratica
Owner: Alan Barry Carrus
Ocala, FL
Courtesy of Alan B. and Linda Carrus
Photo by Bravo Equine Enterprises

Color: ***CHESTNUT PINTO***

INSOLITO DE ESTABAN

* *US 2004 and 2005 **PFHA** National Champion Paso Versatility, 2005 **PFHA** Hi-point Paso Versatility. US 2004 **PFHA** National Champion Paso Western Pleasure. US 2005 **PFHA** 2nd place National Champion Paso Western Pleasure. US 2005 **PFHA** National Champion Paso Driving.*

Registration number: 30,535 (PFHA)
Foaling date: 06/07/1998
Sire: Pegasus Estaban
Dam: Espectacla Estaban
Breeder: El Rancho de Estaban
Owner: Estero Verde Dev. Co, LLC
Farm: Wild Magnolia Ranch, LLC
Bonita Springs, FL
Courtesy of Randy and Donna Wilkerson
Photo by Bravo Equine Enterprises

Color: ***BLACK PINTO***

AMADIS DE ESTABAN

Registration number: 35,482 (PFHA)
Foaling date: 08/07/2000
Sire: Amadeus de Estaban
Dam: Sombra La Caro
Breeder: El Rancho de Estaban
Owner: Estero Verde Dev. Co, LLC
Farm: Wild Magnolia Ranch, LLC
Bonita Springs, FL
Courtesy of Randy and Donna Wilkerson
Photo by Bravo Equine Enterprises

Color: ***TRI-COLOR PINTO***

ARCO DE AIRES

Registration number: 26,665 (PFHA)
Foaling date: 07/01/1992
Sire: Chulo de Pastorale
Dam: Navarra Elegante
Owner: Jorge Montenegro
Farm: Galaraga Ranch
Dade City, FL
Courtesy of Jorge Montenegro
Photo by Bravo Equine Enterprises

Color: ***WHITE ON PINTO***

Before dark areas turned white

EL RUBIO DE GELISA

Registration number: 32,460 (PFHA)
Foaling date: 01/09/1999
Sire: Anfitrion del Conde
Dam: Flint Oak Genevieve
Breeder: George L. Hernandez
Owners: Mike and Tina Tripoli
Farm: Adam's Grove Paso Fino Farm
Drewryville, VA
Courtesy of Mike and Tina Tripoli
Photo by Tina Tripoli

Color: **CREMELLO**

WHITE MARKINGS

Neither white markings on the legs and/or the head, nor flecks (marble markings) on the back and/or croup, affect the definition of color.

The white markings on the bottom of the horse's legs have different names, depending on the distance from the hooves. A white marking extending from the hoof to the upper end of the cannon is known as **white full-stocking**; a white marking extending from the hoof to half of the cannon is called **white half-cannon** or **white half-stocking**; a white marking extending from the hoof to the lower third of the cannon is a **white sock**; a white marking extending from the hoof up to the fetlock is a **white fetlock**; a white marking extending from the hoof to the upper end of the pastern, just below the fetlock is a **white pastern**; a white marking extending from the hoof to half of the pastern is a **white half-pastern**; and a single white marking, like a ring, just above the hoof's coronary band is a **white coronet ring**.

It is important to note that horses with white marked legs have yellowish, beige or pink hooves because they have no presence of melanin pigment. The rare exception of a black hoof with a white marked leg occurs when a small area of skin above the coronet has a dark area (black or brown).

The white markings on the horse's head also have different names according to the extension and location. A single white marking of any shape on the horse's forehead, usually not very big, is known as a **star**; a white marking between the nostrils is called a **snip**; a white marking on the lower lip that may include the chin is a **white underlip**; a thin white stripe from the forehead's lower edge to the muzzle's upper edge is a **white face stripe**; a wide stripe from the forehead to the muzzle, which may be close to the eyes and nostrils, but does not include them, is a **blaze**; a white spot all over the face, including the eyelids of one or both eyes and the upper muzzle, and one or both nostrils, is called an **apron face**. When an apron face is present, one eye (or both) within the white marking is (are) usually blue (known as "glass eyes").

SHOW RULES BASED ON THE HORSE'S COLOR

There is no restriction on the horse's color (eyes, coat, mane/tail, and legs, including white markings or pink skin all over the body), for a Paso Fino horse in *Paso Fino Horse Association* sanctioned shows *(PFHA – Constitution and Rule Book, Chapter Two, Section IV, Subsection B).*

CONFEPASO (*Confederación Internacional de Caballos de Paso*) does not allow horses to compete with white markings (white hair on pink skin) over the body except on the face/muzzle and legs *(Reglamento de Competencias de Caballos de Paso - CONFEPASO, Chapter 4, Article 7, Sections 26 and 28).* Thus, solid-colored (black, seal bay, bay, buckskin, dun, blue dun, chestnut, palomino, and chestnut with flaxen mane and tail), grey/white, flea-bitten, and roan horses may participate in *CONFEPASO* sanctioned shows, but pintos, cremellos, and perlinos cannot participate. Additionally, there are some restrictions regarding white markings on the face/muzzle and legs, and eye color for horses to be shown in *CONFEPASO* sanctioned shows:

- **White markings on the legs**: A white marking on one or more of the legs, extending from the hoof to over the perimeter line of the joint's transversal section at the carpus (false knee) of the forelegs or at the hock of the hind legs is not allowed. Likewise, an isolated, non-continuous white marking on any part of a leg is not allowed *(Reglamento de Competencias de Caballos de Paso - CONFEPASO, Chapter 4, Article 7, Sections 26 and 27).* A white marking from the hoof to over the carpus or the hock is known as "**Stocking Plus**."

Note: The perimeter line of the joint's transversal section at the carpus (false knee) and at the hock may easily be seen where a wrinkle of skin is produced when the leg is completely flexed at the respective joint.

- **White markings on the face and muzzle**: Neither a white marking on the face that includes the eyelids of one or both eyes (as occurs in an apron face) nor a white marking involving both nostrils and extending from the upper to the lower lips is allowed *(Reglamento de Competencias de Caballos de Paso - CONFEPASO, Chapter 4, Article 7, Sections 29 and 30).*
- **Eyes**: Horses with eyes of different colors cannot be shown in *CONFEPASO* sanctioned shows *(Reglamento de Competencias de Caballos de Paso - CONFEPASO, Chapter 4, Article 7, Section 24).*

Note: In the countries where Paso Finos were originally developed, dark skin is more desirable than pink skin because pink skin has a greater risk of developing cancer due to exposure to UV rays.

BASICS OF COLOR GENETICS

Knowing some basics about color inheritance is important for at least three reasons:

- When the breeder desires specific colors in offspring.
- When the breeder wants to avoid specific colors.
- In some cases, when the breeder wants to determine if the parentage of a horse, and its attributed parents or offspring, has been misrepresented.

With any explanation of genetics, it is first necessary to define the terms, genotype and phenotype:

- **Genotype of a horse**: This term refers to the genes transmitted from parents to offspring. Genes are present in pairs and determine all characteristics of the horse, such as sex, size, color, conformation, etc. For easy understanding and for calculating probabilities, genes are named with letters. If both genes are named with capital letters, this pair of genes is known as "Dominant Homozygous." If, conversely, both genes are named with lower case letters, this pair of genes is known as "Recessive Homozygous." When one gene is named with a capital letter and the other is named with a lower case letter, that pair of genes is known as "Heterozygous."

- **Phenotype of a horse**: This term refers to the entire appearance of a horse (including its color), which is the visible expression of the genotype.

Currently, there are a number of theories about color inheritance; most theories agree that several genes interact to produce a horse's color.

The **gene *Extension* (*E*)** determines if the horse has a phenotype with black skin and black hair (on the coat and/or the mane/tail and bottom of the legs) or not. The dominant form of this gene, either dominant homozygous

(***EE***) or heterozygous (***Ee***), causes the eumelanin (black pigment) to be present. This occurs in the following colors: black, seal bay, bay, buckskin, dun, and blue dun.

Conversely, the recessive homozygous genotype for black (***ee***) causes the pheomelanin (red/yellow pigment) to be present. This produces a phenotype with no black, but red/yellow, such as chestnut, palomino, and chestnut with flaxen mane and tail.

Therefore, the offspring produced by crossing two red/yellow-factored horses (chestnut, palomino, and/or chestnut with flaxen mane and tail) do not have black pigment. However, the offspring of a horse with the presence of black may or may not have black points, depending on the genotype.

The **amount of black color** on the horse is determined by **gene *Agouti*** (*A*), which has three different strengths of expression: ***A***, ***A-***, and ***a***.

- The weakest expression of this gene (***aa***) produces full black horses.
- The intermediate expressions of the gene (***A-A-*** or ***A-a***) produce seal bay horses.
- The strongest expressions of the gene (***AA***, ***AA-***, or ***Aa***) produce horses with black points only (black mane, tail, and bottom of the legs).

This is why black horses are less common than seal bay horses, and seal bay horses are less common than other horse colors with black points (bay, buckskin, dun, and blue dun).

The **gene *Cream*** (***C***) affects intensity of coat color for brown/red and yellow hair as follows:

- When the genotype of the horse is dominant homozygous (***CC***), the coat is dark (black, seal bay, bay, or chestnut).
- When the genotype is heterozygous (***Cc***), the dark brown color becomes lighter (yellow), either buckskin or palomino.
- If the genotype is recessive homozygous (***cc***), the yellow color (from buckskin and palomino) turns to a false albino, either perlino or cremello.

Thus, crossing buckskin x buckskin, buckskin x palomino, or palomino x palomino gives a 25% chance of obtaining perlino or cremello colors. Additionally, crossing a cremello or a perlino-colored horse with a solid-colored horse gives the best chance of obtaining palomino or buckskin. Conversely, if perlino or cremello colors want to be avoided, crossing buckskin x buckskin, buckskin x palomino, palomino x palomino, and perlino/cremello x buckskin/palomino are not recommended.

The **gene *Dun*** (***D***) affects intensity of coat color for both black and brown/red patterns, as well as the dorsal stripe:

- If the genotype is recessive homozygous (***dd***), the coat is dark (black, seal bay, bay, or chestnut).
- When the genotype of a horse is dominant homozygous (***DD***) or heterozygous (***Dd***), the coat is lighter and has a dorsal stripe: blue dun, dun, and dun chestnut.

A **chestnut horse with flaxen mane and tail** is produced by the recessive homozygous form (***ff***) of the **gene *Flaxen*** (***F***). The dominant homozygous form (***FF***) and the heterozygous form (***Ff***) do not have any effect. As a result, chestnut horses with flaxen manes and tails are not very common. This gene only affects chestnut-colored horses (including chestnut pinto-colored ones), but not horses with black points or grey horses.

Gene *Grey* (***G***) produces **Grey** horses:

- When the genotype of a horse is dominant homozygous for grey (***GG***) or heterozygous (***Gg***), the horse's coat turns grey.
- If the genotype is recessive homozygous (***gg***), the horse stays solid-colored.

Therefore, a dominant homozygous grey horse always produces grey offspring. A heterozygous grey horse produces grey and solid-colored offspring. In addition, a grey horse is produced from at least one grey horse (sire or dam), and a grey horse is never produced from two solid-colored parents.

Gene *Roan* (***Rn***) is responsible for the **Roan** color, as follows: Roan horses are produced by the heterozygous form of the gene (***Rnrn***). The recessive homozygous form (***rnrn***) produces a solid color, and the dominant homozygous form (***RnRn***) is not viable. Therefore, a roan may only be produced by at least one roan horse (sire or dam). Moreover, because a flea-bitten color horse has both roan and grey genes, it may produce roan, grey, flea-bitten, or solid color offspring, depending on the color and genotype of the other horse being crossed.

Pinto, in the Paso Fino breed, is produced by the **gene *Tobiano*** (***T***). The dominant homozygous form (***TT***) and the heterozygous form (***Tt***) produce a pinto horse. The recessive homozygous form (***tt***) produces a solid color. This is why a tobiano, with the dominant homozygous genotype form, always produces tobiano offspring. Additionally, pinto horses, with heterozygous form (***Tt***), may produce either pinto or solid-colored offspring, depending on the genotype.

In conclusion, based on a horse's phenotype, it is possible to presume its genotype for color. Moreover, knowing the colors of the horse's parents, and preferably also its grandparents, ensures the most complete genotypic map for the color of a horse. This information helps calculate the probabilities of color for the offspring. Additionally, it helps the breeder plan crosses in order to obtain, or avoid, specific colors in offspring.

SPECIAL CARE OF THE COAT, MANE, AND TAIL

Some daily practices help maintain the horse's coat, mane, and tail in the best condition.

- **COAT CARE**
  The condition of the coat is a sign of the nutritional state and the general health of a horse. When the coat is soft, shiny, and silky, it indicates that the animal is well cared for and healthy. A dry, bristled, and opaque coat indicates the opposite. There are some practical routines that help to maintain a beautiful coat.

- **Daily grooming**: Some important tools for daily grooming and their proper use are explained below:

The rubber **curry comb** has a series of ´teeth´ on the surface that come in contact with the horse's coat and skin when being used. The proper way to use the rubber curry comb is by rubbing vigorously in circles all over the horse's coat.

This activity serves five functions at once:

- Removing the old hairs of the coat that is being shed, so that the horse will replace them with new ones.
- Removing dirt, dust, dry sweat, and old cells from the surface of the epidermis, so that the skin will be in better condition and the perspiration process will be easier.
- Massaging the skin to improve the flow of blood with its nutrients to the dermis, so that the result is healthier skin.
- Massaging the sebaceous glands to make them increase the production of cebum (oil) that helps the coat bccome shiny and silky.
- Reviewing the entire skin, inch by inch. If the horse refuses to be "scratched" with the rubber curry comb in a specific area, it is important to determine if there is a sore, wound, inflammation, or any other abnormality.

After using the curry comb, the horse should be brushed all over the coat, in the direction of the hair growth, with a **stiff brush** made of polypropylene or palmyra fiber. The purpose is to comb the coat and remove the rest of the old hair and dust. After every three strokes across the coat, it is important to clean the brush by chafing it two or three times against the "teeth" of the rubber curry comb.

Note: These activities (using the rubber curry comb and the brush) lift particles into the air; this may be prevented by rubbing the coat with a wet piece of cloth before using the curry comb and also before brushing. Slightly wetting the surface of the coat prior to grooming causes particles to form into "pellets" and, therefore, does not produce any discomfort to the groomer or the horse.

Next, the horse's face may be brushed gently with a **soft bristle brush**. Additionally, it is very important to clean the horse's eyelids, face, and nostrils with a **wet towel**. Finally, rubbing the coat with a **dry piece of cloth** helps the coat become very silky. When the rider gently grooms the horse, this gives the horse and the rider pleasure, so a favorable relationship begins, and the horse starts to trust the rider.

Using a separate curry comb, brush, and towel for each horse avoids spreading skin infections among horses. All grooming implements should be washed and disinfected periodically.

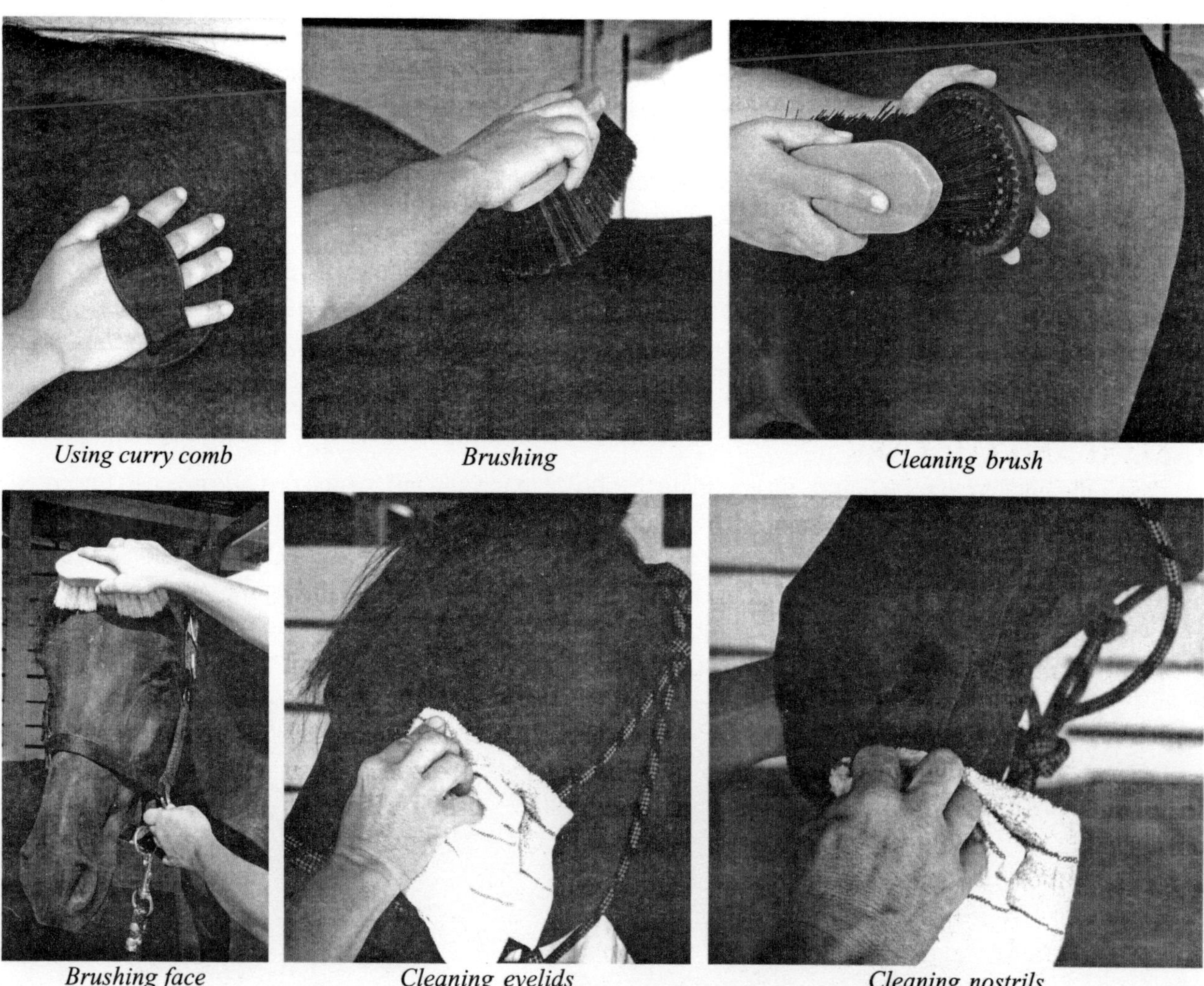

Using curry comb *Brushing* *Cleaning brush*

Brushing face *Cleaning eyelids* *Cleaning nostrils*

- **Giving the horse a bath**: A horse does not need a bath as frequently as it needs grooming. Giving the horse a bath, with abundant water and mild soap or shampoo once or twice a week, is very effective for cleaning the horse's coat and skin. However, when a horse is bathed more often, the action of the soap/shampoo removes the natural sebum of the hair, resulting in a dry and opaque coat. The pH of the skin also may be altered, causing some types of dermatitis. Further, increased coat hair growth is a normal response to frequent bathing, either with or without soap/shampoo.

  When the horse is sweaty after working during cold weather, rinsing certain areas of the horse, preferably with warm water, is recommended rather than complete bathing. The face should be gently rinsed. The forelegs should be rinsed from the elbows to the hooves. The hindquarters should be rinsed under the tail, from the perineum (between the anus and the scrotum in the male, and between the vulva and the udder in the mare), and the internal surfaces of the thighs to the hooves. The sweat on the rest of the body should be removed with a scraper (stick). Then, when the sweat dries (either the same day or the day after), it may be removed by grooming, which helps to shed old hair from the coat.

  Conversely, if the horse is very sweaty during hot weather, the entire body may be rinsed, including the face, with warm water (but not with cold water). The water on the horse's coat should be removed with a **scraper**.

- **Tips to accelerate coat shedding**: Shedding may be accelerated by wetting the horse's coat (neck, trunk, and legs) with salted water (two pounds of salt to two gallons of water), using a piece of cloth and letting the coat dry while the animal is tied. Vigorous grooming after three days, during which time the horse has been kept dry and not groomed, makes the coat shed a great amount of hair. If necessary, this process should be repeated two or three weeks later. Clipping the horse's coat after winter is another way to make the coat shed old hair.

  Offering commercial nutritional supplements based on fatty acids, vitamins, and minerals help shed the old coat and cause the coat to become shiny. Additionally, some products intensify the coat color, making it a deeper black, golden (for palomino horses), or white, depending on the horse's natural color.

- **MANE AND TAIL CARE**
  Paso Fino horses have, by nature, an abundant, beautiful mane and tail, which provide grace to the breed. The mane and tail should be kept, therefore, in the best possible condition. Mane and tail hair grow healthier and stronger when the skin areas are clean. Washing them carefully the day of the horse's regular bath with a soft soap or shampoo (which may contain conditioner), and rinsing the mane and tail with abundant water, is recommended. In addition, in order to stimulate mane/tail hair growth, some people use a mixture of coconut oil and rum (the liquor) on the skin of the mane and tail once a week.

"Candeloso de Casta" exhibiting his beautiful mane and tail. Owner Rebecca V. Anderson, Criadero Hidalgo, LLC. Jay, FL. Photo by Olga García.

The mane and tail should not be detangled with a brush or comb on a daily basis, because this breaks many hairs each time it is done. To see that damage, check the number of hairs trapped on the brush or comb after just one session of detangling. The mane and tail may be detangled easily using the fingers after applying any commercial product that contains substances for this purpose (e.g., silicone coat spray).

For special occasions (e.g., photos, showing), the mane and tail may be detangled fully as follows:

- Applying abundant detangling spray.
- Removing shavings/hay attached to the mane and tail with the fingers and detangling the knots.
- Washing the mane and tail with a shampoo and rinsing them with abundant water
- Applying more detangling spray.
- Detangling the mane and tail carefully, first with a soft brush and then a comb. This should be started at the bottom (of the hair), working your way up.

CHAPTER 6

NUTRITION

All horse breeds, domestic and wild, are **herbivores.** After 60 million years of evolution, the horse's teeth and digestive system have changed and adapted to obtain the required nutrients from forages. Thus, feeding horses is more than offering some daily feed; it's also guaranteeing that all the horse's needs are met, according to its age, reproductive stage, body condition index (score), and physical activity.

IMPORTANCE OF A GOOD FEEDING PROGRAM

Proper feeding is one of the most important aspects of providing a good environment for a horse. Other basic requirements are daily care, lodging, hoof care, and prevention of illnesses. The importance of proper feeding is explained as follows:

- Feeding a horse is about 25% to 50% of the total cost of keeping a horse. From this point of view, designing a feeding program is necessary for two purposes: investing resources properly and providing the best nutritional support.
- Good feeding is one of the best ways to keep a horse healthy because the horse's immune system works better and metabolic problems may be prevented.
- A healthy, well-fed horse is easy to identify by its vivacity, shiny and silky coat, hardness of its hooves, proper body condition index (a score correlated to weight), appropriate growth and development rates (in young horses), reproductive activity, and working capability.
- It is important to note that overweight horses are not really healthy, and their feeding program might be wrong. Of course, if the horse is an athlete, extra weight does not help.

HORSE'S GASTROINTESTINAL TRACT

The **DIGESTIVE** system is formed by the **gastrointestinal tract** (mouth, esophagus, stomach, and intestines) and the **liver**. The functions of the digestive system are eating and digesting the food, absorbing the nutrients and sending them to the bloodstream, and excreting the non-digested material. The **URINARY** system is closely associated with the digestive system. The urinary system is formed by the **kidneys**, **ureters**, **bladder**, and the **urethra**. The functions of this system are controlling the water balance and levels of electrolytes in the horse's body, and excreting waste substances out of the body.

The horse's gastrointestinal tract may be compared with the gastrointestinal tract of ruminants and with humans. When compared with a ruminant (e.g., a cow), the horse has a slightly smaller and less efficient gastrointestinal tract. The big rumen of a ruminant animal is the first place where food is carried by the esophagus in order to ferment the fiber with millions of specialized bacteria and protozoa. Thus, fermentation is the first stage of digestion for a ruminant animal.

Humans and horses have a relatively similar structure of their gastrointestinal tracts. Their main differences are size and the cecum's activity. Because of a different diet during evolution, humans have a small cecum, with very reduced fermentative action of fiber from salads, grains (cereals), and fruit. Conversely, the horse digests large amounts of fiber from forages (such as grass and legume) in the cecum, by the action of a large microbial population.

The horse's digestion, as in humans, starts with the **CEPHALIC PHASE**, when the brain signals the gastrointestinal tract to receive and digest food, even before eating. This action may start for two reasons:

- Detection of palatable food by the specialized sensory organs.
- Hunger, in answer to the "biological watch," triggered by the horse's daily feeding schedule or an empty stomach.

The cephalic phase of digestion is very important as the gastrointestinal tract gets ready to do its best work. In order to profit from this phase, horses should be fed at the same time every day with palatable and nutritious food.

From the time the horse's gastrointestinal tract actually is in contact with the foodstuff, there are four phases that are explained as follows:

- **ORAL PHASE**: This phase occurs in the mouth. The lips choose the food to be eaten, such as forage or grain. If the horse is grazing in a pasture, the incisors cut the grass. Food becomes wet in the mouth by large amounts of saliva produced by the salivary glands. The tongue carries the food towards the back of the mouth in order to be chewed by premolars and molars and then swallowed.
- **ESOPHAGEAL PHASE**: This is a fast phase that occurs in the esophagus. After food is swallowed, it is conducted by the esophagus to the stomach (whether the horse's head is kept low, while grazing, or kept high), without any physical or chemical change. Curiously, in normal circumstances, horses cannot vomit like humans and other animal species.

- **GASTRIC PHASE**: This phase occurs in the stomach. The stomach is described as a small bag where food is taken from the esophagus. Gastric juices are secreted in the stomach in order to start the hydrolysis of the foodstuff, reducing food into smaller nutrients, which are able to be absorbed by the intestine. Some carbohydrates are fermented in the stomach due to the presence of bacteria. A third function of the stomach consists of controlling the passage rate of the foodstuff to the small intestine.

  Because the stomach is usually not empty at any time (the horse has evolved over millions of years to graze about 17 hours a day), and considering the stomach's reduced capacity (around 1/10 of the whole gastrointestinal tract capacity), any horse kept in a stall or paddock should have free access to grass/hay (unless the horse is an "easy keeper," with a very slow metabolism), and, sometimes, grain in small, frequent meals.

- **INTESTINAL PHASE**: The small and large intestines have the greatest capacity in the gastrointestinal tract, and most changes to the foodstuff occur there. The absorption of nutrients and the excretion of the non-digested portion of the foodstuff also occur in the intestines.

  - **Small Intestine**: The small intestine is a long, thin tube, about 50 feet long. One of its functions is the hydrolysis of proteins and carbohydrates into the most simple absorbable forms due to the action of enzymes secreted by the small intestine's cells. The emulsification of fats (lipids) also occurs in the small intestine, due to the action of bile salts. Another function of the small intestine is to absorb nutrients (amino acids, glucose, fatty acids, vitamins, and minerals).

  - **Large Intestine**: The large intestine is a much wider tube than the small intestine, but much shorter (about 20 to 22 feet long). The large intestine has three main parts that work in very different ways: cecum, colon, and rectum.

    The cecum is an elongated bag (about 4 feet in length), the top end of which joins both the small intestine (at its end) and the colon (at its entrance). The main function of the cecum is fermenting the fiber of forages and those carbohydrates that are passed by the small intestine. Fermentation occurs through specialized microbial populations (bacteria and protozoa), similar to those in the rumen of ruminant animals. Volatile fatty acids (acetic, propionic, butyric, valeric) are the results of this fermentative action. They are absorbed in the cecum to be used later as energy. The cecum also is the primary site in the gastrointestinal tract where water is absorbed.

    The colon, in its different sections (ventral, dorsal, transverse, and small), is the largest portion of the large intestine. The passage rate in the colon is slow, as it is the last opportunity for digesting the foodstuff, and the water content has been reduced in the cecum. The ventral colon also has a small microbial population for fermenting fiber.

    The rectum is the last portion of the gastrointestinal tract. The function of the rectum is to absorb water and compact the material to be excreted as manure.

NUTRIENTS AND THEIR DIGESTION

In order to meet a horse's needs, all the nutrients must be offered in the diet according to the horse's age, reproductive stage, physical activity, etc. Depending on the nutrients, each kind of food may take a different length of time to be eaten, digested, and excreted. The transit time in the gastrointestinal tract mainly depends on the content of fiber, water, and fat.

- **Soluble Carbohydrates**: These are the non-structural carbohydrates of plants (sugars and starch) that are used by the horse as a source of energy. Sugars and starch are broken into smaller particles (monosaccharides), such as glucose, due to the action of carbohydrases (specialized enzymes) secreted into the small intestine. Thereafter, monosaccharides are absorbed into the same intestine and, once in the bloodstream, they are regulated by the endocrine system. However, small amounts of carbohydrates pass through the small intestine without being digested and reach the cecum to be fermented by the microorganisms present in it.

  Soluble carbohydrates are found in plants (especially the young ones), grains, molasses, carrots (and similar roots), sugar (e.g., extracted from cane and beets), and mare's milk in the form of lactose (which is only absorbable by nursing foals and young horses under 30 months of age).

- **Fiber**: This word refers to the structural carbohydrates of plants: cellulose and hemicellulose. Fiber increases with the plant's age in order to support leaves, flowers, seeds, etc. Moreover, as the plant ages, the usable fiber gradually turns into lignin (a hard, non-carbohydrate component), which is not possible for horses to digest. High levels of lignin in the food not only hinder digestibility of some nutrients, and may lead to colic, but also may take up to 60 hours in transit through the gastrointestinal tract.

  Fiber (cellulose and hemicellulose) is very important in the horse's diet for several reasons. Although it is not digested in the small intestine, a proper amount of fiber aids in the passage of foodstuff through the gastrointestinal tract. Once fiber reaches the cecum, the specialized microorganisms in it ferment the fiber. The final product (volatile fatty acids) is absorbed in the cecum and used by the horse as a source of energy. A horse's diet should contain a fiber average from 20% to 32%. The optimal average content of fiber is 26% for adult horses.

- **Fat (Lipids)**: Fat provides 2.25 times the energy (calculated in Megacalories) as carbohydrates, which makes fat a good way to increase the energy in a horse's diet. Therefore, in some circumstances, grain intake may be partially/totally reduced by replacing the amount of grain with the proper amount of fat, based on the calories provided by both sources. Fat is emulsified (fractioned) by the bile salts into fatty acids in the small intestine, where they are absorbed directly by the intestinal walls. Bile salts continuously are secreted by the liver into the small intestine because the horse does not have a gallbladder to accumulate them as humans do.

  In general, fat from animal sources has less palatability and digestibility for horses than vegetable fat. Therefore, grass, grains, and vegetable oil are the most common sources for providing fat to a horse. However, fish oil may also be used as a fat source, which also provides the benefit of omega-3 fatty acid.

  Fat, which is stored in the horse's tissues as a result of extra energy supplied in the regular diet, may also be used as a source of energy during exercise.

- **Protein**: The quality of protein in any kind of food depends on the type and amount of amino acids in it. Protein is fractioned (hydrolyzed) into amino acids, primarily in the small intestine, by the action of proteases (specialized enzymes); the amino acids are then absorbed by the intestinal walls. The antibodies from the broodmare's colostrum (the first milk produced by the mare after foaling) are the only kind of protein that are absorbed intact by the foal's small intestine, and only during the first 24 to 36 hours of life (see Chapter 8: "Reproduction").

The main function of amino acids in a horse is to build the tissues (organs, muscles, tendons, skin, hair, hooves, cartilage, blood cells, etc.), by constructing new chains of amino acids (proteins), according to a given genetic code.

Therefore, for proper growth and development, young, growing horses need a greater amount and higher quality of protein than horses in other physiological stages. Lysine is the most important amino acid in growing foals. Pregnant mares and lactating mares also need a great amount of good quality protein in their diets.

- **Water**: Although it is not a real nutrient, water is essential to the horse's diet because it is the means by which all solutes of the body are diluted for chemical reactions. Thus, approximately 68% - 72% of the horse's weight is water.

  Because the horse needs to replace the internal water that is lost in urine, manure, sweat, and through breathing, water always should be available. During normal conditions, an adult Paso Fino horse will drink from four to ten gallons of water every day, depending on the weather, exercise, moisture contained in the food, and reproductive stage. Pregnant and lactating mares and working horses need a greater amount of water than other horses. The horse must drink good quality water, free of chemical and biological contaminating agents; therefore, the water source (even a spring) needs to be evaluated before being used for consumption. Based on this evaluation, special filters may be installed on the pump.

  Water may be flavored by adding a small amount of sugar, salt or electrolytes, starting, at a minimum, two to three weeks before the horse travels to another location. When the horse arrives at the new location, the same flavoring may be added to the water to prevent the horse from objecting to the water's taste. This recommendation is important because, if a horse does not drink enough water, it may become dehydrated and stop eating.

- **Minerals** and **Vitamins**: These nutrients are essential for metabolism because they facilitate most of the biochemical reactions; therefore, deficiency or excess may create severe problems for a horse. Horses need some minerals (calcium, phosphorus, magnesium, potassium, and sodium chloride) in greater amounts than others. These are known as "macro minerals." The other minerals (copper, iodine, iron, manganese, selenium, sulfur, and zinc), known as "trace minerals" or "micro minerals," are also required by the horse, but in lesser amounts. Macro minerals should be provided in the horse's diet, but not trace minerals (because the amount the horse needs is too little and they usually are present in most food).

  Vitamins are classified according to their solubility, either in fat or water. The fat-soluble vitamins are A, D, E, and K. The water-soluble vitamins are: B1 (thiamin), B2 (riboflavin), B12 , and biotin.

  Healthy adult horses obtain most vitamins from forage or synthesize them from precursors (a substance that allows another to be formed) contained in the forage through the action of bacteria in their intestines.

However, young, growing horses, pregnant and/or lactating mares, horses in training, and horses of any age kept in stressful situations need the addition of vitamins to the diet.

Note: Appendix A consists of four tables that summarize information regarding minerals and vitamins, including their function in the body, common sources, signs of deficiency, and signs of excess.

Only one part of the food is digested and absorbed into the horse's gastrointestinal tract. The usable fraction of a nutrient, compared with the total amount of that nutrient contained in the food, is called "digestibility." Of course, feed with a high level of digestible nutrients is more valuable. For example, legume hay is more digestible than grass hay.

On the other hand, teeth in bad condition lead to low digestibility of nutrients, especially when sharp points or unleveled areas (such as ramps) are present in the premolars and molars, because the horse cannot chew properly. Gastric ulcers and/or high internal parasitism levels also lead to a lower rate of digestion. In addition, hard work diminishes digestibility, probably because of increased peristaltic movements (contractions) of the intestine that make the foodstuff pass too fast.

FEEDING SOURCES

There are several feeding sources that, when properly mixed, will meet the nutritional needs of horses of any physiological stage.

- **Forage**: This term refers to all the species of plants that horses and other herbivores eat as their normal source of nutrients, including grass, legumes, and grains (the full plant). Eating forage keeps the gastrointestinal tract functioning. Forage may be offered green or dry (e.g., hay, pellets, cubes, and blocks). After weaning, the young horse must eat forage as a high proportion of its daily diet.

  Forage contains different forms of energy (fiber, sugars, and fat), protein, minerals, vitamins and/or their precursors, and some water. These nutrients vary depending on plant species/variety, soil fertilization, season, and plant maturity. Additionally, if the forage is in dry form, the nutrients may vary depending on both the drying and storage processes.

  Green forage contains more water (78% - 82%) than hay (15% or less). Thus, the dry matter, which actually contains the nutrients, is more concentrated in hay than green forage. The amount of dry matter in any forage may be calculated by subtracting the water content from the total weight of the forage.

  Green, cut forage is turned into hay after drying most of the water content either by exposure to the sun or by any physical means. Horses fed with hay need to drink more water than horses fed with green forage. In addition, horses fed with green forage, which contains more water, spend more time eating in order to obtain all the required nutrients that are more diluted.

  The most common way to offer green forage is by keeping the horse in a pasture, either part-time or full-time. In the pasture, the horse grazes according to its preferences. In addition, grazed forages are more digestible than their hay forms. This is reasonable because a horse selects the young, growing plants in the pasture, which have a higher nutritive value and digestibility, compared to mature plants.

Hay is the most common way to offer dry forage to horses. When hay is not produced on the farm where the horse is housed, customers should obtain thorough information about the hay available on the market (species, dry matter, protein, fiber, length of storage) in order to evaluate the price versus the quality. Alternatively, pellets, cubes, and blocks are other options of dry forage for horses.

Changing the forage source for horses must be done gradually over three to four days, either from green grass to hay or vice versa, or to a different plant species of hay. This is an important consideration because hay distributors may change the species of hay according to the season.

- **Pastures for horses**: From the nutritional point of view, a good pasture is the best place for a horse to live because the animal chooses exactly the most nutritious plants, or parts of plants. However, the amount of grass eaten by a horse everyday depends on the plant's palatability and the dry matter content, as well as the horse's needs.

From a psychological point of view, the pasture provides a healthy environment for the horse without the stress of being in a stall all day long; thus, the horse has less opportunity to develop vices due to boredom/stress. While being in the pasture, the horse learns how to deal with an environment in motion (such as branches being shaken by the wind, birds and squirrels moving around, and rain pouring down), which teaches the horse to be more confident when working. Additionally, if sharing the pasture with other horses, a horse learns how to interact in the herd, which leads to better behavior with other horses.

From a physiological point of view, the horse's skeleton improves its bone density and becomes stronger because of both exercise and exposure to sunshine (which promotes vitamin D synthesis). In addition, Paso Fino horses may benefit by living on inclined pastures that help them to develop muscles related to both slow and quick contraction.

From an economical point of view, pastures may produce the cheapest high quality forage for horses, except if the land price and taxes are very high. Nevertheless, well- managed pastures increase the land's value in the real estate market.

A horse in the pasture grazes about 17 hours a day because it takes time to carefully choose favorite plants and chew them perfectly before swallowing. Thus, the horse's gastrointestinal tract has some foodstuff to digest all the time. Because equines have developed this habit (eating carefully many hours daily) over millions of years of evolution, it must be respected when raising domestic horses. Thus, horses kept from good pastures, either in stalls or paddocks, always should have some good quality forage (such as hay) to eat, and be fed small amounts of grain several times a day, if so required: two times, at a minimum, three times is better.

Ruminants, like cattle, spend about eight hours a day grazing, eight hours ruminating, and eight hours resting. They cut the grass with the tongue or the eight lower incisor teeth (cattle do not possess upper incisors), and swallow it after a little chewing with the molar teeth. When full, they start to regurgitate, chew, and swallow the foodstuff. Additionally, fiber is fermented by millions of microorganisms in the first stomach (known as the "rumen"), making a very efficient digestive process for obtaining nutrients from forages.

Because horses graze many hours daily and horse pastures recuperate slowly, many people erroneously think that one horse eats the same amount of forage as three or four cows. Actually, an adult Paso Fino horse, that has an average body weight of 870 lbs. (391.5 kg.), may eat about the same amount of forage daily as an adult cow that has an average body weight of 1,111 lbs. (about 500 kg.). Pastures for horses take longer to recuperate than pastures for cattle because equines cut the plants shorter. Grass cut shorter (by horses) needs to use stored nutrients to survive while new leaves grow.

Due to the different grazing habits of horses and cows, both herbivore species may be kept in good pastures, either mixed at the same time or alternated, in order to take the most advantage of the grass. The recommended ratio is about one horse to three to four cows because the grass eaten by horses is cut shorter, and thus, takes longer to grow back.

Note: The total number of horses and/or cows that a pasture will sustain depends on several factors, such as acreage, plant species, fertility of the soil, rain, temperature, and sunshine.

Although a pasture must provide enough nutrients for horses of all ages (except for salt and some minerals), young growing horses, lactating mares, and horses in training may need supplementation with grains or concentrates because of their higher nutritional requirements. Logically, horses kept full-time in the pasture and supplemented with grain spend less time grazing than non-supplemented horses because grain fills part of their needs.

The horse pasture must contain plenty of nutritious and palatable plants that, ideally, cover the soil. Either one single species of grass or a mix of several species of grasses and/or legumes makes up the pasture forage. Although legumes are more nutritious than grasses, horses actually prefer to eat grasses. Legumes planted in pastures, that are not fertilized with nitrogen, take this nutrient from the air and put it into the soil, which improves soil fertility and, therefore, the grass quality.

Some common grass species for horse pastures are Argentine, Bahiagrass, Bluestem, Bromegrass, Callie, Carpet, Coastal Bermuda grass, Fescue (not recommended for pregnant mares), Kentucky Bluegrass, Orchardgrass, Pangola, Para, Pensacola, Ryegrass (annual and perennial), Tifton varieties, and Timothy. Some common legume species for horse pastures are Alfalfa, Clover, and Trefoil.

Selection of any grass and/or legume species, however, is limited by the type of soil, severity of weather within the seasons, and management capability. Therefore, before planting any kind of grass or legume for horse pastures, getting advice from the closest County Agricultural Extension Office or the State University Agronomy Faculty/Department is recommended.

The horse pasture should be kept free of weeds, especially before they seed, because equines also eat some of them. These seeds go through the gastrointestinal tract to be finally planted in the manure. Then, the weeds gradually invade the pasture, which reduces the nutritious plants for horses. "Weed" is the generic word used to define undesirable plants because of their toxicity, non-palatability, or very low nutritional value.

Because the horse is a selective grazer in the pasture, preferring young, growing plants, horse pastures commonly have areas with mature forage that horses do not eat except if there is no other option. Conversely, because horses keep eating young, short plants from certain areas of the pasture, even digging to reach the plant roots, horses should be rotated periodically to other pastures to maintain the integrity of the pasture.

The care and culture of a pasture includes dispersing the manure piles with a drag pulled by a truck, four-wheeler, or a tractor; rotational use; fertilization; irrigation; mowing; and weed and insect control. These activities depend on the weather (season), the plant species, and the soil. As with selecting grass and legumes, contacting the County Agricultural Extension Office or the State University Agronomy Faculty/ Department is also recommended to obtain advice on proper care and culture of the pastures.

Having trees spread out in the pasture provides shade to horses during the hottest hours of summer days. Additionally, it allows for more efficient nutrient recycling in the pasture because the tree roots take nutrients from the deepest levels of the soil, which are not reached by the grass/legume roots. Moreover, after old leaves from the tree fall, they become reduced to simple nutrients by the action of microorganisms, that thereafter become available for the pasture.

- **Hay for horses**: Hay consists of dehydrated grass, legumes, or grains (the plant), or a mix of them, in order to improve its overall quality.

  - **Grass hay**: Some common grasses used to produce commercial hay for horses in the United States are Coastal Bermuda grass, Kentucky Bluegrass, Orchardgrass, and Timothy. With proper fertilization, these grass species may be cut every three to five weeks (in the most productive season) to produce enough dry matter to contain 7.5 to 12% of protein.

    Timothy is very popular for horses due to its palatability and because it stays free from mold and dust. Feeding horses Coastal Bermuda grass hay is also popular in the United States, although there is some disagreement about whether this hay may cause colic in some horses. Therefore, horses with a recurrent history of colic should not be fed this hay. Additionally, coastal hay may become moldy if it is not properly stored.

  - **Legume hay**: Alfalfa hay is probably the best legume hay offered to horses because it is rich in high quality protein (from 12 to 16%), energy, and calcium. Besides the traditional hay bales, big blocks of compressed, dehydrated Alfalfa are becoming more popular for feeding horses in the pasture, especially during the winter when the grass does not grow, and for horses staying in small paddocks. In addition, Alfalfa cubes and pellets are two other ways to offer this legume, which contain around 90% dry matter and similar nutrients and digestibility as hay.

    Note: Timothy (grass) and Alfalfa (legume) combined in different proportions, is a popular hay for horses offered in the market, known as T&A. Thus, the higher content of protein in Alfalfa increases the total protein offered to the horse.

    Clover is a legume offered to horses as hay which, like Alfalfa, is rich in protein and calcium. Perennial Peanut hay is another legume species that is fed to horses. Perennial Peanut is highly palatable, but has slightly fewer nutrients than Alfalfa.

- **Grain plant hay**: Some grain plants, such as oats and barley, are also used for hay, usually mixed with grass; these should be supplemented with hay or concentrates that are rich in protein.

- **Grains**: Oats, corn, barley, wheat, and rice are very rich in starch (soluble carbohydrates), which is a form of energy. They are also rich in phosphorus, intermediately rich in protein, and poor in calcium. Dry matter from grains is about 90%.

  Both the entire grain and the bran of these grains are commonly used as an energy supplement for horses, when forages do not provide enough energy. Protein from grains, however, does not have a high nutritional value because it contains little of the essential amino acid, lysine.

  Oats and rice are commonly offered to horses after being rolled, which consists of breaking the husks. Corn is offered to horses in several forms, such as broken into small pieces, boiled, kept wet from the day before, or flaked. Barley is offered either bruised or boiled. Wheat is commonly offered to horses as bran, which is the outer husk of the grain.

  When pure grains (or a mix of them) are offered to horses, soybean meal may be added to improve the quality and the amount of protein. Soybean is a legume, highly rich in good quality protein, that is available for feeding after removing the hulls of the seeds. Therefore, it is commonly used in concentrates. On the other hand, due to an inadequate amount of calcium in grains, addition of a good calcium source is required to balance the high content of phosphorus.

- **Concentrates**: A planned mix of nutritional sources is called a “concentrate” or “compound feed.” This kind of product is designed to improve horse nutrition according to the physiological stage of the animal. There are several companies that produce concentrates for horses in the United States, with a wide variety of products designed for different purposes.

  The primary sources used in concentrates are grains, such as corn, oats, wheat, barley, and rice. Therefore, the dry matter of concentrates is around 90%. Other sources in concentrates include soybean meal, dehydrated alfalfa meal, sugar beet pulp, corn oil, molasses, amino acids (lysine and methionine), minerals, vitamins, and propionic acid (used as a preservative). Additionally, some concentrates designed for foals may also contain dried skim milk as a source of protein.

  Based on the sources of energy used, concentrates are classified into three main categories:

  - **Sweet feed**: All the ingredients, including starch from grains, are balanced, mixed, and combined with molasses. Molasses also makes the concentrate more palatable for horses. Vegetable oil is usually added, as well.

  - **Pelleted feed with no molasses**: All the ingredients, including starch from grains, are processed, balanced, and mixed before they are made into small cylindrical pieces (pellets or nuggets). This type of concentrate contains no molasses. Instead, this type of concentrate is supplemented with vegetable oil and sometimes with sugar beet pulp.

- **Pelleted feed with low starch and no molasses**: This type of concentrate is becoming very popular for horses that become ′hot′ when being fed starch/sweet sources of energy, and for horses with metabolic problems. The sources of energy used in this type of concentrate are dehydrated alfalfa, highly digestible fiber (e.g., sugar beet pulp), and vegetable oil, among others.

Although concentrates are actually excellent products that improve the diet, they should never replace forage completely, which is considered the primary food for horses. Thus, concentrates should be considered as supplements to enrich the horse's diet.

- **Fat**: Although grass contains a certain amount of fat (as oil), this important source of energy may also be supplied to horses using vegetable oil extracted from corn, soybean, rice, or sunflower. Fat is especially helpful as a safe form of energy for horses with high energy requirements, reducing the risk of founder and colic. Additionally, because this energy source does not break down into sugars, it provides the horse with a "calm" amount of energy, that does not make the animal become difficult to control ("hot").

Feeding fat is recommended for horses that need to gain weight, horses under moderate to high physical activity, and horses over 15 years of age. Feeding fat is recommended for broodmares during the last three months of pregnancy and the first three months of lactation. Broodmares over 12 years of age (before breeding and during their entire pregnancy) also benefit from fat supplementation. A healthy and shiny coat is another advantage of adding fat to a horse's diet.

Although most concentrates for horses contain 3% to 4% fat, some of them may contain 6% to 7% fat. Special concentrates for high performing horses may contain as much as 10% fat. Oil (vegetable or fish sources) may be added to low fat concentrates in order to increase calories, but the total amount of fat should not exceed 10% of the concentrate. Offering cooked linseed is another way to supply some vegetable oil to the horse's diet.

- **Other horse feed options**: Carrots, apples, and turnips are also used for feeding horses (as supplementation) because they are very palatable. These have a high concentration of soluble carbohydrates, diluted by high moisture, so dry matter is just 10%. Thus, these "vegetables" are not very efficient for providing large amounts of nutrients to horses; however, they may be used as a "treat" for horses in order to improve the appetite, reward the horse, or as a regular treat.

Sugar beet pulp is a source of energy for horses in the form of fiber (about 13%) and sugars (over 22%). Because of its sweet flavor, sugar beet pulp is accepted very well by horses; therefore, one to two pounds of sugar beet pulp may be added to each meal of grain or concentrate to make it more palatable and to provide some extra energy. Sugar beet pulp is recommended as a complementary source of energy for horses older than 14 years of age.

Maize (the entire corn plant) is an excellent kind of forage for horses, with highly digestible energy and good palatability. Maize may be cut into small pieces before offering it to the horse to make it easier to eat.

Molasses and sugar are two sources of energy that are digested easily by the horse. Cane molasses commonly is used in sweet concentrates for several reasons, such as improving palatability, providing energy, and binding particles. Molasses, however, should not be offered to horses when diluted in large amounts of water because the animal will drink an excess of liquid at one time, thereby "washing" the gastrointestinal tract and preventing the digestion of many nutrients. Sugar also may be added to grains or concentrates as an energy supplement.

Note: As described above, there are many types of horse feed available, some more conventional than others. Therefore, before choosing one or more items, several elements should be considered: nutritional quality, availability in or around the farm, palatability, risks of use, conservation requirements, and price.

- **Mineral supplements**: Salt (sodium chloride) should be included in the horse's diet in order to replace what is lost in sweat, urine, and milk (for mares in lactation). Therefore, iodized salt (the same kind used for cooking) should be supplied to horses in "salters" placed away from the rain, where the animals may eat the required daily amount, (around 20 grams). Some Paso horse breeders prefer to give a dessert spoon of iodized salt, mixed with the grain, daily to each horse.

  The other macro and micro minerals are usually supplied by offering a mineral supplement mixed with the food, according to the needs of the horse. Of course, the mineral supplement should be calculated based on what is provided in the rest of the diet.

  If offering minerals and salt using these methods is not possible, the other option is to supply them to the horses by means of a mineral salt block/brick. However, this method makes the intake of minerals dependent on the horse's salt needs.

THE PROPER DIET

Most people associate the word "diet" with restricted food intake in order to lose weight. The word diet, however, also means the right feeding plan to assure the best health and physical condition of a person or an animal.

The proper diet for a horse may vary due to several factors:

- Physiological stage, such as rest (a non-reproducing, non-working, adult horse that is not gaining weight), growth and development, and reproduction (breeding season, pregnancy, and lactation).
- Body condition index (related to appearance of fat deposits and, therefore, correlated to weight).
- Physical activity (exercise).
- Individual needs.

Based on these factors, the Paso Fino owner/manager must consider three important elements in designing a horse's diet:

1. **Total intake**: Each Paso Fino horse should eat a daily amount of food, consisting of forage and possibly supplemented by grains and/or concentrates, as follows.

    - Young Paso Fino horses:
      A two-month old nursing foal will eat from 3 to 6 lbs. of hay and grains/concentrates (containing 85% to 90% of dry matter) daily, plus the mare's milk, which, at this time, is in peak production.

      A four-month old nursing foal eats from 6.5 to 10 lbs. of hay and grains/concentrates (with 85% to 90% of dry matter) daily, plus the mare's milk.

      An eight-month old weanling foal eats from 9 to 12 lbs. of hay and grains/concentrates (with 85% to 90% of dry matter) daily.

      A twelve-month old Paso Fino horse eats from 11 to 16.5 lbs. of hay and grains/concentrates (with 85% to 90% of dry matter) daily.

      A twenty-four-month old (*not working*) Paso Fino horse eats from 12.5 to 18 lbs. of hay and grains/concentrates (with 85% to 90% of dry matter) daily.

    - Adult Paso Fino horses (870 lbs. = 391.5 kg. average weight):
      An adult horse at rest (horses being used for reproduction or horses that need to gain weight *not included*) eats from 13 to 18 lbs. of hay and grains/concentrates (with 85% to 90% of dry matter) daily.

      A horse under light work (pregnant/lactating mares *not included*) eats from 15 to 20 lbs. of hay and grains/concentrates (with 85% to 90% of dry matter) daily.

      A horse under heavy work (pregnant/lactating mares *not included*) eats from 18.5 to 25 lbs. of hay and grains/concentrates (with 85% to 90% of dry matter) daily.

      A pregnant mare (during the last three months of pregnancy) eats from 15 to 20 lbs. of hay and grains/concentrates (with 85% to 90% of dry matter) daily.

      A lactating mare (not at work) eats from 17 to 25 lbs. of hay and grains/concentrates (with 85% to 90% of dry matter) daily.

    Notes:

    - The information above is applicable to confined horses.
    - The intake of horses grazing in good pastures, either part-time or full-time, must be determined based on type and availability of grass.
    - The appropriate proportion of forage and grain (grains/concentrates) is explained in "Recommendations for a good feeding program."

2. **Body condition index**: All horses have some fat deposits throughout the body. The location and appearance of these fat deposits is known as the "horse's body condition." The following table describes different body conditions correlated to a given score:

Score/Body Condition	Description
1 *Poor*	Animal extremely emaciated Spinous processes, ribs, tailhead (where tail meets the body), hip bones, and buttock bones projecting prominently Bone structure of withers, shoulders, and neck easily noticeable No fatty tissue is felt
2 *Very Thin*	Animal emaciated Spinous processes, ribs, tailhead, hip bones, and buttock bones prominent Withers, shoulders, and neck structures faintly discernable Slight fat covering base of spinous processes; transverse processes of lumbar vertebrae feel rounded
3 *Thin*	Fat build up on spinous processes about halfway; transverse processes cannot be felt Slight fat cover over ribs Spinous processes and ribs easily discernible Tailhead prominent, but individual vertebrae cannot be identified visually Hip bones appear rounded, but easily discernable Buttock bones not distinguishable Withers, shoulders, and neck accentuated
4 *Moderately Thin*	Ridge along back Faint outline of ribs discernible Tailhead prominence depends on conformation; fat may be felt around it Hip bones not discernable Withers, shoulders, and neck not obviously thin
5 *Moderate*	Back is level Ribs cannot be distinguished visually, but are easily felt Fat around tailhead beginning to feel spongy Withers appear rounded over spinous processes Shoulders and neck blend smoothly into body
6 *Moderate to Fleshy*	Slight crease down back Fat over ribs feels spongy Fat around tailhead feels soft Fat beginning to be deposited along sides of the withers, behind shoulders, and along sides of the neck
7 *Fleshy*	Crease down back Individual ribs may be felt, but noticeable filling between ribs with fat Fat around tailhead is soft Fat deposited along withers, behind shoulders, and along neck
8 *Fat*	Prominent crease down back Difficult to feel ribs Fat around tailhead very soft Area along withers filled with fat Area behind shoulder filled with fat Noticeable thickening of neck Fat deposited along inner buttocks (thighs)
9 *Extremely Fat*	Extremely obvious crease down back Patchy fat appearing over ribs Bulging fat around tailhead, along withers, behind shoulders, and along neck Fat along inner buttocks (thighs) may rub together Flank filled with fat

Adapted from Henneke, D. R., G. D. Potter, J. L. Kreider, and B. F. Yeates. 1983. A scoring system for comparing body condition in horses. *Equine Vet. J. 15:371-372.*

Following are some recommendations for Paso Fino horses with body conditions that are described in the table above:

- Poor and very thin (scores 1 and 2) are not desirable body conditions for any Paso Fino horse, independent of age or gender. Horses with these two scores need to gain weight urgently and should not work before significant improvement, nor are they recommended for reproduction.
- Thin and moderately thin horses (scores 3 and 4) also need to gain weight, but they may work lightly. Reproduction is usually not successful.
- Moderate, moderate to fleshy, and fleshy adult Paso Fino horses (scores 5, 6, and 7) may work moderately to intensively, with the proper diet and endurance adjusting program. These are the optimal scores for mares to be bred successfully. The optimal body condition for pregnant mares to foaling and for lactating mares is fleshy (score 7).
- Young, growing horses should have a body condition score of 5 to 7, with 6 and 7 more desirable. Any lower body condition score (from 1 to 4) is not recommended because this would mean a lack of nutrients/feed. On the other hand, a higher body condition score (8 or 9) is also not recommended because this would mean the horse has a hyper-caloric diet that is risky for growth and health.
- The ideal body condition score for Paso Fino horses during the show season (since the horses are being ridden regularly), is between fleshy (score 7) and fat (score 8), because the horse looks well and may have good deposits of glycogen and fat that are used during the intense training/competition.
- A fat body condition (score 8) is not healthy for Paso Fino horses of any physiological stage. Because pregnant mares may reach this condition easily due to the anabolic effect of the pregnancy hormones, they may need physical activity everyday and, in some cases, a controlled diet.
- Extremely fat (obese) Paso Fino horses (score 9) are not acceptable for any reason, and they are at high risk to develop different types of diseases, including laminitis (described in Chapter 10: "Health basics").

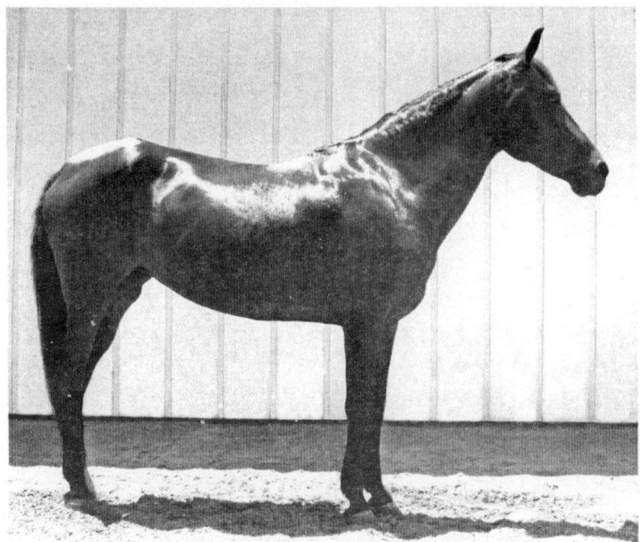

Minimal recommended body condition (moderately thin - score 4)

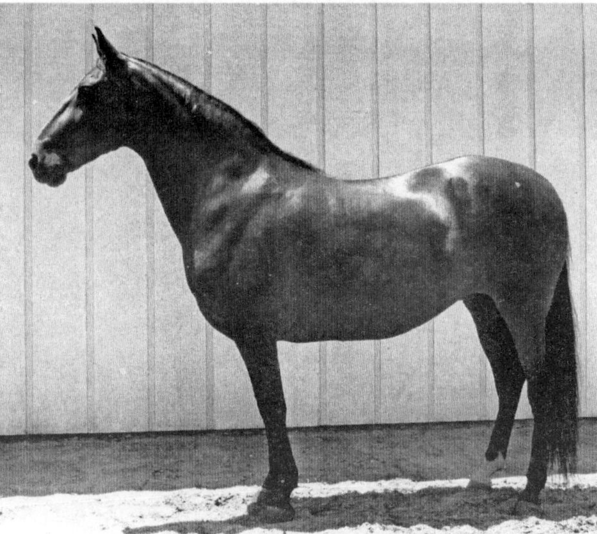

Ideal body condition during the show season (between fleshy - score 7, and fat - score 8)

3. **Some nutrients to keep in mind**: According to their physiological stage and/or physical activity, some horses need a greater amount of certain nutrients to fill their requirements.

- To calculate diets for horses, the energy content of feed is commonly represented as "Digestible Energy" (DE) and expressed in Megacalories per kilogram of feed (DE: Mcal/kg). Likewise, a horse's daily requirement of energy may be expressed in Megacalories of digestible energy.

  An adult Paso Fino horse (based on 870 lbs. = 391.5 kg. of body weight) at rest (neither working, nor reproducing, nor gaining weight) needs about 13 to 13.5 Mcal. of digestible energy per day, that is usually provided with good forage. This requirement, however, may have minor variations according to **individual needs**. "Easy keepers," for instance, are horses that maintain a highly scored body condition with less than this amount of energy due to their metabolism. Conversely, others need a greater amount/ quality of feed to be in proper condition.

  Young, growing Paso Fino horses (yearlings), lactating mares, and moderately to highly exercised horses have greater energy requirements of 25%, 75%, and 100%, respectively, more than what is required by an adult horse at rest. Young, growing horses may fulfill the high energy requirement with a more caloric feed. Lactating mares and highly exercised horses fill the high energy requirements with both a higher feed intake (dry matter) and a more caloric feed.

  For a horse of any age to gain weight requires a diet with a greater amount of energy than is required for a well-conditioned horse of the same physiological stage. The greater the energy fed, the faster the weight gained. However, an excess of grain (which is rich in energy) must be avoided to prevent laminitis (see Chapter 10: "Health basics").

  The energy supplemented from carbohydrates (sugars and starch) should be reduced/eliminated on some days for horses in training or horses that are regularly being ridden, when they become difficult ("hot"). Once the horse starts to work well, carbohydrates gradually may be increased.

  Because the energy required by some horses is not always supplied by forage, grains/concentrates are excellent sources for these needs when offered up to 50% (under supervised conditions) of the entire diet. Fat is another source of energy for lactating mares and highly exercised horses. Adding fat increases calories in the diet; therefore, feeding grains/concentrates may need to be reduced.

  Notes:

  - Some adjustments to diets, according to the horses' physical activity, are explained in more depth in Chapter 12: "The horse as an athlete."

  - The "Percentage of Total Digestible Nutrients" (% TDN) is another way to describe the energy content of horse feed. If the total digestible nutrients (TDN) is used to calculate a horse's diet, the following conversion from digestible energy (DE) may be used:

  1 kg. of TDN = 4.4 Megacalories of DE = 4,400 kilocalories of DE.

- Protein is not highly required by horses, compared to other species. An adult Paso Fino horse at rest needs about 9% of crude protein in its diet. Protein requirements are greater for mares during the last three months of pregnancy (10.5% due to the fetal development), lactating mares (no less than 12% because milk produced contains a great amount of protein), and growing horses (about 12% to 14% for growth and development). Additionally, the amount of the amino acid, lysine, is extremely important in the diet of young, growing horses (about 0.55%, equivalent to approximately 30 g., daily).

  Good quality grass hay generally provides the protein required by adult Paso Fino horses at rest. Grass hay mixed with legume hay and/or concentrate containing 12% to 16% protein will fulfill the higher amount of protein required by pregnant mares in the last trimester of pregnancy, lactating mares, and growing horses.

- Horses of all ages should have free access to sodium chloride (salt), found in iodized salt, sea salt, mineral salt, salt block, or salt brick. Other minerals are important for all horses, but especially for stallions during the breeding season, pregnant mares, young, growing horses, horses working moderately and intensely, and lactating mares. For example, the needs for absorbable calcium for Paso Fino horses in these physiological stages range from 20 to 40 g. per day.

RECOMMENDATIONS FOR A GOOD FEEDING PROGRAM

- If possible, the horse should live in a good pasture with a water supply and a roof or trees, where the horse may be protected from rain and hot sunshine. A supplement of salt and minerals should be offered according to the horse's needs.

- Confined horses should have clean/fresh water and salt (free-choice), minerals, and good quality forage (also free-choice, except for "easy keepers").

- Grain given to confined horses should be distributed twice a day at a minimum, but more frequently, if possible.

- Forage is the main feed for the horse; grains (grains/concentrates) are supplements. Forage should be from 60% to 100% of the Paso Fino horse diet; grains, when used, should not be more than 40% of the entire diet. In addition, grains should never be offered free-choice to horses. Due to the high risk of metabolic illnesses, ONLY in special situations, and under supervised conditions, should some horses be fed 50% forage and 50% grain.

- Grain supplementation should be reduced for working horses during one or more days of rest.

- Similar amounts of feed should be offered at the same time every day (except grain when the horse rests one or more days).

- A foal older than 30 days of age may be supplemented with an intermediate-to high-protein concentrate (14% to 18%) in a separate feeder from the mother.

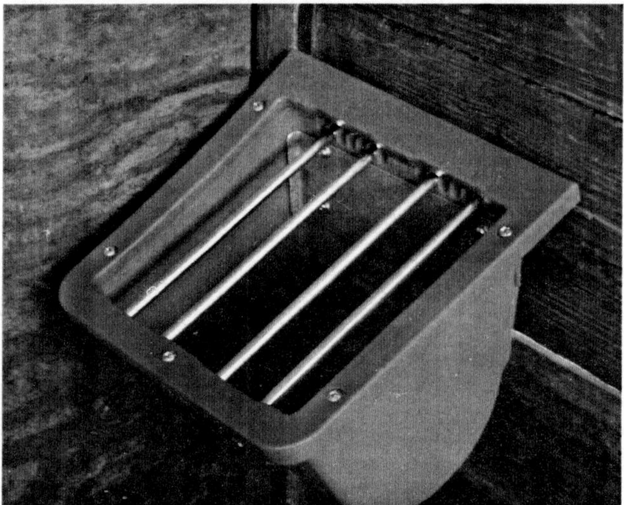

This foal feeder keeps the dam from eating the foal's concentrate

- Each horse should be fed according to several parameters: physiological stage, body condition index, physical activity, and individual needs.
- A balanced diet is based on feed nutrient and dry matter content.
- The horse's diet should be evaluated and/or adjusted once or twice a month to keep the animal in optimal condition, neither under- nor overweight.
- Feeding should be made by weight of feed; feeding by volume causes mistakes that could result in an excess or lack of nutrients and/or dry matter.
- A horse should rest (not work) for a minimum of one hour after eating a full meal.
- When the horse is hot after working, it may eat a small ammount of forage and drink a few sips of water after 15 minutes of "cool down." The horse may eat grain after one hour of rest.
- The calcium/phosphorus ratio should be balanced between 1.3/1 to 1.85/1, and based on the feed content.
- Grain for horses that are "fast eaters," optimally, should be divided into several meals per day.
- Changes in either feed or feeding schedule should be made gradually over one week.
- During winter, the horse needs more forage in order to obtain the energy required to keep its temperature constant.
- Feeders and water suppliers should be cleaned regularly in order to avoid contamination.

Note: Several feeding and metabolic disorders, most of them caused by inappropriate feeding, are explained in Chapter 10: "Health basics."

CHAPTER 7

HOOF TRIMMING AND SHOEING

THE HOOF

While a horse is standing, only the **wall** of each hoof may be seen. This hard wall is composed of keratinized cells, which are not sensitive, similar to human finger nails. The hoof wall's color may be black, light yellow, or beige to pink. The **coronet** (also called "**coronary band**") is at the top of the wall, where the hoof joins the pastern's skin. Because the coronet is responsible for wall growth, any injury caused to it could produce a scar on the wall.

Seen from the side, the front inclined edge of the hoof is the "**toe profile.**" The back edge of the hoof is called the "**heel profile.**" This is also inclined, but shorter than the toe profile. Both profiles are almost parallel to each other, but the toe profile is about twice as long as the heel profile.

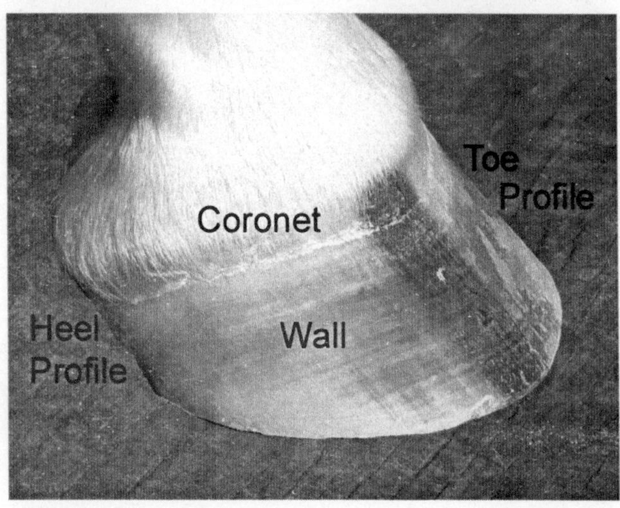

The "**stepping surface**" (or "**bottom surface**") of the hoof is divided into three even sections (or areas) from the front point to the back point: The front third is the **toe**; the back third is the **heel**; and the intermediate third is the **quarter**.

The stepping surface of the hoof has several external structures. The wall is the outside ring of the hoof, about 1/4 to 3/8 of an inch (0.63 to 0.95 cm.) wide, from the bearing edge toward the center. The inside area of the wall is the **white line**, which is much narrower than the wall. The white line marks the border between the hard laminae of the wall and the internal sensitive laminae. The white line starts at one heel, circles around the wall toward the toe, and ends at the other heel. Both ends of the wall, next to the heel, turn back toward the center to form a **bar**.

The **frog** is not as hard as the wall and the sole. The frog is a slightly elastic, prominent, isosceles triangle-shaped structure of the hoof. Its even sides (of the triangle) project from the two bars (next to each heel) toward the area between the toe and the quarter, to join at the apex of the frog. The uneven side of the frog projects from one bar to the other (below the bulbs). The top of the frog has a **cleft** or **central sulcus** projecting from back to front. Each hoof sheds the frog approximately every six months. The two **bulbs** of the hoof, located above the back side of the frog, are slightly elastic.

The **sole** projects from the white line toward the center of the hoof in a concave manner. The sole is the same color as the wall because they both are composed of the same kind of hard tissue (keratinized cells). Additionally, the sole is as thick as the wall.

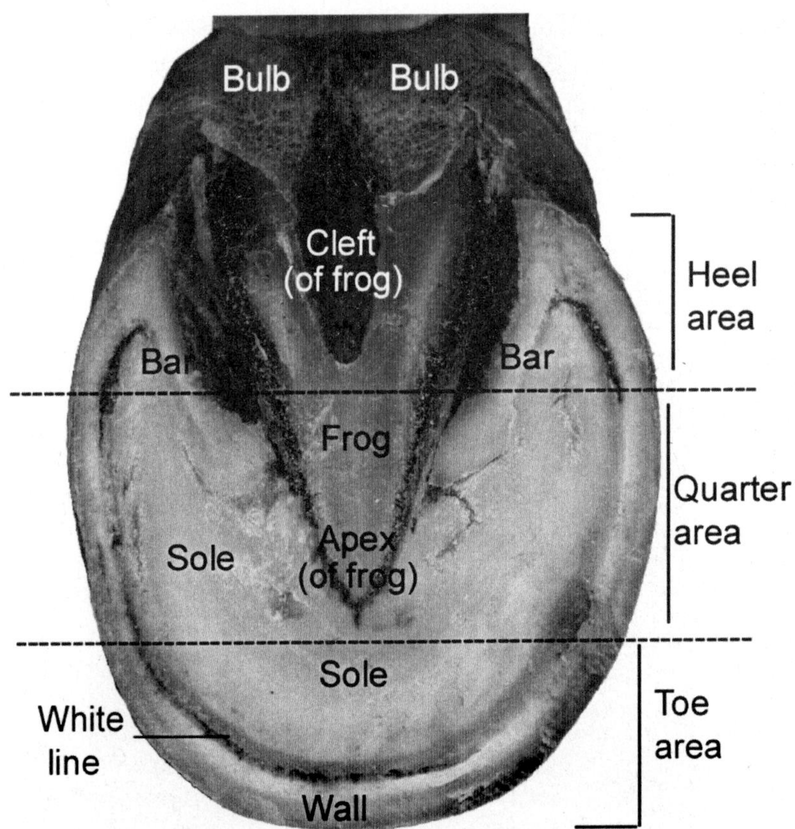

Un-shod hooves support the horse's weight on the hoof walls. However, when an un-shod Paso Fino horse is overworked on an abrasive floor (such as asphalt, concrete, or stones), the walls of all the hooves become more worn than desired, forcing the soles to provide support, which is not their function. This situation may cause sole bruising, hoof abscess, or laminitis.

Although the outside structures of the hoof are hard and not sensitive, they contain many sensitive internal structures, such as the **sensitive laminae**, the **navicular** (bone), the **coffin bone**, and the lower small portion of the **second phalange**. Additionally, the hoof has nerves and blood vessels inside.

SPECIAL HOOF CARE

Healthy hooves are very important for good performance of the horse. For this reason, hooves cannot be neglected and practicing good maintenance is a necessity:

- **Cleaning the hooves**: Because the hooves are in contact with manure and urine, especially when the horse is in a stall, they need to be cleaned regularly (ideally every day) to remove the pathogen microorganisms that will affect their good health. Additionally, removing the polluting material stuck to the hoof's sole helps the rider to assure that there is not any object that may generate trauma. This is also the opportunity to inspect the health of the hooves; special attention is necessary if they smell very badly or appear to have thrush (see Chapter 10: "Health basics"). Likewise, during hoof cleaning, the state of the horseshoes may be reviewed to determine if they are properly attached or loose, or if they are worn and need to be replaced.

  The proper tool used to clean the hooves is a hoof pick with a tip that often is like the tip of a flat screwdriver. In addition, some hoof picks have a brush attached. Using separate hoof picks for each horse avoids the diffusion of pathogens from one horse to another. The habit of regular hoof cleaning should begin with foals from the first month of life. This will make the foal comfortable with this activity and facilitate later shoeing.

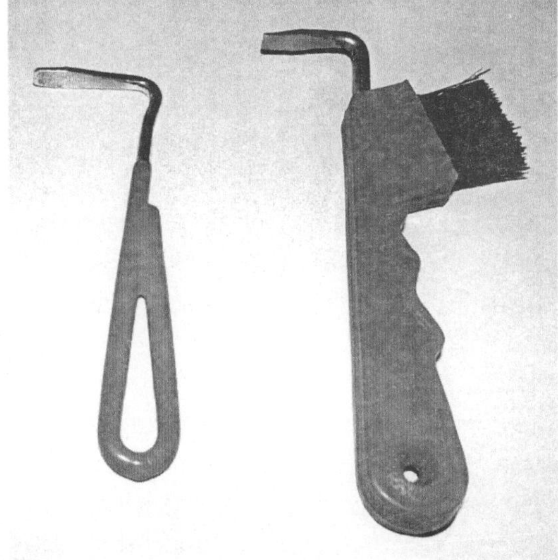

Hoof picks

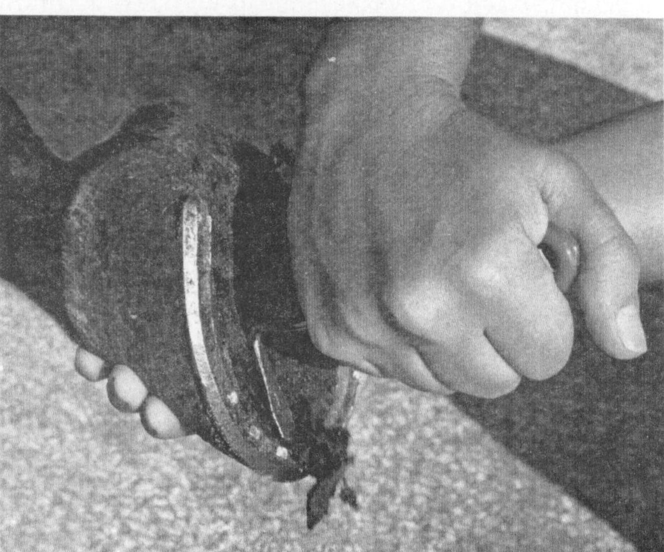

Using a hoof pick

- **Keeping the hooves free of pathogens**: Frequently applying products that keep the sole free of bacteria helps to prevent infectious illnesses of the hoof. Two products to use are clear iodine or diluted chloride.
- **Lubricating the hooves**: The application of a lubricant, cream-type or oil, on the hoof wall, from the coronet, seems to be helpful in improving hoof elasticity, hardness, and growth. There are many good products on the market for this purpose.
- **Promoting hoof growth**: When hoof growth or consistency needs to be improved, there are some specific products on the market with biotin, methionine, and other nutrients that may be added to the horse's food.

IMPORTANCE OF HOOF TRIMMING

Wild horses do not need hoof trimming; the hooves grow at the same rate as they are worn. However, domestic horses, either shod or not, require frequent hoof trimming every 40 to 55 days (depending on the age, the activity, and individual hoof growth) to keep the hooves in the best possible shape.

The foal's hooves grow about 3/8 inch monthly (0.95 cm.). They need to be trimmed for two reasons: removing dead tissue and correcting any incorrect balance of the hooves or the entire legs, which may affect the normal movement.

Because the leg bones grow on the epiphyses (ends of long bones), any inexact distribution of the foal's weight on those epiphyses of a leg, caused by incorrect balance, increases the imbalance and, therefore, causes more problems to the still growing bones. Correction of the hoof/leg balance of a foal consists of trimming the hooves to achieve appropriate conformation of the legs, which allows the foal to progressively achieve a perfect execution of leg movement. These corrections should be carried out at an early age, when the epiphyses are still malleable.

Depending on the orthopedic problem, the correction must start before the epiphyses become fully developed and harder. This correction should be done during the first six months of age to fix any deviations below the cannon bone. During the first 12 months of age is the time to correct any conformation problems of the carpus (or "false knee") or the tarsus (or "hock"). During the first 18 to 24 months of age is the time to correct deviations of the forearm or the gaskin. Corrections done after these ages are much less successful.

Having a corrective trimming program requires the cooperative effort of the farrier, veterinarian, and trainer (for horses in training). For the most successful results, the trimming program should be backed by proper nutrition and free outdoor exercise. Having accurate recorded information allows good tracking of changes to orthopedic problems.

The adult horse's hoof grows ½ inch (1.27 cm.) monthly or slightly less. Therefore, the hooves (kept shod or not) also require trimming to maintain a proper shape. In contrast to young, growing horses, improper conformation of the adult horse's legs neither may be corrected with trimming nor with shoeing, because the mature horse's bones are fully developed. The purpose of corrective trimming of the adult horse's hooves is only to compensate for any abnormal hoof growth in order to allow the leg to be used in the most natural way, which in turn allows for healthier and more efficient movement. Therefore, proper corrective hoof trimming requires an analysis of each leg to evaluate the horse's balance while it both stands and moves.

Drastic changes to the hoof of any horse should be avoided because they may cause either excess strain or pressure on certain bones, tendons, and foot structures, which may lead to more severe problems. Therefore, when it is necessary to remove an excessive amount of hoof wall through corrective trimming, it should be done gradually, in more than one session.

HOOF AND LEG BALANCE

When a hoof and its leg are conformed properly and balanced, the same amount of weight is supported by both sides of the limb, while standing and moving. Viewed from the front, the rear, and the top, the horse's foot (hoof and pastern) should point forward and be balanced.

When the foot points outward, it is commonly because the outside hoof wall is higher than the inside hoof wall. This type of conformation makes the hoof perform an inward curved movement when the horse is walking or gaiting, which is not appropriate. This may be corrected by trimming the outside hoof wall of the toe and the quarter, on both the stepping and the lateral surfaces.

If the foot points inward, it is usually because the inside wall of the hoof is higher than the outside one. This conformation makes the hoof perform an outward curved movement, when the horse either is walking or gaiting, which is not appropriate. This may be corrected by trimming the inside wall of the toe and the quarter areas, on both the stepping and the lateral surfaces.

Viewed from the side, the toe profile of the hooves of the Paso Fino horse should have an angle to the ground of about 55-56 degrees, which is the most common inclination of the scapula (shoulder) in the breed. Normally, the inclination of the toe profile should be the same as the shoulder. Moreover, the angle of the hoof should be as close as possible to the angle of the corresponding pastern, neither lower than 49 degrees, nor higher than 62 degrees.

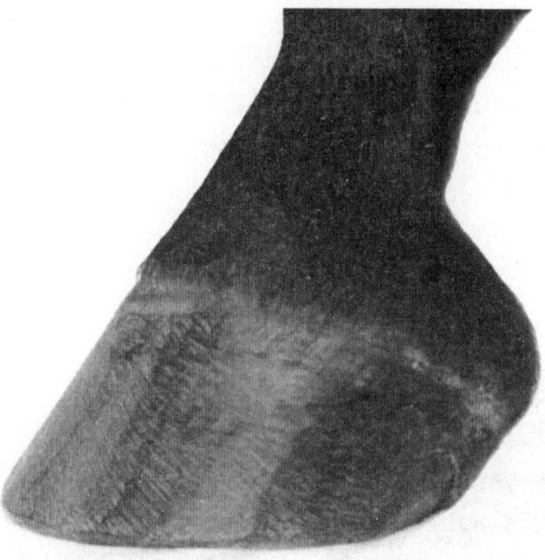

When the angle needs to be increased because the toe is long and the heel is low, the toe is trimmed on the stepping surface as shown in the figure below.

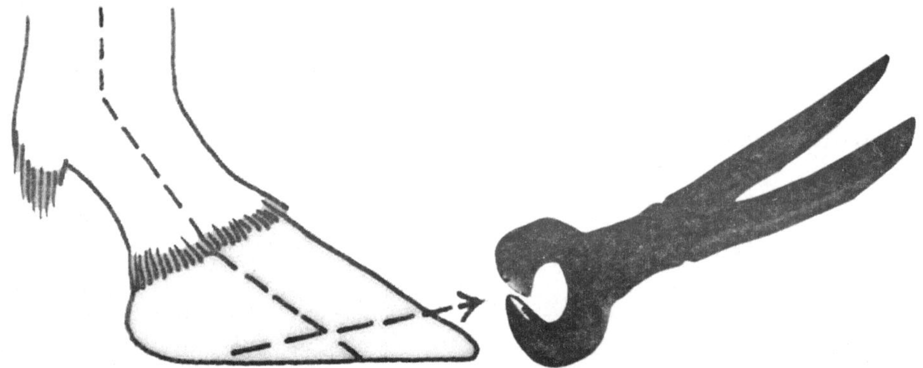

When the angle needs to be reduced because the toe is short and the heel is very high, the heel is trimmed on the stepping surface as shown in the figure below. However, when the heels need to be trimmed, they cannot be over-trimmed because they commonly grow more slowly than the toe.

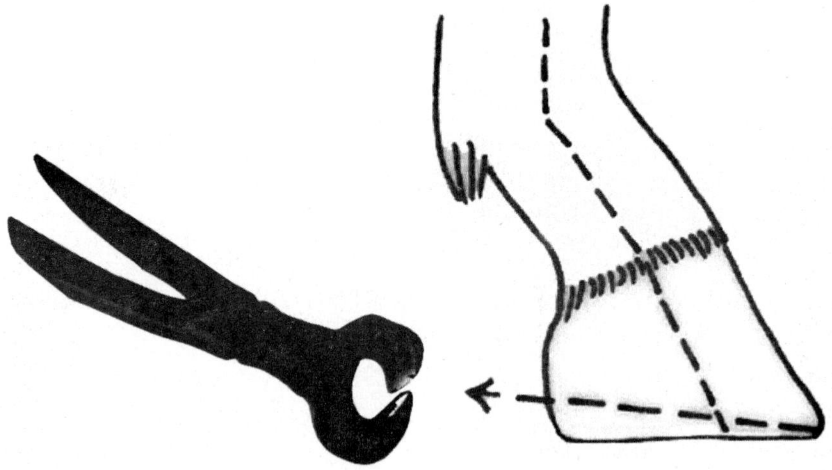

The stepping surfaces of the front hooves have a round shape because the forelegs have a supporting function during movement. Conversely, the stepping surfaces of the hind hooves are slightly longer and more pointed at the toes because the hind legs propel the horse forward.

TOOLS FOR HOOF TRIMMING

The set of tools used for trimming the hoof are as follows:

- **Hoof pick**: This tool is used to clean the hoof's bottom surface.

- **Hoof knife**: This is used to cut the sole, frog, and small pieces of the wall, when required. Because the entire blade is slightly bent, the hoof knife allows the farrier to trim the sole in a concave manner. The hoof knife's end is not pointed, but bent over to cut tissue only as desired, preventing the farrier from cutting the hoof too deeply. Most farriers use two hoof knives, one designed for the right hand and one designed for the left hand. Additionally, a "**loop knife**" may be used for the same purpose as the hoof knife.

- **Hoof nippers**: These are sharp in order to cut the wall of the hoof.

- **Hoof rasp**: This tool is used for filing the hoof wall, in order to make it level on the stepping surface, and to give the hoof a rounded shape on the edge. The hoof rasp has a rough side (used first to file the hoof roughly) and a smooth side (used to finish the hoof). A handle made of wood, plastic or metal is fixed to the hoof rasp in order to make it more comfortable to use.

- **Hoof Stand**: The farrier places the hoof on top of this stand to support the leg for rasping the hoof. This tool is used on Paso Fino horses 20 months or older. Additionally, the hoof stand is used to support the hoof when working on clinches during the shoeing process.

- **Gauge** or **hoof leveler**: This tool is used to measure the angle between the profile of the toe and the stepping surface (known as the "angle of the hoof").

- **Metal ruler**: This tool is used to verify the length of the toe and height of the heels.

- **Apron (made of leather or nylon)**: The apron keeps the farrier's legs from being injured by any sharp tool during trimming, or by a nail or a warm horseshoe while shoeing.

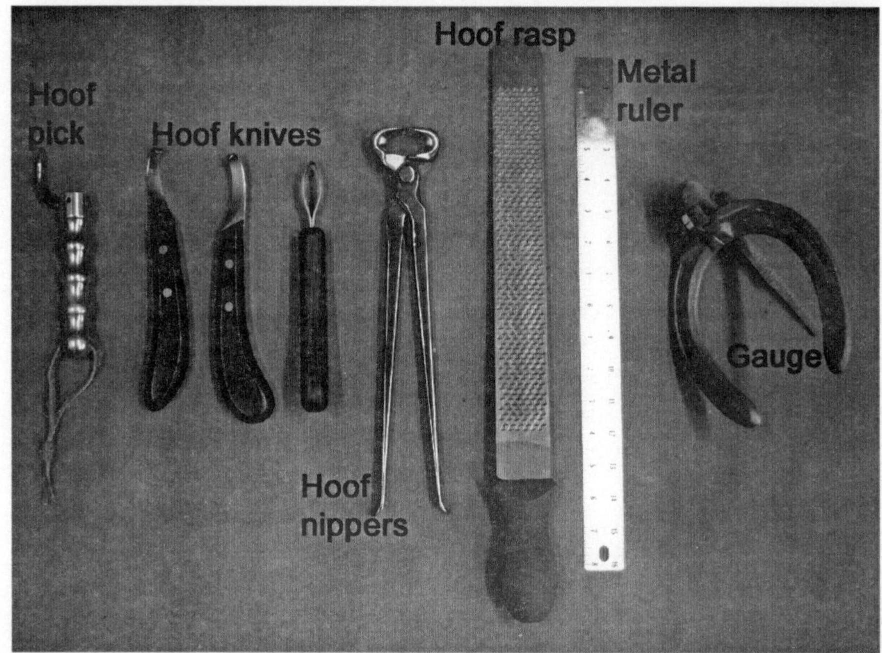

Trimming tools

Leather apron

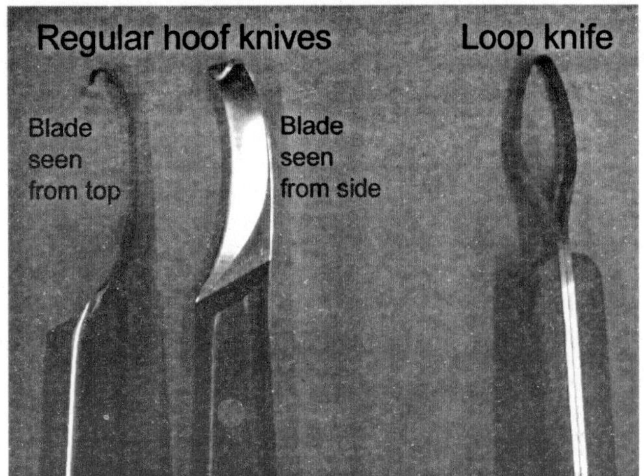

PROCEDURE FOR TRIMMING

The stepping surface of the hoof needs to be cleaned (with the hoof pick); then, any dead tissue from the sole should be cut concavely with the hoof knife.

The frog should be cut (with a hoof knife or a loop knife) as little as possible, preferably only the torn, dead or loose pieces. If the frog is properly cut, it is level with the wall, after the wall is trimmed. Straight, pointed knives or pocket knives should never be used to cut any hoof tissue.

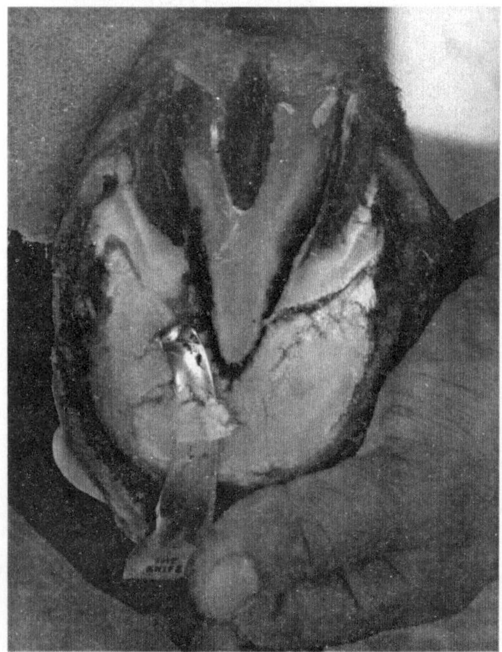

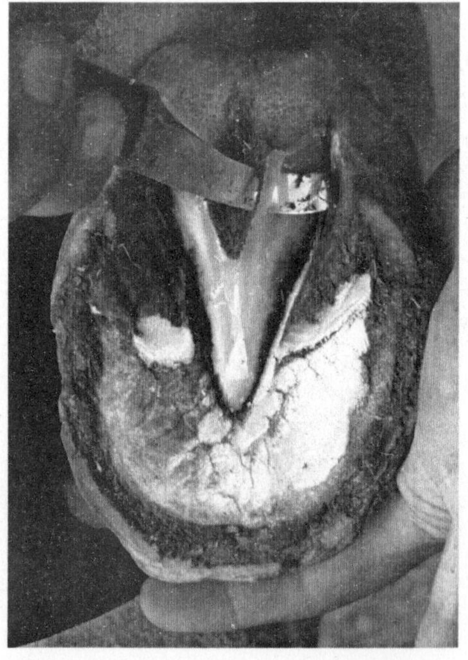

The excess hoof wall on the bottom must be cut with either the hoof knife or the hoof nippers, making sure it is never higher of the ground than the level of the sole. Because in Paso Finos the toe of the hoof usually grows faster than the heels, the stepping surface hoof wall is cut only at the quarters and toe areas. The heels generally do not need to be cut (except in special cases when the hoof needs to be at a lower angle). Hoof nippers are preferable to the hoof knife when there is a great deal of hoof wall to cut.

For showing Paso Fino horses in *PFHA* sanctioned shows, the hoof's toe profile should not exceed 4 inches long (10.2 cm) in un-shod horses and 4 ½ inches long (11.5 cm) in shod horses (this includes the height of the shoe) *(PFHA - Constitution and Rule Book, Chapter Two, Section IV, Subsection C).*

In *CONFEPASO* rules, the hoof's toe profile should not exceed 4 inches long (10.2 cm) in un-shod horses and 4 ½ inches long (11.5 cm) in shod horses (this includes the height of the shoe). Additionally, the hoof's coronary band cannot be higher than 1 ½ inches (3.81 cm) from the bottom of the heel *(Reglamento de Competencias de Caballos de Paso - CONFEPASO, Chapter 4, Article 7, "Medida de la altura del casco"* and *"Herrajes," 4).*

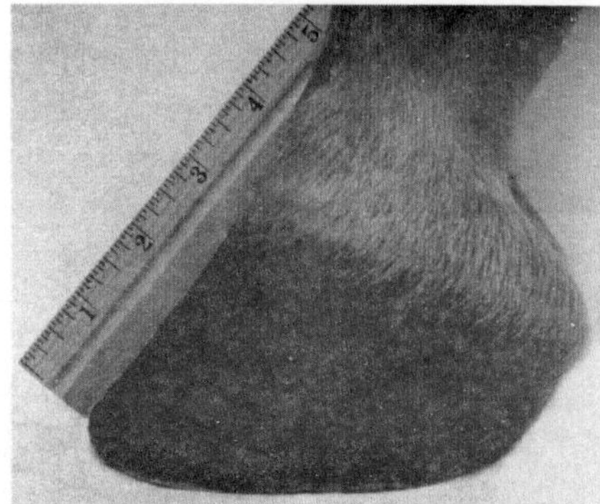

Measuring toe profile (bare hoof)

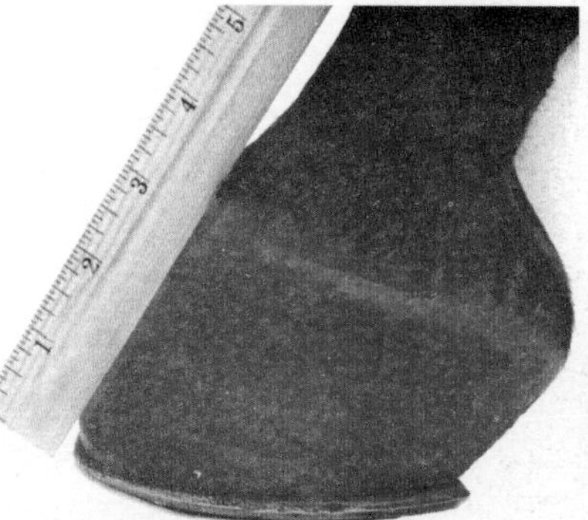

Measuring toe profile (shod hoof)

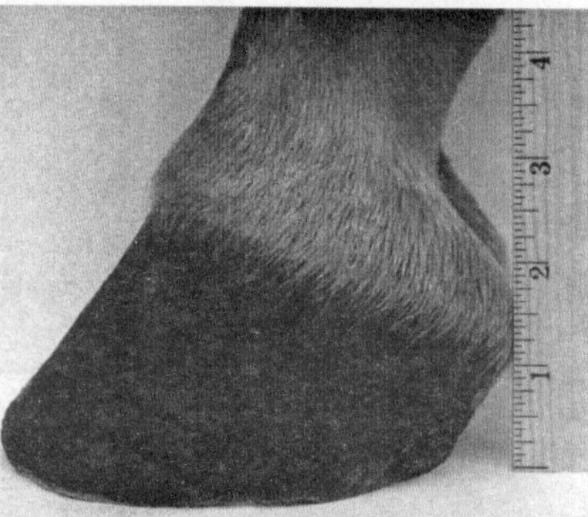

Measuring heel profile

The stepping surfaces of the hoof wall and the bars are rasped with the hoof rasp in order to make them level. The edge of the hoof wall is rasped to round it off. At this time, for the farrier's comfort, the hoof stand may be used to support the horse's hoof.

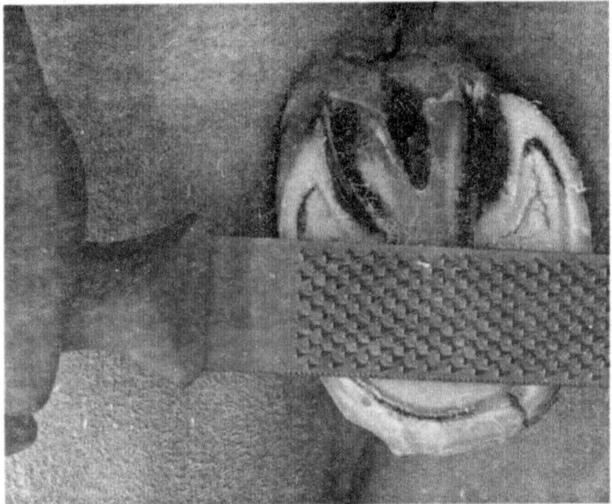

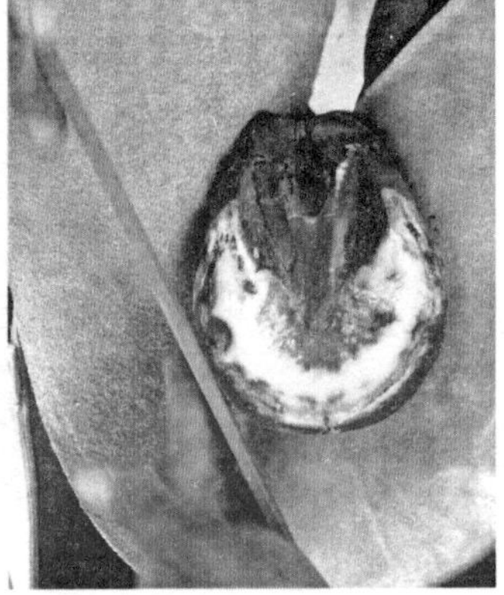

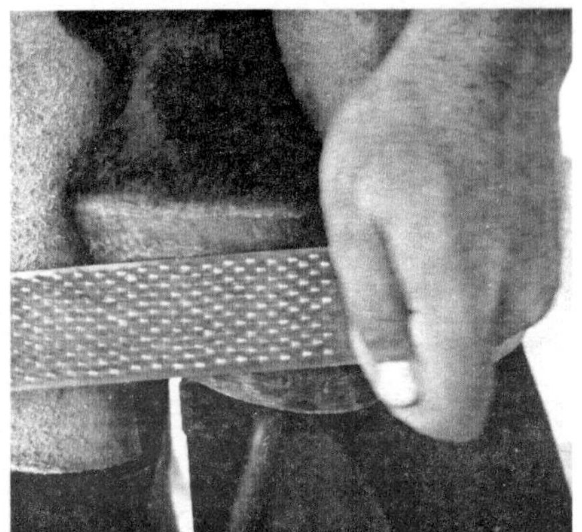

The sole is cut concavely with the hoof knife to make it deeper than the hoof wall. This ensures that the horse supports its weight on the hoof wall instead of the sole, which is not for supporting weight. Thus, the sole is kept from being in contact with the ground.

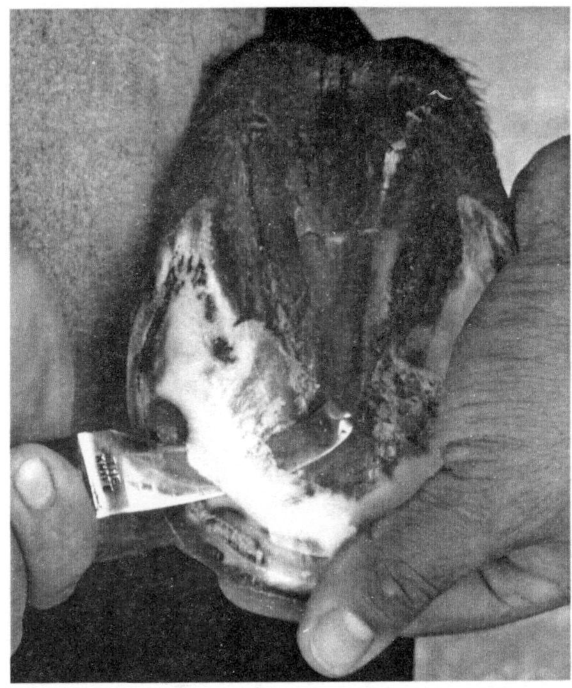

The angle of the hoof may be determined by using a hoof leveler (gauge). For comfort, the two front hooves should have even angles. This is also true for the back hooves.

SHOEING

The horse in training and/or at work needs horseshoes to protect the hooves from excessive wear and breaking, when working on abrasive grounds. In some cases, horseshoes allow the farrier to modify the action of the hooves and legs to improve the gait. Corrective trimming and shoeing is part of the treatment of some hoof diseases, such as navicular disease, white line disease, contracted heels, founder, and grass cracks, among others.

Shoeing should be done every 40 to 55 days, not only because shoes may become loose and worn out, but also because hooves do not wear out at all and continue to grow, due to the fact that they are protected by shoes from abrasive surfaces. Within such a period of time, some hooves will lose the exactness of their balance due to irregular growth. Because the toe has the tendency to grow faster than the heels, this affects the angle of the hooves and the gait as well; therefore, the farrier should trim the hooves within the recommended time in order to keep or improve their balance.

TOOLS FOR SHOEING

In addition to those tools used for hoof trimming (hoof pick, hoof nippers, hoof knife, hoof rasp, gauge, and hoof stand), the process of shoeing requires other tools, described as follows:

- **Buffer**: Before taking the old shoe off, some farriers use the buffer to straighten or cut clinches from the nails on both sides of the hoof.

- **Nail puller**: This is used to remove nails from the hoof, either when taking an old shoe off or when a nail has been wrongly driven into the shoe/hoof during the shoeing process.

- **Pincers** (also called **shoe pullers**): This type of nippers removes the old shoe by pulling it off the hoof.

- **Anvil**: This steel tool is used to shape the horseshoes.

- **Rounding hammer**: This type of hammer is used to pound the horseshoes in order to round them against the anvil.

- **Farrier's tongs**: These are used to hold the shoe when it is being rounded on the anvil. These are also used for holding a warm horseshoe.

- **Hoof hammer**: This light hammer is used to drive the nails into the hoof. It has "claws," which are used to bend the sharp pointed end of the nails over the hoof wall, immediately after they are driven into the hoof.

- **Clinch cutters**: These are small nippers used to cut the sharp pointed end of the nails, after all of them are driven into the hoof and bent over the wall.

- **Clinch block**: This is used to begin setting the clinches of the nails, after they are driven into the hoof and cut. However, pincers may also be used as a clinch block.

- **Nail clincher**: This particular tool is used to bend the clinches tightly over the wall. There are two styles of nail clinchers: One looks like an alligator (also called curved jaw clincher) and the other looks like a gooseneck.

- **Shoeing box with wheels**: This allows the farrier to carry all the tools and to have them accessible when shoeing a horse.

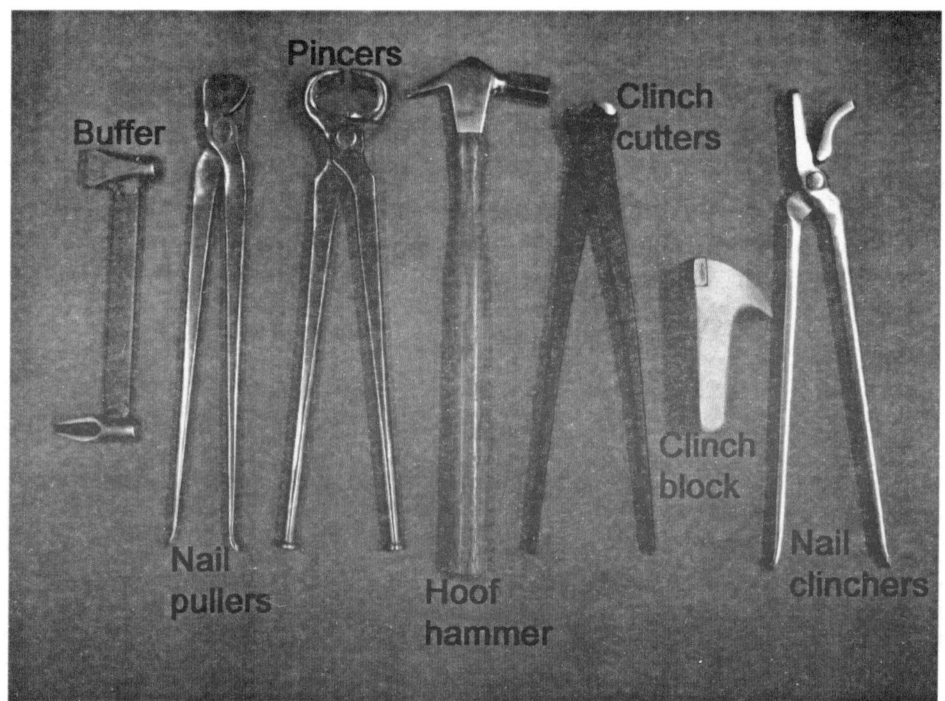

Shoeing tools

Anvil

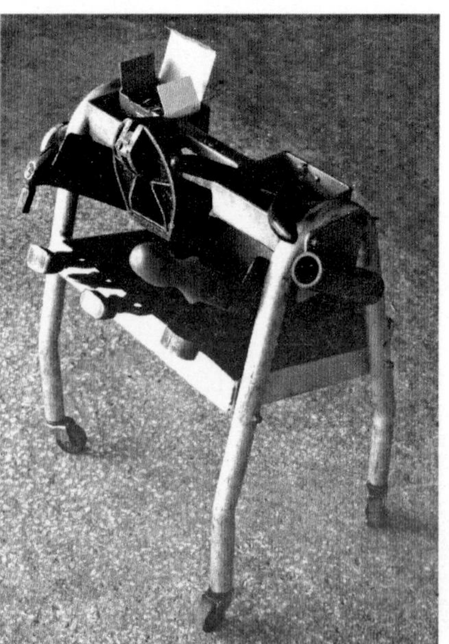

Shoeing box with wheels

HORSESHOES AND NAILS

The most common horseshoe for Paso Finos is comprised of a flat plate of metal up to 3/8 of an inch in height (1 cm). Some horses may need special horseshoes with traction devices (calks or ice nails, for example) to increase hoof traction on certain terrains, such as clay, mud, snow, ice, etc. The horseshoe may have one clip at the toe or clips at each side, which are bent over the hoof wall. Toe/lateral clips are made by the farrier when the horseshoe is not made with them. This type of clip, commonly used on the shoes of the hind hooves of Paso Finos, offers a better fit and holds the horseshoe on the hoof. The horseshoes used for showing Paso Finos are flat plates, either made of steel or aluminum.

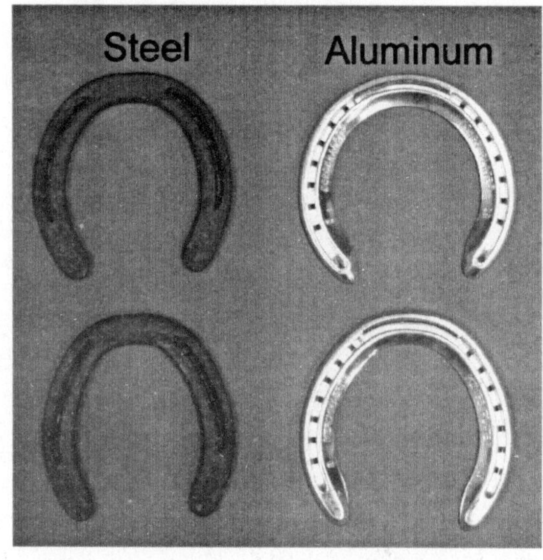

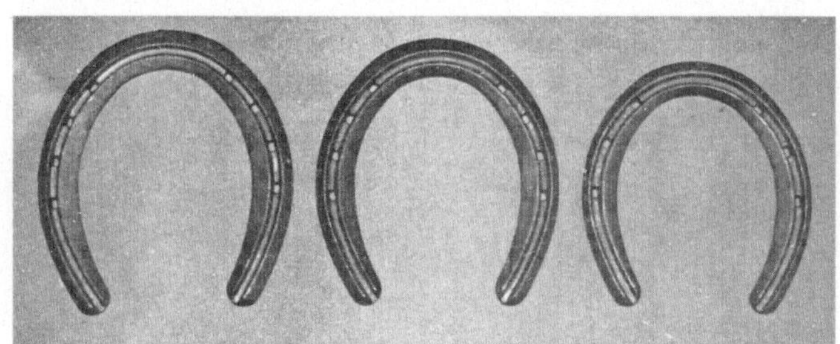

Horseshoes are made in different sizes and thicknesses for the many horse breeds. The size of horseshoes for Paso Fino horses runs in most brands from **0000** for animals with very small hooves, **000** for animals with small to regular size hooves, and **00** for animals with regular size to big hooves. In some brands, horseshoes for Paso Finos run from #1, #2, and #3 for the same sizes of hooves. Steel horseshoes may be very thin (ultra-light), thin (light), intermediate thick (plain), and thick.

Horseshoes for the front hooves are more rounded than those for the hind hooves in order to fit the stepping surfaces. This difference in shape is necessary because hooves are rounded on the front legs and slightly pointed at the toes on the hind legs.

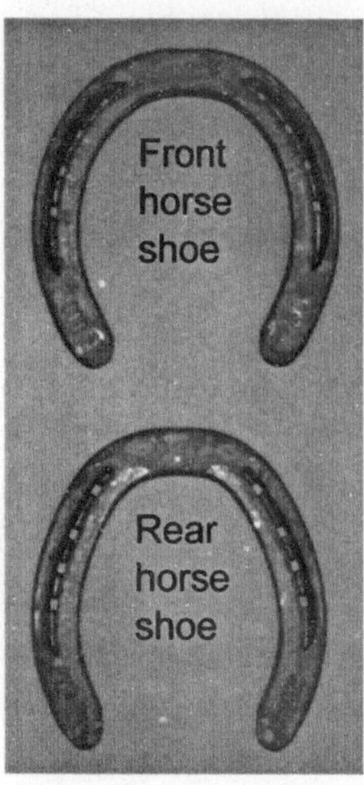

To protect a sensitive/worn sole of the hoof, the horseshoe should be wider than usual. Additionally, an orthopedic "egg horseshoe" may be used to correct several problems of the horse's foot.

The horseshoes for Paso Finos have holes for six to eight nails (three or four on each side). The farrier commonly applies six nails per horseshoe. The heads of the horseshoe nails should fit perfectly into the holes of the horseshoe, which makes it hold more securely. If the heads of the nails are smaller than the holes, the horseshoe could become loose in a few days, due to movement. Conversely, if the heads of nails are bigger than the holes, the horseshoe also could become loose in a few days after the heads of the nails become worn.

One of the two widest sides of the horseshoe nail's head has a brand engraved on it, which varies depending on the producer. The farrier must drive the nail into the hoof making the brand name face the sole in order to take advantage of the nail's special design, which has a sharp end that makes it curve outward while being driven. The body of the horseshoe nail is flat so that it makes a narrow hole in the hoof wall when it is applied.

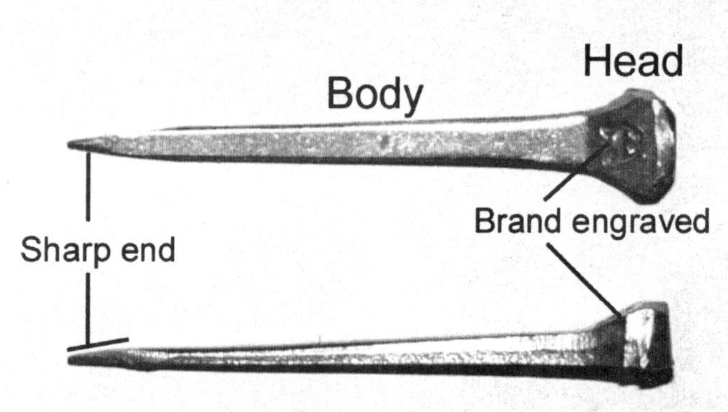

Therefore, once a nail is applied to the bottom of the hoof wall (just outside the white line), it curves slightly outward to stay within the non-sensitive hoof wall. Finally the pointed end of the nail breaks through the wall about 5/8 to 7/8 of an inch (1.5 to 2.2 cm) high.

SHOEING PROCESS

Before removing the old horseshoes, the farrier must observe the horse from the front, rear and the two sides while the animal stands, walks, and performs the gait. After determining the balance of the horse's legs and the way each hoof moves, the farrier is able to look at the way each horseshoe is worn. At this time, it is possible to determine the proper corrections for trimming and shoeing.

Removing the old horseshoes must be done carefully in order to prevent damaging the hoof. First, clinches of the nails have to be opened or cut at both sides of the hoof, using the buffer and the hoof hammer (see below on left) or by rasping them with a hoof rasp (see below on right).

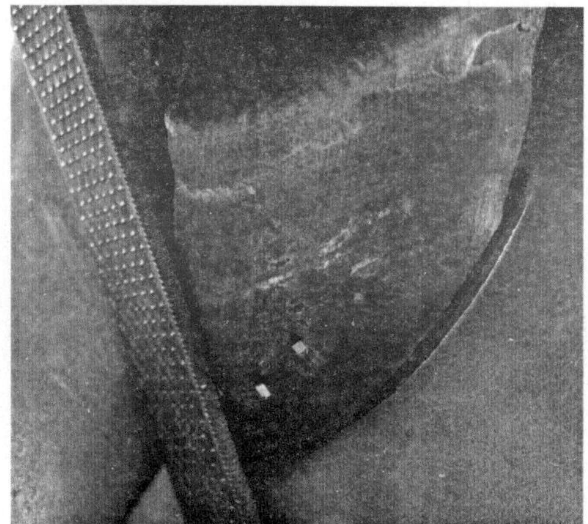

After opening/rasping the clinches of the nails, they are removed one-by-one with the nail puller. This makes the old horseshoe come off without breaking the wall of the hoof.

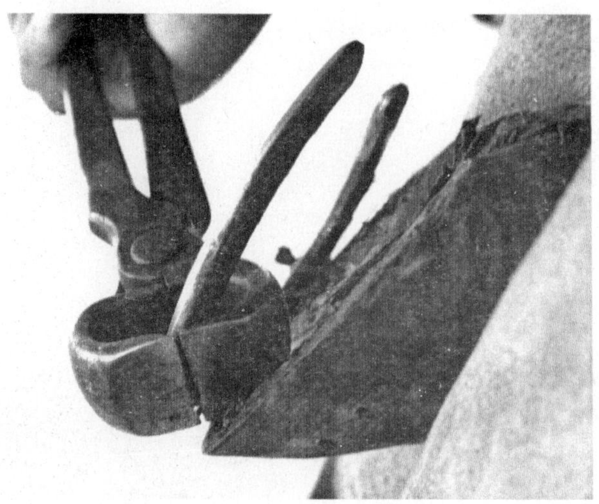

However, after opening/rasping the clinches of the nails, an old horseshoe also may be removed from the hoof using pincers. After pincers are inserted between the hoof and the horseshoe at one end, the pincers are pulled first toward the toe and then toward the frog, until the horseshoe starts to be released. The same process is done at the opposite end of the horseshoe and continued, alternating both sides of the horseshoe toward the toe, until the horseshoe is loose and comes off.

The hoof is then ready to be trimmed (sole, frog, bars, and wall) in order to prepare it to be shod. During trimming, the farrier has to ensure that each set of hooves (meaning the two front hooves or the two hind hooves) have an even size, shape, angle, length of toe, and height of heels.

After the hooves are trimmed, the horseshoes are chosen according to size and purpose. It is important to note that the horseshoe should have a shape that properly fits the hoof. The anvil, farrier's tongs, and rounding hammer are used to give shape to the horseshoe in order to make it fit the respective hoof.

The back end of each horseshoe should be about 3/16 of an inch (4.7 mm) longer than the back end of the hoof. These short extensions of the shoe heels keep the shoe under the hoof wall after the toe grows. Conversely, if the shoe were the exact size of the hoof at shoeing, this would cause the horseshoe to slip forward once the toe grew.

Putting on a "cold" shoe is the most common way to shoe horses, which consists of applying a non-heated horseshoe to a properly trimmed and leveled hoof. On the other hand, putting on a "hot" shoe is used for optimal fitting between horseshoe and hoof because a heated horseshoe is more moldable (with the anvil and rounding hammer) than a cold horseshoe. Additionally, when the heated horseshoe is placed on the bottom surface of the hoof to see if they fit each other, it is easy to see those points where either the hoof wall or the horseshoe needs to be leveled.

After the horseshoe is sized properly and fitted to the bottom surface of the hoof wall (applying either a cold or a hot shoe), the farrier drives one nail in each side of the hoof in order to anchor the horseshoe in position. As said previously, nails must be driven into the hoof wall and break through about 5/8 to 7/8 of an inch (1.5 to 2.2 cm) above the bottom edge of the hoof.

After assuring that the horseshoe is in the right place and fits the hoof correctly, the farrier drives in the remaining nails. At this time, toe/lateral clips of the hind horseshoes (if present) are bent over the hoof by hitting them with the hoof hammer.

Note: If the horseshoe was not made originally with the toe/ lateral clip, the farrier will make it by heating the horseshoe and pounding it with the rounding hammer over the anvil in order to pull the front/lateral edge out.

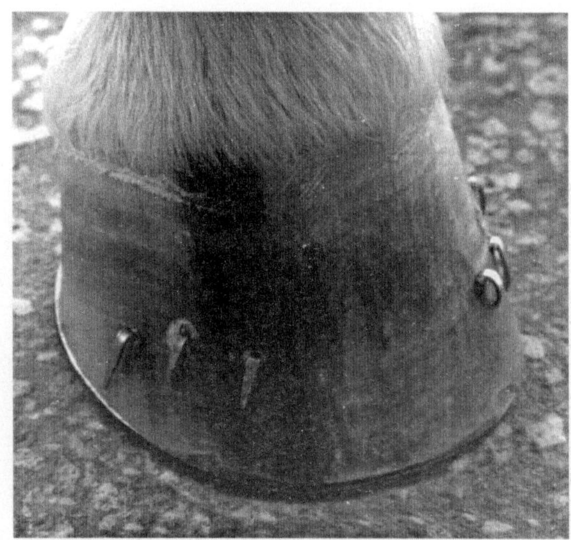

After each horseshoe nail is applied, its end is bent over the hoof wall with the claws of the hoof hammer in order to avoid cutting either the farrier or the horse.

Note: When a horseshoe nail is accidentally driven into the hoof's sensitive laminae (or near them), the horse will immediately jump due to the acute pain. This nail must be removed immediately (either with the hoof hammer or the nail puller). If bleeding or not, the hole made in the hoof should be treated with tincture of iodine or Venice turpentine.

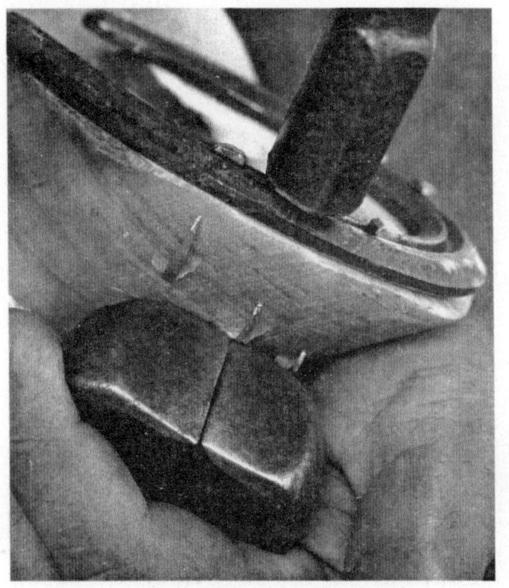

Once all horseshoe nails are driven into the hoof (and ends of the nails are bent over the wall), clinches are set by holding either the clinch block or the pincers under the tip of each nail and hitting its head with the hoof hammer. This also helps the head of the nails to be set perfectly into the holes of the horseshoe.

After that, the sharp pointed ends of the horseshoe nails are cut with the clinch cutters, except for a little tip of nail of about 1/8 of an inch (3 mm).

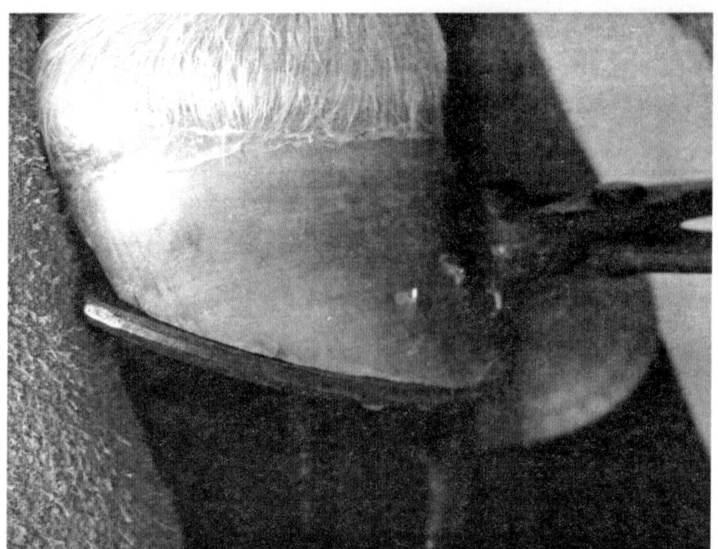

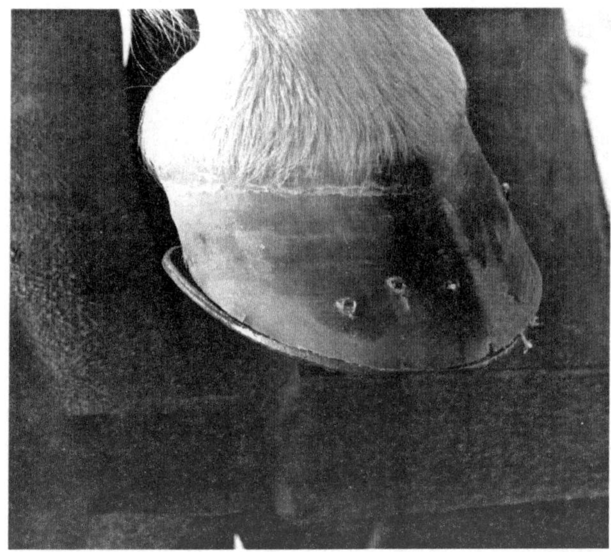

Then, any overhang of the wall beyond the horseshoe must be rasped in order to keep hoof and horseshoe aligned. At this time, the hoof stand may be used to support the horse's hoof.

The smooth side of the hoof rasp should be used to file a small groove on the hoof wall where each clinch will be set.

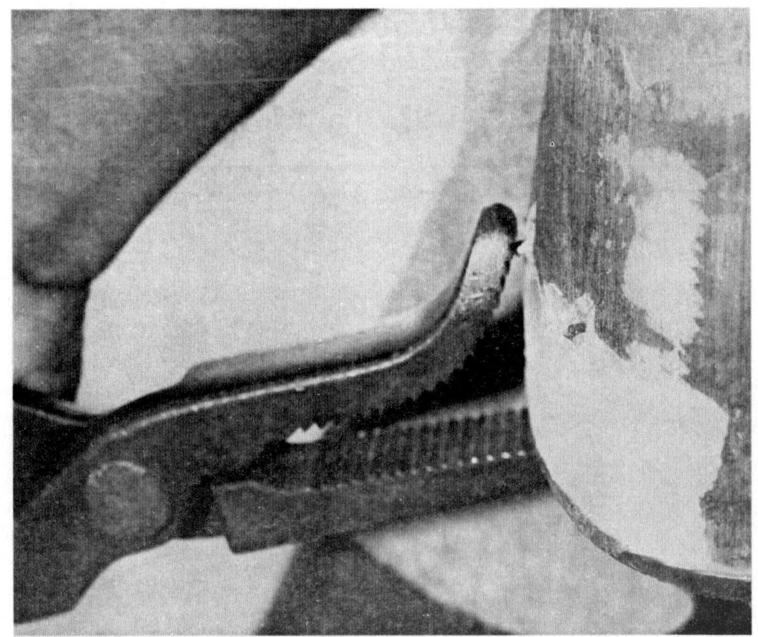

Thereafter, nail tips (clinches) are ready to be set (bending them over the hoof wall tightly) by using the nail clincher (alligator or gooseneck style).

Note: If after the hoof is shod, it has a crack or a broken chip, this space may be filled with a material developed for that purpose, to give the hoof more resistance, to prevent more damage, and for aesthetics.

To make clinches smooth and safe for both the horse and any person who picks the hooves up, clinches should be carefully filed with the smooth side of an old, worn hoof rasp.

TIPS TO REMEMBER DURING TRIMMING AND SHOEING PASO FINOS

- Before corrective trimming, the horse has to be observed carefully, while standing, walking, and gaiting from the front, rear, and both sides to define the proper correction for each hoof/leg.

- Neither a pointed knife nor a pocket knife should be used to cut any structure of the hoof; only properly designed hoof knives, with ends that are not pointed but bent over, should be used.

- The frog should be cut as little as possible, preferably trimming only torn or loose pieces.

- Hoof heels should be trimmed the minimum amount possible because they usually take longer to grow than the hoof toes. Heels are cut only when absolutely necessary to adjust (reduce) the hoof's angle.

- Measuring tools should be used to verify the angle and size of the hooves during trimming; these tools are the hoof leveler (gauge) and the metal ruler.

- Horseshoes must fit the respective hoof. In addition, each pair of hooves (front or back) must be as even as possible.

- Nails must never be driven inside the white line due to the risk of a "hot-nail," which may hurt the hoof's sensitive laminae.

- When filing small grooves on the hoof wall where clinches will be set, the farrier should *NOT* file a continuous line joining the nails on one side (as shown in the picture) because it weakens the hoof wall. A groove should be filed separately for each nail.

- Clinching the nails too tightly should be avoided because it may cause pain in the hoof.

- Any hoof crack or broken chip should be filled with a material developed for that purpose after the horse is shod.

- For aesthetics, some farriers rasp the hoof wall between the coronet and clinches after shoeing a horse. This should be avoided due to the fact that it causes a systematic reduction of the hoof wall width, that will severely weaken the hoof after time.

Note: The pictures in this chapter were taken with the help of *Mr. Luis Acosta*, a professional Paso farrier from Ocala, FL.

CHAPTER 8

REPRODUCTION

The horse's reproductive ability is commonly considered lower than other domestic animal species. However, effective practices, such as good management, an excellent feeding program, and proper reproductive technology may improve productivity. This chapter provides guidelines for obtaining the best reproductive results.

The function of the **REPRODUCTIVE** system is to guarantee perpetuation of the species. A description of the reproductive systems of stallions and mares follows. The **ENDOCRINE** system shares some glands with the reproductive system, such as **hypothalamus**, **pituitary**, **testes** (stallion), and **ovaries** (mare). **Adrenal glands**, **thyroid**, **parathyroid**, and **pancreas** are other glands of the endocrine system. The functions of the endocrine system are producing hormones to control a variety of body functions and maintaining internal balance and sexual behavior.

THE STALLION

The most important function of the domestic stallion in reproduction is providing the semen, from which spermatozoa have the genes that he may pass to his offspring. A colt is able to breed mares and reproduce when he reaches puberty. At this time, the colt shows a strong sexual desire and production of "mature" semen. Puberty also is associated with an increase of muscle mass in the neck, shoulders, back, and hips due to the presence of testosterone in the blood that is produced in the testicles.

Puberty of the Paso Fino colt is commonly reached between 14 and 24 months of age, depending on the colt's development. Nutrition is one of the primary factors; underfed colts reach puberty later than properly fed colts. Additionally, underfeeding may result in the testicles being permanently undeveloped. Although during puberty a colt may impregnate mares, it is not recommended that a colt reproduce before the "bitting" stage of the training process has started. If the colt breeds mares before this time, he may become more difficult to train. Thereafter, the young stallion should be used cautiously in reproduction. At five years of age, a stallion reaches full reproductive capability.

The stallion's reproductive system is described in the following table:

ORGAN	*MAIN CHARACTERISTICS*	*FUNCTIONS*
Penis	The penis is kept in the **Prepuce** (also known as the "sheath") and the abdominal cavity most of the time. The prepuce is a double-folded piece of skin with no hair that extends forward from the scrotum to 3 inches behind the umbilicus.	The penis is extended outside the prepuce up to 13 inches during urination. During reproduction, the penis is the stallion's copulatory organ that becomes erect and rigid when all its sinuses are filled with arterial blood. The penis increases in size during erection to about 23 inches.
Testicles or **Testes**	Two bean -shaped glands (4 ½ x 3 x 2 inches) located in the inguinal region and protected by the **Scrotum** (a four -layer bag with no hair covering it). The left testicle is slightly larger and lower than the right one in most stallions.	Produces spermatozoa in the seminiferous tubules. Also produces the testosterone hormone, which causes spermatogenesis and the stallion's libido (sexual desire). The testicles move up (closer to the abdominal cavity to warm them) or move down (away from the abdominal cavity to cool them) by means of the cremaster muscle contraction or relaxation.
Ducts for storing and/or transporting the spermatozoa	**Epididymis**: A three -portion duct (head, body, and tail) attached to the testicle's seminiferous tubules by the head end and to the vas deferens by the tail end.	Spermatozoa coming out of the testicle are stored to mature in the epididymis until they are expelled during ejaculation.
	Vas deferens: A duct that joins the tail of the epididymis on one side and the urethra on the other side.	Transports mature spermatozoa from the epididymis to the urethra during ejaculation.
	Urethra: A single duct inside the penis. The vas deferens that transports spermatozoa from the testicles and all the ducts that transport the seminal fluids from the five accessory sex glands enter the Urethra.	During urination, the urethra is the duct that transports urine from the bladder. During Reproduction, the urethra transports the semen during ejaculation. Semen is made up of spermatozoa and seminal fluids.
Accessory Sex Glands that produce seminal fluids	**Prostate gland**: A single gland consisting of two portions (each shaped/sized like a tangerine section) located on both sides of the urethra. Several ducts that come out from the prostate gland reach into the urethra.	Secretes a fluid that cleans the urethra immediately before ejaculation, and which reaches the urethra through the ducts. Alkalinity of this fluid neutralizes any acidity in the urethra due to urine remains and bacteria.
	Seminal vesicle glands: Two glands (each shaped/sized like a medium size cucumber) located above both sides of the bladder.	They secrete the largest amount of whole seminal fluid (like gel) that includes some nutrients. This slightly acidic gel (containing citric acid) reaches the urethra through the vesicle ducts.
	Bulbourethral glands: Two glands (each shaped/sized as a dove's egg) located on both sides of the urethra.	They secrete a thick fluid (like mucus), which gets into the urethra by means of 16 ducts, just behind the prostatic ducts.

LIBIDO OF THE STALLION

The libido (sexual desire) is one of the factors associated with the stallion's fertility, which is affected by many factors:

- Size of the testicles: Small and undeveloped testicles do not produce enough testosterone for proper libido.
- Disease: The libido, and therefore the production of spermatozoa, is lower when the stallion is sick. Further, a disease involving a fever causes death of the stored spermatozoa.
- Poor nutrition: Excess or deficiency of some nutrients causes a lower libido.
- Presence of other horses: When a stallion is surrounded solely by other stallions, its testosterone level lowers and so does its libido. On the other hand, when the stallion is surrounded by mares, especially when the mares are in heat, its libido increases due to increased testosterone production.
- Exercise: Over-exercised stallions exhibit a lower libido and a higher proportion of abnormal spermatozoa. Conversely, stallions that run in a pasture by themselves exhibit a higher libido and better production of normal spermatozoa.

THE SEMEN

The stallion's semen consists of spermatozoa produced in the testicles and the seminal fluids produced by four of the accessory sex glands (seminal vesicles and bulbourethral glands). The seminal fluids (mixed in the urethra) dilute and transport the spermatozoa and allow them to survive for a few days in the mare's reproductive tract. As a whole, a stallion's semen has a pH of 7.5 and its color is like diluted cow milk.

The process of spermatozoa production in the testicles is known as spermatogenesis, which takes 49 days. However, because the spermatozoa spend five additional days maturing in the epididymis, 54 days is the time required for a complete spermatogenic cycle. Certain diseases that produce a fever may cause the spermatozoa that already are formed and stored, and those being formed, to die or to be unable to fertilize the mare's ova. Therefore, the stallion's fertility is affected negatively. Then, when the stallion becomes well, another complete spermatogenic cycle is necessary to produce new fertile spermatozoa.

The normal volume of semen per ejaculate is 60 ml, but it may vary with each stallion from slightly lower to almost three times this volume. A concentration of 30 to 700 million spermatozoa per milliliter of semen is normal. The total amount of spermatozoa in an ejaculate may be calculated by computing the total volume of semen and the sperm concentration per milliliter. However, a more important criteria in evaluating semen is the percentage of morphologically normal, progressive motile spermatozoa in the whole ejaculate, which should be 60%, at a minimum. The expression "progressive motile spermatozoa" indicates that the stallion's normal spermatozoa move in a straight or circling direction, instead of in a zig-zag manner.

Evaluating semen from a stallion, using the parameters described above, indicate the horse's fertility. However, only the percentage of pregnant mares of the total number of mares bred, and the actual offspring produced, demonstrate the stallion's ability to reproduce.

CASTRATING A STALLION

Castration is an operation that consists of cutting and removing the stallion's testicles and their epididymis. This decision is made for one or more of the following reasons:

- Neither the horse's quality nor its pedigree is considered outstanding.
- Although the stallion exhibits some good qualities, it has one or more undesirable, transmissible characteristics, such as conformational defects.
- The stallion's existing offspring have repeatedly exhibited transmissible health problems, such as umbilical hernia and leg deformity, among others. Or, the offspring are not of proper quality.
- The stallion exhibits out-of-control behavior.
- Certain diseases in the testicles (e.g., tumors) may require the stallion's castration in order to save his life.
- Some Paso Fino owners, who are not interested in offspring and want to enjoy their male horses, either for show or pleasure, opt for castration. Thus, the owner does not have to be concerned about having any problems with mares in heat during a trail ride or when males (geldings) are kept together with mares in a pasture/paddock.
- The stallion has either bilateral cryptorchid (both testicles are retained in the abdominal cavity or into the inguinal canal) or unilateral cryptorchid (one testicle is retained).

  Note: In a normal stallion, both testicles should descend into the scrotum no later than 24 months of age.

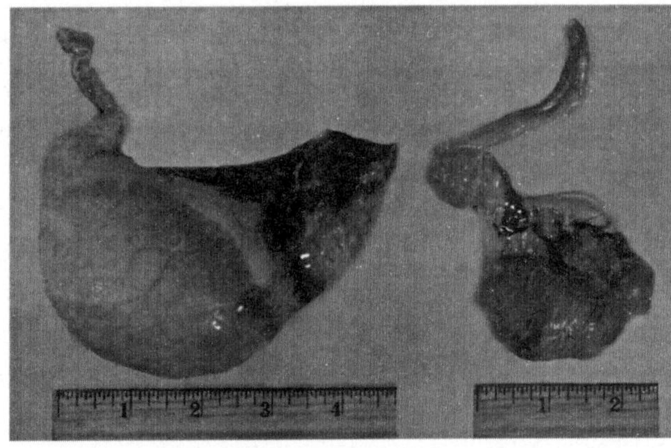

The testicle on the left side is of normal size since it descended properly into the scrotum. The testicle on the right side is undeveloped since it was retained in the abdominal cavity.

Paso Fino geldings are becoming more popular for showing in both *PFHA* and *CONFEPASO* sanctioned shows. At the *PFHA* National Show, Classic Fino, Paso Performance, and Paso Pleasure geldings participate in "Geldings for Gold," which pays substantial prize money to the winners. Additionally, as the old saying goes: *"To have a good quality gelding, a good quality stallion must be gelded."*

THE MARE

The domestic mare provides the egg, allows fertilization, carries the pregnancy (unless the mare is a donor of embryo transfer technology), lactates, and "educates" the foal. At 12 to 18 months of age, the filly reaches puberty, which is marked by the first heat and the ability to ovulate. A filly may become pregnant at the time of puberty, although it is not recommended that this occurs at such an early age. Although the filly continues to cycle after reaching puberty, the reproductive maturity of the average mare is around 36 months of age.

The mare's reproductive system is formed by the reproductive tract and the udder. Externally to internally, the reproductive tract of the mare is described in the following table:

ORGAN	*MAIN CHARACTERISTICS*	*FUNCTIONS*
Vulva	This is the most external part of the mare's reproductive tract. The vertical labia of the vulva (about 5 ½ inches long and 2 inches wide) are located below the anus with a vertical opening about 4 ½ inches long. The clitoris (a small erectile structure like the stallion's penis) is located about 1 inch inside the lowest end of the vulva's labia. The vulva (and anus) are not covered by hair.	The vulva should stay well closed and vertical to protect the rest of the reproductive tract from external contamination. The vulva extends about 4 inches deep inside to where the urethra ends. ***Note***: The urethra is the duct that takes urine out to be expelled through the vulva.
Vagina	The vagina is located between the interior vulva and the cervix and is 9 inches long and 4 inches in diameter. However, it has very dilatable tissue that will open wider for foaling. Although the vagina does not have glands, some specialized cells produce the mucous that lubricates it during copulation. The angle where the vagina and cervix join is known as "fornix."	The vagina is part of the birth canal through which the foal passes during birth. This is also the location where the stallion's penis gets stimulated to ejaculate. The fornix provides a limit for the stallion's penis to penetrate into the vagina and helps the penis glans expand to twice its size during ejaculation.
Cervix	This is a thin duct of about 2 to 3 inches long that separates the vagina from the uterus. The cervix (also called the "uterine neck") has a strong muscular layer that will be extremely dilated during foaling.	Once the filly reaches puberty, the cervix's lumen is filled with a dense mucous to keep any substance or pathogen from penetrating to the uterus, except during heat and delivery. During the mare's estrus (heat), the cervix is relaxed and the mucous becomes liquid to allow the entry of semen into the uterus.
Uterus	In an empty mare, the uterus body is about 8 inches long and 4 inches in diameter. The uterus has two cylindrical horns, about 10 inches long and 3 ½ inches in diameter each.	The uterus provides a perfect, comfortable and safe place for the fetus to grow. The uterus secretes prostaglandin (hormone).
Fallopian tubes or oviducts	These are two very thin tubes of about 7 inches long and 1/6 to 1/3 of an inch wide, located between the ovaries and the uterine horns.	At its end, each oviduct surrounds an ovary (like an inverted umbrella) in order to catch any egg as soon as it is released. The oviduct is the site where fertilization occurs; about five days later, the fertilized egg is conducted by the oviduct to the uterus.
Ovaries	These two glands are twice the size of a bigger soybean seed (about 2 ½ inches long and 1 ½ inches wide). They may be smaller in mares during "anestrus" (no cycling period) and mares with nutritional deficiencies.	The ovaries produce hormones (estrogens and progestins) to control the estrous cycle. They produce and release the egg (also called ova) during each estrus.

REPRODUCTIVE CYCLE OF THE MARE

The reproductive cycle of the mare, known technically as "**estrous cycle**," is the period of time between the first signs of estrus (heat) to the time a new estrus starts again. Most mares have an estrous cycle of 20 to 23 days. Rarely, however, some mares exhibit very short cycles of about one week and others exhibit very long cycles of about six months. These unusual cycles are usually related to a pathology of the reproductive tract (such as an infection or an ovarian tumor).

The estrous cycle is divided into two periods that are regulated by the hormones and influence the sexual behavior of the mare:

- The **Estrus** (also called "heat") is the shortest period of the estrous cycle, consisting of four to seven days during which the mare shows signs of accepting the stallion and being bred. One or more follicles in the ovaries display rapid growth from which one egg is released during the last 24 to 48 hours of the mare's heat. Some mares are able to release two eggs at the same time, which usually allows fertilization of both eggs. However, mares rarely maintain a twin pregnancy to full term.

  Although estrus (and follicular growth) implies ovulation in most mares, some mares may exhibit signs of heat without any ovulation. This may be caused by low energy and mineral intake, among other things. Conversely, some mares may present a ′silent′ estrus, which consists of ovulation with no signs of heat.

  The common signs of estrus are as follows: the vulva's labia look slightly thicker; there is frequent opening of the vulva's labia, exhibiting the clitoris, alternating with closing of the labia; the tail often is kept up; there may be nervousness and excitation in the presence of other horses; the upper area of the tail appears scratched; and frequent short urination may occur.

  There are additional signs of heat, in the presence of a stallion: When the stallion starts the courtship (see "Direct Mounting"), the mare commonly makes a short, acute whinny that reveals moderate acceptance of the stallion; this is usually accompanied by alternating periods of swishing and raising the tail.

  When she is completely receptive to the stallion, the mare turns her hips slightly downward and raises her tail (to completely exhibit the vulva), followed by a short period of urination and intermittent opening/closing of the vulva and exposure of the clitoris.

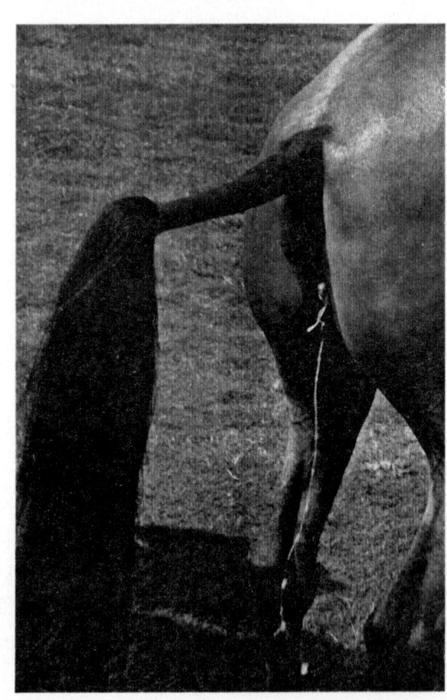

- The **Diestrus** is the longest period of the estrous cycle (15 to 18 days) that extends from the end of a heat to when the mare comes into heat again. During this period of time, the mare is neither interested nor receptive to the stallion.

The area on the ovary where the follicle releases the egg (during estrus) starts to turn into another structure, known as "corpus luteum," 12 to 24 hours after ovulation. Once the yellowish corpus luteum is formed, it starts to produce progesterone, allowing diestrus to occur. If the mare is not pregnant, the uterus releases prostaglandin about 12 to 13 days after ovulation, to destroy the corpus luteum and inhibit its production of progesterone. At this time, a gonadotropin releasing hormone (GnRH) is secreted from the hypothalamus into the blood, which causes the pituitary gland to release a follicle stimulating hormone (FSH) and a luteinizing hormone (LH). A few hours later, FSH causes one or more follicles to start growing in one of the ovaries. Once a follicle is fully grown (sometimes two follicles grow simultaneously), LH causes ovulation and thereafter it assures development of the corpus luteum.

Mares that stop cycling may have a prolonged diestrus (due to a persistent or prolonged corpus luteum in the ovary that continues to release progesterone) or may be in anestrus. This condition (anestrus) may be caused by a hormonal imbalance, having limited exposure to daylight, and/or nutritional deficiencies.

Because of shorter daylight hours during winter, most non-pregnant mares (also known as ′open mares′ or ′empty mares′), and mares foaling during the middle of the winter, stop ovulating and start a seasonal anestrus. However, this may be changed in some mares by increasing the daily photoperiod (period of time exposed to light) from November until March. The mare should be taken outside of the stall during daylight and thereafter kept in the stall with the light from one or more bulbs (a total of approximately 200 watts) to assure 16 to 18 hours of light per day. As a result of this treatment, non-pregnant mares in winter anestrus start cycling soon for the next breeding season.

Mares normally have a transitional cycling period in early spring and some follicular activity in the ovaries with corresponding signs of estrus. However, mares do not necessarily ovulate during this transition. Therefore, looking at a mare's behavior may not be an accurate sign when breeding; the first ovulation of the spring should be confirmed by a veterinarian.

FACTORS AFFECTING THE MARE'S FERTILITY

Properly breeding a mare in heat with a stallion (either by direct mounting or artificial insemination) does not guarantee pregnancy. Some common factors for reduced fertility in mares are as follows:

- Ovarian cysts or tumors that inhibit ovulation.
- Recurrent infections of the uterus.
- Closed or torn cervix that keeps the semen from entering the uterus.
- Blocked oviducts that do not allow the sperm to reach the egg to be fertilized.
- Endometrial cysts in the uterus.
- Rupture of the prepubic tendon.

- Genetic problems associated with chromosomes causing permanent infertility.
- An inclined vulva that permits air aspiration (known as "pneumovagina") and contamination. This may be resolved with a "Caslick's suture," that consists of stitching the upper 2 ½ to 3 inches of the vulva's labia, in order to reduce the entry size and, thus, contamination. Before breeding the mare by direct mounting, the suture is removed; for artificial insemination, however, it does not need to be removed. The Caslick's suture should be removed around the 300th day of pregnancy for foaling.

SELECTION OF THE STALLION AND THE BROODMARE

The first step in producing a good quality horse is to select a mare and a stallion that will provide the required genetic combination to obtain the most desirable offspring. In addition, proper environment, training, and management are necessary to obtain, as a result, a good Paso Fino horse.

Because the Paso Fino stallion and broodmare each provides 50% of the offspring's genes, both should have positive characteristics that may be transmitted to their offspring:

- Normal conformation that allows the species to survive.
- Proper phenotypic characteristics, including average height, that allow the horse to work under saddle and perform its gait.
- A smooth and very consistent gait, according to the standard of the breed. This includes powerful and high elevation of the hind legs for impulsion.
- Brio and kindness.
- Beauty.
- Trainability.
- Longevity and good health.

If the stallion and/or mare have already produced offspring with those positive characteristics, chances of having more good foals are increased. At this point, many domestic animal breeders use statistics as a tool for evaluating the offspring to select the horses that transmit the best characteristics, and, thus, improve the breed more rapidly. Unfortunately, this method is not used consistently in Paso Fino breeding.

In fact, some Paso Fino horse breeders are solely concerned with using outstanding stallions based on their "show ring" awards. Certainly, several famous stallions have produced outstanding specimens. However, using statistics allows breeders to evaluate the percentage of good offspring from a stallion to determine if he is actually improving the breed as expected. Using statistics to evaluate the offspring of a stallion must also include the quality of the broodmares that are the dams of the stallion's offspring.

The importance of the broodmare in producing good horses is not only related to the genes transmitted to each foal, including the always present chromosome X (associated with the transmission of physical characteristics), given to both gender offspring. The mare is also in charge of gestation and lactation, which are the first foal environments, both before and after birth (except in cases of embryo transfer). Therefore, in addition to the positive characteristics described above that may be transmitted to the offspring, and strong pedigree, the broodmare carrying her own foal should have other physical qualities:

- Good health that allows the mare to have normal gestation and foaling.
- Normal level of hormones that promote ovulation and foaling, and maintain gestation and lactation.
- Proper size and body condition index (based on proper nutrition) that allows for proper fetal development in the uterus in order to produce a well-sized foal at birth.
- High milk production during lactation, which is the only food for the foal during its first days, and also the main food during the first few months.

The mare's status in the social structure of the herd is also important because the dam is in charge of the 'foal's education'; in fact, it has been shown that a foal imitates its mother's behavior, as either dominant or submissive in the herd. This situation becomes important for two reasons:

- Dominant horses in the herd have more of a chance of obtaining food and water than others.
- From a competitive point of view, dominant horses try to show superiority over other horses when they share the show ring. In contrast, submissive horses may become shy in the show ring in the presence of dominant horses.

Thus, in a program of embryo transfer, recipient mares should meet both the physical and behavioral qualities described above, in order to provide the best environment for their 'adopted' foals.

THE USE OF INBREEDING

This practice consists of breeding a horse with a relative (in terms of parentage). If the inbreeding is properly planned, the two related specimens should share some outstanding characteristics and not exhibit any genetically transmissible defect. The goal is to produce offspring with genes that may replicate desirable phenotypic characteristics. Therefore, inbreeding is a technique that has been used to develop many horse breeds throughout history, including the Paso Fino. Depending on the degree of kinship between the stallion and mare, inbreeding may be classified in two ways:

- Close-breeding is when the stallion and mare have a very close kinship (about 50% parentage, or more), such as full brother with sister, father with daughter, or mother with son, in order to increase rapidly the offspring's pureness, in terms of obtaining similar phenotypic characteristics and a concentration of desired genes.

  Although close-breeding was a very common way to purify some horse breeds in the past, it is not commonly used today because of the risk of perpetuating some undesired traits in the offspring, such as inherited diseases, lesser resistance to an adverse environment, and reduced size.

- Line-breeding is when the stallion and mare have a certain degree of kinship, but are not too closely related (about 25% parentage or less), such as half brother with sister, grandmother with grandson, grandfather with granddaughter, aunt with nephew, uncle with niece, or cousins. The goal of line-breeding is to produce offspring with highly desirable characteristics in order to retain specific genes in the breed.

Development of the Paso Fino breed (and the three Colombian diagonal Paso horse breeds) has involved both kinds of inbreeding (close-breeding and line-breeding) for at least the past six decades. This has resulted in very important bloodlines (with a high concentration of desirable genes) for producing offspring with well-defined qualities.

Line-breeding is still used successfully at some farms. However, this type of inbreeding must be planned carefully and the offspring evaluated to determine if results are successful. Thereafter, only outstanding specimens resulting from inbreeding should be used in further reproduction. Conversely, if low or just average quality specimens resulting from inbreeding are used in reproduction, there is an increased chance of decreased quality in the next generation.

DETECTION OF THE MARE'S HEAT

Proper detection of the mare's heat, based on the signs described above, is the first step to breeding. Using a ´teaser´ stallion to check the mare every other day is a way to determine whether the mare is in heat, because all the signs will be more obvious. The teaser should be separated from the mare by means of a wall, which guarantees the safety of both animals and handlers. For Paso Finos, this wall should be approximately 3 ½ feet high. During the breeding season, large Paso Fino farms, with many broodmares to be bred, may keep a teaser in a central stall surrounded by the mares to be teased (either in stalls or a pasture).

Moreover, at the current time, both rectal palpation and ultrasound (ultrasonic ecography) are the determining technique and tool, respectively, to follow the mare's cycle and pregnancy, and to apply the best of the reproductive technology.

For different reasons, such as synchronizing the mare's heat or assisting in timing ovulation close to insemination or direct mounting, some mares may require the intervention of a veterinarian to control the estrous cycle. This requires the injection of hormones, on specific days of the estrous cycle, and watching the changes of the mare's ovaries and uterus with ultrasound.

TIPS FOR BREEDING

The mare's egg survives up to 24 hours in the mare's oviducts. The stallion's semen will survive about 48 hours in the mare's uterus and/or oviducts. Therefore, the mare should be bred as closely as possible to the time of ovulation, which coincides with the time she is most receptive to the stallion. This allows semen to survive long enough to fertilize the egg.

In order to increase the chance of conception and use the stallion's semen more efficiently, the veterinarian may palpate/ultrasound the mare's reproductive tract (through her rectum) to determine the condition of the ovaries and the uterus. The structures found in the ovaries, and the status of the uterus, allow the veterinarian to diagnose when the next ovulation should occur and to calculate the time for the mare to be bred. On the other hand, if the mare has not been examined by a veterinarian before breeding, she should be bred the second day of heat (no later than the third day), and the breeding repeated every 36 to 48 hours while she is receptive to the stallion.

The mare may be bred either by direct mounting or artificial insemination:

- **Direct Mounting** (or **Live Cover**): With this method, the stallion serves the mare and ejaculates into the vagina. Hand breeding, which consists of controlling the stallion and the mare during direct mounting, is a relatively common method in the Paso Fino breed because it reduces the risk of injuries to both the mare and stallion. For the same reason, free breeding, in which the stallion and the mare are free in a corral/pasture, is rarely used.

  Before breeding, the stallion's penis should be washed with water from his own bucket, softly rubbed with his own sponge, and then dried with a paper towel. The mare also requires some hygienic procedures prior to breeding. The tail should be wrapped with any wrapping material, such as flexible cohesive bandage, in order to reduce penis contamination and to prevent the penis from becoming injured by the strong hairs of the mare's tail. The mare's vulva, anus, perineum, and buttocks should be washed with a mild soap, properly rinsed, and finally dried with a paper towel.

  Mares should have a negative uterine culture, both to increase the probability of pregnancy and to prevent the stallion from becoming contaminated and infecting other mares. In addition, a current "Coggins test" should be obtained for both stallion and mare before direct mounting occurs.

  Even though the mare is in heat, she may become nervous during the breeding process and may try to kick the stallion. Thus, to protect the stallion from injuries, the mare's hind legs should be hobbled properly, either using pastern-hobbles or hock-hobbles, that are tied to the chest/neck with a cord and a safety snap (see Chapter 13: "Tack and attire"). The mare is able to move, but she cannot kick the stallion. In addition, some aggressive mares need to be controlled more effectively during mating, either with a "twitch" around the upper lip or a chain attached to the halter and passed under the upper lip.

  Floors made of pavement, concrete, or rubber matting are not recommended for breeding. Anti-slippery rubber floors, properly designed for the purpose, are an excellent option for breeding, although they are expensive. Other options are either well-mowed grassed terrain or ground covered with a bed of non-dusty shavings.

  For the breeding, the handler slowly leads the stallion with a halter or jaquima that provides proper control. After seeing the mare, the stallion starts the "courtship" by arching his neck, moving very elegantly, exhibiting a ′puffed up′ appearance, expanding his nostrils, and snorting. When close to the mare, the stallion starts to sniff and nuzzle her in different areas and sometimes will bite. If the stallion bites the mare, especially above the hocks, the handler should pull the stallion's lead rope in order to avoid that behavior. When sniffing the mare's vulva, the stallion tests to see if the mare is in heat by raising his upper lip next to the vulva and then raising the head to expose the inside lip to fresh air (all of which is known as the "Flehmen reflex"). If the stallion becomes aggressive by trying to strike or kick the mare, the handler should yank the lead rope and make the stallion stay off the mare until he calms down.

  The handler allows the stallion to mount the mare's croup only after several minutes of courtship, with the assurance that the mare is completely receptive, and when the stallion's penis is fully erect. If necessary, the handler will indicate to the stallion when to mount the mare by gently pulling the lead rope up over the mare's croup, which allows the stallion to get on her. When the stallion has mounted, the handler may move the mare's tail to one side in order to permit easier penetration of the penis into the vagina.

After some intravaginal thrusts (about ten), the stallion ejaculates, which may be determined by observing the stallion's tail flagging up and down about eight times. When the penis comes out of the mare's vagina, its glans appears twice the normal size. Immediately after, the mare should be moved carefully three or four steps forward in order to help the stallion dismount easily and safely. After breeding, the stallion's penis again should be rinsed with water. Afterwards, the mare and the stallion should be put away.

Although breeding is instinctive, the ′bachelor′ stallion should be trained for breeding with a non-aggressive mare in heat. Proper training may require more than one session for some stallions.

- **Artificial Insemination (A.I.)**: The use of fresh or frozen semen, put into the mare's uterus (by a person), is currently a very common method for breeding Paso Fino mares. One billion progressive motile spermatozoa is the minimum amount shipped for each mare; thus, the number of mares bred from one ejaculate depends on the semen volume and the concentration of motile spermatozoa in it. The semen of some Paso Fino stallions cannot be frozen for storing because the spermatozoa do not survive severe temperature changes.

  Some advantages of artificial insemination are listed below:

  - Several mares may be bred with only one ejaculation of the stallion (usually five mares per ejaculate); this prevents overuse of the stallion when he has to serve several mares during the same day.

  - An increased number of offspring from the best stallions rapidly may improve the breed.

- A.I. eliminates the spread of disease transmitted by sexual contact.

- There is a reduction of lesion risks, for both stallion and mare, that may occur during direct mounting.

- For breeding, neither the mare nor the stallion needs to be moved from the farms where they live; only the semen needs to be transported. Fresh cooled semen may be stored from six to 72 hours at 39 °F to 43°F (about 4 to 6°C).

- This technique solves breeding problems when the stallion suffers arthritis, lameness, or weakness that makes mounting difficult, as well as when the mare cannot support the stallion's weight.

- Frozen semen from some stallions may be stored for a long period of time and used later, even though the animal has been sold or is deceased.

Note: A.I. is not allowed in all horse breeds. In the Thoroughbred breed, for example, only direct mounting is permitted.

A well prepared artificial vagina, lubricated inside, and kept at an optimal temperature of 109°F (about 43°C) is used for collecting the semen. Some stallions may prefer the artificial vagina at a higher temperature of 111°F (about 44°C) to 122°F (50°C), which is not recommended because it may cause damage to the sperm cells.

Before collecting the semen, the stallion's penis must be washed and dried as explained for direct mounting. The stallion is induced to mount a hobbled mare in heat (or a very gentle mare), but the penis is deviated from the mare's vagina and introduced into the artificial vagina. The artificial vagina is held firmly while the stallion thrusts against it and finally ejaculates. Then, the operator moves the artificial vagina forward to take the penis out.

After that, the artificial vagina is taken to the laboratory in order to start work on the semen, including evaluation (volume, concentration of spermatozoa, etc.), dilution, fractioning, cooling/freezing, and shipping. Some stallions are trained to mount on a dummy (phantom) instead of a real mare that makes the collection both easier and safer.

Before insemination, the mare's external genitalia should be washed, rinsed, and dried as described for direct mounting. For the insemination, the veterinarian passes a speculum (previously sterilized) or a gloved arm (previously lubricated with non-spermicidal product) through the vagina. Then, a brand new, sterile catheter is passed through both the vagina and the cervix until it reaches the uterus. An already prepared disposal syringe containing the semen is connected to the outside end of the catheter, in order to inject the semen through it into the uterus.

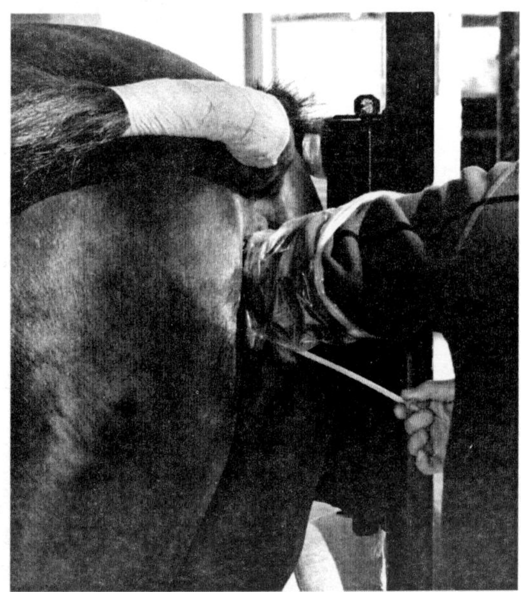

Passing a sterile catheter through the vagina and the cervix

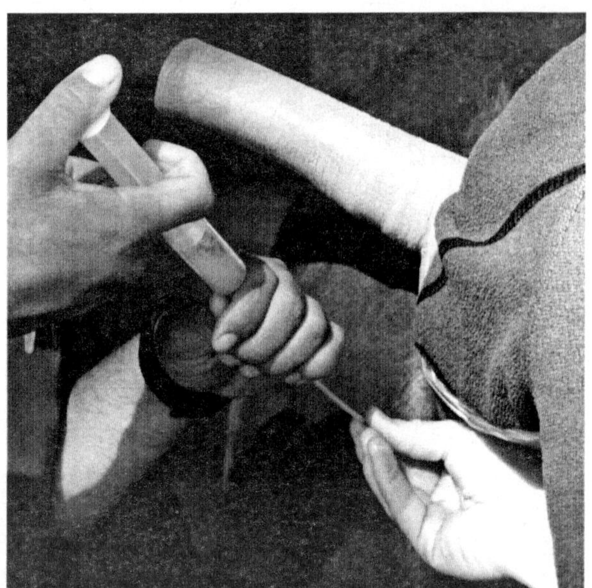

Injecting the semen

THE EMBRYO TRANSFER TECHNIQUE

This consists of removing a fertilized egg (also known as an "embryo") from a recently pregnant mare and putting it into the uterus of another mare, which sustains the entire pregnancy, delivers the foal, and thereafter nurses and takes care of the foal. The mare from which the embryo is removed, known as the ′donor,′ passes her genes to the future foal, even though the fetus does not develop in her uterus . The mare that receives the embryo, known as the ′recipient,′ does not provide her genes, but provides the nutrients and space for fetal development, gives birth, and raises the foal. The recipient mare does not need to be of the same breed as the donor, but ideally slightly bigger. For example, Quarter Horse mares commonly have been used as recipients for Paso Fino embryos, with excellent results.

By means of the embryo transfer technique, it is possible to produce a greater number of foals from outstanding mares each year. Mares dedicated to competition do not need to stop performing during the show season because of a pregnancy, but may be used to produce embryos to be ′adopted′ by recipient mares. This method also keeps in reproduction those superior mares that, because of health problems, cannot sustain an entire pregnancy.

The process for embryo transfer is as follows:

- Synchronizing the estrous cycle of both mares, donor and recipient, by injecting hormones, in order to accomplish a simultaneous heat and ovulation.
- Breeding the donor mare with an outstanding stallion just before ovulation.

- Collecting the embryo from the donor mare at six to eight days after ovulation. The most common method is to drop a special liquid medium into the uterus by means of a catheter that is passed trough the vagina and cervix. Then, the medium, with the embryo floating in it, is taken out from the uterus through the same catheter and collected in an embryo filter.
- Depositing the embryo directly into the recipient mare's uterus is accomplished using a technique similar to artificial insemination. Another option consists of freezing the embryo, storing it, and later depositing it in a recipient mare.

Embryo transfer in the Paso Fino breed is currently an important and successful reproduction method in Colombia, the United States, and Puerto Rico. From a genetic point of view, embryo transfer will result in significant improvement of the breed over the years. However, producing Paso Fino horses by using embryo transfer technology should be watched carefully to avoid over-production that negatively may affect the market.

DETERMINING THE MARE'S PREGNANCY

In the past, the most common method of diagnosing pregnancy consisted of checking/teasing the already bred mare every other day, 14 to 23 days after the last breeding, in order to look for signs of heat. If found to be in heat, the mare was considered to be open (empty), but if the mare did not come into heat, she was considered to be pregnant. However, this method is not foolproof. For example, although most pregnant mares do not come into heat, some mares may show estrus behavior two or three times during gestation, more commonly around the fifth month of pregnancy, because the fetal gonads (sexual glands) are secreting a large amount of estrogen. Moreover, some empty mares do not show signs of heat due to winter anestrus, silent heat, reabsorbed embryo, prolonged corpus luteum, minimal exposure to daylight, or nutritional deficiencies.

A rectal ultrasound, made by a veterinarian within 13 to 18 days after the breeding, helps to determine if the mare is pregnant. This is also the ideal time to determine if a twin pregnancy is present and rectify this undesirable condition by either pinching one of the embryos (known as "pinch twin") or stopping the pregnancy and re-breeding the mare during the following heat. If the mare is empty, the veterinarian may determine the next heat and ovulation time in order to repeat the breeding. A rectal ultrasound, made 30 days after breeding, shows a small fetus with heart activity. However, it is difficult to rectify successfully a twin pregnancy at this late time.

Note: A twin pregnancy is not desirable because it is rarely maintained full-term and both fetuses generally die.

Rectal palpation of uterine tone and ovarian structures is another option for diagnosing pregnancy at 28 to 30 days after breeding or later. The veterinarian must be very careful, when moving a hand into the mare's rectum and palpating structures, to avoid damaging the intestinal walls. This technique, however, does not allow detection of a twin pregnancy.

After eight months of pregnancy, some fetal movements may be felt under the mare's skin on her flanks. Sometimes, fetal movements will make the mare very uncomfortable or even cause colic.

GESTATION

About five days after the egg is fertilized in one of the oviducts, it migrates into the uterine lumen, where it is mobile for 16 to 17 days. About 14 days later (35 days after fertilization), the embryo moves into one of the uterine horns where it stays. Its first attachment to the uterine walls starts about four days later (39 to 40 days of pregnancy), but the membranes of the placenta are only developed completely during the fourth month of gestation.

The average gestation for horses is 335 days, but the range extends from 300 to 380 days. Foals born between 300 and 315 days of gestation are considered premature. They are usually small, weak in standing and walking, and have difficulties with thermoregulation. A premature foal also may exhibit some signs of underdevelopment, such as soft ear cartilage and/or short coat hair.

Care of the pregnant mare includes the following:

- Permanent access to fresh and potable drinking water.
- Proper nutrition according to the stage of gestation, that aids proper fetal development without affecting the mare's health.
- Free exercising in the pasture, working under saddle, or longeing.
- Healthy teeth (see Chapter 3: "The horse inside and out").
- Proper trimming/shoeing of hooves (see Chapter 7: "Hoof trimming and shoeing").
- Necessary regular management practices, as well as vaccinations and dewormers (see Chapter 10: "Health basics").

ABORTION

This term describes those situations in which a fetus is expelled from the uterus through the vulva between 45 and 300 days of gestation. The common causes of abortion are described below:

- Hormone imbalance, mainly associated with progesterone deficiencies.
- Chronic endometritis before pregnancy that causes insufficient development of the placenta.
- A bacterial or fungal infection of the placenta (known as "placentitis"). This is caused when an already pregnant mare is bred again or when a weak cervix is lacerated prior to pregnancy (known as "incompetent cervix"); thus, allowing entry of an infection into the uterus.
- Pathogens infecting the mare which kill the fetus:
  - Bacteria, such as *Streptococcus zooepidemicus, Brucella abortus*, *Salmonella abortus equi, E. coli*, and *Leptospira spp.*
  - Viruses, such as rhinopneumonitis (also known as equine herpes virus) type EHV-1, and equine viral arteritis.
- Strangulation of the fetus caused by the umbilical cord.
- Pregnancy with twins; abortion of both fetuses usually occurs after the eighth month of gestation.

- Ingestion of toxic or contaminated plants.
- Genetic incompatibilities between mare and fetus.
- Fetal deformities.
- Illness of the mare, such as colic, laminitis, and respiratory infections, among others.
- Severe blow to the mare's abdomen that kills the fetus.
- Severe dehydration over a period of time.

In the case of abortion, a veterinarian must be called, both to determine the cause and to attend to the mare. The fetus and placenta should be kept refrigerated and taken to a veterinary laboratory for proper diagnosis of the cause of the abortion.

FOALING PROCESS

The best place for foaling should be either a quiet clean pasture (only if the weather is mild) or a quiet, illuminated, and well disinfected stall with new, abundant, straw or non-dusty shavings for bedding. The mare should be taken to the foaling area three to seven days before she is expected to foal.

The stall is a better place for foaling, either when it is going to occur during the winter or the summer (due to the extreme weather) or the farm is located where wild predators (such as coyotes or wolves) may reach the horses in the pasture. In addition, the use of a closed circuit television set in the foaling stall is very helpful for supervising the birth, without irritating the mare, and detecting whether the mare or foal has any problem during the birthing process.

Most mares exhibit the following signs before foaling: The udder enlarges from one to five weeks before foaling, but the nipples only become enlarged about five days before foaling. From one to three weeks before foaling, the hips start looking less rounded, with the bones more noticeable. About one week before foaling, the croup appears slightly more inclined downward. The mare's vulva enlarges and relaxes gradually one to five days before foaling in order to permit the foal's expulsion. The nipples fill with milk, and may start to drip slightly a few hours before foaling. In addition, some mares start to develop a soft swelling from the udder toward the abdominal area about four days before foaling, known as "pre-parturition ventral edema."

When the foaling signs are identified within 24 hours of birth, the mare's udder and genitals may be washed gently with a mild soap and then rinsed properly. The foaling process is as follows:

- Once the cervix starts dilating and the uterine muscles begin to evidence the first contractions to deliver the foal, the mare starts walking nervously, often looking at her sides and her udder. Walking helps the foal take position for delivery. Sweating profusely also is common at this stage of foaling.
- When the yellowish allantois and chorion membranes (the first placental membranes also known as "allantochorion" together) break, amber- to brown-colored liquid is released (known as "breaking the water").
- Then, the mare starts to deliver the foal with strong, rhythmic contractions of the uterus and a large group of abdominal muscles. The mare does this lying on one side and rolling in order to position the foal into the

birth canal; some mares prefer to stand or alternate lying down/rolling and standing while foaling. The white-translucent amniotic placenta (or amnion) appears first at the mare's vulva followed immediately by the foal's forelegs. Thereafter, the head, neck, body, and the hind legs are expelled with the rest of the amniotic placenta, which finally breaks to allow the newborn to breathe for the first time. This process usually takes 15 to 25 minutes, but may take longer. If the mare takes longer than one hour, this may be considered problematic.

- The umbilical cord stays connected on one end to the foal's abdomen and on the other end to some remains of the placenta (allantochorion) that stay attached to the mare's uterus endometrium. This allows some blood to be passed to the foal through the umbilical cord.
- The umbilical cord usually breaks 15 to 30 minutes after birth because of the movements of both the foal and the mare. It breaks about 1 ½ to 2 inches from the foal's abdomen.
- Finally, the rest of the allantochorion placenta and the main part of the umbilical cord are expulsed, as a result of more uterine contractions, usually within the next hour, but this may occur during the first three hours after foaling. If the placenta is not expelled within that period of time, a veterinarian should attend to the mare.

When the placenta is expelled, it must be inspected carefully in order to verify that all parts of it were delivered and there are none remaining attached to the mare's uterus. This should be observed carefully because a retained placenta may affect the mare after foaling, and cause serious chronic diseases. After all verifications are made, the entire placenta should be buried in a three to four foot deep hole with lime on top.

PROBLEMS DURING FOALING

A problem at birth (technically called "dystocia") usually occurs for several reasons: a foal's malformation, a foal's incorrect position when being expelled from the uterus, a mare's pelvic malformation, a small opening in the mare's pelvis that allows a very small space for delivery, weak/failed uterine contractions, or foaling twins.

Although most cases of dystocia bring severe problems to the foal and even death, some dystocias may be attended to successfully by a veterinarian, when requested on time. Another problem occurs when the allantochorion placenta separates prematurely from the uterus endometrium and is expelled previous to/simultaneously with the foal. In most of these cases the foal dies due to a lack of oxygen in the birth canal.

Other severe problems and even death may occur to the mare during foaling: an internal hemorrhage due to an uterine artery rupture, an external hemorrhage caused by lacerations to the reproductive tract (cervix, vagina, or vulva), a rupture of the large intestine (recto-vaginal fistula), or a rupture of the prepubic tendon (that holds the heavy uterus and fetus in position during pregnancy).

If the mare shows signs of colic after foaling, an intravenous injection of an analgesic/antispasmodic drug may solve the problem. However, a very severe colic post- foaling may also be caused by a large twisting of the colon, a ruptured uterus, or an uterine artery hemorrhage, for which a veterinarian should be called.

FIRST ATTENTION TO THE NEW FOAL

If a person stays with the newborn and the mare for the first two to three hours after birth, this will help the foal in many ways, as described below. In addition, during this time, the same person will make a positive imprinting on the foal. Thus, the foal should trust people and should be easier to handle in the future (see Chapter 15: "Horse psychology and training" – The foal's training).

As soon as it is born, the foal should be breathing properly. If any material, such as placenta, mucus or shavings, is found in the nostrils or the mouth, this should be removed immediately. Sometimes, the amnion placenta does not break and may be covering the foal's face and muzzle. This does not allow breathing and causes the foal's death if it is not removed or broken in time. If the foal is not breathing after birth, some strategies may be used, such as artificial respiration (by blowing air into its mouth) and rubbing its ribs. Additionally, rubbing the whole body of the foal with a towel helps to dry its coat, stimulate blood circulation, and rapidly improve tendon and muscle strength.

If the mare's and foal's movements do not make the umbilical cord break within 20 to 30 minutes after birth, the cord should not be cut with a sharp instrument, such as a scissors or a knife. It should be separated carefully by just the pressure of fingertips at the thinnest part of the cord, located about 1 ½ to 2 inches from the foal.

As soon as possible, the foal's navel stump should be treated with chlorohexidine solution or tincture of 2% to 10% iodine, in order to reduce the risk of a severe, fatal infection known as septicemia of the newborn. The tincture of iodine must never be in contact with the skin on the foal's abdomen because it is very caustic and irritating. 3/4 of the stump length should be immersed in a small container filled with the solution. This treatment should be done three or four times within the first day, and reduced to two times for the next two days.

The two mammary glands of the mare are externally seen as the udder, which has no hair covering it and is located between the thighs in the inguinal region. Each gland ends in a nipple, 1 ½ to 2 ½ inches long, that is tilted forward slightly. Each nipple has from two to five narrow ducts that permit milk to flow, when the foal is nursing. About 24 hours prior to foaling, the mare begins to produce a unique kind of milk called "colostrum" that gradually turns normal 36 to 48 hours after foaling. Color and properties of colostrum are very different from regular milk because it contains, among other substances, immunoglobulins (antibodies) and laxatives.

Because the foal is a natural prey of predators, it usually stands and nurses 45 to 90 minutes after birth, but some foals do it much sooner. The foal should drink colostrum within the first three hours of life and drink frequently during the first 24 hours after birth. Immunoglobulins from its dam provide the foal with a passive immunity against most infectious diseases during the first three to four months of life. Nevertheless, the veterinarian should check the foal's and mare's conditions within the first 24 hours after birth and test the foal's blood in order to determine the level of immunoglobulin G (IgG).

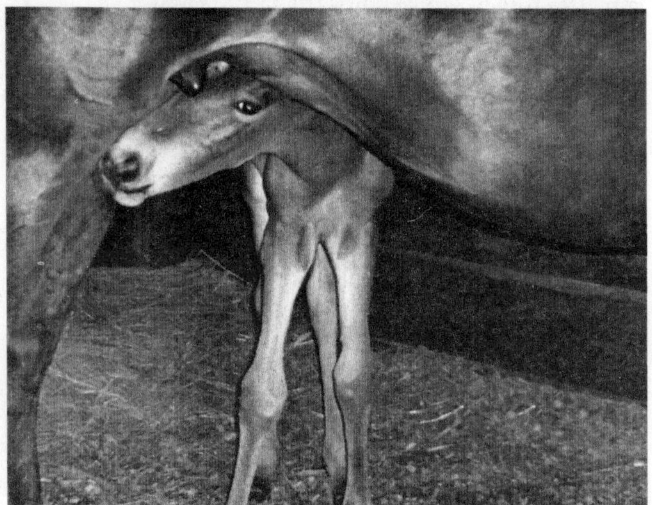

When the foal is not able to nurse within the first two hours, it needs some help, either in standing or finding the mare's udder. This also may be caused by a mare that does not produce milk or a mare that refuses to let the foal suckle because this hurts the udder.

If everything looks normal after the first two to three hours, both mare and foal should be left alone for proper recognition and rest; however, observing them periodically from a distance or outside the stall helps to ensure that everything is going well. A first birth mare must be observed more often to detect any sign of aggressiveness or disinterest in the foal.

The foal should urinate normally with no strain and the first excrement (called "meconium") should be eliminated within the first 12 hours of life. Because the colostrum contains a laxative substance, it usually is the only substance needed for the foal to pass the meconium. If, during the first twelve hours after birth, the meconium has not passed or there is a sign of colic or constipation (the foal raises its tail and strains to defecate with no success), this requires the application of one or more phosphate enemas that are used for humans.

If the pregnant mare did not receive a tetanus toxoid shot about 45 days before foaling, the newborn foal and its dam should receive a tetanus antitoxin shot as soon as possible. The mare should be dewormed 24 hours post foaling.

MORE CARE FOR THE NEW FOAL

If weather permits, mare and foal should have free exercise in a paddock/pasture for at least two daylight hours per day (but preferably for eight to twelve hours) starting at the second or third day after foaling. This helps to reduce the pre-parturition ventral edema of the mare, when it occurs, and allows her to teach the foal how to be outside and run. The free exercise helps the foal to improve its athletic abilities, such as heart/lung activity, muscle strength, and coordination. Additionally, exposure to sunlight permits the foal to synthesize vitamin D.

"Fiesta de Capuchino" (Capuchino x Coqueta de Aristocratica) at five days old. Owned by Mildred Arent, Criadero Aristocratica, Ocala, FL. Photo by Olga García.

The foal may need supplemental nutrition starting at one month of age, in a separate feeder from its mother's. This should provide all the required nutrients that the mare's milk cannot supply for proper foal growth, which occurs at a very fast rate. This supplemental nutrition, that includes forage, grain, and vitamins/minerals, should be adjusted for the foal's stomach capacity according to its age (see Chapter 6: "Nutrition"). In addition, the foal needs free access to fresh, clean water to drink after the first week of life.

The foal develops its own immune system at three to four months of age, when it is able to produce its own antibodies. That is why the first vaccines are administrated at three months of age (see Chapter 10: "Health basics"). The foal should be dewormed the first time at two months of age, at the same time as its dam and the other horses that share a space, such as a corral or a pasture.

THE PREMATURE FOAL

Although life is much harder for a premature foal, the foal usually recovers completely after one to two weeks with proper care. To keep the foal's body temperature from decreasing, the foal should be put in an enclosed stall, with dry, abundant bedding, and provided with one or two heat lamps, like those used for other animal species, such as poultry or pigs.

To feed the premature foal, first the colostrum and then the regular milk must be extracted from the dam's udder (the entire content) every 90 minutes and given to the foal with a bottle ending with a lamb's nipple. This allows the foal to grow and become stronger until it can stand and drink milk by itself. Regularly milking the mare during these first days, and keeping her close to the foal, maintains enough brain stimulation to make the mare keep producing milk during the entire lactation period.

Extremely weak, premature foals with a poor suckle reflex may require hospitalization for placement of a stomach tube for feeding and to rectify additional problems associated with prematurity.

THE ORPHAN FOAL

A foal becomes an orphan in a number of situations: when its mother dies, either while foaling or a few hours later; when the mare does not produce milk (condition known as "agalactia"); or when the mare rejects the foal (more common in first birth mares than in experienced mares). The orphan foal may be introduced to another lactating mare that accepts the foal for nursing. If, however, a substitute mare is not available, the foal needs to be fed with mare milk or a milk replacement, initially by means of a bottle with a lamb's nipple and later with a bucket.

If the newborn foal is unable to drink colostrum from its mother, feeding colostrum from another mare (either fresh or frozen), as many times as possible during its first 24 hours of life, may provide the amount of immunoglobulines needed. Other methods include either an intravenous transfusion of plasma from a healthy adult gelding horse or a relative, or the use of a commercial IgG product. These practices always should be supervised by a veterinarian.

Although cow's milk, with the addition of some nutrients (dextrose, lactose, and calcium), is an option for feeding the orphan foal, a commercial milk replacement may be used for four to six months. Commercial milk replacements come in two different forms: a powder converted into liquid by the addition of water, and a pellet feed offered in a feeder to older foals that eat well. The amount of milk should be fractioned into multiple portions during the day, and increased gradually to the maximum amount the foal should have for its age, but assuring that this increase does not cause diarrhea. Supplemental nutrition based on forage, concentrate, vitamins/minerals, and fresh, clean water must be included, starting with small amounts at eight to ten days of age.

THE MARE'S FOAL HEAT

This is the expression used when referring to the mare's first heat after foaling, that starts at the seventh to eleventh day after parturition. The mare may be bred during the foal heat except if there was a problem during delivery or a retained placenta more than three hours after parturition. Other exceptions include the presence of any yellowish vaginal discharge or any laceration to the vagina. Paso Fino mares, previously examined by a veterinarian, are commonly bred during the foal heat with a good percentage becoming pregnant.

WEANING THE FOAL

The foal should be weaned between four and a half and seven and a half months of age, depending on some factors, such as the dam's body condition index, the foal's development, the amount of milk produced by the mare, the space (pasture or stall) available for the weaned foal, the season (related to the weather), and the availability of other foals to be weaned simultaneously so that they may share the same space.

In addition, two important elements should be taken into consideration before weaning the foal to reduce the stress caused by this event:

- Making sure that the foal eats its own daily ration in a different feeder than its mother eats.
- Developing a confident relationship between the foal and the person who will take care of it after weaning.

Among the many methods for weaning a foal, progressively separating the mare and the foal for about one to two hours daily (for instance keeping the foal in the stall while the mare is out), and gradually increasing the time of separation, is a good way to build the foal's independence. For weaning, the foal should be left in the same stall/pasture that it once shared with its mother for at least three to four weeks; this well-known place gives the foal confidence. However, if the weaned foal is going to be left in a pasture, the foal requires the company of another horse, preferably one weaned at the same age. The foal's diet, feeder and overall routine initially should be kept the same. Ideally, the mare should be moved to another barn, pasture, or farm where they (dam and foal) will neither see nor hear each other.

Three days before weaning, the mare should not be fed grain or alfalfa (only green grass in the pasture or grass hay), so that milk production rapidly will be reduced; this strategy should continue for one week or more after weaning, to ensure that the mare stops producing milk. If after weaning, the mare's udder becomes inflamed because of the milk stored in it, gently hosing the udder for about ten minutes with cold water three or four times a day, within the next two or three days, will provide comfort to the mare. If inflammation is serious, the veterinarian may prescribe an antibiotic to prevent mastitis and an analgesic drug to reduce pain.

The foal of a lactating, pregnant mare should be weaned no later than seven and half months of age. This will give the mare enough time to recuperate for the next foaling and lactation. If a mare is not pregnant when its foal is weaned, it usually comes into a fertile heat the sixth to eleventh day after weaning, depending on the mare's body condition index and season.

Applying the information in this chapter, and enlisting the assistance of a veterinarian, helps assure better reproductive efficiency of horses and healthy offspring.

CHAPTER 9

FACILITIES FOR HORSES

Just as any other domestic animal species, the horse needs adequate facilities to be productive. Facilities for horses must offer protection from adverse weather and from wild, dangerous animals.

PLANNING FACILITIES

The farm owner/manager must plan carefully the type of facilities (to build or renovate) that meet both current and future needs. When planning facilities many factors should be considered:

- Related to the horses:
  - The current number of Paso Fino horses and the planned number in the future. Therefore, possible expansion should be considered.
  - Physiological stage, age, and gender of the animals.
  - Primary use of the horses (such as showing, reproduction, trail riding).
- Related to the land and the environment:
  - Type of terrain, including topography and soil texture (for drainage and fertility).
  - Space available.
  - Amount of potable water available.
  - Predominant climate in the area (temperature, sunshine, wind, rain, snow) and its variation in different seasons.
  - Orientation according to sunrise and sunset.

  - Accessibility from the outside and to the different areas inside the farm during all seasons (even when raining or snowing).
  - Availability of electricity or other sources of energy (such as coal, gas, wind, sun).
  - Sanitary, architectural, and/or social laws in the County/State for horse farms, or additional requirements in the area (e.g., equestrian developments).

- Related to administration:
  - Availability of workers (labor).
  - Availability of building and equine supplies, and feed.
  - Management (keeping horses stalled or outside).
  - Estimated finances needed for this investment.

Because safety for people and horses is a priority on the Paso Fino farm, special attention must be paid to the following:

- Building fences, walls, doors, gates, and all the elements at proper heights. Additionally, doors, gates, aisles, and passage-ways should be built at the correct width, preferably wider than narrower.
- Using strong materials.
- Making walls, doors, floors, etc., easy to disinfect.
- Avoiding dangerous floors, appliances or obstacles that may cause a variety of injuries to either people or horses. To achieve this, avoid slippery and/or uneven floors, sharp/pointed edges or elements (such as nails), and hoof-sized holes in walls, gates, or fences.
- Having well-illuminated areas during both day and night.

Facilities for horses are a good investment if they are constructed with the following in mind:

- Designed technically for the purpose.
- Functional for efficiency.
- Safe for people and horses.
- Made with durable materials.
- Constructed in compliance with all County/State regulations.
- Aesthetically pleasing.

It is important to note that the luxuriousness and expense of horse facilities is not a guarantee that they are well-designed for their purpose. Following are recommendations for facilities for Paso Fino horses.

BARN AND STALL

Horses and other domestic animals have been living close to people for many generations, and that has allowed them to share part of the human lifestyle. Therefore, just like humans, a horse should have a ′house′ for protection from adverse weather (burning sunshine, extreme heat or cold, wind, rain, snow, and lightning).

Adverse weather may affect the horse negatively:

- Cold increases energy requirements and makes the horse's coat grow longer. That is why stalled horses usually have shorter and shinier coats than horses kept outside during late fall, winter, and the beginning of spring.
- Cold wind may induce the horse to develop respiratory diseases.
- Heat reduces the horse's appetite and increases water intake. In addition, intense sun bleaches ad dries out the horse's coat.
- A horse usually does not graze in heavy rain. Additionally, being wet and cold requires the horse to use stored energy to keep its minimum required body temperature.
- Horses may be killed by lightning when they are kept outside during an electrical storm.

The barn may be considered the horse's house, and the stall its room. Besides protecting the horse from bad weather, other purposes for adequate shelter are protecting the horse from wild animals (predators), allowing each horse to be fed (or supplemented) individually, and offering a quiet place for rest. Additionally, an owner may take advantage of the energy stored by a stalled horse, either for work or recreation.

Pasos del Cielo Ranch, Anthony, FL. Photo courtesy of Allen and Glenna Struthers.

The barn (as well as any other building on the farm) should be built on high ground. This helps protect it from flooding. The barn should be designed and located according to the wind direction. In a properly designed barn, the wind should blow the heat out of the stalls during the summer. Conversely, cold wind should not blow directly into the stalls during winter because it may cause respiratory diseases in horses.

Good ventilation is imperative to prevent respiratory problems. This may be provided using several strategies. Building a high roof allows for excellent ventilation in the barn during all seasons. Stall windows are a notable alternative for providing adequate ventilation and natural light. In addition, windows placed 4 ½ feet above the ground allow the horse to see what happens outside its ′home.′

Windows should be closed during the coldest hours of the winter to avoid cold wind blowing directly into the stalls and then opened during the summer to improve ventilation. The use of fans in the barn, installed on the walls, gates, or ceilings, helps to keep the horse cooler during the hottest hours of summer days, and improves ventilation to control moisture and odors.

Because the barn is one of the most important buildings on the horse farm, it requires water and electricity. Professional or large barns also need a telephone and restroom facilities. Aisles in the barn should have flat, leveled, and non-slip floors. Additionally, aisles should have sufficient room for any vehicle/equipment needed (e.g., a truck with a manure spreader attached).

The most common size of a stall for Paso Finos worldwide is 13 x 13 feet (4 m. x 4 m.), but the bigger the area, the better. The minimum size recommended for Paso Fino yearlings is 10 x 10 feet and for older horses is 10 x 12 feet. The stall should be dry and well-illuminated with sunlight if possible. Unfortunately, building dark stalls for Paso Fino horses was recommended for many years and some horses still live in these conditions due to this misconception.

The ideal stall floor is flat, level (or slightly inclined), and dry. The stall should have a drainage system according to the natural drainage in the barn. Although packed clay is very good flooring for the stall, a one-piece mat made of rubber (or another synthetic material) is also good flooring for a stall when put on top of packed clay or concrete. This is sanitary and comfortable for the horse and easy for daily cleaning of manure, wet bedding, and urine. Independent of the type of flooring, the stall requires a bedding material (such as shavings), spread all over the floor, in order to absorb liquids and offer a soft and comfortable surface for the horse to stand and to rest.

Stall walls may be made of different materials such as concrete block, wood, or metal. Stall walls for Paso Fino horses should be strong, durable, flat, and 5 ½ feet high, at a minimum. The stall door should be 4 ½ tall, at a minimum, to keep the horse from jumping over it, and 4 ½ feet wide to allow a pregnant mare to move in and out safely. The slope of the roof and the stall's entry should be 7 ½ feet high, at a minimum.

Horses should be fed (hay and grain) at the ground level of the stall because it is the horse's natural position when eating; this prevents the horse from developing back/neck problems. However, if the bucket/tub used for grain is taken out of the stall after the horse finishes eating each meal, it should be placed higher than the ground level, up to 3 feet. The proper location for the grain feeder in the stall is at the easiest access point for the person in charge of feeding, not only for safety but also for more efficient labor.

The waterer should be located in the opposite corner from the feeder and at about 3 to 4 feet above the ground (depending on the horse's age). Any type of waterer should be cleaned every day and kept full with fresh, clean water. Installing an "automatic" waterer will provide a permanent supply of water to the horse and save labor; however, it requires daily checking to verify that it is working properly. During winter, for example, water quickly may turn to ice. On the other hand, the use of a plastic bucket as a waterer helps control the amount of water the horse drinks daily; this also requires regular inspection and refilling.

The stall should have a salter (a small bucket or bowl) to offer salt (iodized or with minerals added) to the horse at all times; the salter should be placed in a corner of the stall at about 3 to 4 feet above the floor.

For safety, a moderate size area where the horse barn is built should be enclosed by fences and gates, which should be opened only when required for a vehicle or a horse (under control) to pass. This prevents a horse from becoming loose on the farm (which may cause problems with vehicles or other horses) or from leaving the farm (which may cause serious accidents).

The "open shelter" is a stall built in a paddock where the horse may go in or out as it desires. This shelter should include a waterer, feeder, and salter. An individual open shelter system is common for stallions. A "pole barn" consists of a roof held on poles in a pasture with access from all directions. This is useful for small groups of horses (e.g., pregnant mares).

FIRE PREVENTION

The horse barn has a risk of fire due to the many combustible materials in it, such as wood, shavings/straw, hay, and horse manure. The following strategies will help prevent barn fires:

- Keeping fire extinguishers at the barn with instructions on proper use and maintenance.
- Storing bedding material (shavings/straw) and hay in separate buildings away from the barn. The same is true for storing fuel and oil for the farm equipment and machinery.
- Painting the barn's wooden walls and posts with a "flame retardant" paint.
- Prohibiting smoking in or around the barn.
- Installing fire detectors in different areas of the barn.
- Installing lightning protection systems.

STALL VERSUS JAIL

Although the stall offers many benefits for the horse, it cannot be used like a ′jail′ to keep the horse confined permanently. The horse should spend some time each day out of the stall. The boredom and stress of a horse kept permanently in a stall is easily imagined. Boredom and stress from confinement may cause the horse to develop vices/bad habits:

- **Walking in the stall**: This habit, in which the horse walks in the stall close to one or more walls many hours a day, is caused by boredom, and/or stress. This keeps the horse from gaining weight. As soon as the horse starts to develop this vice, the horse should be put in a large pasture full of grass, as a correction. **Weaving** (also called the **"vice of the bear"**) is a variation of stall walking, but instead of walking close to the walls of the stall, the horse stands in front of a wall and shakes its neck and head side-to-side for hours.

- **Cribbing**: The horse takes hold of any solid item with its incisors (the fore teeth) and swallows air; therefore, the incisors of a cribber horse may become worn irregularly. Just before swallowing air, the cribber arches its neck and pulls backward. Some cribbers are so compulsive that they share the time between eating and cribbing. Cribbing tends to release endorphins, which gives the horse a pleasant feeling. Thus, cribbing is difficult to control once it has begun.

  A horse that cribs is capable of reaching any body condition index (weight), except if the horse's incisors are too worn, and cutting grass from the pasture (for horses living outside) is difficult. The stress and boredom that make the horse crib in the stall may cause gastric ulcers, which will keep the horse from gaining weight and eventually may cause colic.

  There is a less traumatic variation of cribbing (also caused by boredom) in which the horse only swallows air. It is known as "**wind-sucking**." In this case, the horse does not grab anything with the incisors.

  Some horses will eliminate these habits (cribbing/wind-sucking) when kept in large, good pastures. Using an electric fence, where the horse cribs, may also be helpful to partially solve this problem. Because the horse does not crib on items placed below its carpus level (false knee), feeders, waterers, and salters for the cribber horse should be placed low. Additionally, the use of a special collar (there are different designs of collars for cribbers), that places a little pressure on the horse's throat, may help the horse to stop cribbing.

- **Pawing**: Due to the stress of being confined, the horse paws the floor of the stall. In this case, the foreleg used to paw may be injured. This habit more commonly is seen in horses that once lived in pastures and then are confined to barns. Keeping the horse half-time in and half-time out of the stall may help eliminate this vice. If the horse digs holes in the ground while pawing, the use of a rubber mat in the stall, as flooring, keeps the horse from causing damage.

- **Eating manure**: The nursing foal usually eats small amounts of manure from its mother because it needs to obtain the beneficial microorganisms for its cecum. When the adult horse eats its own manure, however, it is caused by the stress of being kept in the stall, being hungry, and/or having food with a low fiber content. Taking the horse into a paddock or a pasture for several hours daily, and providing a good diet distributed over many meals a day, usually solves this habit.

- **Masturbation**: The stallion rubs his abdomen with his erect penis, for a few minutes, many times a day. The boredom of spending excessive time in the stall is a common cause of this vice in a stallion. However, this occurs more commonly when the stallion is able to detect the presence of mares in heat (from spring to fall).

  Masturbation is thought by some to make stallions infertile because it is assumed that they have several ejaculations every day; fortunately, only a small number of stallions ejaculate in these circumstances. In the case where the stallion actually does ejaculate, its fertility is reduced.

  To decrease the boredom of confinement, the stallion should be turned out in a paddock/pasture a few hours per day. Placing a "stallion ring" above the penis glans also works with more difficult cases. This ring is only removed from the penis for breeding or cleaning the penis and prepuce (every three to four weeks), and placed back on the penis.

Another helpful strategy to reduce the boredom and stress of a confined horse, and to keep the horse from developing vices, consists of giving it toys with which to play (e.g., a rubber ball, rubber cones) and/or giving it a companion to share its stall. Any small domestic animal, such as a sheep, goat, rabbit, hen, duck, etc. may accomplish this purpose.

IMPORTANCE OF PASTURES FOR HORSES

Just like any other breed of horses, Paso Finos are real athletes that need to walk, run, and jump freely. They are always happier when they spend some free time out of the stall.

Allowing the horse to spend several hours daily in a good pasture not only keeps the animal from developing the many vices caused by the boredom/stress of confinement, but also offers other important advantages. It allows the horse to spend some time eating the most palatable and nutritious grasses or legumes available in the pasture, thereby enriching the diet. Grazing in the pasture is also helpful for keeping the teeth in good condition, the digestive system working properly, and the muscles of the legs, neck, and back healthier and stronger.

The horse in the pasture develops a stronger skeleton and better leg conformation because of both free exercise and exposure to sunshine. Furthermore, free exercise keeps the circulatory and respiratory systems much healthier. Unfortunately, some small farms do not have enough space for adequate pastures. In this case one or more smaller paddocks may suffice.

Pastures and paddocks must be fenced properly to keep horses, either individually or in a group, in the given space. Good fencing also beautifies the property and increases its value. Fences must be designed and built for the most challenging horse expected to be in the paddock or pasture. A variety of fence materials are available: wood, metal (pipe, screen, or wire), solid plastic, and diverse electric systems. Before choosing any material, the cost should be balanced with durability, safety, and beauty. No matter what material is selected, fences for horses must be strong and tight (to avoid horses reaching through them), high (to avoid horses jumping over them), clearly visible (to prevent horses from crashing into them), and free of dangerous sharp edges or improperly driven nails. The minimum fence height for Paso Fino horses is 4 feet, but the higher the better.

Note: Barbed wire, a common fencing material used for cattle, is inappropriate for horses.

Horses kept in pastures, corrals, or paddocks (full-time or part-time) need a permanent water supply, especially during hot days. Trees and/or roofs offer protection against the sunshine during the hottest hours. Installing water sprayers in the pasture allow the horses to "shower" themselves during summer.

STORAGE

The horse feed and tack, bedding material, farm equipment (including fuel and oil to be used) and tools, cleaning products, etc. must be stored properly for protection against damage.

Hay should be stored in a covered, enclosed, dry, clean and ventilated place, preferably away from the barn. Grain, mineral and vitamin supplements should be stored in a clean, cool, ventilated, dry room (feed room), preferably close to the stalls. Some people use an extra stall to store hay, grain, etc. The feed room (for hay or grain) must **NEVER** be accessible to horses that may accidentally escape from either the stall or the pasture. If allowed, a horse may eat enormous amounts of feed in a short period of time. This may cause founder or another serious illness.

The tack should be stored in the tack room, which must be dry and cool. The halters, lead ropes, hobbles, jaquimas, bits, reins, and all the tack for training should be hanging from hooks to keep them organized and away from rodents. Metal or wooden saddle racks, mounted on the tack room walls, make good use of space for storing saddles. Although saddle floor stands (made of metal or wood) require more space in the tack room, they are portable for events.

Pasos del Cielo Ranch, Anthony, FL. Photos courtesy of Allen and Glenna Struthers.

Saddle pads and/or blankets should be placed in a dry ventilated place for easy drying. After drying, they should be placed in the tack room. Blankets, cooling sheets, and shipping tack (halter and boots) may be kept in a cabinet or closet in the tack room. Helmets should be kept in their original boxes and/or in a cabinet (or closet) in the tack room. Chaps, zamarros, and all the attire required by the rider should be placed in the tack room away from the horse tack.

First-aid supplies (see Chapter 10: "Health basics") should be on a shelf, that may be located in the tack room; a small size refrigerator is also helpful to store medicines that may be affected by changes in temperature.

The equipment (such as tractor, mower, four-wheeler, manure spreader, drag), tools, cleaning products, fuel, oil, insecticides, paint, brushes, nails, screws, new fence boards and posts, etc. should be put in a well-organized shed. Cabinets and/or shelves may be a good place for small items. The new bedding material should be kept in the shavings bin away from the barn; if not permanently covered with a roof, the bedding material should be covered with a tarp during rainy/windy days.

Although they may be separated, the location of all the storage places (feed room, tack room, shavings bin, etc.) should be close to where the horses stay (stalls, pastures, etc.) for efficiency.

FACILITIES FOR TYING THE HORSE

"H" shaped posts (for cross-tying) are very important on the Paso Fino farm to tie horses for grooming, bathing, shoeing, injecting, etc. "H" shaped posts should be installed in different places on the farm for these diverse purposes. Additionally, the washing/bathing "H" posts may have rubber mats on the ground for the horses to stand safely. This area should also have adequate drainage.

One chain or rope attached to each post should have a safety snap at its free end to attach to each side of the horse's halter. This way the horse is held evenly-distanced between the two posts. The horizontal piece of the "H" keeps the horse's neck from becoming hurt if the animal should try to run forward.

Pasos del Cielo Ranch, Anthony, FL. Photo courtesy of Allen and Glenna Struthers.

Note: The Colombian leather jaquima is not designed to cross-tie the horse by using the chain-snap sets on the posts; therefore, when wearing a Colombian leather jaquima, the horse should be tied to the post by using its pisador (see Chapter 13: "Tack and attire").

A strong post, firmly placed in the ground, may be necessary for tying certain difficult horses. It should be located in the middle of a large space (such as paddock) with at least a 15 foot radius of free space. The post/pole must be resistant to the strength of an adult horse. The posts for tying (either for the "H" shaped or the single post) may be made of metal, wood, or PVC pipe filled with concrete and steel bars. Any type of post must be cylindrical and free of any protrusions (such as spikes or nails).

A palpation chute (or rectangular stock), with front and rear gates at the narrower ends, is ideal for rectal palpation of a mare, ultrasound, and hygiene prior to breeding, so the veterinarian/technician is able to accomplish these activities safely. This structure is particularly important at farms where many broodmares are kept during breeding season. The mare enters the stock through the open rear gate, while the gate in front of her is closed. Once the rear gate is closed, the veterinarian may attend to the horse. When finished, the front gate is opened and the mare exits.

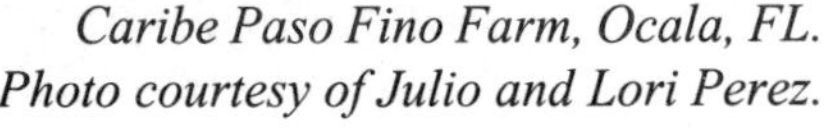

Caribe Paso Fino Farm, Ocala, FL.
Photo courtesy of Julio and Lori Perez.

The palpation chute is not recommended as a restraint for injecting, cleaning wounds, clipping, giving a bath, etc. because the animal may easily hurt itself by hitting the sides or the gates while trying to avoid the activity; moreover, the person attending to the horse may be severely injured if a hand and/or arm is squeezed against the structure.

THE QUARANTINE AREA

The farm should have a dedicated area for sick horses. This area preferably should have stalls and be located in a peaceful, isolated place from the other horses on the farm. For hygiene, the quarantine area needs to be disinfected more frequently than other areas of the farm.

New horses entering the farm should first be kept in the quarantine area for at least two weeks; otherwise, they may spread diseases to the other horses. Additionally, if the farm has stallions at stud for outside mares, these mares should be kept in the quarantine area.

The foaling stall may be located in the quarantine area. The pregnant mares going to foal should be moved to the foaling stall at least three to seven days before the birth, according to the date of breeding or depending on the foaling signs (see Chapter 8: "Reproduction").

USING MANURE

Once manure is removed daily from the stables, corrals, and arenas, it needs to be put in a proper place. If manure is stored to be fermented for compost, and used like fertilizer later, it has to be put either in bags or in a covered container away from all farm buildings. This type of manure storage area should be built with no access for domestic animals or wild birds. To prevent fly reproduction in manure, an application of a powder insecticide product may be required. Additionally, any possible liquid draining from manure in fermentation must be kept from contaminating water sources (including streams or ponds). The use of a manure dumpster, that is emptied when it is full by a company that specializes in this, is a good choice for small/intermediate size farms.

When the farm has a rotational pasture system for horses and/or other domestic grazers, fresh manure from stalls and corrals may be spread like fertilizer on the pastures at rest. A manure spreader, pulled by a four-wheeler, tractor, or small truck, may be used to spread the manure uniformly and to minimize the size of the particles. This keeps flies from reproducing and worm larvae from surviving. Although warm weather is ideal for fertilizing with fresh manure, because parasite eggs die when exposed to sunshine, manure may also be spread in cold weather, except when the ground is covered with snow.

TRAINING AREAS

"H" shaped posts (for cross-tying), or a single strong post, set up in the tacking area are necessary to tie the horse. One or more saddle racks (made of metal or wood) should be mounted on the wall close by, as well as hooks to hang jaquimas, reins, bits, etc. The floor either may be concrete or covered with a rubber mat.

The round pen (25 to 30 feet radius) is a very safe place for young horses to be started in training. The round pen is useful also for those horses more advanced in the training process that need some time to quiet down.

Pasos del Cielo Ranch, Anthony, FL. Photo courtesy of Allen and Glenna Struthers.

Working the horse on both flat and inclined ground allows the animal to develop strong legs, coordination, and balance. Riding the horse in different places, such as trails, pastures, next to roads, around buildings, etc., not only exposes it to different situations that promote mental maturation, but also helps make the training session more interesting.

Having an arena with flat ground, sounding board, and cones allows the horse to be trained in different exercises, which improve responsiveness, balance, and collection. This space also may be used for showing horses to visitors and buyers.

Pasos del Cielo Ranch, Anthony, FL. Photo courtesy of Allen and Glenna Struthers.

INSURANCE AND LIABILITY

Because facilities for horses are expensive, the farm owner should consider investing in an insurance policy to cover, at a minimum, the most valuable buildings and equipment. The insurance should cover any loss due to theft, fire, or natural disaster. The policy should include liability coverage for possible employee or visitor accidents. If outside horses visit the farm, the liability insurance should cover accidents or death. Additionally, workman's compensation insurance should be considered for farm employees.

CHAPTER 10

HEALTH BASICS

This chapter does not intend to be a veterinary handbook, however, it does provide guidance for keeping the Paso Fino horse in good health, with the assistance of a veterinarian.

Maintaining healthy horses is not based on luck, but rather on systematic care of the animals to prevent health problems and to assure early attention to emergencies. Although having a "health maintenance plan" means investing time and money, the advantages are obvious:

- Reduces long-term expenses (treatment of a sick horse may cost a great deal of money).
- Helps to assure optimal physical condition of the horses (growth, development, weight gain, reproductive efficiency) and work capability.
- Reduces stress and enhances overall management of the farm.

THE HEALTH MAINTENANCE PLAN

A successful health maintenance plan consists, at a minimum, of the following elements:

- Having a proper feeding plan, based on the horse's needs, that promotes a good body condition index (score), increases immunity against microbial diseases, and prevents metabolic problems.
- Reducing grain supplements for any horse requiring rest (due to lameness or another health problem) in order to avoid metabolic problems.
- Allowing the horse to exercise freely in the sunshine, which increases the metabolism, permits synthesis of vitamin D, promotes stronger bones and legs, builds endurance, and helps mental health.

- Designing a vaccination program, with the assistance of a veterinarian, as well as a plan for controlling internal and external parasites, assuring appropriate preventative measures are taken.
- Training all personnel working with the horses to identify health problems by recognizing symptoms of disease or behavioral changes, and training one person, at a minimum, to administer first aid until a veterinarian arrives, preventing further serious complications.
- Scheduling an annual veterinary examination, thus, solving health problems before they become serious. The physical examination should be thorough, and subsequent diagnostic tests performed when abnormalities are suspected or identified.
- Maintaining updated records of preventative actions and treatments, providing baseline information on each horse.
- Having available the emergency telephone numbers of at least two veterinarians in the area, assuring that, in emergencies, help may be contacted quickly.
- Reading labels of all medicines, before using them; thus, knowing the proper dosage, method of administration, cautions, expiration date, and storage conditions.

VITAL SIGNS

This term refers to the pulse rate, respiratory rate, and temperature a horse exhibits at rest. The normal vital signs for a Paso Fino horse at rest and the way to determine them are as follows:

- **CARDIAC RATE**: The heart beat rate (or "cardiac rate") is 36 to 45 beats per minute in adult horses and 60 to 90 beats in nursing foals. Cardiac rate should be taken by using a stethoscope that is placed on the ribs behind the left elbow. Another way to judge the cardiac rate is by taking the **PULSE** (the immediate reaction in the arteries after blood is pumped by the heart). The pulse may be taken by placing one or two fingertips on the inside of the mandible, or on the groove under the tail.

- **RESPIRATORY RATE**: 8 to 20 breaths per minute is normal. Pain, fever, or exercise may increase the respiratory rate. Using a stethoscope to listen to the "wind pipe" (trachea) is the most accurate way to determine the respiratory rate. Additionally, counting the movements of the flanks and/or the nostrils, when the horse is excited, may determine the respiratory rate.

- **RECTAL TEMPERATURE**: 99 to101°F. This may be determined by inserting the bulb end and ¾ length of a large animal thermometer (mercury or digital) into the horse's rectum, while its tail is raised. The bulb end of the thermometer should be lubricated with mineral oil before being inserted into the horse's rectum. The thermometer should be held in place with two fingers for two minutes. After the horse's temperature is determined, the thermometer should be cleaned with alcohol, especially the part introduced into the rectum.

Although a few individual variations of these ranges may occur, vital signs are generally very predictable in the same horse. Therefore, reviewing the horse's vital signs is the first step in determining the animal's condition, either during a regular examination or during diagnosis of a disease. If the horse is sick, the vital signs may increase or decrease, depending on the body systems involved. Dramatic changes in vital signs, when the horse is resting, are considered abnormal and require the attention of a veterinarian.

Abnormal vital signs in an adult horse at rest are a cardiac rate (or pulse) greater than 48 beats per minute; a respiratory rate greater than 30 breaths per minute; a rectal temperature above 102.5° F; and a cardiac rate (or pulse) with an equal or lower rate than the respiratory rate.

Vital signs may change due to several factors:

- The three vital signs increase during exercise, but they become normal after two hours of rest.
- Hot weather causes the vital signs to increase, although they usually stay within the normal range; cold weather (not due to greater altitude) makes the vital signs decrease slightly.
- Cardiac rate (and, therefore, pulse) and respiratory rate may increase to the highest normal range, due to excitement or altitude (more than 4,700 feet above sea level).

DEHYDRATION

Dehydration is a clear sign of a problem in a horse. Dehydration occurs when fluid from the blood goes into the tissues in order to compensate for a loss of fluids.

Cause: Dehydration may be caused by diarrhea, diminished drinking of water, excessive sweating (see Chapter 12: "The horse as an athlete"), colic, or peritonitis.

Symptoms: After a loss of fluids, the horse appears very thirsty and drinks more water (if available). Depression and weakness are often symptoms of severe dehydration, sometimes accompanied by increased cardiac rate (or pulse) of 55 beats per minute or more. A veterinarian will diagnose a horse's dehydration from a blood test, that shows whether the PCV (Packed Cell Volume) and total protein are increased.

The "skin pinch test" may also reveal if a horse is dehydrated. This test consists of picking up a fold of the horse's skin from its neck with the finger tips. If the skin fold returns to place immediately, the horse is not dehydrated. Conversely, if the tissues have lost more than ten percent of body fluid, the skin fold will take some seconds to return to its original position. In this case, the horse requires prompt attention from a veterinarian to administer intravenous fluids.

Checking the "capillary refill time" is an additional method to detect not only dehydration, but also circulatory problems. This test consists of pressing a finger firmly on the horse's pink- to red- colored upper gum, for a few seconds, until that spot becomes creamy-colored. Once the pressure is released, the creamy-colored spot should turn pink- to red- colored in no longer than four seconds, if the horse is in normal condition. Conversely, if the creamy-colored spot takes longer to turn pink-to red-colored after the finger pressure is released, this is a sign of a problem that may include dehydration.

MEDICAL SUPPLIES FOR FIRST AID

A veterinarian may provide a list of essential first-aid supplies and the proper way to use them. Some suggested supplies are listed below:

- **Disposable syringes** of different sizes (3, 6, 12, and 20 c.c.) and **needles**, for trained personnel only.
- **Latex examination gloves** for cleaning wounds, applying topical medications, etc.
- **Anti-inflammatory** oral tablets or paste.

  Note: Some anti-inflammatory drugs have restrictions for pregnant mares.
- **Anti-spasmodic** oral paste for initial treatment of colic.
- **Pain killer** medication.
- **Iodine tincture** for treating both the newborn foal's navel and some hoof diseases.
- **Betadine** soap and solution, as a disinfectant for skin diseases and instruments.
- **Antimicrobial ointment** or **spray** for wounds.
- **Insect repellent** for keeping insects off the horse.
- **Sanitary pads** for pressing against bleeding wounds.
- **Sterile gauze** for placement over wounds.
- **Flexible cohesive bandage**, such as Co-Flex or Vet-Wrap.
- **Rolled cotton**, either for cleaning the injection sites or padding for bandages.
- **Large animal thermometer**.
- **Mineral oil** or **Vaseline** for lubricating a thermometer.
- **Rubbing alcohol** for cleaning the site of an injection or a thermometer.
- **Epsom salt** for use as a laxative or heat therapy.
- **Scissors**.
- **Adhesive tape**.
- **Blankets** sized for Paso Fino horses (see Chapter 13: "Tack and attire").
- **Protective hoof boots** for keeping hooves clean while treating hoof infections.
- **Calibrated horse weight tape** for estimating the horse's weight before drug applications.
- **Regular towels** for drying the newborn foal and for applying heat therapy.
- **Paper towels** for drying and cleaning.

INJECTIONS

Vaccines and some drugs may be injected by means of a syringe and a needle, but only by properly trained personnel. Disposable syringes and needles are highly recommended. Once used, they should be disposed of properly and kept away from children. The size of the syringe must be appropriate for the amount of drug that is injected. The needle should have the correct caliber (in terms of length and diameter) for the type of injection and viscosity of the drug. Three types of injections are given to horses:

- **Subcutaneous** (**SC**): The product is injected under the skin of the neck. For this, a fold of skin is lifted to insert the needle (already attached to the syringe), making sure it is not inserted into the muscle.
- **Intramuscular** (**IM**): The product is injected into a big muscle. Options include the muscle located 4 inches behind and below the hip bone, the largest muscle at either side of the neck (usually under the mane), or the rear muscle of the thigh.
- **Intravenous** (**IV**): The product is injected into the horse's jugular vein in the neck.

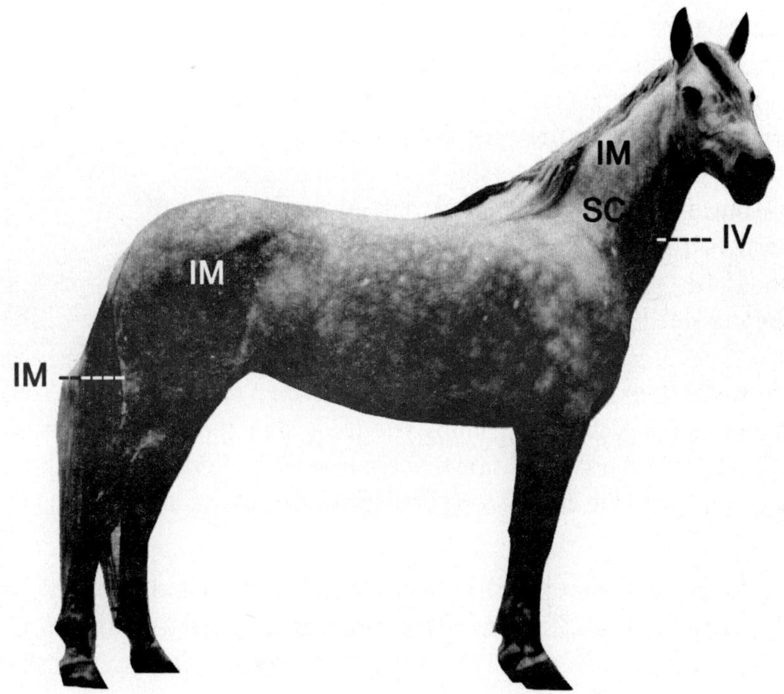

Sites of injection: Subcutaneous (***SC***)*, Intramuscular* (***IM***)*, Intravenous* (***IV***)*.*

BLOOD TEST

A blood test allows the veterinarian to diagnose diseases or alterations to the horse's physiology. The veterinarian takes the blood sample from the horse's jugular vein. A blood test may be recommended for the following reasons:

- To count the red blood cells (RBC) and the white blood cells (WBC) in order to determine several blood cell diseases and/or infections.
- To determine the amount of hemoglobin to verify anemia.
- To determine the packed cell volume (PCV) to verify dehydration.

- To detect diseases in plasma (infectious equine anemia, for example).
- To determine enzyme and/or hormone levels in plasma.
- To detect the presence of prohibited substances (dope)

METHODS OF RESTRAINT

During examination of a horse, injection, rectal palpation, shoeing, taking a blood sample, giving a dewormer, or other procedures, a method of restraint often is necessary for the safety of both the person and the horse. The most common methods of horse restraint are as follows:

- For giving an oral drug or a dewormer, one person should use a halter and a lead line to control the horse. Injections in the neck (SC, IM, or IV) may also be given to some horses by using only a halter and a lead line for control.
- For a routine examination and taking a blood sample, enlisting the help of an assistant, to control the horse with a halter and a lead line, makes it easier and more practical. Sometimes, a lead line ending with a chain is used for better restraint; the chain is passed through the left ring of the halter's bosal, over the nose, then through the right ring of the bosal, and finally attached to the right ring above the halter's cheek piece. Next, the chain is placed either over the nose or under the upper lip (on the upper gum), and the lead line is used to control the horse. 
- Tying the horse to one post, or cross-tying the horse between two posts, is the most common way to control a Paso Fino for grooming, clipping, bathing, trimming/shoeing, giving intramuscular injections in the hindquarters, and cleaning a wound. Additionally, some strong, spooky horses should be tied/cross-tied for simple activities, such as giving an oral drug or a dewormer, giving injections in the neck, and taking a blood sample.
- For very difficult cases, grasping the upper lip either with a "metal lip twitch" (which should be tied to the halter) or with a "stick twitch" made of a cord (or a chain) attached to a stick, provides good control. However, these twitching tools never must be applied for more than five minutes because of the risk of damage to the lip tissue.
- Using hobbles to prevent the horse from kicking (during rectal palpation/ultrasound, examining/treating a hind leg, or breeding). This is usually enough restraint in most cases (see Chapter 13: "Tack and attire").
- Using a palpation chute will be more efficient and safer during rectal palpation/ultrasound, artificial insemination, vaginal examination, and embryo transfer technology. However, a palpation chute is not recommended for other practices, such as injections, cleaning wounds, etc. because it may be dangerous for both the person and the horse.
- Giving an intravenous tranquilizer for controlling a horse when the restraint methods above do not work.

Note: Because cartilage is not as hard as bone, it is not recommended that foals be held by their ears as a method of restraint. The ear's shape may be affected and the young horse may develop a fear of being touched on the ears.

COMMON DISEASES OF THE PASO FINO HORSE

Most diseases and parasites affecting Paso Fino horses are explained in the following pages of this chapter.

- **FEEDING AND METABOLIC DISORDERS**: Improper feeding and changing the natural diet of this constant grazer may lead to several disorders that may cause death.

  - **COLIC**: This is the term used for any pain in the abdomen that may be caused by digestive or non-digestive causes.

    Causes: Digestive causes of colic are eating moldy or contaminated feed, lack of fiber in the diet, working the horse immediately after eating a full meal, allowing a ′still hot′ horse to drink a lot of water or eat grain after working, sudden feed changes (either in schedule or kind of feed), eating an excessive amount of hay/grass, having a high content of potassium (K) in the diet, or drinking contaminated water. Also, an intestinal impaction/blockage may be caused by feeding the horse hay comprised of old plants with a high content of lignin instead of usable fiber (cellulose and hemicellulose), missing water for several hours, improper chewing of food (due to teeth that are in bad condition), eating sand or another type of soil, or eating bedding shavings.

    Non-digestive causes of colic include intestinal spasms caused by worm blockage of blood vessels that supply blood to the intestine, kidney problems, urinary obstruction, or a mare's intestinal discomfort during the last months of pregnancy or after foaling.

    Symptoms: Poor or no appetite, nervousness, pawing at the ground, abundant sweating for apparently no reason, frequent lying down and getting up, looking at or biting one side of the abdomen, raising a hind leg with discomfort, and/or violently rolling on the ground. In addition, when a horse is showing signs of colic, it usually has not urinated or defecated for a long time.

    First aid: Calling a veterinarian; putting the horse on a halter and lead rope to keep the animal from rolling, eating, or drinking water; giving the horse a pain killer/anti-spasmodic drug either in paste form (by the mouth) or by intravenous injection; and leading the horse at a walk for about 30 minutes.

    Treatment: The person attending to the horse should explain to the veterinarian all the signs of colic observed, the last feeding time, kind of food offered, last time the horse was dewormed, etc. Based on that information and a complete examination (that may include rectal palpation), the veterinarian may prescribe different treatments, such as giving more analgesic and anti-spasmodic medicine, administering mineral oil through a stomach tube, giving anti-gas medication, re-hydrating the horse, administering an enema, or recommending surgery.

  - **LAMINITIS**: This serious inflammation of the hoof's sensitive laminae causes acute pain to the affected foot. Although any leg may be affected, front legs are more commonly affected than hind legs.

    Causes: Dietary causes include overfeeding grain to an overweight horse with low physical activity, maintaining an overweight horse in a very rich pasture during the spring or summer season (due to a high content of sugar in the young plants), having a horse that eats an excess of grain (e.g., by breaking into the feed room), or sudden feeding changes. Other causes include colic that lasts a long time, retained placenta after foaling (in mares), an exhausting workout, or working an un-shod Paso Fino horse on a hard surface (such as concrete), for a long period of time.

If a horse with laminitis is not attended to promptly within the first 36 hours, many sensitive laminae die and separate from the hoof wall because of tension put on the the deep flexor tendon; thus, causing the coffin bone to rotate downward. This condition of phalanx rotation is known as **founder** (or chronic laminitis) and may affect the horse for the rest of its life. A severe case of white line disease (see "Lameness" below) also may lead to a similar rotation of the coffin bone.

Symptoms: General stiffness of the legs, refusing to walk due to pain, and/or trying to lean back on the heels; increased pulse, especially in the affected foot; increased respiratory rate; sweating and, sometimes, fever. An affected hoof is usually warmer than the rest. If two or more feet are affected, the horse prefers to lie down.

A foundered hoof (chronic laminitis) exhibits several changes, such as irregular rings on the hoof wall and a curled toe; additionally, the sole becomes thinner and is either flat or convex (instead of concave).

First aid: Discontinue feeding the horse (including grazing), put the affected leg in cold/iced water up to the carpus (knee) or hock, and call a veterinarian.

Treatment: Proper diagnosis and treatment of laminitis, within 12 to 36 hours after inflammation of the sensitive laminae has begun, may prevent the occurrence of founder (rotation of the coffin bone). The treatment includes analgesic, anti-inflammatory, and vessel-dilator drugs. Some cases require passing mineral oil through a stomach tube. The horse should be kept in a sand floor stall with a soft bed of shavings. Cold therapy on the affected foot helps to reduce pain. Feeding should consist of grass (green or dry) and water. X-rays of the foot help to identify any degree of rotation of the coffin bone. Therapeutic shoeing, combined with the use to either a rubber frog pad or certain acrylic resins, helps prevent rotation.

- **AZOTURIA**: This condition is also known as **tying up**, **paralytic myoglobinuria**, and **Monday morning disease**.

  Cause: Azoturia is associated with everyday hardworking horses whose diet is richly supplemented with soluble carbohydrates (grains and/or sugars). When one of these horses is supplemented with the same amount of carbohydrates during one or two days of rest, the big muscles keep storing large amounts of glycogen. Then, when the horse needs energy for a highly demanding physical activity (during the first day of work), there is a rapid anaerobic use of the abundant glycogen, and this produces a great amount of lactic acid.

  Symptoms: After some exercise, the acidity hurts and damages the muscle fibers, causing severe pain that makes the horse sweat and be very anxious. Due to the rigidity and pain of the muscles of the loins and the legs, the horse may refuse to move. Additionally, the horse's urine may become either difficult to pass or very dark-colored (brown).

Prevention: Reducing grain supplementation and/or sugar/molasses during days of rest is the primary method of prevention. Cooling the horse down at the end of a work session allows the metabolism to consume the substances produced during exercise.

First aid: Calling a veterinarian, keeping the horse from walking, keeping the horse warm with a blanket, and withholding grain until full recuperation.

Treatment: The veterinarian may confirm the diagnosis of azoturia with a blood test to determine if there are high levels of enzymes caused by muscle cell damage. The treatment consists of complete rest, a low soluble carbohydrate diet, giving anti-inflammatory and diuretic drugs, and offering either electrolytes or iodized salt. Some daily walking sessions are needed, depending on the improvement. The horse should only return to normal work and diet after total recuperation.

- **BIGHEAD DISEASE**: This is a nutritional disease secondary to hyperparathyroidism, also called **bran disease** or **Miller's disease**.

  Cause: This is a progressive disease that gradually makes the skeleton weaker because of a phosphorus and calcium imbalance. It is caused by excessive intake of phosphorus, indirectly given to a horse in grains that, in general, are rich in this mineral. When phosphorus goes into the blood, the horse uses the amount needed for normal functions; the excess is later excreted and joined to calcium that is circulating in the blood. When the calcium level in the blood decreases, the parathyroid gland releases a hormone (parathyroid-hormone) that allows calcium to be freed from the bones, until a normal level of the mineral is regained in the blood. The daily loss of calcium makes the bones soft and weak.

  Symptoms: Although this disease develops in the whole skeleton, the main signs are visible only when the facial bones become enlarged and rounded. In addition, temporary or permanent lameness may occur.

  Prevention: The horse needs a normal calcium-phosphorus ratio of 1.5-1 to 3.5-1 in the whole diet, depending on the physiological stage and physical activity.

  Treatment: In young animals suffering from this disease, the facial bones may be improved with a high quality calcium and magnesium supplement and reduction of phosphorus in the diet over a period of a few months.

- **ANEMIA**: This condition refers to a deficiency of hemoglobin and there also may be an associated reduction of red blood cells. It negatively affects the horse's capability to work because hemoglobin is the red pigment in red blood cells that transports oxygen to all the cells of the body. In addition, the anemic horse has a reduced metabolism, which affects all its vital functions.

  Causes: The nutritional causes of anemia are related to a severe deficiency of some of the following nutrients: iron, vitamins (E, B6, and B12), copper, and protein. Other causes of anemia are previous hemorrhage, infestation of adult roundworms in the intestines, or a systematic destruction of red blood cells in the body caused by equine infectious anemia disease and/or equine piroplasmosis (also called babesiosis).

Symptoms: The anemic horse has a reduced appetite, low weight, depression, and low energy. The membranes of the mouth (including the gums) and eyes become light pink or yellow-colored when anemia is advanced.

Prevention: Having a proper nutritional plan, controlling internal parasites, and preventing equine infectious anemia and equine piroplasmosis.

Treatment: For proper diagnosis of anemia, the veterinarian takes a blood sample to verify whether the hemoglobin level is low. The treatment for anemia (not caused by equine infectious anemia or equine piroplasmosis) consists of deworming the horse and providing a balanced diet that includes protein, iron, vitamins (E, B6, and B12), and copper. The anemic horse should not be worked for a few weeks until full recuperation, but should be turned out in a good pasture a few hours a day.

- **GASTRIC ULCERS**: Some acid is secreted in a horse's stomach at all times. This is not a common problem for wild equines and domestic horses kept in well-cared for pastures because they may graze at any time and, therefore, any acid acts on the foodstuff, but does not irritate the stomach walls.

Causes: Stabled horses, and those horses kept in corrals with no grass, are susceptible to gastric ulcers because they are fed pre-scheduled meals every day, sometimes making them spend too long with nothing to eat. Thus, the presence of acid in the stomach, in the absence of food, irritates the stomach walls, which later may develop ulcers. Overcrowded pastures/corrals may also cause gastric ulcers, especially among the weakest horses of the group, including nursing foals.

Horses in training, or active during the show season, are susceptible to developing stomach ulcers because of stress. Additionally, a heavy infestation of stomach worms may cause gastric ulcers. A nursing foal may develop gastric ulcers, caused by a depleted appetite due to another disease. The stress of being weaned will also cause gastric ulcers in some foals.

Symptoms: The most common signs of gastric ulcers are decreased appetite, depression, weight loss, and grinding the teeth. Sometimes, gastric ulcers also may cause colic. For proper diagnosis of gastric ulcers, a veterinarian should examine the horse's stomach using an endoscope.

A foal with a gastric ulcer exhibits additional symptoms, such as having a periodic light colic (during which the foal rolls around to find a comfortable position on its back, with its legs in the air, to avoid pain), attempting to chew while not eating, and having diarrhea. A foal with gastric ulcers also looks under-developed and in poor condition.

Prevention: Every horse should spend some time in a good pasture every day. When stabled, the horse needs free access to good forage. Proper deworming is another measure to prevent ulcers caused by worms.

Treatment: The sick horse should be placed in a good pasture to graze for 45 to 60 days in order to allow the ulcers to heal. If the horse's diet includes grain, it must be provided in an independent feeder, where other horses cannot compete to eat it. Administering specific drugs, daily, in paste form is part of the treatment for equine gastric ulcers.

- **STUNTED** or **SLOW GROWTH**: A young Paso Fino needs to grow at a proper rate in order to reach the minimum height of the breed standard. During the first year of life, the young horse reaches 90% of its adult height.

  Causes: Stunted or slow growth of a young horse mainly is caused by improper nutrition (excess or lack of nutrients), disease, or incorrect management programs. In addition, some Paso Fino bloodlines transmit this characteristic to the offspring.

  Symptoms: The young Paso Fino horse looks shorter than others of the same age, and its height is inadequate for its age.

  Prevention: Proper nutrition and management of the young horse promotes the growth and development of all tissues in the correct order: nervous, skeletal, muscular, integumentary, circulatory, digestive, urinary, respiratory, endocrine, reproductive, and fatty.

  Treatment: When a young horse is not growing/developing at a proper rate, it needs special treatment consisting of a very well-balanced diet, based on highly digestible sources of nutrients, accompanied by all the proper daily management practices. This treatment encourages the horse's metabolism to start "compensatory growth," allowing the young animal to reach maximum size, according to its genotype.

  Unfortunately, when a young horse is not growing at the expected rate, some owners inject them with anabolic steroids, which actually do not help the horse to grow; furthermore, treating fillies with anabolic steroids may alter their behavior in a negative way.

- **POISONING BY PLANTS**: Horses living in pastures without proper weed control are at risk of eating a variety of potentially toxic plants.

  Cause: Horses in the pasture carefully choose the most palatable plants to eat. Having too many horses in a pasture, that cannot produce enough good forage, may cause the animals to eat toxic plants. In addition, a hungry horse (for example, after a long trip or a long work time), put in a pasture with weeds, may eat toxic plants just because of eating too quickly. Sometimes curiosity causes the horse to eat toxic plants.

  Symptoms: Poisonous plants cause diverse kinds of damage to the horse: systematic destruction of red blood cells; gastrointestinal tract irritation (that may lead to death); diarrhea that may contain some blood; damage to the liver; severe damage to the nervous system that may lead to death; heart failure; photosensitization; difficulty breathing; laminitis; and poisoning and death caused by toxic substances (alkaloids, cyanide, glycosides, selenium, etc.).

  Prevention: Asking the County's Agricultural Extension Office or the State University Agronomy Faculty/Department about poisonous (toxic) plants for horses in the area where the farm is located, learning how to recognize those toxic plants and the problems they cause for horses, and having proper pasture care and weed control, including under the fence lines.

  First aid: If any abnormal symptom is observed in a horse grazing in the pasture, look for any strange plants in the field (and under the fence lines), and call a veterinarian.

- **FOAL DIARRHEA**: This is when the foal's feces have a liquid consistency, which may lead to dehydration.

  Causes and symptoms: Diarrhea may be caused by excessive milk intake, when the foal's dam is a high milk producer; however, this does not affect the foal seriously. Foal heat diarrhea commonly occurs within seven to fifteen days after the foal is born (which coincides with the mare's foal heat), but it normally stops after three to four days.

  Virus is another common cause of diarrhea in a foal, which mostly affects stabled foals at one to three months of age. This type of diarrhea usually lasts three days. Other signs accompanying viral diarrhea are low appetite, depression, and fever, in some cases. To prevent viral diarrhea from reoccurring, the foaling stall must be disinfected before using it again (all stalls should be disinfected every two to four weeks). In addition, worm infestation by *Strongyloides westeri* and/or *Parascaris equorum* also may cause diarrhea in a foal.

  Treatment: The first method for stopping diarrhea consists of giving the foal an oral medicine for that purpose. For reducing discomfort and fly attack, the foal's buttocks, anal region, and hocks should be washed with warm water and a mild soap, and then rinsed gently. A veterinarian should attend to the foal when fever is a complementary symptom of diarrhea, the foal presents signs of dehydration, or diarrhea persists for more than five days.

- **RESPIRATORY DISORDERS**: The horse's respiratory system may be affected by both pathogens and external agents that may cause severe diseases.

  - **EQUINE INFLUENZA**: This is the most common infectious respiratory disease of horses, which may be compared to influenza in humans (flu).

    Cause: Different types of viruses that may be transmitted by inhalation of the aerosol form of the virus, either directly from a sick horse, or from particles left by a sick horse.

    Symptoms: Fever (102.5° F or higher), low appetite, depression, increased respiratory rate, clear nasal discharge, eye mucous membrane inflammation, and sometimes a dry cough. Although the viral disease usually is not fatal, poorly attended or unattended horses may have complications, due to secondary bacterial invasions by *Streptococcus* or *Staphylococcus*. If there is a secondary infection with bacteria, the clear nasal discharge becomes yellow-green, and thicker.

    Prevention: Injecting a vaccine at four to six months of age, and giving a second dose 45 days later. Repeating vaccinations for all the horses on the farm every six months also is recommended. Isolating new horses coming to the farm is a complementary preventive measure to avoid spreading the virus from any infected animal.

    Treatment: The sick horse must rest and be kept in an isolated and ventilated stall, but protected from the wind, for three to six weeks. During cold weather (winter), using a blanket on the horse helps to keep it warm, especially at night. Analgesics and bronchodilators are given to reduce fever and cough; additionally, some veterinarians prescribe antibiotics (such as penicillin) for preventing complications from a secondary bacterial infection. Feeding green grass, cut carrots, and a mass of wet grain improves the appetite.

- **STRANGLES**: Although in its early stages strangles may be confused with influenza, strangles is an extremely contagious infection that soon causes inflammation of certain areas around the horse's jaw.

  Cause: A respiratory infection caused by *Streptococcus equi* (bacteria), that is spread by infected horses through their nasal discharges in waterers, feeders, pastures, stalls, and fences.

  Symptoms: The first symptoms of strangles are the same as with influenza. The main differential sign of strangles occurs four to eight days after the first symptoms appear, in which the lymph nodes at the throat and/or under the lower jaw become abscessed and filled with thick pus. This causes the larynx and pharynx to become inflamed, making it difficult for the horse to breathe and swallow. A few days later, a purulent discharge comes out through the nostrils. Some lymph nodes may burst through the skin, letting the pus drain. In severe cases, some lymph nodes in other body areas may abscess.

  Prevention: Disinfecting the facilities, especially if any infected horse was located there; isolating for four to six weeks all new horses coming to the farm; and giving a nasal vaccine to all horses once a year, starting at three to four months of age.

  Treatment: Any infected horse must be isolated in a stall and treated with penicillin by a veterinarian who also should design a plan to avoid spreading strangles. Offering feed free of dust is recommended. If abscesses rupture, or the veterinarian opens them to let the pus drain, daily disinfection of the wounds with Betadine solution is necessary.

- **PNEUMONIA**: A respiratory disease that causes an inflammation of the lungs.

  Causes: A weak, sick horse living in a cold, windy place is vulnerable to pneumonia caused by pathogens (such as a virus, bacteria). For example, *Rhodococcus equi* is a bacteria that causes severe pneumonia in foals. It produces abscesses in the lungs and requires a long treatment plan with a specific antibiotic. In addition, any improperly attended horse suffering a respiratory infection may develop pneumonia.

  Aspiration pneumonia is caused by the inhalation of liquids (or saliva), worm larvae, or food particles into the lungs. Several circumstances may cause aspiration pneumonia: an oral liquid medication improperly given (dewormer or vitamins); a medicine (such as mineral oil) deposited into the lungs instead of the stomach by means of a stomach tube incorrectly placed; inhaled worm larvae; or saliva/mucous passed into the lungs when a horse suffering a respiratory disease coughs, while being unable to put its head down (because of the way its head is tied).

  Symptoms: Loss of appetite; loss of weight; painful, dry cough; very difficult breathing (which increases the horse's respiratory rate); nasal discharge; and temperature of 102° F or higher. In addition, congestive heart failure and ventral edema (soft swelling at the girth or abdomen area caused by fluid retention) may occur in severe cases.

  Prevention: Several practices may help to reduce/prevent pneumonia:

  - Guaranteeing a proper feeding program for all horses, including adequate milk intake for nursing foals.
  - Having a proper vaccination and deworming program.

- o Avoiding dusty hay, grain, and bedding material, because dust may easily irritate the lungs.
- o Regularly disinfecting facilities.
- o Properly administering oral drugs.

Treatment: The veterinarian may hear congestion in the lungs by using a stethoscope on the horse's thorax, which is the best way to diagnose pneumonia. The sick horse must be kept warm, protected from wind, rested, and fed green grass or wet hay and wet grain. Treatment with antibiotics is effective when pneumonia is caused by bacteria. Unfortunately, viral and aspiration pneumonia are often fatal.

- **EQUINE HERPES VIRUS** or **RHINOPNEUMONITIS**: Horses may contract different diseases caused by the herpes virus.

Cause: From several types of equine herpes virus, two types, EHV-1 and EHV-4, cause the most serious problems for horses of all ages (not people or other animals). Equine herpes virus may be transmitted by direct contact with a sick animal or a deceased fetus (killed by the disease) or its placenta; fly/mosquito bites following their ingestion of blood from a sick horse; sharing facilities or tack with sick animals; or by transporting the infectious agent in vehicles, clothes, boots, tools, etc.

Symptoms: Horses infected with EHV-4 have symptoms similar to influenza: high fever of about 105° F, watery nasal discharge (if there is not a secondary bacterial infection), and, sometimes, a dry cough. These symptoms may lead to abortion in weak, pregnant mares. Although this form of the disease usually is not fatal in adult horses, it causes a high rate of mortality in young horses (up to one year old), especially when they are not attended to properly.

EHV-1 not only affects horses in the respiratory form (similar to EHV-4), but it also may cause abortion to infected pregnant mares, commonly during the last trimester of pregnancy. If a foal is born, it dies soon after birth. Although less common, the EHV-1 neurological form causes a gradual loss of coordination, followed by paralysis and death.

Note: Due to the respiratory symptoms caused by EHV-1 and EHV-4, this disease is also known as "Rhinopneumonitis."

Prevention: Foals at three to four months of age should be vaccinated with EHV-1 and EHV-4 vaccines and re-vaccinated 45 days after. Horses of all ages should be re-vaccinated once or twice a year as needed, depending on specific recommendations, and whether there is an outbreak in the area. Show horses should be re-vaccinated more often with EHV-1 and EHV-4 vaccines, ideally every three months during the competition season. Pregnant mares should be vaccinated at five, seven, and nine months of pregnancy with EHV-1 vaccine.

Diagnosis: Any form of the equine herpes virus can be detected in the laboratory from a blood sample of an infected horse. After abortion, the herpes virus can be found in the placenta or the remains of the fetus.

Treatment: A horse with respiratory symptoms should be isolated in a warm stall for three weeks and kept free of dusty feed/bedding material. The veterinarian may recommend the use of antibiotics to control and prevent a secondary bacterial infection.

If a mare aborts, a veterinarian should be called to determine if the abortion is caused by EHV-1. Likewise, if a horse shows neurological signs (loss of coordination) a veterinarian should be called to determine the cause, the treatment, and the additional precautions to be taken to avoid spreading of the disease.

- **HEAVES**: This disease, mainly present in stalled horses, also is called **chronic obstructive pulmonary disease (COPD)**.

  Causes: Heaves is generally caused by feeding horses either moldy and/or dusty hay, or very dusty grain. In addition, dusty bedding in the stall may cause the problem. Constriction of bronchioles keeps the lungs from working efficiently because of an allergic reaction to dust and/or mold.

  Symptoms: The main symptom is a constant, or intermittent, cough that makes the horse unable to work. Sometimes there is a clear, watery discharge through the nostrils. The sick horse may start to lose weight because of the discomfort from coughing and the increased efforts to breathe.

  Note: Infestation with lungworms has the same symptoms as heaves.

  Prevention: Avoiding the odor of ammonia from urine and eliminating dusty/moldy feed and bedding.

  Treatment: Call a veterinarian if a horse has an acute attack of cough. When properly diagnosed in an early stage of heaves, most horses affected by heaves recuperate in one to four weeks after the causes of the allergy are removed. For faster recuperation, a sick horse should be moved to a pasture full of good grass. If there is no pasture available, all sources of dust and mold should be avoided, either in the stall or in the corral.

• **MICROBIAL ILLNESSES**: Horses may be infected by several pathogens which may lead to death.

- **EQUINE INFECTIOUS ANEMIA (EIA)**: This untreatable disease only affects the equine species and is also known as **swamp fever**.

  Cause: A *Retroviridae* virus that is transmitted from one infected horse to others by secretions, such as saliva and nasal discharges; blood passed by some vectors like mosquitoes and blood-sucking flies; sexual contact; and sharing elements (such as tack, needles, syringes, and dental floats) between EIA carriers and healthy horses.

  Symptoms: A horse with the **acute** form of EIA exhibits depression, high fever (above 104° F), low appetite, weakness, loss of weight, and a watery discharge from the nostrils and eyes. Other signs, evident when the red blood cells start to be destroyed rapidly, include a ventral edema, increased respiratory rate, and more frequent urination. Although these symptoms finally may cause the horse's death, the already weakened horse easily may be infected by pathogens that will accelerate its death.

  A horse with the **chronic** form of EIA may not die from the disease. The horse exhibits intermittent attacks of much less severe symptoms of the disease, but seems to recuperate for periods of time. However, a horse with this condition is a silent, dangerous, carrier of the virus and is able to infect other horses.

Prevention: Because there is no vaccine available for prevention, all horses must be tested for this disease (Coggins test), which is determined through a blood test. Horses that test positive, usually are euthanized to avoid spread of the disease.

A current, negative Coggins test is required for horse transportation throughout the United States; for exportation, importation, and showing; and for entering any horse farm/facility. In most States, a negative Coggins test is valid for one year, but specific rules of the State where the farm is located, or where the horse is going to be transported, should be reviewed. In addition, a current negative Coggins test for both stallions and mares is required before breeding using direct mounting.

<u>Note</u>: There is no effective treatment for infected horses.

- **EQUINE VIRAL ENCEPHALOMYELITIS**: Also known as **sleeping sickness**, produces a severe brain inflammation (technically defined as encephalitis). Three forms of the disease are Eastern (EEE), Western (WEE), and Venezuelan (VEE).

  Cause: Three different types of *Togaviridae* viruses may cause the disease, not only in the equine species, but also in humans. Each type of virus is transmitted by different vectors, especially mosquitoes and less commonly by other blood-sucking insects. The common intermediary hosts of the virus are small wild animals (such as birds, snakes, frogs, raccoons, etc.), which actually are not affected by the disease. Once a vector sucks the blood from any reservoir host, it easily may transmit the virus to a human or to a healthy horse.

  Symptoms: The initial symptoms are depression, intermittent fever (103° to 106° F), decreased appetite, loss of weight, weakness after a period of excitement, stiffness, and lack of muscular coordination. Thereafter, the horse relaxes its lips and tongue, keeps its head down, starts walking in circles (as if it were blind), and exhibits drowsiness. Before dying (about four to five days after the first symptoms appear), the horse has severe paralysis of the lips, tongue, pharynx, larynx, and legs. Proper diagnosis must be made by a veterinarian, through verifying the symptoms of the disease and the presence of antibodies in a blood sample. When equine viral encephalomyelitis is the suspected cause of a horse's death, the body (and any fluids) should be burned and buried.

  Prevention: The combined vaccine of EEE and WEE should be given to all horses in the United States once a year, starting at three to four months of age. The use of insecticides helps to control mosquito attacks. A VEE vaccine must be given only if any cases of the disease occur in the area.

  <u>Note</u>: VEE is the most common type of disease in South America (such as Colombia and Venezuela), and annual vaccination of all equines in these countries is mandatory.

  Treatment: Although there is no current treatment for viruses, some sick horses with any type of equine viral encephalomyelitis survive with very good medical attention.

- **TETANUS**: This fatal disease (also known as **lockjaw disease**) affects the nervous system of animals and humans.

  Cause: This disease is caused by the bacteria *Clostridium tetani* that commonly is present in horse manure, in any material (bedding) or soil contaminated with manure, and in sharp, rusty pieces of metal exposed to the bacteria. Some bacteria enter the body through a surgical site that does not have proper disinfection, or a wound. Once in the body, bacteria produce a neurotoxin that causes increased muscular rigidity.

Symptoms: The first symptom is severe rigidity of the masseter muscles that prevents movements of the jaw (which gives it the name of "lockjaw disease"). Thereafter, the third eyelid covers the ocular globe and the ears appear erect. Rigidity involves other muscles progressively (neck, legs, and even tail), affecting the horse's locomotion. Death occurs from four to seven days after the first sign of disease is seen. Paralysis of all muscles involved in respiration cause the horse to asphyxiate and die.

Prevention: All horses over three months of age should be vaccinated with **tetanus toxoid** once a year. This stimulates the horse to make the tetanus antitoxin in its body. Pregnant mares should receive another dose of tetanus toxoid about 45 days before foaling. If the mare does not receive the toxoid before foaling, the newborn foal and the mare will need a **tetanus antitoxin** shot as soon as possible after foaling.

When a non-vaccinated horse is wounded, it should receive a dose (1,500 units) of tetanus antitoxin, which protects the horse against the tetanus toxin for two to four weeks. One month before any horse is having surgery, such as a castration, it should receive a dose of tetanus toxoid. However, if the horse was not vaccinated before the surgery, both tetanus antitoxin and tetanus toxoid should be injected in two different places following the surgery.

Moreover, because of the common presence of *Clostridium tetani* in the horse environment (e.g., manure), people working with equine species also should be vaccinated with tetanus toxoid every two years.

Treatment: Although the treatment is not very successful (only about 20% of sick animals being treated survive), it consists of giving a "tetanus antitoxin," and opening and severely disinfecting the wound that permitted the entry of the bacteria. Muscle relaxant drugs and tranquilizers are given. Feeding usually is through a stomach tube. Unfortunately, all untreated horses die.

- **RABIES**: Although this fatal disease is commonly associated with dogs, cats, and wild animals, it may infect all warm-blooded animals, including horses and humans.

Cause: A virus in the saliva of infected wild animals (bats, foxes, raccoons, etc.) or infected dogs and cats. The virus may be transmitted to horses or people by the bite of a sick animal. After a variable period of incubation (from one to six months), no matter where the bite occurred, the virus reaches the brain through the nerve cells. Once in the brain, the rabies virus causes death in a few days.

Symptoms: Severe difficulty swallowing water and saliva (which causes profuse drooling) and facial paralysis. Other symptoms vary from lack of coordination, blindness, and weakness to furious aggression, although this rarely occurs in horses. In some cases, however, the horse dies before showing any outward signs.

Note: Unfortunately, there is no test to diagnose rabies in live animals.

Prevention: Giving a vaccine to all horses over four to six months of age, every year, in those areas with a high incidence of rabies.

Treatment: Infected people usually are treated successfully, but not infected horses.

- **WEST NILE VIRUS (WNV)**: Because the horse's brain swells, some symptoms of this disease easily may be confused with others, such as equine encephalomyelitis and rabies.

  Cause: The virus is carried by several species of infected wild birds, including some migrating species. A mosquito becomes a vector of the virus after biting an infected bird; the mosquito then transmits the disease to a person or a horse through a bite.

  Symptoms: The most common symptoms of the disease gradually appear and include fever, loss of appetite, depression, weakness, walking in circles, difficulty swallowing, and lying down. Convulsions and coma are present before death.

  Prevention: Vaccinating all horses over three months of age, once a year, in those areas with a greater incidence of the disease; reducing mosquito attacks with repellents/insecticides; and eliminating mosquito breeding places (such as stagnant water).

- **SEPTICEMIA OF THE NEWBORN FOAL**: This severe infection of the foal may affect most of its organs and tissues. When the disease reaches one or more of the foal's joints, it is known as **joint ill**.

  Cause: This serious bacterial infection enters the body through the newborn foal's umbilical stump when it is improperly/not treated with chlorohexidine solution or tincture of 2 % to 10% iodine after birth.

  Symptoms: Fever, weakness, depression, disinterest in sucking milk, and inflammation and warmth of the umbilical stump within the first week of life. The infection progresses rapidly and reaches the gastrointestinal tract, causing diarrhea. The infection also may be spread to most internal organs and to the central nervous system. When the infection reaches one or more joints, they become warm, swollen, and painful. Some infected foals may die before showing these signs. When the foal survives this disease, the affected joint usually develops arthritis.

  Prevention: Proper disinfection of the foal's umbilical stump after birth and the following days with chlorohexidine solution or tincture of 2 % to 10% iodine (see Chapter 8: "Reproduction" - First attention to the new foal).

  Treatment: Although most foals suffering this type of infection die, the use of antibiotics helps to reduce the spread of infection through the body.

• **VACCINATION PROGRAM FOR HORSES**: A vaccine is a substance given to the horse (usually injected) to stimulate the development of antibodies (immunity) against a microbial disease. Vaccines usually are manufactured, based on the organism that produces the disease, either live-modified or dead. The vaccine also may be manufactured using specific molecules from the contagion involved.

  Although a toxoid is given to the horse to develop immunity, it is not an actual vaccine. A toxoid does not stimulate the horse to develop antibodies, but stimulates the horse to produce an antitoxin against the toxins produced by a specific microorganism. Additionally, an antitoxin may be injected in order to block serious side effects of a toxin.

  For prevention, horses must be vaccinated against some microbial diseases each year. Depending on age, physiological condition, or exposure to the disease, some horses need more than an annual vaccination.

The following table describes the complete vaccination program for horses

VACCINE/ TOXOID/ANTITOXIN	METHOD OF ADMINISTRATION	AGE AND FREQUENCY OF APPLICATION
TETANUS TOXOID	Intramuscular injection	Foal at three to four months of age and a second shot 45 days later. All horses (repeat once a year). Pregnant mares require another shot 45 days before foaling. Any horse requires a shot one month before a surgery. Non-vaccinated horses right after surgery or wound.
TETANUS ANTITOXIN	Subcutaneous or Intramuscular injection	Foal at birth and dam, if dam was not vaccinated with tetanus toxoid 45 days before foaling. Horses that were not vaccinated with tetanus toxoid, (right after surgery or being wounded).
EQUINE HERPES VIRUS or ***RHINOPNEUMONITIS*** ***(EHV-1*** and ***EHV-4)***	Intramuscular Injection	**EHV-1** and **EHV-4** vaccines: Foal at three to four months of age and a second shot 45 days later. Horses of all ages should be re-vaccinated once or twice a year. Show horses need a shot every three months during the competition season. **EHV-1** vaccine: Pregnant mares at five, seven, and nine months of pregnancy.
EQUINE ENCEPHALOMYELITIS *(*three types: ***EEE, WEE, VEE)***	Intramuscular injection	**EEE** and **WEE** shot to foal at three to four months of age and a second shot 45 days later. Repeat once a year, unless the veterinarian recommends a shot every six months, due to a prolonged season of mosquitoes in the area. **VEE** shot to all horses (only if there is a case of disease in the area). In Colombia and Venezuela (South America) vaccinating all horses against **VEE** once a year is mandatory.
EQUINE INFLUENZA	Intramuscular injection	Foal at four to six months of age and a second shot 45 days later. Repeat vaccination every six months.
STRANGLES	Nasal vaccine	Foal at three to four months of age. Repeat to all horses once a year.
WEST NILE VIRUS	Intramuscular injection	Foal at three to four months of age in those areas with greater incidence of the disease. Repeat to all horses once a year in areas with greater incidence.
RABIES	Intramuscular injection	Foal at four to six months of age. Repeat once a year only in those areas with high incidence of rabies.

Note: Vaccines may be purchased/given independently (such as tetanus toxoid, rabies, and VEE encephalomyelitis) or combined together (such as tetanus, equine influenza, and EEE -WEE encephalomyelitis).

Although vaccines are produced with the proper quality to protect the horse from these diseases, their application may not be 100% effective for several reasons:

- The horse does not respond properly to the vaccine, either because it is already infected by the disease, or its immune system is weakened.

- The vaccine does not work because it was not properly stored.

- The dosage applied is not given as recommended.

• **HORSE LAMENESS**: This general term encompasses a number of leg problems involving serious pain in one or more legs.

When there is severe pain in the hoof structure, the horse keeps minimal weight on it, places only the toe on the ground, and tries to move as little as possible. This is in contrast to laminitis when the horse leans back on its heels, rather than on its toes. Other less obvious signs of lameness may be observed when the horse moves in a straight line at a walk, and shortens the step of one foot (in comparison to the others), or takes the weight off of it, indicating pain. When the horse is led in circles at a walk or at a Paso Fino, the lame horse takes the weight off a sore leg when circling in the direction of that leg, but probably not when circling to the other side.

When the horse is led straight ahead in Paso Fino gait, it behaves differently depending on which leg is sore. If a foreleg is sore, the horse's head nods when the healthy foreleg hits the ground, so as to support the most weight on the sound foreleg. If a hind leg is sore, the hips sink once the healthy hind leg hits the ground, so as to support the most weight on the sound hind leg. Another kind of lameness is when the horse lifts one hind leg higher than the other, either at a walk or Paso Fino, caused by "Stringhalt syndrome" (see below).

When a horse is lame, a veterinarian should be called. Before the horse's exam, the veterinarian should be informed of all the events leading to the lameness. The veterinarian examines the whole lame leg, starting with the hoof, for heat, pain with pressure, swelling, or increased digital pulse. Different joints may be flexed in order to help locate the lameness and determine its cause. When the hoof seems to be the problem, the veterinarian uses a "hoof tester" to produce localized pressure. The pain produced by this pressure may be a sign of laminitis, a fractured coffin bone, an abscess, or a sole puncture/bruise. Additionally, the veterinarian may require the help of special technology, such as X-rays ("radiographs"), ultrasound (for soft tissues, such as tendons), and/or arthroscopy, for proper diagnosis and/or treatment.

The main causes of lameness are as follows:

- **HOOF LESIONS and INFECTIONS**
  - o **HOOF WALL CRACKS**: The **sand crack** is a vertical wall crack extending down from the coronet of the hoof, caused by an injury to the coronary band; additionally, it may be caused by an excess of selenium in the horse's diet. A **grass crack** is a vertical wall crack extending upward from the bottom of the hoof, which usually occurs on a bare hoof, with long toe.

    Symptoms: These conditions cause lameness if the crack becomes very deep, infected, or too long, eventually causing the hoof wall to split.

Treatment: Disinfecting the crack and treating any possible infection. A hoof with a grass crack should be trimmed properly and probably shod. The crack must be kept from growing and deepening by filling it with a specific material for this use.

- **BRUISED SOLE**: A bruise in the sole of the hoof is very painful because the internal sensitive laminae are affected.

  Cause: Bruising often is caused by the impact of a hard object (commonly a stone) on the sole of the hoof. Excessive trimming of the sole increases the risk of bruising.

  Prevention: Painting the bottom of the hoof with Venice turpentine hardens the hoof, which is helpful when the horse is trimmed too short or when the hoof becomes too soft.

  Treatment: The horse should rest either in a pasture or in a well-bedded stall and the hoof should be protected with a boot or bandage. Applying cold or ice therapy to the hoof during the first 48 hours should be followed by soaking the hoof, in warm water, with an Epsom salt solution. Another strategy to draw out soreness is packing the bottom of the hoof with Epson salt and iodine, with a carrier such as mud or poultice, covered with brown paper. Giving analgesic and anti-inflammatory drugs for two or three days may be helpful.

- **WHITE LINE DISEASE**: This severe hoof infection is also called **seedy toe.**

  Cause: The disease is caused by several pathogens, such as bacteria and fungus/yeast. Usually it occurs in shod horses living on wet ground, and mainly affects the toe section.

  Symptoms: The sole of the hoof starts to disintegrate from the toe toward the back. If the white line is disintegrated from the bottom to the coronary band, this damage may lead to founder.

  Treatment: The infected area of the hoof must be removed and kept disinfected with a solution of copper sulfate or iodine. The hoof must be kept dry and the horse must stay in a dry place. The use of "egg shoes" may help prevent founder. Injections of Penicillin may also help.

  Note: Due to the high toxicity, copper sulfate should be handled carefully and people and animals must be kept from ingesting it.

- **GRAVEL**: This is another type of infection of the hoof's white line.

  Cause: An infection occurring after a puncture wound is made, either with a shoe nail incorrectly applied or a piece of stone encrusted in the hoof's white line. The infection usually causes a small abscess around the white line, travels up the white line, and later may drain pus at the coronary band.

  Symptoms: Black spots are seen in the white line when the lame hoof is inspected without a shoe. The abscessed area is very painful when pressure is made with a hoof tester.

  Treatment: Digging/cutting the black spots to find the abscess in order to drain pus. Treating the hole with diluted iodine and packing it with gauze that is saturated with iodine. Protecting the hoof with a boot or bandage is recommended.

- **THRUSH**: This condition is a painful infection of the hoof's frog and sole.

  Cause: This bacterial infection usually occurs when the horse stands on wet ground or manure. When wet bedding is not properly removed from the stall every day, ammonia from the urine aggravates thrush.

  Symptoms: The main characteristic of thrush is the presence of a black-colored discharge with a terrible smell. When the infection has eroded the frog, it may extend into the sensitive, internal laminae, causing lameness.

  Prevention: Keeping the horse on dry ground, cleaning the hooves daily, and removing manure and wet bedding from the stall on a daily basis.

  Treatment: Cutting the affected tissue, cleaning the hoof everyday, and applying diluted copper sulfate, iodine solution (7% to 10%) or a product containing copper naphthenate. If the horse cannot be kept on a clean, dry floor, putting the affected hoof in a protective hoof boot or bandaging is needed.

- **HOOF ABSCESS**: Although the hoof looks very hard, an abscess may grow in the softer internal structures.

  Cause: An infection by anaerobic bacteria that enters the hoof through a puncture or a crack.

  Symptoms: The infection causes severe pain in the hoof and may result in serious damage to the sensitive laminae and/or the coffin bone.

  Treatment: The veterinarian should locate the entry point to make a drainage hole; otherwise, the pus will drain through the coronary band, the weakest point of the hoof. The drainage hole must be treated with diluted iodine. Thereafter, the hole must be packed with gauze that is saturated with the same iodine solution. The horse must be kept in a dry, clean stall and given antibiotics and anti-inflammatory drugs. The horse should rest until it recuperates completely.

- **HOT NAIL**: This is the expression used for a shoe nail applied too far inside the hoof's white line, which injures the sensitive laminae during shoeing.

  Symptoms: The horse's discomfort and lameness usually will be noticed immediately during shoeing or a few days after.

  Treatment: The "hot nail" is detected by either applying pressure with a hoof tester or tapping each nail with a farrier's hammer. The nail must be removed, and the hole treated everyday with diluted iodine, until it heals completely.

- **OVER-CLINCHED NAIL**: This is the expression used to describe one or more nails that are clinched too tightly.

  Symptoms: Because of the nail pressure, the hoof is uncomfortable and the foot appears lame.

  Treatment: The tight nail(s) must be reset or loosened.

- **TENDON PROBLEMS**: In a horse, a tendon is defined as a band of non-stretching fibers that allow locomotion by connecting a leg bone to a muscle. When a tendon, either flexor or extensor, becomes injured, it causes lameness. Although any tendon may be affected, most tendon injuries occur below the carpus in the forelegs.

  - **TENDONITIS**: This is an inflammation of a tendon, caused by overstretching.

    Causes: A tendon strain occurs when the horse missteps into a hole, on a slippery surface, or on stony ground that is not level. It also may occur when the horse's hooves are kept at a very low angle for a long time.

    Symptoms: Once the injured tendon becomes warm, inflamed, weak, and painful, it causes lameness. Ultrasound may be used for proper diagnosis.

    Treatment: When the injury is recent, it requires cold therapy for five days, administering anti-inflammatory drugs, bandaging, and having the horse rest in a stall for two weeks. Thereafter, the horse should start gradual physiotherapy, which may consist of leading the horse, at a walk on a flat surface for a few minutes twice a day, for one week. During the second week, the horse should be led at a Paso Fino. Then, the horse should be walked gently under saddle for short periods of time, every day, until it is able to perform Paso Fino with no lameness. Swimming is an alternative to physiotherapy, in which the horse does not need to hit its hooves against the ground. When tendonitis persists, the horse needs longer rest, immobilization, heat therapy, and corticoid infiltration.

  - **TORN TENDON**: This is a severe injury of the tendon that may cause permanent lameness.

    Causes: An over-flexion or an over-extension of a joint.

    Treatment: Includes surgery, immobilization, antibiotics, analgesic, and anti-inflammatory drugs, prolonged rest, and special shoes. Physiotherapy (starting with swimming) is recommended after the tendon and the skin have healed properly.

  - **CUT TENDON**: This is a critical situation in which a tendon is cut with a sharp object. This may cause permanent lameness.

    Cause: This condition is caused by a deep cut to the leg that involves the tendon.

    Treatment: The tendon may need stitches. If not, a local antiseptic should be applied and the wounded area should be bandaged to keep it clean. Prognosis is guarded.

  - **STRINGHALT SYNDROME**: The Stringhalt syndrome is an involuntary over-flexion of one or both hocks, like a spasm, in which the affected leg is suddenly raised forward and higher than normal. A horse with Stringhalt may transmit this problem to a portion of its offspring.

    Cause: Among other possible tissues involved, this problem affects the lateral digital extensor tendon of the hind leg.

Symptoms: The affected hind leg suddenly is raised higher than normal when the horse steps forward. When the animal is asked to back up or turn to the side of the affected hind leg, the spasmodic contraction easily is observed.

Treatment: Stringhalt syndrome may only be treated with surgery, by cutting the lateral digital extensor tendon of the affected leg and taking it out. Due to the fact that an affected horse may transmit this problem to some of its offspring, the horse should not be used for reproduction.

Note: A horse with Stringhalt syndrome is not allowed to compete in *CONFEPASO* sanctioned shows *(Reglamento de Competencias de Caballos de Paso - CONFEPASO, Chapter 4, Article 7, Section 21).*

- **LIGAMENT PROBLEMS**: A ligament is a band of fibers like a tendon, but slightly elastic, that joins two or more bones together (at a joint). Due to a sudden turn on a slippery ground, and/or over-bending a leg joint, the ligament fibers of the joint may tear. The severity of the lameness depends on how the ligament fibers are affected.

  - **LIGAMENT SPRAIN**: This is a severe injury to the ligament because some ligament fibers are torn.

    Symptoms: The ligament is swollen and very painful and the joint movement is limited seriously, causing severe lameness. Bleeding inside the ligament also may occur.

    Treatment: Giving anti-inflammatory drugs, bandaging the affected joint or casting the leg (in severe cases), providing long periods of rest, and providing physiotherapy after pain and inflammation disappear.

  - **RUPTURED LIGAMENT**: Once a joint is severely bent, a complete rupture of the ligament may occur, and this usually causes a luxation (dislocation of the joint).

    Symptoms: The horse is unable to walk due to extreme pain and joint dislocation.

    Treatment: Although surgery, casting the leg, giving antibiotic and anti-inflammatory drugs, long periods of rest, and physiotherapy may be successful, the prognosis is guarded.

- **MUSCLE OVERSTRETCHING**: Some muscles may be pulled (overstretched), causing lameness. The most common muscles that are pulled (strained) on Paso Fino horses are as follows:

  - **HINDQUARTERS MUSCLE STRAIN**: Strains in the hindquarters may occur at the croup muscles or above the hocks.

    Symptoms: Asymmetrical, weak steps with one hind leg.

    Treatment: Rest, massage, and administering analgesic and anti-inflammatory drugs.

- **BACK MUSCLE STRAIN**: This is a sore muscle at the back or loins, caused by a poorly designed saddle (including a saddle with panels that are too far apart), or a very heavy rider who is not balanced on the saddle.

  Symptoms: Painful reaction to pressure, stiffness, short steps, and lameness.

  Treatment: Rest, anti-inflammatory drugs, massage, and heat therapy. The initial cause of the problem should be corrected before the horse starts working again.

  Note: Some veterinarians believe that **acupunture** works well with horses that demonstrate muscular/neurological problems.

- **BONE INJURIES**: Injuries caused to the bones may be classified into two groups: periostitis and fractures.

  - **PERIOSTITIS**: This is an inflammation of the periosteum, that is the layer of tissue covering the bones. Periostitis also may lead to a fissure of the bone. The most common types of periostitis are as follows:

    - **SPLINT**: This is a kind of periostitis on the foreleg which involves the small metacarpals (or splint bones) and their covering periosteum.

      Cause: Young horses with poor leg conformation, starting horses in training too young, training on hard ground, or an injury to the splint bone area (for example, when a foal tries to climb a fence to escape, or to reach its mother who is on the other side).

      Symptoms: A hard inflamed area on the foreleg, just on the inside surface of the cannon bone, about 2 inches bellow the carpus. This usually is painful. Proper diagnosis requires X-rays.

      Treatment: During the initial stage, cold therapy, pressure bandages, anti-inflammatory drugs, cortisone injections, and rest. When the "splint" interferes with the suspensory ligament of the carpus, causing lameness, it may be treated with freeze firing.

    - **BUCKED SHIN**: Although less common on Paso Fino horses than splints, this type of periostitis affects the front of the cannon bone.

      Cause: This may occur when a young, growing horse is worked on hard ground, or due to trauma to the cannon bone.

      Symptoms: A hard swelling of the affected area, heat, pain, and lameness that increase with exercise. Proper diagnosis requires X-rays.

      Treatment: Cold therapy, pressure bandages, anti-inflammatory drugs, cortisone injections, and rest. Severe cases may be treated with pin-firing.

- **FRACTURES**: A fracture involves the inner bone tissue. When there is any doubt about whether a horse has a fracture, the horse should be kept immobile and a veterinarian should be called for a proper diagnosis. X-rays are taken from two or three angles of the suspected broken bone. Fractures are classified into two groups: **closed fractures** and **open fractures**.

  - **CLOSED FRACTURES**: These are fractures where the affected bone (or bones) never break(s) out of the skin. The least severe types of fractures are those where the bone presents a fissure (called a "stress fracture"), but is not broken completely, or a small piece of bone comes apart from the rest (called "chip fracture"). When the bone is completely broken into two or more pieces, the fracture is considered very severe.

    Causes: Fractures are commonly caused by severe pressure on a bone.

    Treatment: A fissure on the bone may be treated by immobilizing the bone with a cast and full rest for about six weeks, until the bone is fully joined. A chip fracture may be removed by mean of arthroscopy. Swimming is good physiotherapy for horses that have suffered these types of fractures. A fracture, where the bone is completely broken, has a more complicated treatment and has a guarded prognosis.

  - **OPEN FRACTURES**: These are fractures where the bone is broken, in two or more pieces, that displace and break out of the skin.

    Cause: A very hard hit to a bone or overstretching when running.

    Treatment: Prognosis is guarded because, in addition to the broken bone and the other tissues affected (muscles, ligaments, tendons, nerves, blood vessels, skin), the bone may become contaminated by pathogens that cause an infection, called osteomyelitis.

- **BURSITIS**: This is a painful inflammation of a joint's bursa. Several cushioning bursas are located in the joints to avoid friction among the bones. Additionally, bursas secrete a viscous "synovial" fluid to make the movement of the joint smoother. Carpal hygroma (bursitis of the carpus joint) is the most common bursitis which affects Paso Fino horses.

  Cause: A traumatic hit to the joint, or stress produced on the joint by working the horse on an uneven surface while carrying a heavy load (including a heavy saddle and rider).

  Treatment: This condition usually is resolved when promptly treated with anti-inflammatory drugs, injections of cortisone, and rest. A sample of synovial fluid may be taken by using a syringe-needle set, in order to test for infection. If the horse is not treated properly and the joint continues to be stressed, the bursitis persists and becomes chronic. The bursa then becomes harder and affects the normal flexibility of the joint.

- **ARTHRITIS**: This is a chronic inflammation of the joints that usually becomes degenerative with age.

  Causes: Although any joint may become arthritic, as the result of trauma or age, some cases of arthritis occur on the equivalent joints of either the front or the hind legs, such as both hocks. Newborn foals may also develop an infectious arthritis called **joint ill** (caused when the navel is not treated properly after birth).

  Symptoms: Lameness and/or stiffness that reduces movement. For proper diagnosis, the veterinarian requires X-rays of the affected joint (or joints).

  Treatment: Instead of curing the disease, treatment is focused on preventing degeneration of the joint. During the initial stage of arthritis, feeding the horse a supplement containing glucosamine sulfate and chondroitin sulfate improves the horse's condition and prevents quick degeneration. Severe cases require anti-inflammatory drugs, corticoids, analgesic drugs, bandaging, corrective shoeing, long rest, and progressive return to work.

  As a preventive measure, when a leg trauma involves a wound, it should be attended to carefully in order to prevent a bacterial infection of the closest joint, which could become arthritic.

- **CONTRACTED HEELS**: This is a term used to describe narrow heels that grow very close together.

  Cause: Improper hoof trimming.

  Symptoms: Lameness of the affected leg, because of excessive pressure on the coffin bone. In addition, the frog of the hoof with contracted heels cannot grow properly and may become atrophied.

  Treatment: Contracted heels may be fixed with several sessions of proper corrective trimming/shoeing.

- **SCRATCHES** or **GREASE**: This condition is an eczema that appears on the back of a pastern.

  Cause: Accumulation of sweat and mud that irritate the skin and may become infected by bacteria or fungus.

  Symptoms: A swollen, oozing eczema that causes lameness of the affected leg.

  Prevention: Rinsing the legs of sweaty horses after exercise, ideally with warm water and making sure that the horses are not living in muddy places. Additionally, horses with a history of scratches need a regular application of Vaseline on the back of the pasterns, before working.

  Treatment: If there is no secondary infection, treatment consists of cleaning the affected area daily, applying Vaseline on the back of the pastern and heel before working, and rinsing the sweaty legs of the horse after working. If there is any infection, the treatment mentioned above is required, in addition to washing the affected area with Betadine soap and applying an antimicrobial healing cream.

- **SKIN WOUNDS**: Horses may suffer skin wounds, caused by several factors, such as herd battles in the pasture, unsafe facilities, accidents during training, poorly designed tack, etc. A wound may or may not need veterinary attention, depending on the size and depth of the wound.

  - **ABRASION**: This term refers to a superficial cut of the skin that usually has minimal bleeding.

    Treatment: Hosing the affected area (without using a hose nozzle) for six to ten minutes with cold, potable water helps to remove dirt and minimize further swelling. Applying a local antiseptic prevents infection. Applying antimicrobial healing cream prevents infection and helps the skin to recuperate more quickly.

  - **NON-BLEEDING WOUND**: This is usually a minor wound which may still become infected by bacteria if not treated.

    Treatment: If 1 inch long/deep or less, the wound needs daily cleansing, with water and Betadine soap, and an application of local antimicrobial healing cream to promote faster healing.

    If much larger than 1 inch, the wound needs the attention of a veterinarian. The veterinarian may need to suture the wound and may recommend daily cleansing, plus the application of an anti-inflammatory drug.

  - **BLEEDING WOUND**: Certain areas of the horse are more irrigated with blood than others, which make them more susceptible to bleeding. Most bleeding wounds require urgent veterinary attention and immobilization of the horse.

    First aid: A wound that is bleeding dark red blood (venous) requires a pressure pad and bandaging, if possible (e.g., a wound on a leg or the tail), to reduce/stop the bleeding, until the veterinarian arrives.

    A wound on a leg or the tail that is bleeding bright red blood (arterial), instead of dark red blood (venous), needs a tourniquet (placed on the leg/tail about 2 to 3 inches higher than the bleeding artery) to stop the bleeding. If the veterinarian has not arrived within half an hour after the tourniquet is tied, it should be removed for a few minutes and retied again.

    Treatment: The veterinarian may suture the wound and recommend antibiotics and anti-inflammatory drugs. If the horse was vaccinated against tetanus more than eight months before, the animal should be given another dose of tetanus toxoid. Conversely, if the wounded horse was not vaccinated against tetanus, both tetanus antitoxin and tetanus toxoid should be injected.

    If a dressing bandage is used for treating the wound, it should be replaced with a new one every day, for five days. The wound should be cleaned with an antiseptic before each bandage change. After this period, the wound still needs cleansing every day and the application of antimicrobial healing cream without a bandage.

    Note: Only a small wound (1 inch long/deep or less) that stops bleeding dark red blood (venous) after 15 minutes of a pressure pad does not require veterinary attention. The wound should be covered with sterile gauze and cleaned every day with an antiseptic for five days.

- **INFECTED WOUND**: A fresh wound easily may become infected by bacteria after a few days if it is not treated properly.

  Treatment: If 1 inch in length/depth or less, the infected wound requires very strict cleansing with water and Betadine soap until pus, necrotic tissue, and dirt are removed completely. Thereafter, daily cleansing and application of local antimicrobial healing cream is the recommended treatment. This type of wound takes longer to heal, due to the initial presence of necrotic tissue.

  An infected wound, that is 1 inch in length/depth or more, needs veterinary attention. The veterinarian may need to remove the necrotic tissue, with a scalpel, until healthy and bleeding tissue appears. Thereafter, the treatment includes daily cleansing, application of a local antimicrobial healing cream, and application of antibiotic and anti-inflammatory drugs.

- **SWELLING**: Horses may get hurt during herd battles, have accidents during training, crash against hard objects when attempting to escape, etc.

  Symptoms: The area becomes swollen and painful.

  Treatment: A horse that has been hurt recently should be treated with cold therapy for the first 48 hours to reduce further inflammation. The third day, the swollen area should be treated with heat therapy (with Epsom salt, for example). The application of anti-inflammatory drugs (local gel, oral paste, or injected drug) helps to reduce pain and swelling. If the swollen area involves bones, this may require X-rays to verify that there is no fracture.

  However, not all swollen areas are caused by injuries. A swelling on the face may be a sign of either a dental problem or a respiratory disease. A swelling on the jaw may be caused by a dental problem or by rubbing by the jaquima during training, but if the swelling is in between the jaw branches, it may be caused by a respiratory disease (such as strangles). A swelling found on the back could be the result of ill-fitting tack. Some insect and snake bites may cause any part of the horse suddenly to swell. Thus, before starting any treatment, the cause of the swelling must be identified properly.

- **HERNIA**: This is the word that describes a portion of the intestine that passes through an abdominal opening. The most common hernia in newborn foals is the umbilical hernia. Additionally, a scrotal hernia may be present in young stallions and recently gelded horses.

  Causes: The umbilical hernia may be caused by various factors, such as accidentally pulling the navel away from the foal's abdomen after birth, resulting in an umbilical abscess. Hernias may be transmitted genetically, such as the scrotal hernia of a young stallion. The scrotal hernia, of a recently gelded horse, is caused by the absence of testicles and their ducts that allow a loop of the intestine to protrude. Although not very common, a stallion may develop a scrotal hernia when being bred excessively.

  Symptoms and treatment: The abdominal opening, at the navel area of a foal, may be palpated through the skin with the finger tips. A small abdominal opening, up to 1 inch long, usually heals with no help within the first six months of life. Conversely, a bigger abdominal opening, or an opening that enlarges gradually, requires surgical correction in order to avoid a loop of intestine passing through it.

  In the scrotal hernia (of a young stallion or a recently gelded horse), a portion of intestine projects through the abdominal ring and the inguinal canal, finally to descend into the scrotal area, causing swelling in the scrotum. This requires immediate surgery.

- **SKIN TUMORS**: Horses may develop five kinds of skin tumors: melanoma, squamous carcinoma, sarcoid, papilloma, and the nostril tumor.

  - **MELANOMA**: This is a skin tumor arising from cells which produce melanin. Although all colored horses (with melanin pigmented skin) could develop melanoma, it occurs mainly in grey/white horses, especially after 12 years of age.

    Symptoms: A melanoma is a hairless lump on the skin that may be as small as a grain of corn or as large as a small size plum (or a group of them). Most melanomas appear around the anus and under the tail, but they may appear in many other places (such as ears, male's prepuce and penis, mare's vulva and udder), including internal organs and the head. Although, initially, a melanoma is only a cosmetic problem, it may be a serious problem later, either when it is wounded (because it usually does not heal), or when it affects a body function (for example, when it covers the anus and blocks normal excretion). In addition, melanomas may grow and, thereafter, spread and metastasize to internal organs, which may seriously affect the horse's health and, eventually, cause death.

    Treatment: A veterinarian may remove an external melanoma by conducting minor surgery, or by treating the melanoma locally with freezing therapy (cryotherapy) by using liquid nitrogen. However, either treatment does not ensure that more melanomas will not appear. Internal melanomas are not easy to detect in living horses and treatment often is not successful.

  - **SQUAMOUS TUMOR**: This type of tumor may occur in horses with pink skin (without melanin), especially on those areas with no presence of hair, such as the muzzle, genital organs, eyelids, and eye membranes. Conversely, horses with dark skin (pigmented with melanin) do not develop squamous tumors.

    Cause: The bare pink skin areas of the body absorb more UV rays than those protected by hair, making them more susceptible to developing malignant cancer.

    Symptoms: The first stage of the disease looks like a small, dry ulcer that turns from a pink color to yellow. Thereafter, it develops into a lump (of variable size) that usually becomes bloody, and does not reduce in size. The biggest problem is that, after time, a squamous tumor may metastasize to the lymph ganglions, which is devastating for the horse. For proper diagnosis, a skin biopsy is needed.

    Treatment: During the first stage, the horse should be protected from direct UV rays by keeping it in a stall and applying sun block lotion/cream to the affected skin. A formed tumor may be treated initially with cryotherapy or radiotherapy (radiation), and then removed by surgery, unless it involves vital organs. A tumor that metastasizes to lymph ganglions has a guarded prognosis.

  - **SARCOID**: This is an enlarged structure, from ½ to 3 inches in diameter, that grows on hairy skin and has the appearance of a pine cone (seed) growing in the skin, either grey to black in color or red.

    Cause: This type of tumor is caused by a virus entering the body through a wound. Transmission is either by direct contact with an affected animal (equine or cattle) or by a vector insect. Once the virus forms a sarcoid on the body, it may spread aggressively; most times it spreads locally, but it may spread to other areas of the horse.

Treatment: Cryotherapy, inside and outside the tumor, facilitates further removal of the sarcoid's structure by surgery. In addition, a vaccine injected into the tumor (or group of tumors) usually leads to an immune reaction that gradually eliminates the sarcoid.

- **PAPILLOMA**: This is a benign tumor (also called a wart) that only affects the aesthetics of certain areas of the horse that have no hair, such as the lips, around the nostrils, eyelids, ears, penis, and udder. It predominantly affects young horses under five years of age.

  Cause: The papilloma virus enters the body through small wounds on the areas of the horse mentioned above and is transmitted by direct contact with infected animals.

  Symptoms: These include small lumps growing on the skin, which begin as red-colored and soft, and thereafter become calloused and grey-colored.

  Treatment: The horse usually develops natural immunity to the virus about six months to a year later, which causes the warts to disappear. Additionally, papillomas may be treated with cryotherapy or cauterization.

- **NOSTRIL TUMOR**: This is a benign, non-transmittable tumor of the horse that appears as an oval-shaped swelling, under the skin, above the nostril opening. It is often about ¼ to 2 inches in diameter. The actual size of the tumor may be determined by placing one or two fingers on the skin inside the nostril and the thumb on the skin above the nostril opening.

  Treatment: For aesthetics, a veterinarian may remove the nostril tumor with minor surgery. This tumor does not spread to other external or internal areas of the horse.

- **OTHER SKIN PROBLEMS**: Horses may develop different kinds of skin infections and allergies.

  - **FUNGUS**: **Ringworm** is the most common fungal infection that affects the horse's skin and may be passed to humans.

    Transmission source: Although spores of the fungus may be carried by strong winds, usually it is transmitted by sharing tack and grooming tools among infected and healthy horses.

    Symptoms: Ringworm causes large circle-shaped patches of hair to fall out. The shape and size depend on the species of fungus causing the infection. The bald skin shows scabs that may become irritated when the animal scratches, and easily may become infected with bacteria. The most common areas affected by this fungus are the back, neck, and croup. Diagnosis should be confirmed by a veterinarian.

    Prevention: Having a saddle pad and grooming implements for each horse helps to prevent fungal transmission from one horse to another.

Treatment: Any horse affected by ringworm should be isolated and washed everyday with Betadine soap, and then a solution of 10% bleach should be applied for three weeks. Afterwards, an antimicrobial, healing cream may be used. Tack and grooming tools of affected horses must be kept apart and disinfected, after being used, with a solution of 10% bleach.

- **BACTERIA**: *Dermatophilus congolensis* causes **rainrot** (or **rain scald**) on horses kept outside during a heavy rainy season.

Transmission source: By rolling in dirt, a horse may get the bacteria, which stays latent until there is enough moisture on the coat for the bacteria to be activated and enter the epidermis. Additionally, direct contact, between infected and healthy horses, may transmit the bacteria.

Symptoms: Most large areas of the horse may be affected, especially the neck, back, and croup. The affected area looses hair gradually and develops a great number of small scabs that are close together. Diagnosis should be confirmed by a veterinarian by means of a culture.

Prevention: Keeping horses inside, during a heavy rainy season, prevents bacteria from being activated. Having a saddle pad and grooming implements for each horse helps to prevent rainrot transmission from one horse to another.

Treatment: Isolating the affected horse, in a dry stall, and applying an injected antibiotic. Daily washing of the affected area with Betadine soap, and applying a local antimicrobial healing cream, helps control this infection.

- **ALLERGIC REACTION**: The horse may show an allergic reaction on its skin, caused by several sources: the ingestion of feed infected by fungus; intolerance of certain sources of protein in the diet; reaction to inhaled pollen, mold or dust; reaction to an injected drug/ vaccine; or insect stings/bites (such as a wasp, bee, spider, scorpion, or several mosquitoes or ants).

Symptoms: Many small bumps are present, spread across one area or over the entire skin, on the neck, barrel, and croup. When the reaction is caused by scorpion or spider bites, the bumps usually will occur on the muzzle, the lower edge of the thorax or the abdomen, or the legs. The horse shakes its skin frequently and appears bothered by anything touching its skin, from a grooming tool to an insect. Swelling of the eyelids also may occur. Acute allergic reactions (usually to insect stings/bites or injected drugs) may cause a lack of coordination, that gradually gets worse, and finally may lead to death, due to anaphylactic shock.

Treatment: After making a proper diagnosis, the veterinarian gives antihistaminic drugs to the horse, either in paste form or by injection, and often recommends giving the horse antihistaminic tablets for about one week. Additionally, the cause of the allergy should be determined and corrected.

- **EXTERNAL PARASITES**: The most common external parasites which attack horses are flies, mosquitoes, ticks, and lice. They will affect the horse's health in several ways: bothering the horse when biting or flying around; transmitting some dangerous viral, bacterial, protozoan diseases, or worms; causing severe blood loss (due to a large infestation of blood-sucking insects) that makes the horse develop anemia; causing the horse to develop allergies to insect bites and/or resulting in infections at the site of the insect bites.

  Different **FLY** species bother horses, especially during warm days. In general, they are classified into two main groups: biting/blood-sucker flies and non-biting flies.

  - **Biting, blood-sucker flies**, such as the stable fly (*Stomoxys calcitrans*), horn fly (*Haematobia irritans*), horsefly and deer fly (*Tabanus sp.*), suck blood through the horse's skin by means of a pseudo-trachea. While biting the horse and sucking blood, they cause pain and may transmit diseases (anthrax, equine infectious anemia, and equine viral encephalomyelitis).

    Eliminating manure piles, and any decomposed organic matter where biting/blood- sucker flies reproduce, helps to control them. Direct application of residual insecticide, on the horse's body and legs, helps to keep horses from being attacked by flies.

  - **Non-biting flies**, such as the housefly (*Musca domestica*), face fly (*Musca autumnalis*), and screwworm fly *(Callitroga Americana*), bother the horse in different ways. While eating on secretions from the eyes (during the day), these flies may cause conjunctivitis and eye-worms. When eating on open wounds, flies may transmit bacteria that cause infections. These flies also lay eggs in open wounds, the un-treated navel stump of a newborn foal, or bleeding bites of insects. When eggs turn to maggots, they eat flesh, keep the infested area from healing, and permit the area to be infected by bacteria.

    For controlling non-biting flies, manure piles and decomposed organic matter should be covered/avoided to reduce fly reproduction. Maintaining good care of wounds (including after castration), disinfecting the newborn foal's navel stump, and using a repellent, limits the ability of flies to lay eggs in the wounds. Using face masks during daylight in summer limits contact with flies.

  MOSQUITOES, **TICKS**, and **LICE** are all blood-sucking parasites, but blood loss is not the only damage they cause to horses.

  - **Mosquitoes** (several species) reproduce in stagnant water. They may transmit a number of viruses, such as West Nile virus, equine viral encephalomyelitis (Eastern, Western, and Venezuelan), and equine infectious anemia. In addition, some horses may have a localized allergic reaction to mosquito bites.

    Methods to reduce mosquitoes include eliminating the stagnant water sources where they reproduce, spraying horses with repellents or insecticides, and turning off barn lights at night, to avoid massive mosquito attacks on stalled horses.

    Note: Installing a fly spray system in the barn, with proper insecticide, helps to control fly and mosquito attacks.

- **Ticks** live in tall grasses, weeds, and bushes. They usually attach to the horse's ears, nostrils, around the anus, and under the tail and mane, on horses grazing in pastures with tall vegetation. Ticks also may attach to horses and riders during a ride in highly infested areas.

  Ticks suck blood from the horse and rapidly grow until they are the size of a slightly flat peanut. A heavy infestation of ticks may cause weakness and anemia, from the constant loss of blood. Ticks may transmit equine piroplasmosis (also called babesiosis). This disease is caused by a protozoan which destroys the red blood cells and leads to severe anemia, hemoglobinuria, and death within two or three days. Ticks may also transmit lyme disease to people, horses, and dogs. This disease is caused by bacteria that affect the joints and may lead to arthritis.

  For the prevention of ticks, pastures with tall grass or plenty of weeds and bushes should be mowed, which makes the environment less hospitable for ticks.

  The recommended treatment for tick infestation is spraying an insecticide, developed for this purpose, all over the horse.

- **Lice** *(Haematopinus asini* and *Damalinia equi*) are more active in cold weather than hot weather because the horse has a longer coat. Lice lay their small, white eggs (nits), "glued" to hair on several areas of the horse, such as ears, neck, back, and croup. Lice are transmitted from infested horses to healthy ones, by direct contact, or by sharing tack and cleaning tools. After the horse scratches the infested area, it causes severe loss of hair and skin irritation. A heavy infestation in a young horse may lead to anemia, due to a severe loss of blood.

  Infested horses should be isolated from healthy ones for three weeks, at a minimum, and be treated every two weeks (for six weeks) with powder or spray insecticides. The same product should be applied to the tack.

• **INTERNAL PARASITES (WORMS)**: Various kinds of worms negatively affect the horse. Their primary damage to the horse is caused when they migrate to different parts of the body, such as intestines (small and large), liver, kidneys, pancreas, and larynx. This leads to one or more of the following symptoms: decreased feed utilization, coughing, reduced athletic capability caused by lower respiratory efficiency, weakness, loss of weight, enteritis and diarrhea, slow growth, distended abdomen, rough coat hair, aspiration pneumonia, colic, peritonitis, and anemia.

  The common types of worms that affect horses are as follows: ascarids (*Parascaris equorum*), lungworms (*Dictyocaulus arnfieldi*), stomach worms (*Habronema muscae*), large strongyles (*S. vulgaris*, *S. edentatus*, and *S. equines*), small strongyles (more than 30 different species may infect the horse's large intestine), strongyloides (*Strongyloides westeri*, *Onchocerca spp.*, and *Draschia spp.*), tapeworms (*Anoplocephala perfoliata*, *Anoplocephala magna*, and *Paranoplocephala mamillana*), oxyuris (*Probstmayria vivipara* and *Oxiuris equi*), and stomach bots.

  While living in the intestine and reproducing, most worm species shed their eggs in manure, which either as eggs or larvae, may infect other horses after being swallowed in hay, grass, or water.

Oxyuris (also known as pinworms) have a different way to infect other horses. The female worms travel from the intestine to the rectum and lay thousands of eggs in a gray cement-colored mass that is deposited on the skin of the anus and perineum, which causes anal itching. While the horse scratches its tail and anus, the worm eggs adhere to everything. Once in the environment, eggs hatch into larvae after one week and infect feed. Thereafter, another horse ingests the larvae in infected feed, and the cycle continues.

Stomach bots infect horses in yet a different way. Flies of genus *Gasterophilus* lay their eggs (usually tan-colored) on the hair of the legs (mainly on the inside of the carpus). When the horse scratches with its teeth and lips, some eggs adhere to the horse's mouth, where they hatch into larvae after few weeks. Thereafter, larvae are swallowed and passed into the stomach. Different larval stages are spent in the horse's gastrointestinal tract and, finally, are passed through in the manure. In the environment, larvae turn into their pupal stage, and then into adult flies that start the cycle again.

To reduce the amount of worms (all species) living in horses' systems and to decrease environmental contamination with worm eggs and larvae passed in the manure, all horses should be dewormed every two months, by rotating three different active agents.

Common active deworming agents are Dichlorvos, Fenbendazole, Ivermectin, Mebendazole, Moxidectin, Praziquantel, Pyrantel Embonate, Pyrantel Pamoate, and Pyrantel Tartrate. Dewormers act against worms by interfering with their metabolism and/or their neuromuscular coordination, but they do not affect the horse's health or its metabolism. Nevertheless, some dewormers must not be used for pregnant mares. This should be determined by reading the label of the product or asking a veterinarian.

Most dewormers for horses are offered in "paste" form to make them safer for the horse and easier to administer. These come in syringes with plungers that have weight marks. After determining the horse's body weight, and calculating the correct amount of the product, the dewormer is given directly from the original syringe into the horse's mouth (on the side and over the tongue).

However, offering dewormers in the "granule" form, to be mixed with the horse's feed on a daily basis, is becoming very common. A palatable pellet product (like alfalfa) containing an active deworming agent, such as Fenbendazole, Mebendazole, Pyrantel Embonate, or Pyrantel Tartrate, is given to the horse everyday. This permanently controls different worms in the intestines.

Broodmares should be dewormed within 24 hours of foaling, with a product containing an active deworming agent against s*trongyloides westeri;* this prevents the foal from being infected by this type of worm in the following days. The foal should receive its first dewormer at two months of age, and repeated every two months, as with other horses. New horses entering the farm should be dewormed no later than one day after arrival.

Note: Giving Ivermectin (a deworming agent) to the horse also controls blood-sucking parasites on the skin, such as ticks and lice.

Other practices, which are recommended to reduce the amount of worm eggs/larvae in the environment, are explained below:

- Picking up manure from stalls once a day, at a minimum. If fresh manure is being used as fertilizer in empty pastures, it must be spread in very small pieces, with a manure spreader, during hot dry seasons. Once worm eggs and larvae are exposed to sunshine, they die because of the dryness.

- Dragging pastures, periodically, in order to break up manure piles and expose worm eggs and larvae to sunshine.

- Disinfecting stall walls, buckets, and feeders, every three to four weeks, in order to reduce the number of eggs and larvae in the stall. Additionally, all bedding material should be removed every three to four weeks.

- Using a "bot knife" to reduce the number of botfly larvae entering the mouth, by removing carefully the botfly eggs that are attached to the horse's legs during late summer and fall.

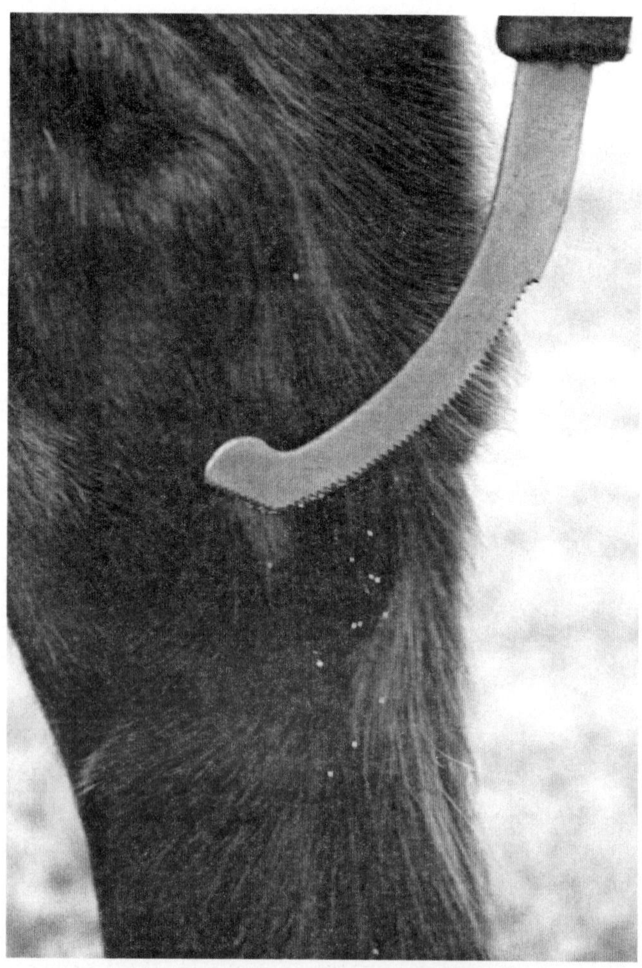

CHAPTER 11

MANAGING EQUINE INFORMATION

Either for hobby or business, the horse is a productive animal that requires proper management; therefore, the horse farm's owner/manager should have a plan with clearly defined goals for the short- mid- and long-term. The plan should include a recording system of daily events. These records should be analyzed periodically to detect deficiencies and weak areas, and the required adjustments/corrections made; otherwise, the horse farm probably will not be successful.

Maintaining the farm plan and complete records of all horse related activities is important for tax purposes. Additionally, this information may be required for obtaining loans or insurance policies, such as horse mortality/theft.

RECORDS OF PASO FINO HORSES

Recorded information should reflect the reality of the Paso Fino farm by listing all day-to-day events; in other words, records are the written history of the farm. All documents, such as contracts, horse certificates of registry, Coggins tests, expense receipts, invoices, and breeding reports should be stored properly in a safe place.

A recording system (paper and/or electronic), helps the farm owner/manager keep track of both individuals and events. Records should be easily understandable, not only for the current owner/manager and staff, but also for anyone who may be visiting, evaluating, or working on the farm in the future.

- **Records of Height and Weight**: Young horses need their height and weight measured periodically. Recording this information allows the owner/manager to evaluate whether growth and development are occurring at proper rates according to the horse's age. Adult horses also need their height and weight measured and recorded.

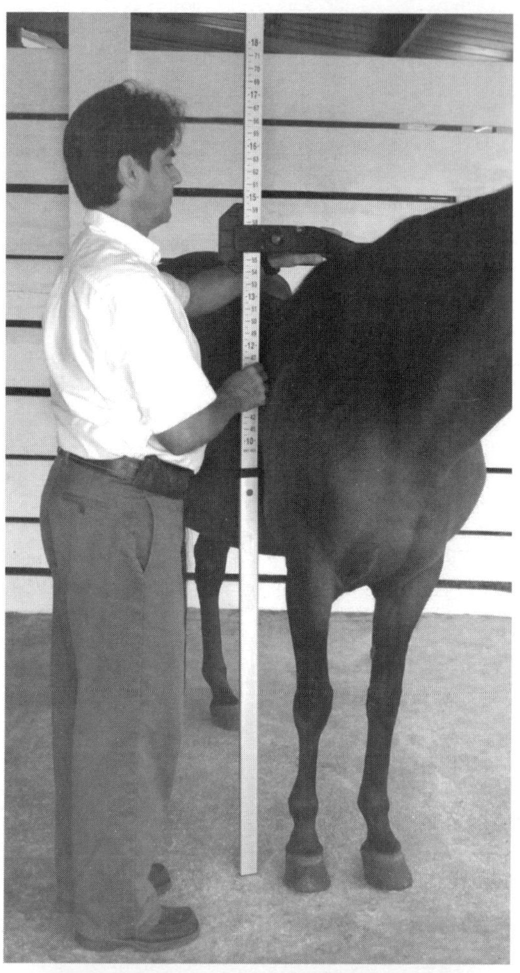

- **Height:** To measure height, the horse stands balanced on flat/level ground. Height is defined as the perpendicular distance between the highest point of the horse's withers and the ground. The "**stick**" is the measuring device used to determine the height of the horse. It consists of a vertical stick with a sliding horizontal level. The vertical stick is divided into inches (and hands) on one side and centimeters on the other. The horizontal level is placed on the horse's withers, and the horse's height is shown on the stick.

  The height may be measured either in hands and inches or centimeters. 1 inch equals 2.54 centimeters; one hand equals 4 inches (10.2 cm.). If, for instance, the height of a Paso Fino horse is 14.1 hands, this means its height is 14 hands and 1 inch.

  It is important to know the height of the adult horse for several reasons: first, the Paso Fino horse (and the Colombian diagonal Paso horse breeds) must reach a minimum height to compete in *CONFEPASO* sanctioned shows according to gender (see Chapter 4: "Unique characteristics of the Paso Fino horse" and Chapter 18: "Other Paso horses"). Additionally, this is a parameter to be considered when choosing foundation livestock because the horse's height may be transmitted genetically to the next generation.

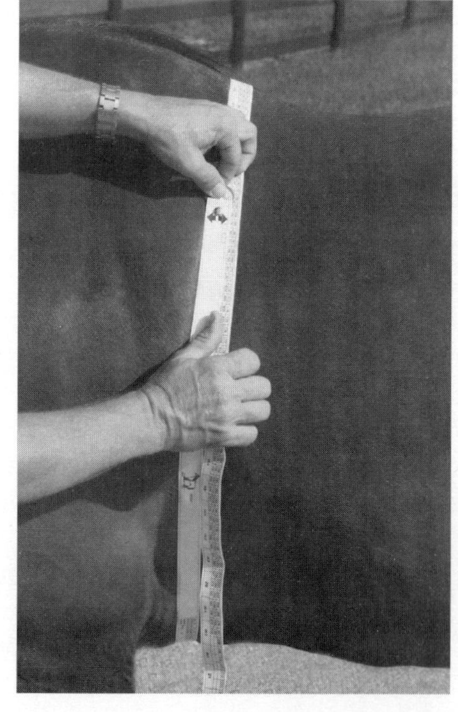

- **Weight**: The most exact way to calculate a horse's weight is by using a scale (ideally a scale for livestock). However, when a scale is not available, using a calibrated horse weight tape for estimating the horse's weight is an acceptable alternative. This is done by measuring the horse's full heart girth (passing behind the front legs). Depending on the tape, the weight may be expressed in pounds (lbs.) and/or kilograms (kgs.).

  Calculating/estimating and recording the horse's weight periodically is important to confirm/adjust the horse's diet and to give the horse correct drug and dewormer dosages.

- **Reproduction Records**: During the breeding season, information must be recorded for both stallion and mare.
  - **For the stallion**: breeding date, mare's name and color, mare's owner's name and contact information (if it is an outside mare), breeding method (direct mounting or artificial insemination), veterinarian in charge, expected date to check for pregnancy, diagnosis of pregnancy (+ or -) and its date, date of next service (applicable for non-pregnant mares), second verification of pregnancy (applicable for pregnant mares), date of birth, foal's sex and color, length of gestation.

    Stallions, whose semen is being used for artificial insemination (fresh, cooled, or frozen), need other records: semen collection date, time, temperature of artificial vagina used, volume of semen collected, concentration of spermatozoa, percentage of (normal) progressive motile spermatozoa, number of doses split, used fresh or way of preservation (cooled or frozen), and veterinarian.
  - **For the mare**: breeding date, stallion's name, color, stallion's owner's name and contact information (if it is an outside stallion), breeding method (direct mounting or artificial insemination), veterinarian in charge, expected date to check for pregnancy, diagnosis of pregnancy (+ or -) and its date, date of next service (applicable for non-pregnant mares), second verification of pregnancy (applicable for pregnant mares), date of birth, foal's sex and color, length of gestation.

    Mares in an embryo transfer program need their own records: breeding date, stallion's name, color, stallion's owner's name and contact information, breeding method and veterinarian, embryo's collection date, recipient mare's name (or other identification) and veterinarian, expected date to check for pregnancy (of the recipient mare), diagnosis of pregnancy (+ or -) and date, second verification of pregnancy (applicable for pregnant recipient mares), date of birth, foal's sex and color, length of gestation, and special notes.
- **Horse Care Records**: Information regarding regular care should be recorded.
  - **Hoof care**: Some information about trimming/shoeing events should be recorded in order to keep the horse's legs in optimal condition and for continuous improvement, either with the same team (consisting of a farrier, veterinarian, and trainer), or another team. Some important records include date, horse's name, work done on forelegs (left-right), work done on hind legs (left-right), names of professionals in charge (farrier, veterinarian, and trainer), special notes, and next appointment date.
  - **Health maintenance plan**: All information about vaccines, internal parasite control, blood tests, and physical examinations should be recorded:

    Vaccines: date, names of horses vaccinated (or other identification), product, serial number of the product, laboratory, diseases prevented, dosage, method of administration, special reactions, veterinarian, and next vaccination date.

    Internal parasite control: date, names of horses dewormed (or another identification), product, laboratory, active agent, dosage, method of administration, special reactions, veterinarian/technician, next deworming date, and next product to use.

    Blood tests: date, names of horses tested, veterinarian, type of test, results, and next testing date.

    Teeth and physical examinations: date, names of horses examined, examination results, recommendation/treatment, veterinarian/dentist, and next examination date.
  - **Health emergencies and treatments**: date, horse's name, condition/disease, probable cause, treatment, veterinarian, and notes.

- **Training Records**: Because proper training is imperative, important information should be recorded as follows: "ground work" starting date, trainer, "ground work" ending date, notes; "breaking" starting date, trainer, "breaking" ending date, notes; "basic training" starting date, trainer, "basic training" ending date, notes; "bitting" starting date, trainer, notes; "collection" starting date, trainer, notes; "finishing" starting date, trainer, notes; and type of show class or other functions for which the horse is trained.

  If the horse is being shown, some information should be recorded as follows: date, city, association/region/club, show classification and location, class, number of contestants, awards obtained, points, and notes for improvement.

- **Administrative Records**: Information about horses staying on the farm, daily activities with horses, facility and pasture management, control of supplies, payments and sales, among others, should be recorded periodically.

  - **Horse inventory and location**: A good recording system allows the farm manager to keep track of horse inventory and location at any time. It should include not only the farm-owned horses, but also the outside horses, either staying for a few days (e.g., mares for breeding), or staying for several months (e.g., horses for sale or training).

    Having an **identification chart** for each horse on the farm that contains the most important information, allows for easier livestock administration. The chart should have, at a minimum, the following information: date of entry, horse's name, sex, color, registration number, foaling date, age (at entry), purpose for being on the farm, microchip number, lip tattoo, freeze mark, and special notes. It also may include a signaling card for drawing the white markings and/or hair swirls, or full color photographs of the horse.

    For outside horses, the chart should include information related to the owner: name, full address, telephone numbers, economic arrangement (e.g., boarding price, consignment price).

    A chart for **general horse inventory** includes the following information: horse's name, sex, color, owner's name (if applicable), current condition, purpose on the farm, identification, and location on the farm. Additionally, if a physical inventory of the farm's horses is made periodically, the same chart may be used to record the horse's weight and height.

    Note: Appendix B includes examples of recording charts.

  - **Daily activities**, such as the feeding schedule, grooming, stall cleaning, etc. must be planned, based on the farm's priorities, and recorded for employees. Other activities that need to be done at specific times/dates, such as health maintenance practices, ultrasounding/palpating or breeding mares, hoof trimming/shoeing, and upcoming events, such as births, also need to be recorded.

  - A **diet** must be designed carefully and recorded for each horse or group of horses. For example, a stalled horse should have its diet written outside the stall door, so farm personnel will feed each horse the recommended amount, without depending on memory. Periodic evaluation of horses' diets (once or twice a month) helps in making important adjustments.

    Developing a **diet summary chart** for all horses on the farm helps in controlling daily, weekly, and monthly use of feed, and planning for new feed shipments.

- Periodic **facility disinfection** should be planned and recorded on a chart with the following information: disinfection date, location, disinfectant (product), special notes, person in charge, and next disinfection date.

- Good pastures are an important resource on the Paso Fino farm (see Chapter 6: "Nutrition" and Chapter 9: "Facilities for horses"). Therefore, proper **pasture management** should be maintained according to the season, and all activities conducted in the pastures should be recorded on charts with the following information: pasture's name or number, area, topography, date (of event), season, predominant weather, activity done (mowing, dragging, fertilizing, seeding, weed/bush control, irrigating), predominant grass/legume plants, occupation date, number of Paso Fino horses (and their ages), daily hours being used, emptying date, total days of occupation, total days of rest (empty of horses and other herbivores).

- **Use of supplies**, such as hay, grain, minerals, vitamins, salt, shavings, and medicines, should be controlled by recording the following information on charts: item, arrival date, amount, brand/supplier, special notes on quality, how long the supplies are expected to last, and next order date.

- **Payments** for labor and supplies must be recorded properly for several reasons: to allow the owner/manager to be clear with employees and professionals who offer specific services (veterinarian, farrier, etc.); to maintain good credit with suppliers; and to maintain all information about farm expenses for analysis and tax purposes.

- The **income from horse sales and services** (as well as boarding, training, stud fees, etc.) must be recorded for analysis and tax purposes.

CONTRACTS

The Paso Fino horse farm's owner/manager should have several contract forms that help to ensure efficient and safe business for both seller and customer. Copies of all the signed forms should be kept in a safe place. Some relevant contracts are listed below:

- **Labor** contracts for permanent and provisional employees, and for professionals who offer special services.
- **Sales** contracts for horses and embryos.
- **Consignment** contracts for horses.
- **Breeding** contracts (should originate with the stallion's owner).
- **Lease** contracts for stallions in stud, mares' bellies (to obtain embryos or carrying foals), recipient mares, and horses being trail ridden or shown.
- **Boarding** and/or **Training** contracts.

Additionally, **Agreement and Liability Release** forms must be kept for workers, customers, and visitors (depending on the State law). As soon as any person comes onto the farm, this agreement should be read, completed, and signed.

Note: The State of Florida requires the horse farm owner/manager to post a liability notice at the farm.

CERTIFICATES OF REGISTRATION

A Certificate of Registration is issued for Paso Fino horses by the *Paso Fino Horse Association, Inc.* (*PFHA*) in the United States. Outside the United States, other associations and federations affiliated with *CONFEPASO* maintain permanent registries of Paso Fino horses in the countries where they are located.

The Certificate of Registration issued by *PFHA* has information about the horse, mainly provided by the owner, through the Registration Application form. The Certificate of Registration's front side has the following information: horse's name, registration number, sex, foaling date, State where it was foaled, color, description (related to white markings and whether the horse was genetically tested), pedigree (including sire, dam, grandparents, and great grandparents), recorded owner, and date issued.

The back side has three sections, as follows: the "Transfer of Ownership" space (section on top), the "Report" space for reporting different events, such as the horse's death, castration, color change, scar or change in markings, and name change (section in the middle), and the "Payment" space (section on the bottom).

The *PFHA* keeps additional information/material related to the horse that is provided by the applicant when obtaining the Certificate of Registration:

- Full color photographs of the horse (properly labeled with the horse's proposed name and date the photographs were taken): head front view, both side views (left and right), and rear of hindquarters view. The photographs must show any white markings and the four legs (*PFHA – Constitution and Rule Book, Chapter Eight, Section III*).
- White markings drawn on the description section of the Registration Application.
- Stallion Breeding Report.
- A copy of the Genetic Test and Parentage Verification based on DNA. A specialized laboratory at U.C. Davis (in California) does this test with a sample of mane/tail hairs sent by the owner. The Genetic Testing kit may be obtained from the *PFHA (PFHA – Constitution and Rule Book, Chapter Eight, Section IV, Subsection G, 4)*.

If a registered horse changes ownership (for example, when the horse is sold), the *PFHA* will issue a new Certificate of Registration with the same information, including the new owner's name. This is accomplished by sending the original Certificate of Registration with the "**Transfer of Ownership**" section (back side, section on top), properly completed, to the Association. It requires the new owner's information (name, full address, and *PFHA* membership number) and the signature and *PFHA* membership number of the current recorded owner *(PFHA – Constitution and Rule Book, Chapter Eight, Section X, Subsection A)*.

The first owner of a foal is considered the recorded owner of the dam at the time of foaling. Therefore, if a foal is sold before it is registered, the recorded owner (of the dam at the time of foaling) must fill out a "**Transfer of Ownership**" section as the seller, as though the foal has been registered previously. A Transfer fee is required in addition to the Registration fee.

When a registered Paso Fino horse dies, its owner must send the original Certificate of Registration with the "**Report of Death**" (back side, middle section) properly completed (indicating both date and cause of death) and signed to the *PFHA* for recording of the event. The Certificate of Registration will be sent back to the owner. Nevertheless, all registered Paso Fino horses will be presumed dead at 30 years of age (based on the recorded date of birth). Thus, the owner should notify the *PFHA* when any registered Paso Fino horse is alive over 30 years *(PFHA – Constitution and Rule Book, Chapter Eight, Section XII, Subsection A, 5, a and b)*.

When a registered Paso Fino stallion is castrated, the owner must send the original Certificate of Registration with the "**Report of Castration**" (back side, middle section) properly completed and signed (indicating castration date) to the *PFHA* in order to change the sex information from "stallion" to "gelding" *(PFHA – Constitution and Rule Book, Chapter Eight, Section XII, Subsection A, 2)*.

When a registered Paso Fino horse has changed its color or white markings, the owner must send the original Certificate of Registration with, depending on the case, either the "**Report of Color Change**" or the "**Report of Scars or Change in Markings**" (back side, middle section), properly completed and signed, to the *PFHA*. Additionally, current photographs that show the changes must be sent. Once approved, the Association sends a new Certificate of Registration to the owner, including the recorded information *(PFHA – Constitution and Rule Book, Chapter Eight, Section XII, Subsection A, 1)*.

When the name of a registered Paso Fino horse is going to be changed, the owner must send the original Certificate of Registration with the "**Report for Name Change**" (back side, middle section), properly completed and signed (indicating the horse's new name), to the *PFHA*. If the change of name is approved, the *PFHA* sends a new Certificate of Registration to the owner, including the recorded information *(PFHA – Constitution and Rule Book, Chapter Eight, Section IV, Subsection I, 3 and 4)*.

Any stallion registered by *PFHA* must have a "**Stallion Breeding Report**" each breeding year. A "Stallion Breeding Report" form should indicate the breeding year, the stallion's registration number and name, and the recorded owner or authorized agent of the stallion during the breeding season. Each year requires a separate form.

Note: "Stallion Breeding Report" forms are available on the *PFHA* website (*www.pfha.org*) or by calling the office to receive forms by mail.

This report should list the registration number and name of each mare that was bred, the method of breeding (natural service, pasture exposed, artificial insemination – off site or on site, or embryo transfer), the breeding dates, and the recorded name of the mare's owner. If a mare is not registered with *PFHA*, but is registered with another association, all the same information should be listed as above. In lieu of a *PFHA* registration number, the registration number and the name of the foreign association should be indicated. There is no charge to list mares that are not registered with *PFHA*.

The recorded owner or authorized agent of the stallion must sign the "Stallion Breeding Report" form. If the ownership of the stallion changes during the breeding year, all owners' signatures are needed to complete the processing. A "Stallion Breeding Report" should be sent to *PFHA* at the end of each calendar year. A "Stallion Breeding Report" postmarked after January 31st of the following year will be considered a late report and late fees will be charged *(PFHA – Constitution and Rule Book, Chapter Eight, Section IV, Subsection D, 1, 2, and 5)*.

IDENTIFICATION METHODS

All horses on the farm (farm-owned or not) should be easy to identify at any time by using one or more identification methods, either provisional or permanent. There are different provisional identification methods that allow personnel on the farm to conduct daily activities for a specific horse or a group of horses, such as feeding, hoof trimming/shoeing, and riding. Provisional identification methods include having a chart with the horse's name outside the stall, a labeled/numbered halter or neck strap, or a tag with the horse's name attached to the halter/neck strap.

Permanent identification methods are more secure than provisional methods. They include a microchip, a lip tattoo, and a freeze-mark.

- **Microchip**: Injecting a microchip in the horse's neck provides the most secure method of identification because each "chip" has a unique number. In equine species, the microchip is injected in the nucal ligament (the muscle at the upper edge of the neck or "crest"), by means of a special needle and syringe set. The recommended site of injection is at the left side of the crest, 1 inch below the upper edge, half or a third the distance between the ears and the withers. The microchip number may easily be read with an electronic scanner. The microchip is a great tool that has helped to identify lost horses, and to return them to their owners, after the devastating hurricanes that have hit some areas of the United States in recent years.

  All Paso horses to be shown in *CONFEPASO* sanctioned shows are required to have a microchip *(Reglamento de Competencias de Caballos de Paso – CONFEPASO, Chapter 1, Article 2, Section G, Subsection 6).*

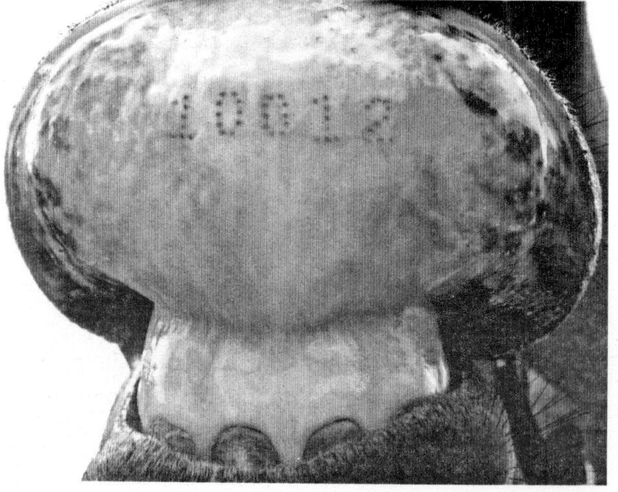

- **Permanent tattooing**: Although less common in Paso Finos, tattooing the inside upper lip of the horse, either with a registration number, the consecutive number on the farm, or the horse's name, allows for easy individual identification.

  This is a common practice for thoroughbreds. In fact, it is required at the racetrack.

- **Freeze-mark**: A freeze-mark provides permanent identification, by contrasting hair colors, that are very easy to see from a distance. Therefore, if one of the farm's purposes is positioning a good, well-known name in the Paso Fino breed, all the farm-owned/bred horses may be freeze-marked. Paso Fino horses are generally freeze-marked on the arm (between the elbow and the point of shoulder), usually on the left side. Freeze-marking a number on a thigh of recipient mares of embryo transfer programs is commonly used as a permanent identification.

  The process of freeze-marking is as follows: Just before freeze-marking a horse, the area to be marked must be shaved. Meanwhile, the metal marker should be kept in a container with a non-caustic solution that maintains a very low temperature from -100 °F to -321 °F (such as liquid nitrogen - LN2, used in tanks to keep frozen semen), for a few minutes, until the metal is frozen. The horse should be restrained properly and the leg opposite to the leg being branded should be lifted by an assistant. Depending on the temperature of the coolant, the frozen metal marker is placed on the skin and held firmly (to keep it from moving) for 10 to 60 seconds.

  Immediately after the iron is lifted, the skin appears grooved in the shape of the marker. A few minutes later, the skin becomes quite swollen and stays that way for a few hours. Five to ten days later, the marked skin begins to shed, while new hair (of the horse's same color) starts to grow surrounding the mark. About thirty days later, the contrasting freeze-mark begins to be seen with white hair growth. However, in some horses with a light coat, the mark has no white hair growth, but just bare skin.

CHAPTER 12

THE HORSE AS AN ATHLETE

This chapter illustrates the importance of recognizing the horse as an athlete in order to understand its physiology, and as a result, to design a proper workout and nutritional plan.

In the wild, all equine species (horses, zebras, asses, etc.) are athletes due to the nature of their life:

- When migrating, they walk long distances each day in order to find better grass and water.
- When escaping from danger, they run fast (about 25 – 35 miles an hour) and are able to maintain a fast speed for a long time and for a long distance.

After horses became domesticated, different breeds were developed in order to refine and improve equine athletic capacities for work, sports, and recreation. Based on their athletic capacities, Paso Fino horses may be compared to marathon runners because they are able to maintain their smooth, powerful gait; energy; elegance; and head-neck posture for long rides.

THE PURPOSE OF TRAINING

When most horse people talk about training, they refer to the conditioned behaviors a horse needs to learn in responding to the rider's commands, based on either positive or negative stimuli (see Chapter 15: "Horse psychology and training"). Furthermore, several physiological processes prepare a horse in training for the endurance to perform physical activity, including:

- Preparing the circulatory and respiratory systems to provide all the substances and gases required in all the tissues at the correct time during the workout.
- Adjusting/developing all the muscles used for performing specific exercises.

- Developing the proper pathways that use the different sources of energy for the physical activity.
- Acquiring a way to metabolize the substances that cause muscular fatigue.

In addition, several factors and circumstances may positively or negatively affect the horse's performance:

- **From the horse**: training level and willingness to work, body condition index (related to weight and fat deposits), individual metabolic rate, and endurance.
- **From the physical activity itself**: duration, cadence, and extension of steps; inclination and texture of the ground; weight added with tack (bit, jaquima, reins, saddle, etc.), the rider, and the shoes; obstacles in the way; and stress.
- **From the diet**: amount and source of nutrients (especially energy) for the physical activity.
- **From the environment**: altitude, humidity in the air, and climate (temperature). These factors affect the concentration of oxygen in the air and its availability.
- **From the rider**: ability to ride the horse while saving energy.

CARDIAC AND RESPIRATORY CHANGES DURING EXERCISE

The cardiac and respiratory systems have complementary functions and, therefore, reviewing them together enhances comprehension of their functioning.

The **CIRCULATORY** system is formed by the **heart**, **blood vessels** (veins, arteries, and capillaries), **lymphatic ganglions** (or **nodes**), **blood** (cells and plasma), and **lymph fluid**. The functions of the circulatory system are transporting all the substances throughout the body, taking oxygen to the tissues by means of the hemoglobin, exchanging oxygen for carbon dioxide, taking carbon dioxide into the heart and then into the lungs to be exhaled, and defense from infections (immunology).

The **RESPIRATORY** system is formed by the **nostrils**, **nasal cavities**, **pharynx**, **larynx**, **epiglottis**, **trachea**, **bronchi**, and **lungs**. The functions of this system are inhaling fresh air through the air passages and taking air into the lungs, passing oxygen (from inhaled air) into the blood, exchanging carbon dioxide for oxygen (in the lungs), and expelling carbon dioxide.

The heart is a pump with four chambers (two atriums and two ventricles), whose function is pumping the blood. The right atrium of the heart collects the non-oxygenated blood coming from the whole body. Without any physical/chemical change, the blood is passed to the right ventricle. The right ventricle pumps the blood to the lungs in order to be oxygenated. After being oxygenated, the blood returns to the heart and enters the left atrium, and then is passed to the left ventricle. At this time, oxygenated blood is ready to be pumped by the left ventricle of the heart and to the rest of the body through the arteries.

The cardiac rate of an adult horse ranges from 36 to 45 beats per minute at rest and the volume of blood pumped during each contraction is from 800 cc to 1 liter. The respiratory rate of an adult horse at rest is between 8 and 20 breaths per minute. When the cardiac rate is increased during physical activity (in order for the hemoglobin in the blood to transport the oxygen to all the muscle cells for the production of energy, and to allow a fast exchange of carbon dioxide), the respiratory rate simultaneously is increased, based on the intensity of the physical activity. This occurs in order to obtain the maximum possible amount of oxygen, that is then passed to the circulatory system.

During the first two minutes of exercise, the horse's cardiac rate greatly increases, and this high rate may be maintained for a long period of time during the workout. The horse's heart rate reaches 120 beats per minute during a moderate workout and may reach up to 230 beats per minute during an extremely demanding workout. The concentration of hemoglobin in the blood, and the number of capillary endings that reach into the muscles to provide oxygen, are the greatest limitations of the circulatory system during a high-intensity workout. A high-intensity workout also is limited by the efficiency of the respiratory system to supply oxygen.

When the intensity of the physical activity is reduced for approximately five minutes, the cardiac rate is slightly reduced, but maintained. The respiratory rate may be reduced even more a few minutes later if the supply of oxygen is paired with the respiratory need. Later, when the physical activity has ended, the cardiac rate usually is dramatically reduced within the first three minutes; thereafter, it takes from ten minutes to two hours to return to the resting cardiac rate, depending on how demanding the exercise was, the length of the work time, and the environmental factors. The respiratory rate reduces more slowly after the physical activity has ended, but it returns to the resting respiratory rate at approximately the same time as the cardiac rate.

Regular training has positive effects on both the respiratory and circulatory systems. When the horse is exercised regularly, the lungs are used at full capacity due to the need for oxygen during physical activity, which in turn leads to more efficient respiration. Likewise, the horse that is exercised regularly has more efficient circulation of blood to all the cells, due to both a stronger and enlarged cardiac muscle to pump the blood and a greater number of capillary endings that reach further into the muscles.

OTHER FACTORS AFFECTING THE CARDIAC AND RESPIRATORY RATES

Besides exercise, other factors affect the respiratory rate of the horse, either at rest or during physical activity. Respiratory and cardiac rates are increased due to fever and/or pain, and during periods of excitement (due to stressful conditions or breeding).

The respiratory rate also may increase directly with environmental factors, such as the altitude, humidity in the air, and/or temperature. When one or more of these environmental factors increases (e.g., the horse is moved to a much higher altitude), the concentration of oxygen in the air is reduced and, therefore, the horse has to breathe more frequently to obtain the required amount.

The environmental factors mentioned above, have an influence on the time required to reach both cardiac and respiratory resting rates after exercise. The higher the altitude, humidity in the air, and/or temperature, the longer it takes to reach resting rates.

Horses exercised regularly at a high altitude generally will perform very easily at a low altitude, but not vice-versa.

SPECIAL ADJUSTMENTS OF RESPIRATION DURING EXERCISE

Although horses breathe through their noses at rest and at work, they make quick adjustments when their oxygen needs are increased during a demanding physical activity, in order to achieve the best airflow:

- Muscles within the nostrils, nasopharynx, and larynx dilate to provide a wider opening of the upper airways, allowing more fresh air to pass to the trachea, and then to the bronchi and to the lungs. The trachea, however, evidences no change in size due to the rings of cartilage that comprise it.

  Note: Even though the rider often may obtain better collection, smoothness, harmony, and elegance from the Paso Fino horse by having the horse's face in a vertical position, the horse still may try to avoid this position by attempting to raise its head. This occurs because bending at the poll causes the larynx to bend, which goes against its initial dilatation and, thus, affects airflow.

- A few minutes after physical activity starts, the horse may "blow air" several times, because of itching caused as the nasopharynx and larynx are dilated, and to clear the air-passages of dust and mucous. Some Paso Fino horses take advantage of this physiological situation and try to gain control of the reins by pulling their heads down while blowing air. This attempt to gain control while blowing air is seen clearly when the horse is anxious and wants to move faster, for example, while going toward the barn.

- In order to breathe with the minimum possible effort while running (galloping) or cantering, the horse adjusts its respiratory rate to its leg movements. Due to several factors that cause negative pressure in the thorax when the forelegs are extended forward in the air, inhalation of air occurs easily, almost effortlessly. Conversely, due to a reversal of the same factors, when the forelegs hit the ground, an easy exhalation of air occurs. This is a physiological mechanism that allows horses to obtain oxygen easily while escaping from predators that follow them for extended periods of time.

  It is important to note that a Paso Fino horse in gait cannot adjust its respiratory rate to its leg movements (as in a canter/gallop), due to its evenly alternated four-beat gait. Therefore, some Paso Fino horses may try to break the proper isochronic gait for a non-isochronic (diachronic) one (canter or a mix with a canter, for instance), when they are asked to perform a more demanding motion, such as a quicker Classic Fino or Paso Largo.

RESPIRATORY PROBLEMS WHICH AFFECT PERFORMANCE

Any respiratory infection and/or allergy may negatively affect the horse's athletic capability, and therefore its performance, because infections and allergies cause inflammation of the air passages and the lungs, and they increase mucous production (see Chapter 10: "Health basics"). Due to inflammation and the presence of excessive mucous, there is a reduction in the diameter of the upper airways, which reduces the amount of air entering the lungs. Additionally, the over production of mucous usually causes coughing that momentarily interrupts breathing and may cause aspiration pneumonia. Therefore, a horse with a respiratory infection and/or allergy should not be exercised until full recuperation to avoid these complications.

Another condition which negatively affects the horse's performance is any reduction in diameter of the nasal passages, the nasopharynx, and/or the larynx as a result of any obstruction. This may make the horse breathe with a noisy sound ("roaring") during exercise.

A partial reduction in diameter of the nasal passages during exercise may be caused by a noseband placed very low and too tight, which will make the horse breathe loudly. This cause of "roaring" may be easily detected and corrected.

Nasal polyps (overgrown tissues in the nasal passages) and/or any damage to the laryngeal nerve (that controls the muscles of the larynx) usually cause the horse to breathe very loudly during a workout and may lead to suffocation of the horse if the physical activity continues. In a case like this, a veterinarian should examine the nasopharynx and larynx in order to diagnose possible causes, the risks of exercising the horse, and to recommend a treatment.

In some cases, when the horse is ridden with its face in a vertical position during a workout, the horse may breathe noisily ("roar") due to associated nervousness/excitation. When this is the situation, the trainer/rider should find a comfortable head position for the horse, and try to calm the horse down while performing, in order to keep it from "roaring."

TYPES OF ENERGY FOR SPECIFIC EXERCISES

The **MUSCULAR** system is made up of **voluntary contracting muscles**, **tendons**, and **ligaments** (that provide locomotion); **involuntary muscles of the heart**; and **involuntary smooth muscles** of the respiratory, digestive, and urinary systems, among others. The diverse functions of the muscles include maintaining the body's structure, providing movement (voluntary contracting muscles, tendons, and ligaments), and performing vital functions (involuntary contracting muscles).

The skeletal muscles and tendons control the horse's locomotion by combined periods of shortening (contraction) and lengthening (relaxation) of the muscle fibers. The muscles involved in any physical activity require a gradual preparation, over several weeks of training, for the horse to perform the required exercises with consistency. Additionally, the diet should provide energy and other nutrients for the physical activity.

Because all muscles involved in exercise require energy for contraction, the more muscle work demanded, the higher the energy required. Paso Fino horses, performing demanding physical activities on a regular basis (e.g., preparing for competition), need, at a minimum, twice the amount of energy as is required for a horse at rest. However, energy requirements depend also on individual needs; meaning that horses of the same physiological stage, body condition index, and physical activity may require different daily amounts of energy, depending on individual metabolic rates.

Carbohydrates, fat, fiber (cellulose and hemicellulose), and protein (although it is not an ideal source) are the nutrients the horse uses to produce energy. Energy is stored by the horse in different ways, depending on the type of regular exercise and diet. Adenosine triphosphate (commonly known as "*ATP*"), the energy molecule required by the muscle cells for contraction, is produced from the different sources of energy, either by aerobic or anaerobic pathways, depending on the availability of oxygen during the physical activity.

Three types of muscle fibers, with different functions and sources of energy, impact muscle contraction in the horse. The first type of muscle fibers is known as "**slow-twitch**," whose source of energy is from aerobic metabolism (aerobic pathway). These are the muscle fibers used by a horse at a walk. Walking is a physical activity of low intensity in which these fibers have enough oxygen provided at all times through oxygenated blood. They produce *ATP* mainly from either fat (fatty acids) or volatile fatty acids (such as, acetate, propionate, and butyrate) that are the final product after fermentation of cellulose and hemicellulose by specialized microorganisms in the cecum. Due to their oxidative pathway for producing energy, "slow-twitch" muscle fibers are not affected by fatigue, even though they keep working for a long period of time.

Thus, horses at rest, or horses whose walking is their only physical activity (for which oxygen is permanently available through easy breathing), may be fed regularly with good quality forage (grass and/or legume), adding some vegetable oil, if desired. Grain is not required in the diet of horses at rest or those horses that engage in low-intensity work, except in special conditions, such as for young horses in growing/developing stages, horses gaining weight, and mares that are pregnant and/or lactating. However, horses fed with poor quality forage (grass/hay) may need supplementation with grain to fulfill their needs.

The second type of muscle fibers is known as "**fast-twitch**," whose energy is produced either from aerobic or anaerobic metabolism (anaerobic pathway), depending on the condition at the time. These are the muscle fibers used by a Paso Fino horse that is required to work in gait. During the first minutes of being in gait, these fibers produce *ATP* through the aerobic pathway. After a few minutes of demanding physical activity (performing a consistent gait), the availability of oxygen becomes limited because the respiratory and circulatory systems cannot supply oxygen to the muscle fibers at the same rate as it is consumed for the production of *ATP* from fat and volatile fatty acids (aerobic pathway). So, when oxygen availability diminishes (anaerobic pathway), these muscle fibers produce *ATP* from glucose (either circulating in the blood or glycogen stored in the muscles and liver). Thus, Paso Fino horses being trained regularly (for example, while preparing for a competition) need to be fed good quality forage and grains/sugars in order to assure a high-storage of glycogen that will provide energy during demanding physical activity. Additionally, when fat is added to this diet (for example, vegetable oil), the horse in regular training increases glycogen storage. During a glycolytic (anaerobic) pathway of obtaining energy, "fast-twitch" muscle fibers are quickly affected by fatigue due to the production of lactic acid.

Note: Glycogen is stored when the horse is being trained regularly and fed soluble carbohydrates (grains/sugars).

There is also **another type of "fast-twitch" fibers**, whose source of energy is solely from anaerobic metabolism (anaerobic pathway). Due to their slightly quicker contraction than the muscle fibers described above, these are the muscle fibers used by a horse in Classic Fino after a few minutes of being in gait. Thus, diets for high performance horses that work regularly in a consistent gait should include carbohydrates.

In summary, a horse at rest or in low-intensity work (such as horses that mainly walk and perform Paso Corto once in a while) may be fed solely with good quality forage, optional vegetable oil, minerals, salt, and water. Horses in low-intensity work, being supplemented with grains, store mainly fat instead of glycogen. This occurs because the normal way that the muscles of these horses produce energy is aerobic (oxidative), and not anaerobic (glycolytic). Conversely, a few weeks before a competition (or a long ride), a horse should be trained with exercises that allow development of endurance for the activity, and be fed according to the intensity of the physical activity, which should include grains/sugars. Hard working horses (during the weeks prior to a show or endurance competition) also benefit from vegetable oil in the diet, in addition to grains/sugars.

A training strategy for a horse that is fed properly, for the purpose of developing endurance while preparing for show competition, is as follows: At the start of the workout, the horse should be warmed up. This allows the horse gradually to increase its body's temperature, cardiac rate, and respiratory rate. Additionally, after that warm-up period, the horse's muscles are stretched, and the animal is ready for heavier physical activity. The horse should walk under saddle the first 6 to 15 minutes of the ride; then, the horse may start performing the gait, but not very intensively, during the next six minutes. Thereafter, the horse may be asked for high-intensity performance for a few minutes. After that, the horse should walk for few minutes and then it may perform intensively again for a few more minutes. After repeating this sequence three or four times during a training session, the horse should be cooled down by asking it to walk under saddle during the final 10 to 15 minutes of the workout.

After the horse is un-tacked and rinsed with warm water (see Chapter 5: "Colors of Paso Fino horses"), the horse should be walked for about 15 to 30 minutes, led by the "pisador" (lead line). If the weather is very cold and the horse is sweaty after being unsaddled, it is best to put on a cooling sheet (see Chapter 13: "Tack and attire"). The cooling sheet allows the animal's high temperature to decrease slowly to become even with the air temperature. After intense physical activity, the horse should rest half an hour, at a minimum, before drinking water or eating grain. This helps prevent colic.

The trainer should alternate long rides (of about one hour) with short rides (of about half hour), one or two per day, five or six days a week.

MUSCULAR FATIGUE

During a low-intensity physical activity, oxygen is permanently available, and *ATP* production does not cause muscular fatigue, because the other end products (water and carbon dioxide) are not accumulated in the body, but exhaled. However, oxygen is not as readily available after a few minutes of a high-intensity physical activity. This reduction of available oxygen activates the anaerobic pathway to produce *ATP*.

Lactic acid, an intermediate product obtained when *ATP* is being produced by glycolytic action (anaerobic pathway), seems to be the primary substance responsible for muscular fatigue during exercise. When lactic acid is produced from glucose, there is no oxygen available at that time, but because the horse keeps breathing and oxygen becomes available again, *ATP* finally may be produced from lactic acid. However, when lactic acid accumulates in muscles during a workout, the muscles become painful unless the lactic acid returns to the oxidative pathway to produce *ATP* (aerobic condition). Thus, to prevent the accumulation of lactic acid in the muscles (and the associated discomfort) after a high-intensity physical activity, the horse should be cooled down properly, as explained above, which assures that all the lactic acid is converted into *ATP*.

DEHYDRATION

In addition to the other causes of dehydration noted in Chapter 10: "Health basics," excessive sweating may also affect the horse under high-intensity physical activity. Hot weather may cause dehydration in horses during intermediate-intensity exercise.

During exercise, the internal temperature of the horse is elevated. As soon as this happens, two physiological processes occur simultaneously. The warm blood flow near the skin increases, and sweat (water and electrolytes) is liberated from the skin by the sweat glands. Evaporation of sweat dissipates the internal heat and, therefore, cools the horse down.

If sweat is not excessive and frequent, the horse should recover the missed electrolytes and fluids with proper diet (that includes salt), drinking enough water, and rest. However, horses that sweat regularly need to be supplemented with electrolytes.

On the other hand, when a horse starts to sweat during physical activity, it is not necessarily caused by a higher internal temperature due to the workout; sweating may be due to high stress caused by a scary environment (such as loud noises, unknown obstacles in the way, vehicles moving) or an aggressive rider.

To prevent dehydration from excessive sweating:

- During hot weather and/or show days, offering grain mixed with water ("soup") increases water intake. Giving the horse about ten lbs. of fresh, cut carrots (which most horses like to eat) twice a day, in between regular meals, also increases water intake.

- Before a long session of high-intensity activity (such as a competition), the horse may be fed hay, but not grain, up to three hours before the exercise. Saliva used to chew and swallow the hay will be absorbed in the intestine and later used to fulfill the need for fluids.

- Just before a ride during hot weather, giving the horse a bath with cool water keeps the horse cool for a considerable period of time, which reduces perspiration during the workout.

When the horse is already dehydrated, either during or after a ride, this condition usually is corrected within one to two hours after drinking water with electrolytes, in small amounts, every 15 minutes, and with rest. If this does not help, a veterinarian should provide hydrating fluids to the horse.

CHAPTER 13

TACK AND ATTIRE

The term "**tack**" describes all the items put on a horse for handling, training, or riding. Tack may also be described as the ′attire′ a horse wears for diverse activities. For example, the bit, reins, and saddle are pieces of tack that, when put on a horse, allow the rider to have a comfortable and a safe ride. Cleaning/grooming implements, such as a hoof pick, curry comb, and brush, are not considered pieces of tack.

Just as feed and medicines are basic supplies for a healthy animal, tack is another important item for controlling and riding the horse. Each piece of tack should fit the horse's anatomy perfectly. Materials must be soft for the horse (for comfort), resistant (because a broken piece of tack may cause an accident), durable (because good quality tack is expensive), and attractive (to highlight the horse's beauty). The photos in this chapter are provided courtesy of the tack store of *Ocala's School of Equestrian Art*.

CLASSIFICATION OF TACK

To better understand its function, tack may be classified into five groups: handling, protection, riding, training, and safety.

- **Tack for handling**: A halter put on the horse's head, either permanently or provisionally, is the proper piece of tack for catching and handling the horse. Once a lead rope is attached to the halter, either with a knot or a snap, the horse may be led safely by the handler, as well as tied to a post or cross-tied for purposes of grooming, hoof trimming/shoeing, bathing, injecting, deworming, palpating, ultrasounding, etc. Both halter and lead rope are the most essential pieces of tack for handling any horse no matter the age, sex, or training stage.

For every day use, the recommended halter for the Paso Fino horse is made of either nylon straps or cords for durability and safety in case the horse pulls when it is tied. A halter made of leather straps is recommended, when the horse keeps the halter on permanently (in the stall or pasture), because it is breakable in case of an accident.

The halter must fit the Paso Fino horse's head properly. The size of the halter varies according to the horse's age. A strap halter with buckles at the upper belt (that is placed on the poll), and the barbada (the belt behind the noseband), may be adjusted for comfort and a better fit. When a horse has a halter on, in the pasture or the stall, the noseband-barbada set must be loose enough for the horse to chew food comfortably. It must not be so tight that the horse cannot move its lower jaw to chew. Conversely, the halter must not be so loose that the horse is able to remove it. Some horses with permanent halters may develop a skin irritation under the halter, during the summer, due to sweating.

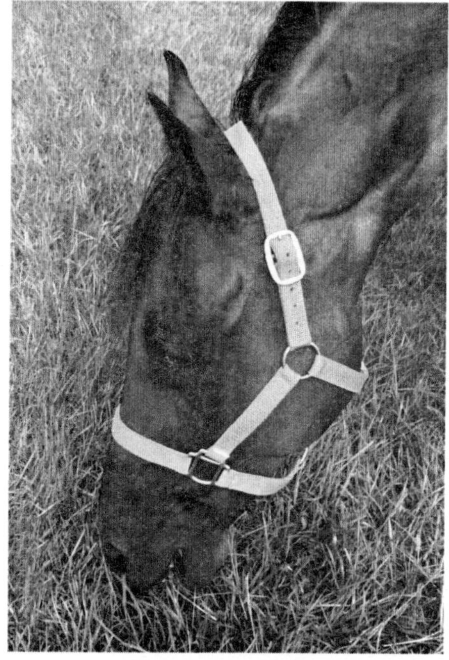

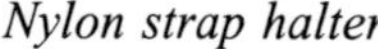

Nylon strap halter

Cord halter

- **Tack for protection**: The tack that prevents the horse from becoming sick or for faster recuperation from disease.

  - **Blanket**: This covering keeps the horse warm and comfortable during cold weather. It is also important for keeping the horse with a respiratory disease warm. Therefore, the blanket is an important "first aid" supply at the Paso Fino farm. A good blanket should fit the horse properly, according to its size. It should be made of a medium-thick to thick material that isolates the horse from cold weather and wind.

  - **Cooling fleece sheet** is used for cooling off a sweaty horse after a hard workout during cold weather. It also helps dry the horse faster after a bath during cold weather. This kind of sheet is made of light wool, or another light fabric, and may be designed to cover the whole body of a horse from its poll.

Blanket

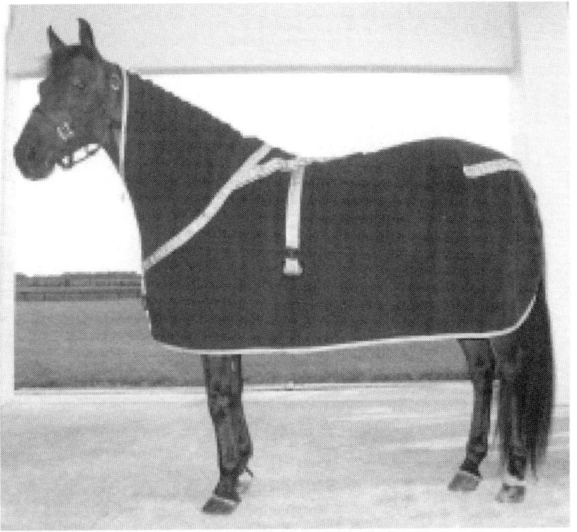

Cooling fleece sheet
(Photo courtesy of Allen and Glenna Struthers)

- **Fly mask** (that covers the eyes and face) keeps insects from reaching the horse's skin or from feeding on the horse's eyes. This piece of tack is especially helpful during the heavy fly seasons. A fly mask is made of a light polyester mesh.

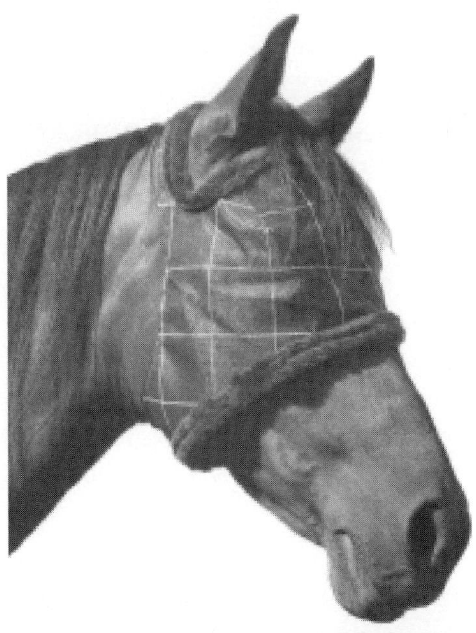

- **Shipping halter**: This type of halter is made of strong, wide, flat nylon straps, and often is covered by a cushioned material, in order to keep the skin from suffering abrasions if the horse pulls during shipment.

- **Shipping boots**: These are designed to protect the horse's legs from injuries when being loaded in a trailer, transported, or unloaded from a trailer. Shipping boots are made of a durable, heavy outer layer (for example nylon) with thick padding inside. They are adjusted on the horse's legs by means of wide, self-fastening straps (Velcro). For the greatest comfort and safety during a trip, the horse should be trained to wear shipping boots a few days before the trip, as well as to load and unload from a trailer.

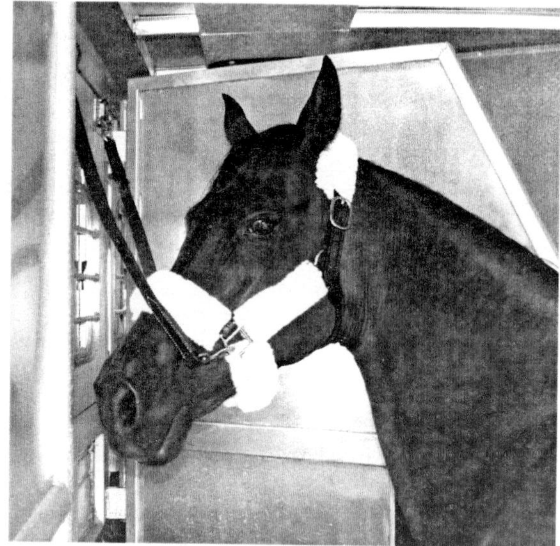

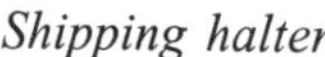

Shipping halter

Shipping boots

- **Shipping wraps**: These wraps are used for the same purpose as shipping boots. However, because shipping wraps consist of two types of bandages for each leg (the quilt and the cover), they take longer to put on the horse than shipping boots. Additionally, the process of putting shipping wraps on the horse's legs requires more expertise, because each bandage must be aligned perfectly to stay in place without affecting the circulation of blood to the foot.

• **Tack for riding**: All the tack that allows the rider to have an easy, comfortable, and safe ride on the horse. Riding tack must fit the horse's anatomy for its safety and comfort. Additionally, good quality tack, properly matching the horse, highlights the horse's beauty.

- **Colombian jaquima** (also called **headgear** in English): This piece of tack, put on the Paso Fino horse's head, is accompanied by the bit, the bit-hanger, and the reins. The jaquima is separate from the bit and bit-hanger; therefore, the jaquima must be put on the horse's head first, before any other piece of tack.

  The jaquima consists of the crownpiece (that goes on the poll), brow band (that goes on the forehead), throat strap (that goes on the throat region), bosal (or noseband), two cheek pieces (that join the lower ends of the crownpiece and the two side rings of the bosal), and the barbada (attached behind the bosal and placed under the horse's jaw). The buckle(s), placed on top of the crown piece and/or the two cheek pieces, the barbada, and sometimes at the throat strap, allow the jaquima to be adjusted on the horse's head for a better fit.

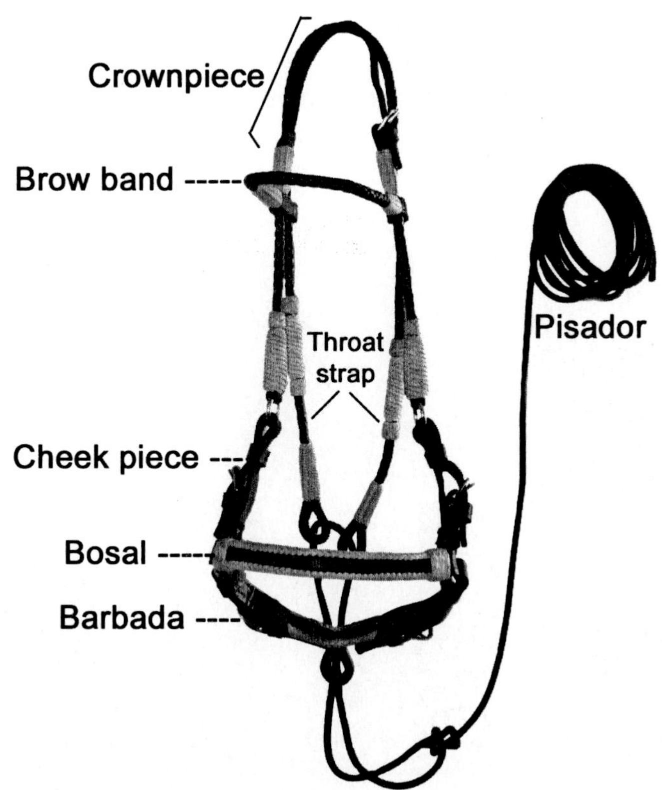

When the jaquima has a pisador (lead line), it is attached to the throat strap and passed through the barbada. The pisador is helpful for both tying and leading the horse. For riding, the pisador should be looped and tied at the left side of the saddle pommel.

The brow band and noseband of the show jaquima may be up to 1 inch wide for showing in *PFHA* sanctioned shows. The cheek pieces may be from 3/8 to 5/8 of an inch wide. The show jaquima may be made of flat leather (plain or stitched), rolled leather, braided leather, or goat skin (only with matching white or cream colored reins). If a pisador is attached to the jaquima for showing, this may be made of rawhide *(PFHA – Constitution and Rule Book, Chapter Two, Section VII, Subsection D, 2)*.

Horses at three or four years of age (in Schooling, Amateur Owner, and Youth classes, except Equitation and Horsemanship classes) may have any training jaquima that is not considered cruel or inhumane by the Judge or Show Committees *(PFHA – Constitution and Rule Book, Chapter Two, Section VII, Subsection C)*. A rawhide leather jaquima is allowed only for Schooling classes *(PFHA – Constitution and Rule Book, Chapter Two, Section VII, Subsection D, 2)*. However, a jaquima made of rawhide is allowed in all Pleasure Division classes.

The show jaquima in *CONFEPASO* sanctioned shows should be made of flat and/or rolled leather (plain or stitched, including rawhide and goat skin as well) and requires a pisador *(Reglamento de Competencias de Caballos de Paso - CONFEPASO, Chapter 2, Article 2, Section 1 "Rienda y Jáquima")*. The pisador is made of rawhide.

Nylon jaquimas (straps or cords) are not allowed for competition in *PFHA* nor *CONFEPASO* sanctioned shows, although, sometimes, they are used for daily riding. Note that any material, leather or nylon, must be soft enough to make the jaquima comfortable for the horse. A pisador made of nylon is another option for daily riding.

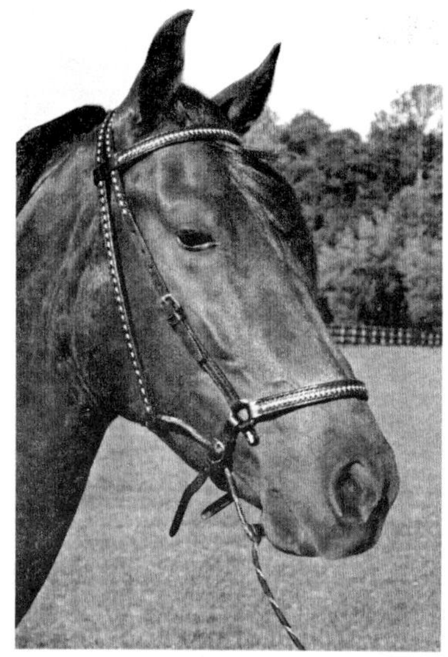

Flat, stitched leather jaquima

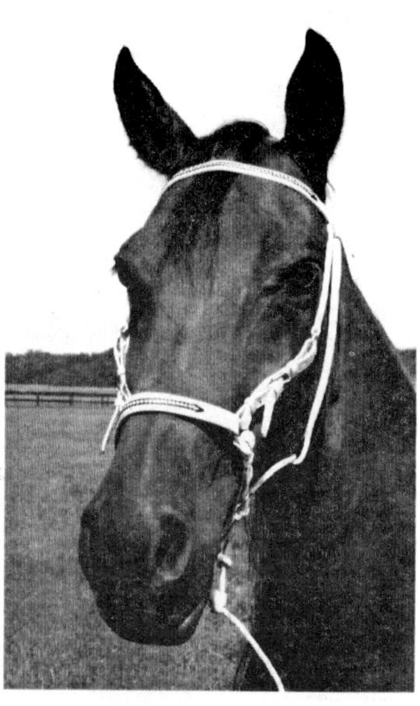

Flat rawhide jaquima with stitched brow band and bosal

Braided, rolled leather jaquima

- **Bit-hanger**: The bit-hanger serves to hold the bit in the horse's mouth. Both of the bit hanger ends are attached to the upper slots of the bit shanks, either by bent-over straps or snaps (not allowed for showing). For aesthetics, the material and color of the bit-hanger should be the same as the jaquima. The bit and the bit-hanger are put on the horse's head after the jaquima.

- **Bridle**: This piece of tack works like a jaquima and a bit-hanger together. The most common materials used for bridles are flat leather, rolled leather, braided leather, and nylon straps or cords.

The **English** style **bridle** has a bit-hanger, a brow band, a throat strap, and a **cavesson**, consisting of the noseband-barbada set, two cheek pieces, and a crownpiece strap (that attaches to the top of both cheek pieces). The **Western bridle** has a bit-hanger, a brow band (or a one-ear hole), often has a throat strap, but has no cavesson.

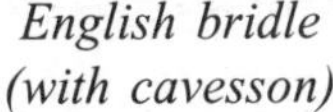

English bridle (with cavesson)

Western bridle with brow band and throat strap

Western bridle with one-ear hole

Like the Colombian jaquima and bit hanger, the English bridle made of leather (flat, rolled, or braided) may be used for showing Paso Finos when English tack is designated. Dimensions of the show bridle are the same as those used for the (Colombian) jaquima: the brow band and the noseband may be up to 1 inch wide and the cheek pieces may be from 3/8 to 5/8 of an inch wide *(PFHA – Constitution and Rule Book, Chapter Two, Section VII, Subsection D, 2).*

A Western bridle is required for showing in the Paso Pleasure Western class of *PFHA* sanctioned shows *(PFHA – Constitution and Rule Book, Chapter Three, Section VI, Subsection B, 3).*

- **Bit**: This piece of tack is put in the horse's mouth for the rider to ′drive′ the horse through the reins. The bit is discussed in detail in the next chapter.

- **Reins**: These allow the rider's hands to have contact with the horse's mouth by using the bit. A fully trained horse will feel and interpret in its mouth the rider's commands that are applied through the bit-reins set. The Paso Fino horse in training (schooling) is ′driven′ by reins attached to the training jaquima on both sides of the bosal and/or the two rings placed toward the center of the barbada (known as "jaw rings"). Once the horse starts learning to work by the bit, two sets of reins are used; one is attached to the training jaquima and the other is attached to the bit (see Chapter 15: "Horse psychology and training").

  Schooling horses (three or four years old) in *PFHA* sanctioned shows may be ridden with two pairs of reins, a pair attached to the bit and the other pair attached to the jaquima (either to both sides of the bosal or to the jaw rings of the barbada). Horses at five years of age, or older, must be ridden with only one pair of reins attached to the bit, except horses in the Pleasure Division classes (at any age), which may be ridden with one or two pairs of reins, and with or without a bit.

Schooling horses (from 30 to 36 months of age) in *CONFEPASO* sanctioned shows may be ridden either with one or two pairs of reins attached to the training jaquima. Older horses must be ridden solely with one pair of reins attached to the bit, except for horses from 37 to 48 months of age, which may be ridden with an additional pair of reins attached to the jaquima.

Reins for Paso Fino horses, either for show or not, are from 7 feet 2 inches (about 2.2 m) in length to 8 feet 2 inches (about 2.5 m.) in length. Reins for showing Paso Fino horses in both *PFHA* and *CONFEPASO* may be flat, rolled, or braided, made of leather, nylon rope, cotton rope, or any other man-made fiber.

For showing a horse in any class of a *PFHA* sanctioned show, the reins may end in leather straps and buckles or snaps, that attach to the bit and/or to the jaquima (at the bosal or the barbada). When nylon reins are used for showing (either ending with leather straps or snaps), they must be the same color as the jaquima or the bridle *(PFHA – Constitution and Rule Book, Chapter Two, Section VII, Subsection D, 3).*

In all the classes of *CONFEPASO* sanctioned shows, horses must be ridden with reins (made of any material explained above) ending in leather straps and buckles that arc attached to the bit and/or to the jaquima. Reins cannot exceed 2.5 m. (8 feet 2 inches) in length *(Reglamento de Competencias de Caballos de Paso - CONFEPASO, Chapter 2, Article 2, Section 1 "Rienda y Jáquima").*

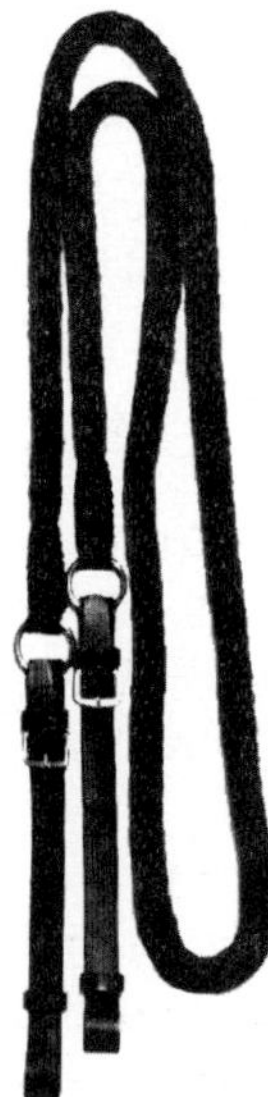

- **Saddle**: This piece of tack is placed on the horse's back in order to give the rider a comfortable and safe ride.

To guarantee comfort, the saddle has to fit both the rider and the horse. A Paso Fino saddle fits the rider properly when the seat is well-cushioned and has enough room to fit the rider comfortably, but should not exceed 3 inches in length (from front to rear) than the correct size for that person. The saddle's seat should be deep enough for the rider to feel the horse's gait. Additionally, a comfortable saddle allows the rider to squeeze the inside thighs easily.

The saddle fits the horse properly when the following requirements are met:

- The cushioned panels allow the weight of the rider to be placed uniformly on both sides of the horse's back.

- It makes no pressure on the horse's shoulders.

- The saddle tree is uniformly kept off the horse's spine from the withers to the front of the loins, which may be seen from the horse's rear, when the saddle is on.

  Note: The "tree" is the internal, hard structure of the saddle made of wood, a synthetic fiber, and/or metal, to which the seat is attached.

Even though Paso Finos have the amazing ability to carry more weight on their backs than many other horse breeds (in relation to their body weight) without altering their gait, the extra weight may affect negatively the horse's back (spine, muscles, and skin). Therefore, the weight of a saddle must be as light as possible to compensate for the weight added by the rider.

Additionally, a light saddle is easier for the rider to place on the horse than a heavy one. In practical terms, 25 lbs. is the recommended maximum weight of a saddle with stirrups for Paso Finos. Most adults should be able to pick up the saddle with the two index fingers.

Each stirrup (either iron-or leather-covered) and its leather strap (either with a fender or not) is attached to the stirrup bar of the saddle that is located under the skirt. Each stirrup should be adjusted to the rider's leg length with the buckle that is located on the leather strap.

Three types of saddles are used to ride Paso Fino horses:

- **English-type**: The main characteristics of an English-type saddle are the concave seat where a rider sits upright, the half rounded flap that projects down and slightly forward from the pommel and under approximately 2/3 of the seat on both sides, and the skirt that covers the stirrup bar on both sides.

  The English-type saddle for Paso Finos includes five main designs:

  - The Paso Show Colombian saddle (also called Colombian Galapago). This is made with matching leather straps and leather covered stirrups, but they may be changed for iron stirrups.

  - The Dressage saddle with straps and iron stirrups.

  - The English pleasure saddle with straps and iron stirrups.

  - The tree-less English saddle.

  - The orthopedic (Paso) saddle.

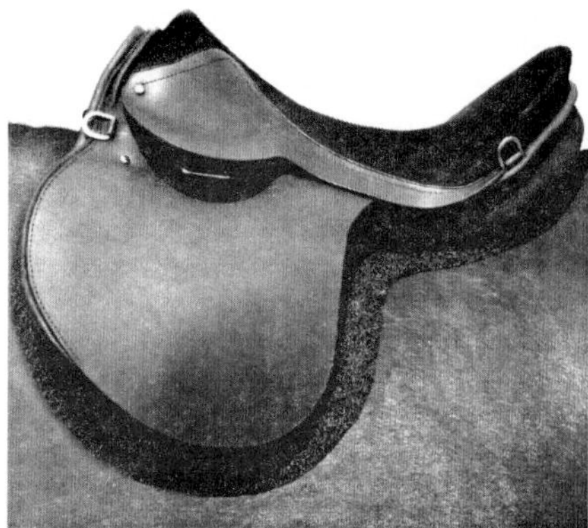
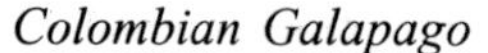

Colombian Galapago

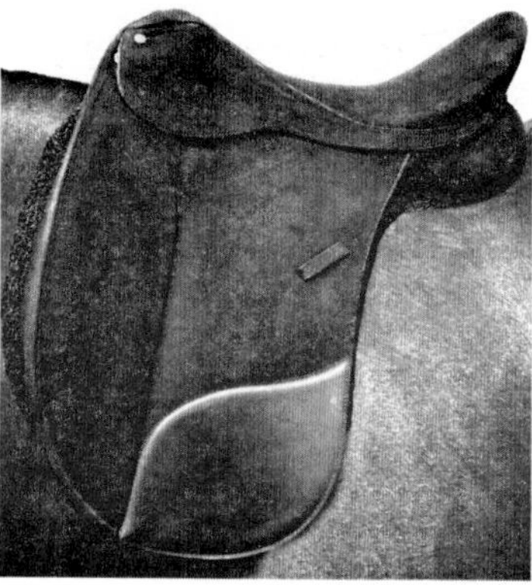

Dressage saddle

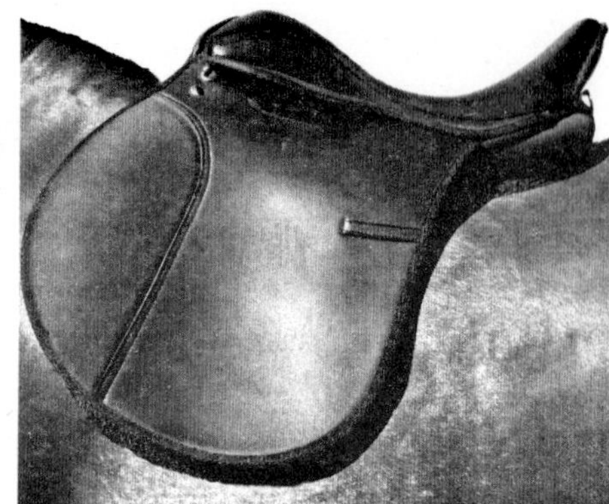

English pleasure saddle

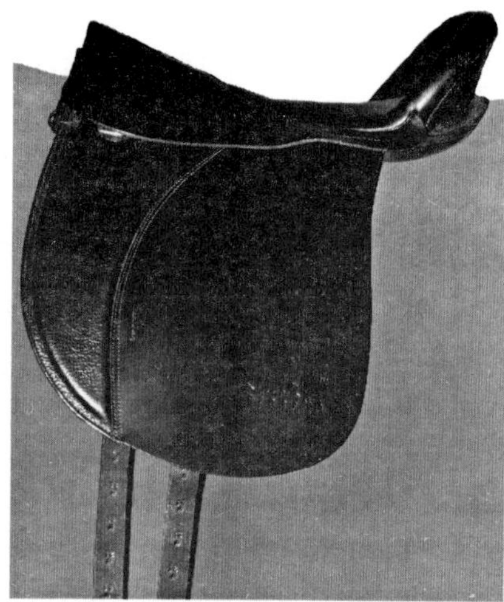

Tree-less English saddle (by KUDA)

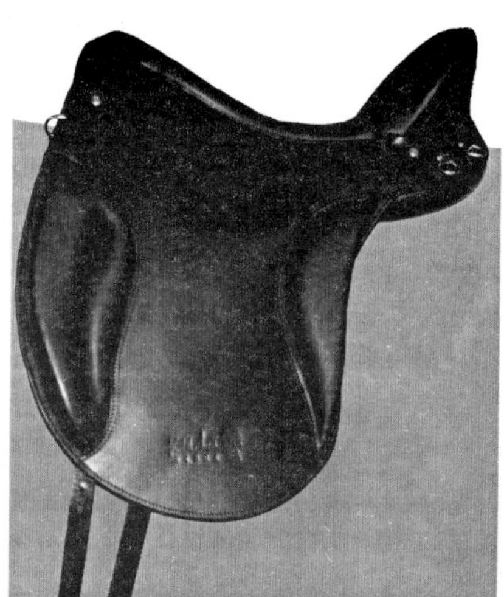

Gold Cup Orthopedic (Paso) saddle (by KUDA)

An English-type saddle is required for showing Classic Fino horses *(PFHA – Constitution and Rule Book, Chapter Three, Section III, Subsection C)*, Paso Performance horses *(PFHA – Constitution and Rule Book, Chapter Three, Section IV, Subsection C)*, and for Equitation competitions in *Paso Fino Horse Association* sanctioned shows *(PFHA – Constitution and Rule Book, Chapter Three, Section I, Subsection B, 2, i)*. The English-type saddle is optional for all the Pleasure Division classes.

The forward seat Jumping saddle is allowed only in those classes when jumping is required *(PFHA – Constitution and Rule Book, Chapter Two, Section VII, Subsection D, 1)*, such as the Paso Versatility class.

An English-type saddle, such as a Colombian Galapago, made of a synthetic material or covered with leather, and in a somber (conservative) color (usually black or brown) is required in *CONFEPASO* sanctioned shows *(Reglamento de Competencias de Caballos de Paso - CONFEPASO, Chapter 2, Article 2, Section 1 "Silla, sillín o galápago")*. Some Paso Fino trail riders like the English-type saddle for long rides.

- **Western-type**: The Western saddle's main characteristic is the presence of a "horn" over the pommel that is used to wrap a rope in order to hold a lassoed cow. The stirrups are leather covered, and the stirrup's leather straps are accompanied by fenders to keep the rider's legs free of sweat from the horse and mud from the trail. The Western-type saddle is used for trail riding and working with cattle, including sports like "Team Penning" and "Cutting."

  This type of saddle is required for showing in the Paso Pleasure Western class of *PFHA* sanctioned shows *(PFHA – Constitution and Rule Book, Chapter Three, Section VI, Subsection B, 3).* The Western-type saddle is optional for the Paso Trail class of *PFHA* sanctioned shows *(PFHA – Constitution and Rule Book, Chapter Three, Section VI, Subsection C, 3)*. The Western-type saddle is required for showing in the Paso Pleasure Western class of *CONFEPASO* sanctioned shows *(Reglamento de Competencias de Caballos de Paso - CONFEPASO, Chapter 5, Article 7 "Accesorios")*.

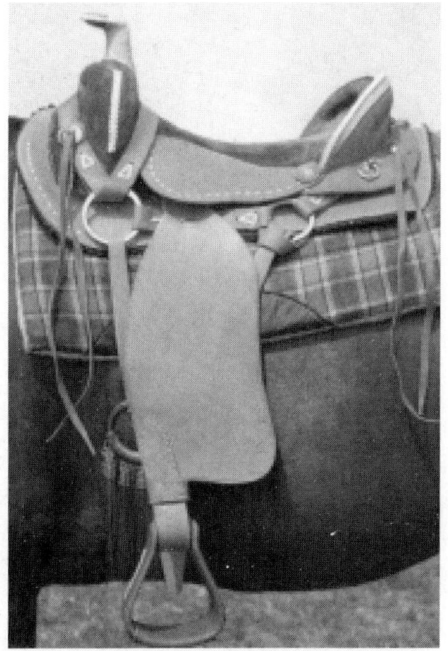

Western saddle

- **Pleasure-type**: This type of saddle may be used for showing Pleasure horses. It is also used for trail rides and endurance competitions. Additionally, this type of saddle is commonly used by Paso Fino trainers for daily riding.

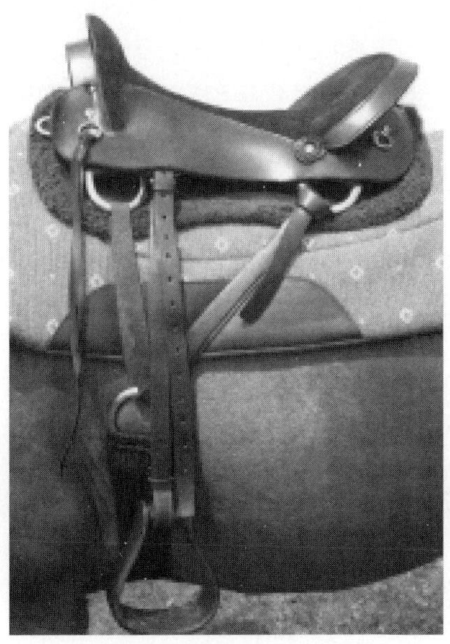

Colombian Tereque

The stirrups of a Pleasure-type saddle are usually leather covered (as in the Western saddle), but the stirrup's leather straps are not always accompanied by fenders. The Pleasure-type saddle includes the Colombian Tereque, the McClellan saddle, and the Endurance saddle.

The parts of the Paso Colombian show saddle and the Western saddle are shown in these pictures.

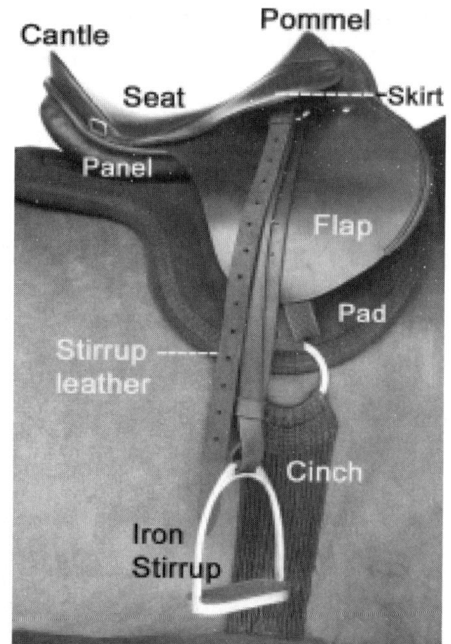

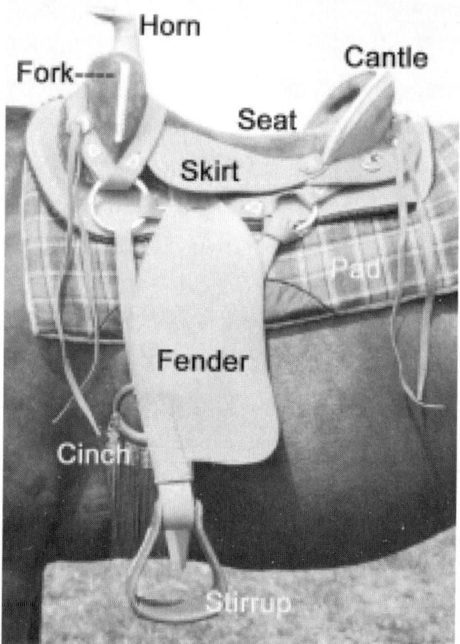

- **Cinch** (also called "**girth**"): This strap (3 to 4 inches wide) holds the saddle in place by passing around the horse's girth area, about 2 inches behind the elbows. The cinch is made of leather, cotton, nylon, or neoprene. If both ends of the cinch have buckles (two buckles at each side), they must be attached to the saddle using the belts (called "billets"), located on both undersides of the saddle. If both ends of the cinch have rings, they must be attached to the one or two rings the saddle has on each underside, by using leather or nylon straps, either with a buckle or by making a special knot.

Most English-type saddles have billets for attaching the cinch; however, the Paso Show Colombian saddle commonly has both options, billets and rings (to attach the cinch using straps). The Western-type and the Pleasure-type saddles have two rings (or a slot and a ring) on each underside for attaching the cinch with straps; one ring (or slot) is placed in front of the stirrup leather strap, and the other is placed behind. Riders can choose to use the front ring or both rings.

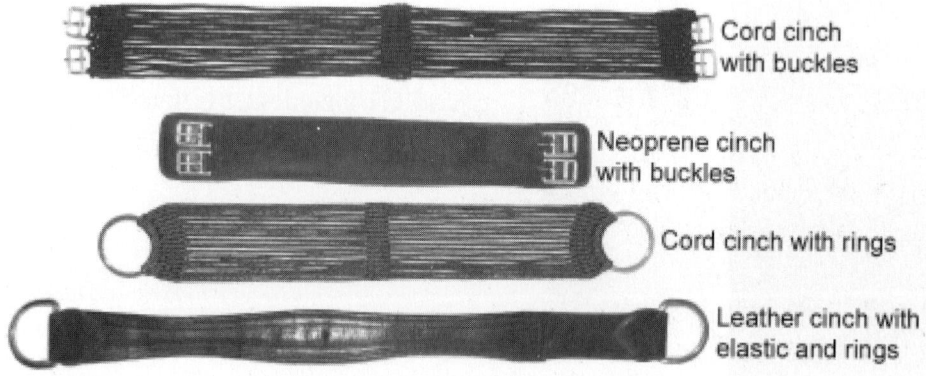

After each ride, when the horse is being un-tacked, the rider should look at the horse's girth area to confirm that there are no abrasions caused by the cinch. If any abrasion is found, the cinch either must be fixed or replaced. The abrasion should be treated as explained in Chapter 10: "Health basics."

- **Breast plate** (also called "**breast strap**"): This piece of tack may be used with any type of saddle to help hold it in place and keep the saddle from moving backwards when the horse and rider are going uphill. Thus, a breast plate is often helpful for trail rides. The breast plate is commonly made of leather, nylon, or cotton straps with buckles that may adjust the breast plate to the size of the horse.

  The "two-point breast plate" wraps around the horse's chest horizontally and attaches to the two rings of the saddle located at the front of both sides, just below the pommel. The "three-point breast plate" (also called "English breast plate") wraps around the horse's chest not only horizontally, but also vertically, allowing the saddle to be held in place more securely. It attaches to the two rings of the saddle like the "two-point breast plate" and also has a strap starting at the center of the chest and ending at the cinch.

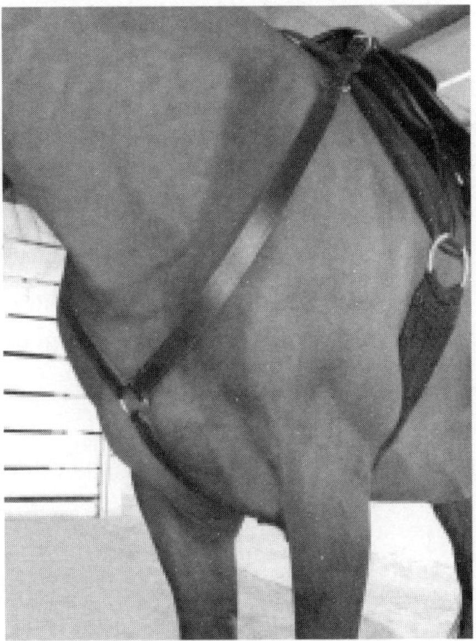

English (three-point) breast plate

  An English breast plate, not exceeding 1 inch wide, may be used for showing in *PFHA* sanctioned shows; however, silver or vinyl or reflective vinyl are prohibited *(PFHA - Constitution and Rule Book, Chapter Two, Section VII, Subsection D, 4)*. A breast plate is not allowed for showing horses in *CONFEPASO* sanctioned shows.

- **Crupper**: This piece of tack holds the saddle in place by keeping it from moving forward when the horse and rider are going downhill. The crupper is made of leather and is adjustable with one or two buckles. The "rabiza" is the part of the crupper that passes under the horse's tail. Two straps on both sides of the rabiza are attached to a ring on the saddle's rear, but in some cruppers, the two straps become one strap before reaching the saddle ring. The crupper is recommended for riding horses on inclined areas.

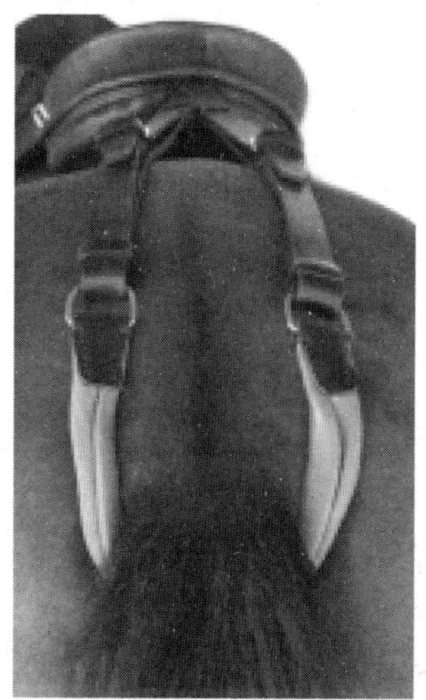

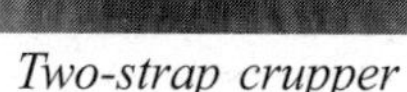

Two-strap crupper

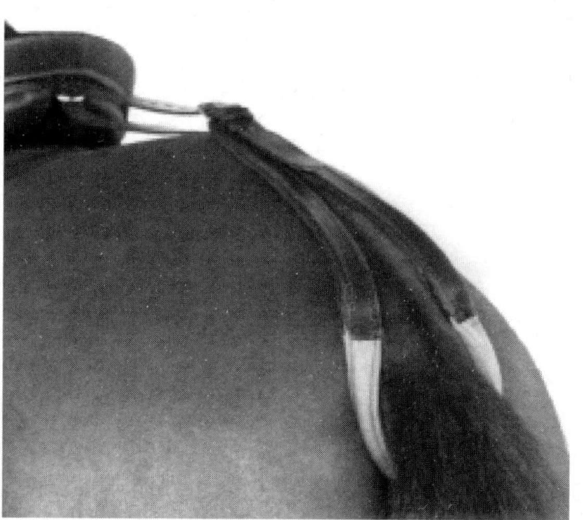

One-strap crupper

A crupper is not allowed for showing horses or in equitation classes in *PFHA* sanctioned shows. On the other hand, the use of a crupper ending in one strap is optional in *CONFEPASO* sanctioned shows *(Reglamento de Competencias de Caballos de Paso - CONFEPASO, Chapter 2, Article 2, Section 1 "Silla, sillín o galápago").*

- **Saddle pad**: This pad is placed between the horse's back and the saddle to protect the horse's back, by cushioning the pressure made by the weight of the saddle and the rider. The saddle pad also protects the saddle panels from sweat, making the saddle more durable.

  Using a saddle pad, that is conservative in color and conforms to the saddle's shape, is optional for showing horses in *PFHA* sanctioned shows *(PFHA – Constitution and Rule Book, Chapter Two, Section VII, Subsection D, 1)*. The use of a saddle pad made of leather, cotton, felt, or any synthetic fiber is also optional for showing horses in *CONFEPASO* sanctioned shows. *(Reglamento de Competencias de Caballos de Paso - CONFEPASO, Chapter 2, Article 2, Section 1 "Silla, sillín o galápago").*

  A good quality, well-designed saddle pad improves the appearance of both horse and rider. Saddle pads are made in different thicknesses and shapes, either rectangular or conforming to the different saddle shapes. They are made of diverse materials, such as cotton, felt, leather, foam, etc. and in a variety of colors, either conservative or bright depending of what is required or desired. Having a saddle pad for each horse prevents transmission of fungus and bacteria from one horse to another.

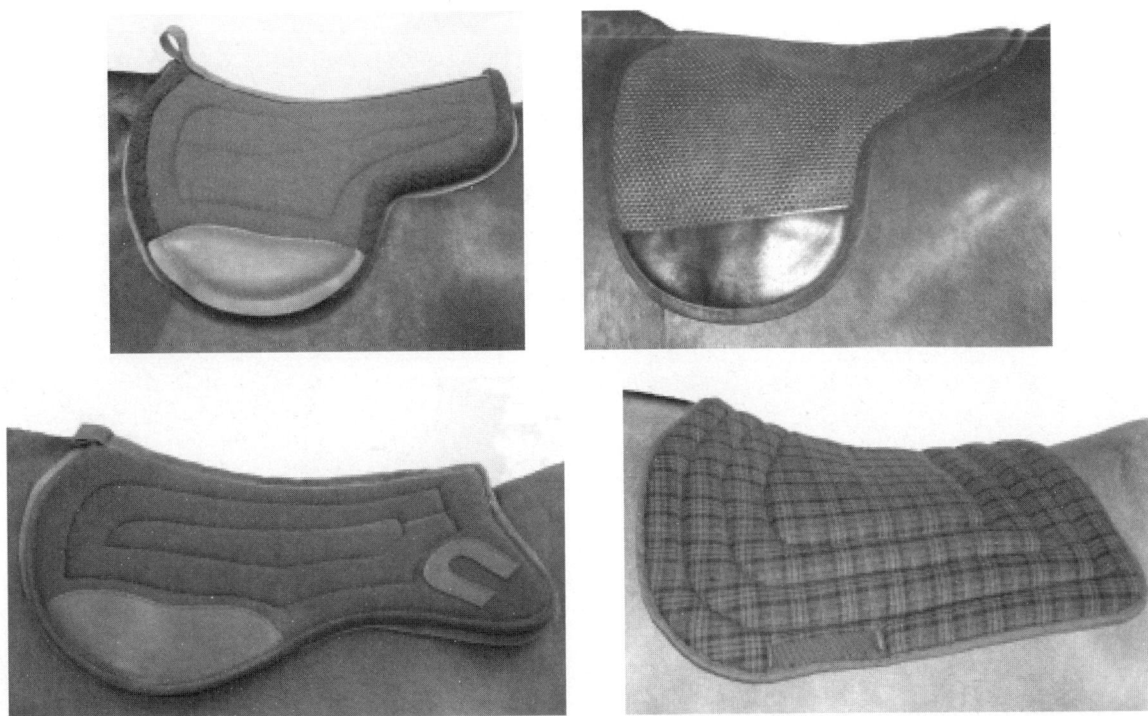

Different designs of saddle pads

The saddle and pad should be checked when the horse is being tacked-up in order to assure that they are in good condition. When the horse is being un-tacked, its back should be inspected in order to assure that neither the saddle nor the pad has caused any lesions.

- A **Saddle blanket** may be used under a Western-type saddle instead of a saddle pad (if so preferred). It is a rectangular blanket, folded in half, with no padding inside.

• **Training tack**: All the pieces of tack that give the trainer special help for training the horse.

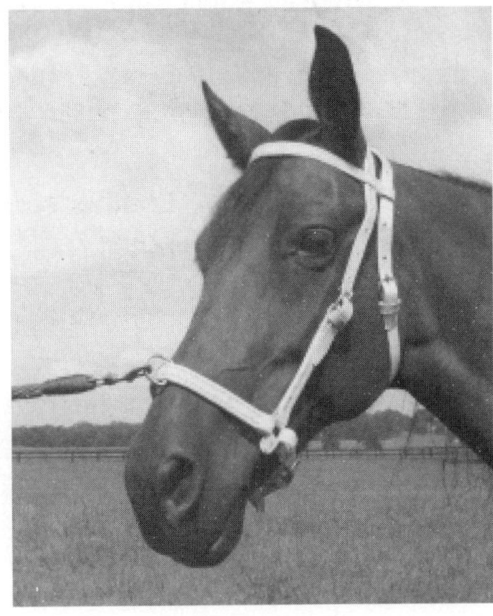

- **Longeing jaquima**: This piece of tack has a ring at the noseband that allows the trainer to longe the horse with its neck and back properly bent.

- **Cord breaking halter**: This is a halter made of cord, that may have a ring on each side of the noseband for attaching reins, if so needed. Because it is not severe and fits the horse's head very comfortably, some trainers use the cord breaking halter during the horse's first rides (see Chapter 15: "Horse psychology and training").

- **Training jaquima**: This piece of tack is used on the horse during the basic training stage. Commonly made of rawhide leather, its straps or cords are no wider than 1 inch. The cheek pieces of the training jaquima have buckles that allow the bosal to be changed for different training purposes.

- **Bosal**: This is the name given to the noseband of the jaquima. During training, the reins are attached to the ring at each end of the bosal. The horse in training may require different kinds of bosals at different stages of the training process. The most common types of bosals, depending on the severity, are described below:

    - **Soft**: Leather strap bosal, leather round bosal, and rope bosal.

The three soft bosals above are allowed when showing in all Schooling classes (Classic Fino, Paso Performance, and Paso Pleasure) in *PFHA* sanctioned shows.

Only leather bosals (flat or round) are allowed for the Schooling classes of Paso Fino and Colombian diagonal Paso horses in *CONFEPASO* sanctioned shows.

- **Intermediate severe**: Cord or rawhide knotted bosal, leather bosal with covered metal balls, and viril bosal (made of bull penis).

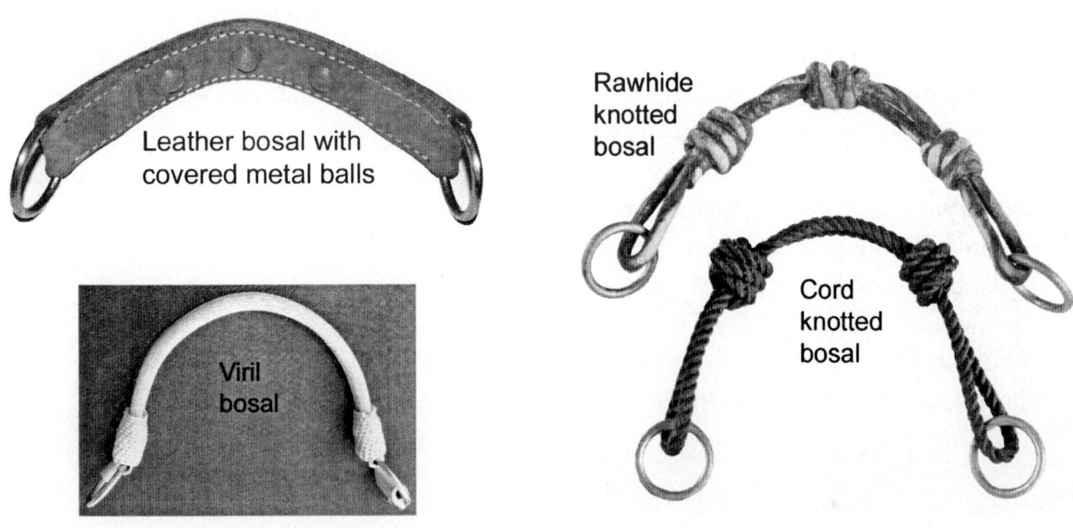

All intermediate severe bosals above are allowed when showing in Classic Fino and Paso Performance Schooling classes in *PFHA* sanctioned shows.

All intermediate severe bosals are prohibited in *CONFEPASO* sanctioned shows for any class.

- **Severe**: Metal curved and jointed bosal, metal flat chain bosal, and metal "serreta" bosal.

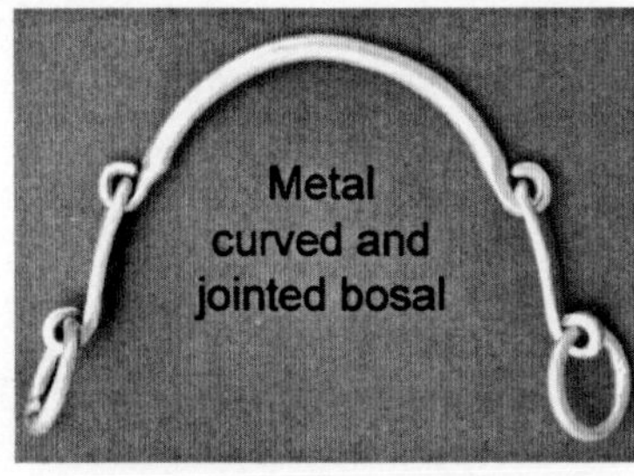

In Schooling classes (Classic Fino, Paso Performance, and Paso Pleasure), metal nosepieces (such as metal curved-hinged and flat chain bosals) may be used if properly covered to ensure comfort for the horse, and not considered cruel or inhumane by the Judge or Show Committee *(PFHA – Constitution and Rule Book, Chapter Two, Section VII, Subsection C)*. However, the metal "serreta" bosal is not allowed.

No metal is allowed on the horse's nose area in *CONFEPASO* shows for Schooling horses *(Reglamento de Competencias de Caballos de Paso - CONFEPASO, Chapter 2, Article 2, Section 1 "Rienda y Jáquima"),* or in any other class.

Note: The metal curved-hinged and flat chain bosals are recommended only to make specific corrections for a few sessions, but ensuring that the horse's nose is not injured. The metal "serreta" bosal is not recommended in any instance.

- **Barbada**: This is the strap placed behind the bosal of the jaquima. Because the barbada is attached to the side rings of the bosal and has two buckles, it is interchangeable. The jaquima for fully trained Paso Fino horses (not for schooling) has a soft plain barbada made of leather (for showing or trail riding) or nylon (for trail riding).

For training (schooling), the barbada has two rings placed toward its center and separated 2 to 3 inches apart ("jaw rings") for attaching a pair of training reins. The horse in training may require different kinds of barbadas, depending on specific training needs as, for example, lowering the face while bending its poll and neck. A braided barbada is commonly used to accomplish this purpose.

In Schooling classes (Classic Fino, Paso Performance, and Paso Pleasure), metal pieces under the chin (attached to the barbada) are allowed for showing, if they are sufficiently covered to ensure comfort for the horse, and not considered cruel or inhumane for the horse by the Judge or Show Committee *(PFHA – Constitution and Rule Book, Chapter Two, Section VII, Subsection C)*. In all Schooling classes, the barbada may have two "jaw rings" for attaching the training reins.

A flexible barbada made of a plain leather strap with two "jaw rings" and two buckles may be used in the Schooling classes (31 to 36 months of age) to attach the training reins at *CONFEPASO* sanctioned shows. Because horses 37 to 48 months of age may be ridden with two pairs of reins (one pair attached to the bit and the other pair to the jaquima), they may have a barbada with jaw rings to attach the optional pair of reins.

- **Jetera**: This is a piece of tack made of cord, thin rope, or horse's mane, with some metal rings attached, that is used in the horse's mouth at the beginning of the bitting stage of the schooling training.

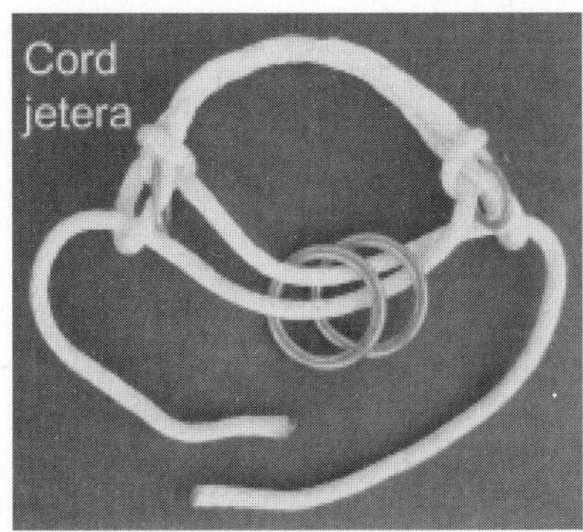

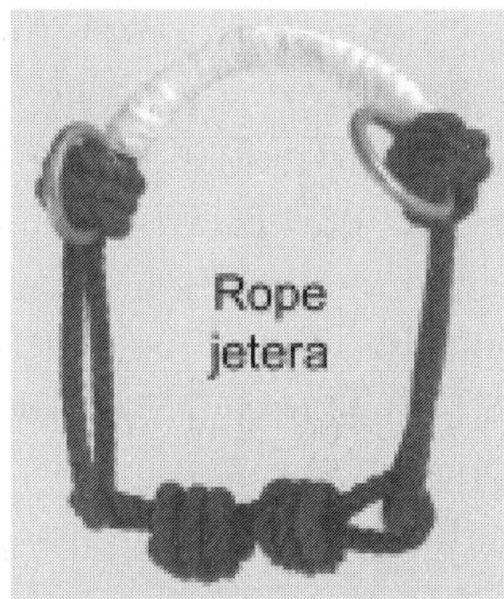

- **Collar**: This Colombian piece of Paso Fino tack encourages the horse to have the proper headset (with the face vertical). The collar is made of leather or nylon straps that wrap around the horse's neck from the chest to the withers and a strap that projects from the chest to the cinch. The collar allows the reins, that are attached from the jaquima and/or from the bit, to pass through a pair of rings placed above both points of the shoulder. The collar may be compared to a martingale, commonly used in many other horse breeds for a similar purpose.

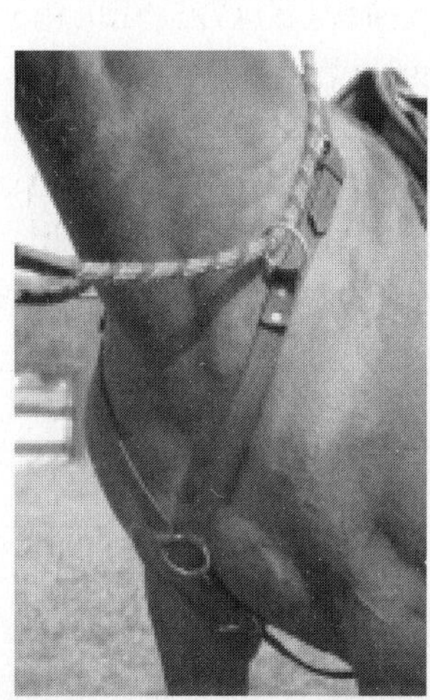

- **Canastilla**: This Colombian piece of tack is made of leather straps, buckles, and snaps; when put on the horse, it covers the horse's hindquarters and encourages the horse to propel its body forward by moving the hind legs under the hips. This helps to improve collection of the gait.

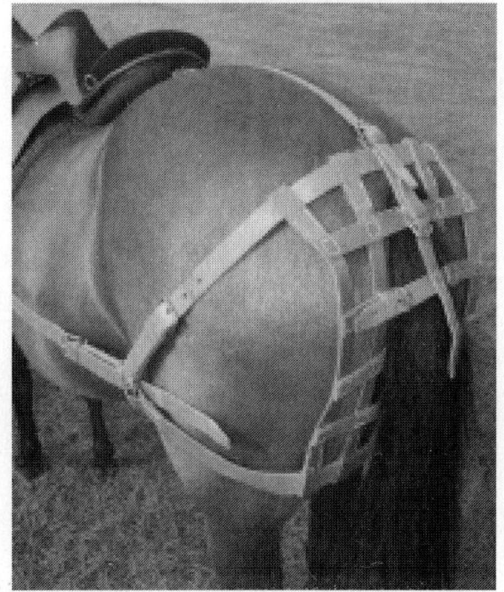

- **Whip** (also called "**crop**"): The rider should use this piece of tack to improve responses in some horses, when natural commands, such as voice, hands, and legs are not enough. When the whip is used on a Paso Fino, the rider should use it on the horse's shoulder or its lower neck, rather than the hips. Abusing the use of a whip may cause the horse to develop a resentment or insensitivity to it.

- **Longeing whip**: This whip may carefully be used for "longeing" the young horse during the longeing stage of training (see Chapter 15: "Horse psychology and training").

• **Tack for safety**: A set of hobbles, put on the horse's legs, keep the horse from kicking during certain activities. For example, the hind legs of a mare are often hobbled to prevent a veterinarian from being kicked when palpating the mare, performing a rectal ultrasound, or inseminating the mare at a farm where there is no palpation chute (see Chapter 9: "Facilities for horses"). The hind legs of a mare also are hobbled during breeding by direct mounting in order to prevent the stallion from being kicked.

Hobbles have three main parts: the set of two pastern-belts (to wrap the horse's pasterns), a breast plate made of nylon (to be placed around the horse's neck-chest area), and a ten foot long, strong cord with a safety snap.

Each pastern-belt has one buckle to fit the pastern and one ring to attach the cord. The pastern-belts must be strong enough to keep the horse's legs from pulling, but also wide enough and cushioned enough to keep the pasterns from being hurt. The cord is attached to the lower end of the breast plate through a safety snap (for easy release) to keep the horse from becoming tangled or injured.

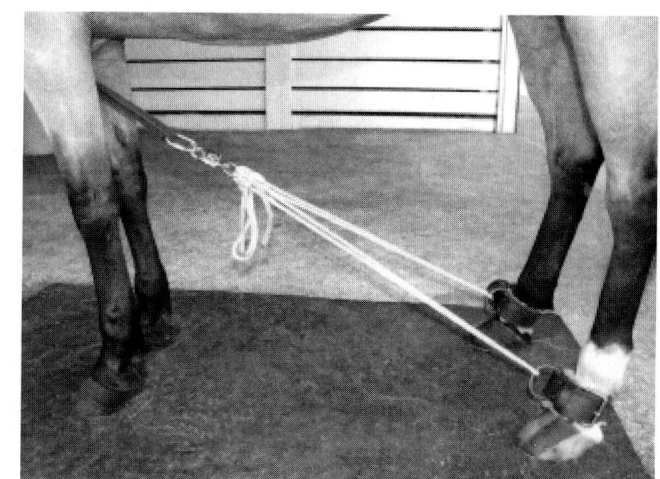

Pastern-hobbles

Note: Instead of having the belts for the pasterns of the rear legs, "hock-hobbles" have belts that are placed at each of the mare's hocks.

TACKING UP

Before tacking-up the horse, all the pieces of tack (jaquima, bit-hanger, bit, reins, saddle pad, saddle panels, stirrups and leather straps, girth, etc.) should be inspected for signs of weakness or damage. A few minutes of inspection may prevent a serious accident. The tacking-up process may be viewed as two different events, "bridling" and "saddling."

• **Bridling**: This refers to putting tack on the horse's head.

- The jaquima (headgear) is put carefully on the horse's head, passing the horse's muzzle through the bosal-barbada set. The crownpiece is then moved up and placed behind the ears, just on the poll, and the brow band placed on the forehead, just below the ears. The jaquima should be adjusted to the horse's head size using the buckles. The horse's forelock should be gathered forward and passed under the brow band. Finally, the horse may be tied to a post using the pisador.

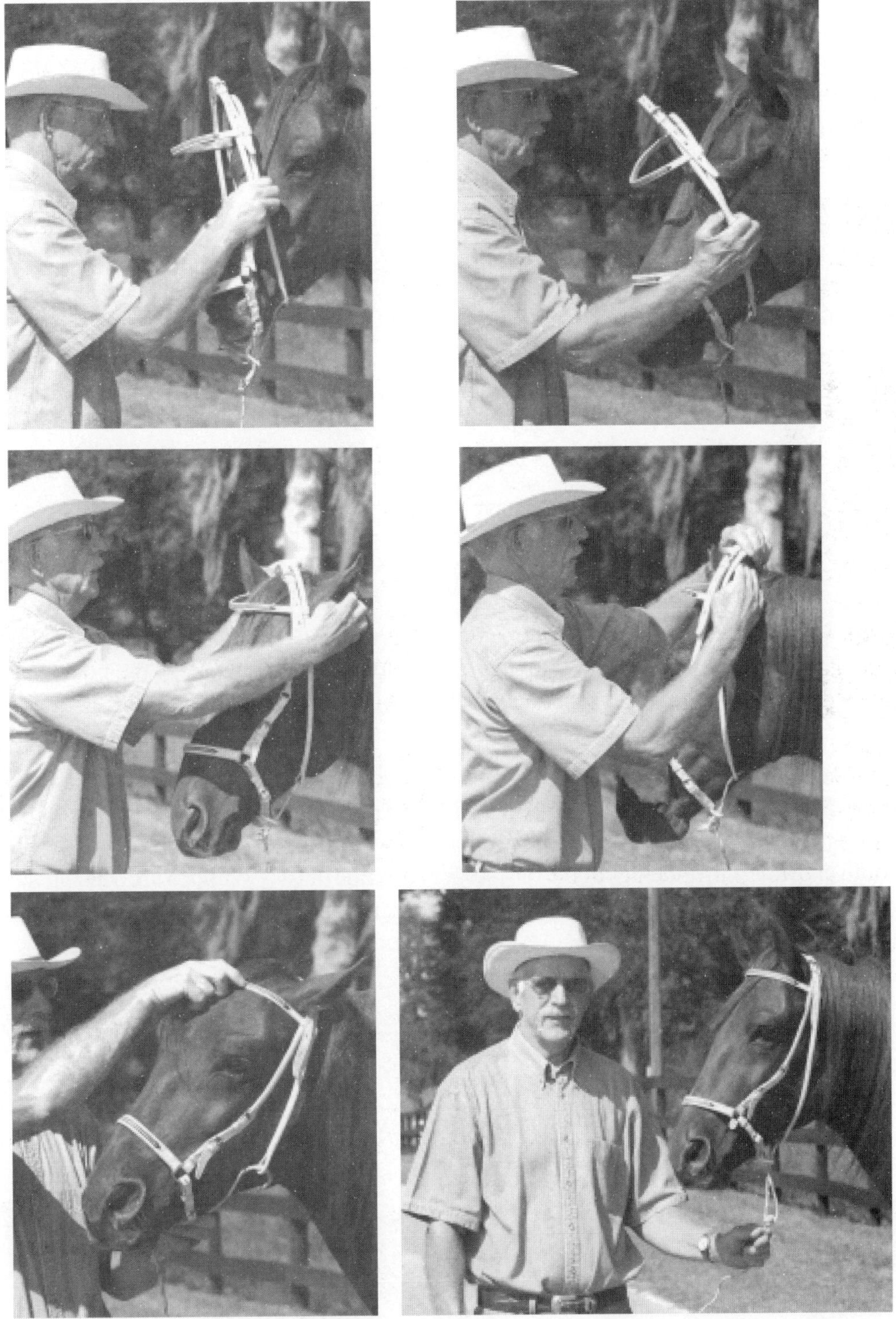

Mr. John Kennedy, a student of Ocala's School of Equestrian Art, shows the appropriate way to put a jaquima on his Paso Fino gelding "Ambisioso de La Katrina" (Ambar del Ocho x Recompensa de Retorno).

- The procedure for putting the bit into the horse's mouth is as follows: The bit-hanger should be attached to the bit. Standing in front of the horse, the rider passes the left forearm through the bit-hanger to let the bit hang from it. After ensuring the rings for the reins are facing toward the horse, the rider holds the bit's left shank with his/her right hand, just where the shank joins the mouthpiece. The rider places the left thumb on the horse's nose and inserts two or three fingers (of the left hand) into the right side of the horse's mouth in order to touch the palate, making the horse open its mouth. The bit is moved toward the horse's mouth, and the bit's mouthpiece introduced in it, keeping the mouthpiece from touching the horse's teeth. Additionally, the horse's tongue must stay under the bit's mouthpiece.

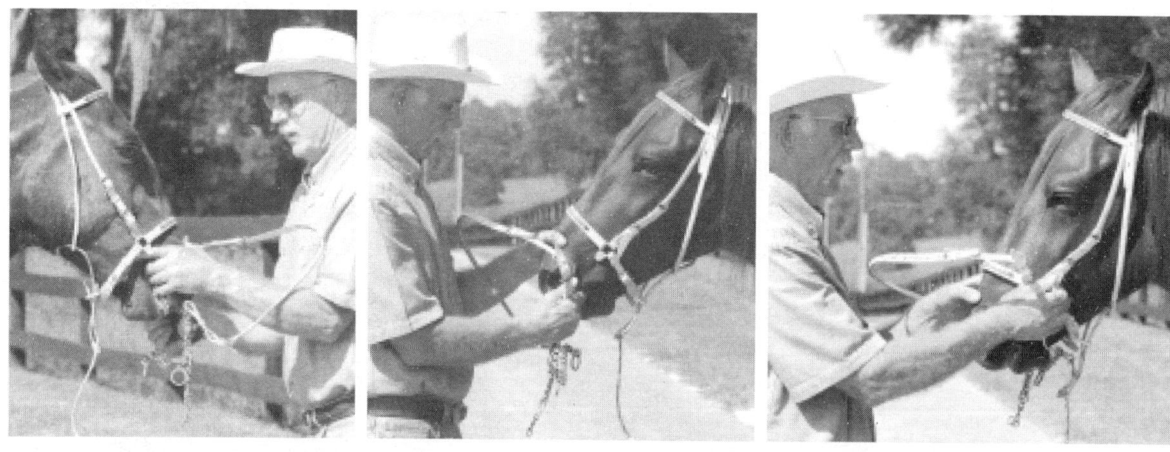

Note: After a time, and as a result of practicing this method consistently, many Paso Fino horses learn to open their mouths for the mouthpieces as the riders touch or squeeze the horses' upper lip on the right side, or sometimes just when the horses see the bit in front of their mouths.

The rider, then, lifts the bit-hanger over the horse's ears with the left hand and places it between the two straps of the jaquima that are already on the horse's poll. The bit's rubber-guards should be checked to ensure that they are placed outside the horse's mouth. The rider has to position the bit in the horse's mouth and adjust the buckles of the bit-hanger until one or two wrinkles are seen on the corners of the horse's mouth, a result of the pressure made by the mouthpiece.

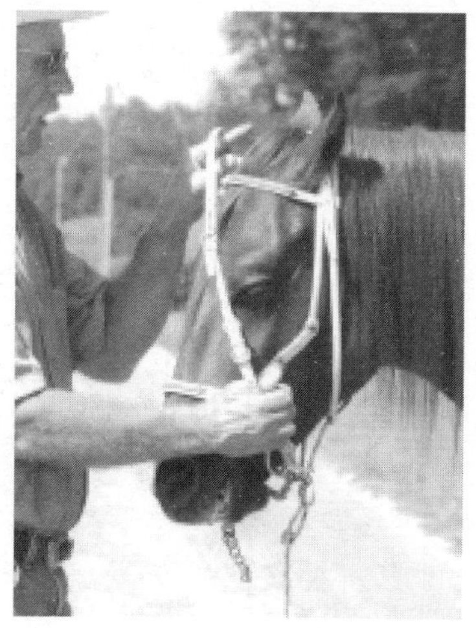

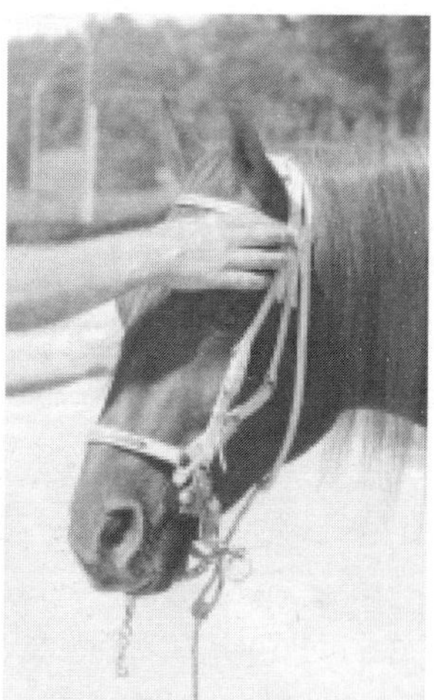

While standing at the horse's left side, the rider's right hand should pass under the jaquima's pisador and barbada to grasp the curb chain that is hanging from the right bit's shank. The curb chain is pulled toward the left bit's shank and twisted to the right until it is completely flat. The curb chain is then attached to the hook on the bit's left shank. The recommended tension for the curb chain is when two fingers, at a minimum, can be passed between the horse's jaw and the chain.

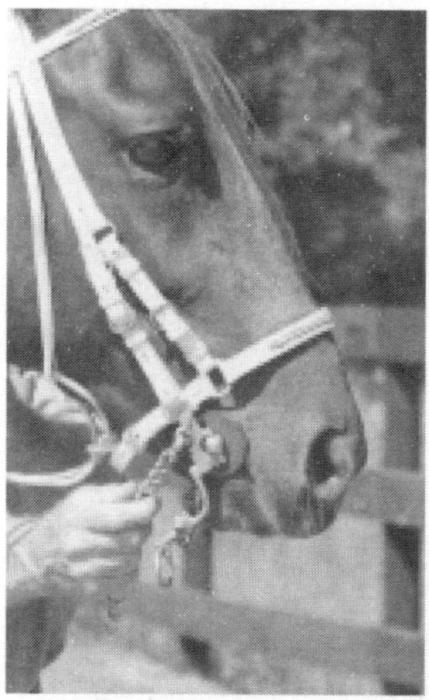
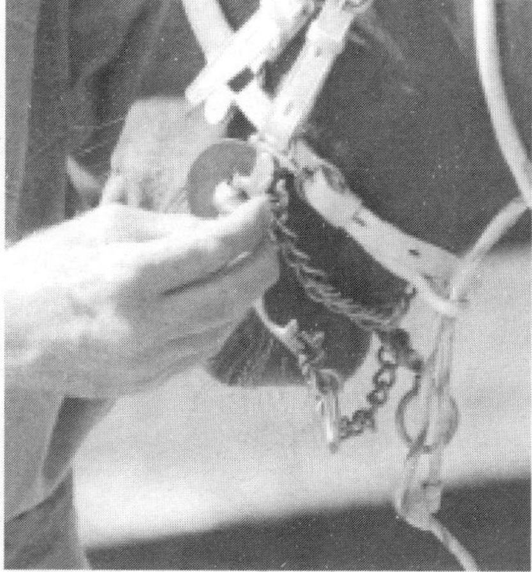
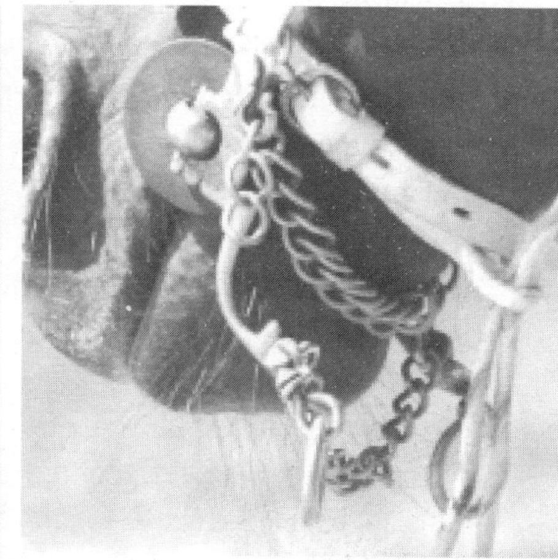

Note: For information about the parts of a bit, see Chapter 14: "The bit – magic or science?"

- The reins should be put over the horse's neck and attached to the rings on the bit (with either snaps or straps), but ensuring that the pisador is placed between the reins.

- Then, after making sure that the reins have even tension on both sides, they are tied over the horse's neck to encourage the horse to begin stretching and arching its neck muscles and tasting the bit's mouthpiece.

In the pictures above, Mr. John Kennedy shows the appropriate way to put a bit on his horse "Ambisioso de La Katrina."

- **Saddling**: This involves putting tack on the horse's back, neck, chest, girth area, and hips.
  - The pad is placed so that the front edge is on the horse's withers. The pad is equally distributed on both sides of the horse's back, with no folds. If some of the horse's mane is under the pad, it should be moved forward in order to keep it free.
  - The saddle must be put over the pad, ensuring that the front edge of the saddle panel is placed just behind the top of the shoulder. This keeps the saddle from interfering with the shoulder's action while the horse is in motion. The belts attached to the saddle (girth, stirrups and leather straps, breast plate, etc.) hang on their corresponding sides.

- The left stirrup should be kept from interfering with tying the cinch as follows: When using iron stirrups, the left stirrup should be secured at the top of the leather strap; conversely, when using leather covered stirrups, the left stirrup should be placed over the horse's neck, rather than the saddle's seat, to assure that the stirrup does not scratch/dirty the saddle.

- The girth (previously fastened on the saddle's right side) is passed under the horse's girth area (about 2 to 3 inches behind the horse's elbows) and then attached to the saddle's left side. Because most horses expand their barrels when the girth is tightened, the rider at first should tighten the girth only as needed to keep the saddle in place; then, when the horse relaxes, the girth may be tightened properly (before mounting the horse).

- If a three-point breast plate is being used, it should be put on the horse and attached to the front of the saddle, on both sides, before tightening the girth. Then, the girth is passed through the loop of the breast plate at the end of the strap that is hanging below the chest. Finally, the girth may be fastened as explained above. If the strap of the breast plate from the chest to the girth ends with a snap, the girth should have a ring located at the bottom (when it is on the horse). When a collar (for training) is being used, it is put on the horse in the same way as a three-point breast plate, except that it is not attached to the front of the saddle; the top strap of the collar is placed on the horse's neck.

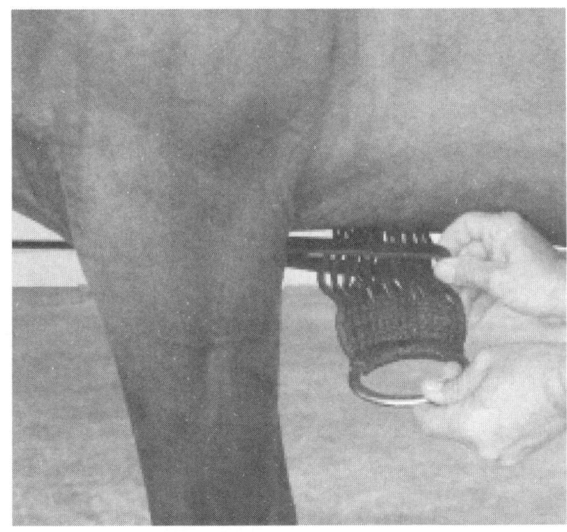

- When using a crupper, the tail must be passed through the crupper's loop while placing the rabiza under the tail's root, ensuring that all tail hair is passed over it. The one or two straps of the crupper, that are projecting forward, must be passed through the back ring of the saddle, and tightened using one or two buckles.

- Before mounting (see Chapter 16: "Equitation – not just sitting pretty"), the rider should inspect both sides of the horse's tack in order to assure that everything is placed properly, attached, and adjusted without disturbing the horse. The length of the stirrups is adjusted according to the length of the rider's legs, which is approximately the same length as the distance from the fingertips to the underarm. The knot of the reins made on the horse's neck should be released before mounting.

  Note: Un-tacking is the reverse process of tacking-up, starting at the horse's rear and ending at the horse's head.

SPECIAL ATTIRE FOR THE RIDER

The Paso Fino rider wears specific attire for safety and/or comfort. Additionally, when showing, the rider must wear the proper attire required for each class.

- **Hat**: For showing in classes requiring the official Paso Fino show costume in *PFHA* sanctioned shows (for example, Classic Fino and Paso Performance), all riders 13 years of age and older should wear a Spanish-type hat (made of felt, leather or suede) with a round, flat crown, a flat or slightly rolled brim, and matching or contrasting hatband *(PFHA – Constitution and Rule Book, Chapter Two, Section VII, Subsection I, 1)*. Riders in the Western Pleasure class, however, should wear a Western-type hat *(PFHA – Constitution and Rule Book, Chapter Two, Section VII, Subsection I, 2)*. For the Paso Pleasure division, the rider may wear a straw hat if the hat matches the rest of the attire and the horse's tack.

  A white straw hat with a black or white hatband is required for all the riders in *CONFEPASO* sanctioned shows *(Reglamento de Competencias de Caballos de Paso - CONFEPASO, Chapter 2, Article 3, Section A)*. In addition, this type of hat is required for riders 12 years of age and older in the equitation show classes sanctioned by *CONFEPASO*.

Spanish-type hat

White straw hats

- **Safety headgear** (or **helmet**): Safety headgear is used to protect the rider's head from injury. For showing, all contestants 12 years of age and under must wear equitation safety headgear in all *PFHA* show classes, as well as contestants of any age who may be required to jump (such as Trail and Versatility classes). Wearing head gear is optional for other riders *(PFHA – Constitution and Rule Book, Chapter Two, Section VII, Subsection I, 3)*.

  All contestants 11 years of age and under must wear safety headgear in the equitation contests sanctioned by *CONFEPASO (Reglamento de Competencias para Amazonas y Jinetes en Equitación – CONFEPASO, Chapter IV, Article 20, Section E)*.

  Wearing safety headgear is recommended for all beginning Paso Fino riders, trail riders, and endurance riders of any age.

Showing helmet

- **Chaps**: Diverse types of chaps are worn by the rider over jeans or britches in order to protect the rider's legs and clothing from the horse's sweat and mud from the trail.

  Long chaps (made of leather, suede, or nylon) are like pants that cover the length of the rider's legs (from feet to thighs). They are adjusted at the rider's waist by using a strap and a buckle, usually at both the front and the back. Long chaps with zippers at the sides fit the rider's legs better than those without zippers.

  The **half chaps** (also called **chinks**) only cover the rider's legs below the knees (calves and ankles). They are made in different sizes for a better fit and are made predominantly of leather or suede.

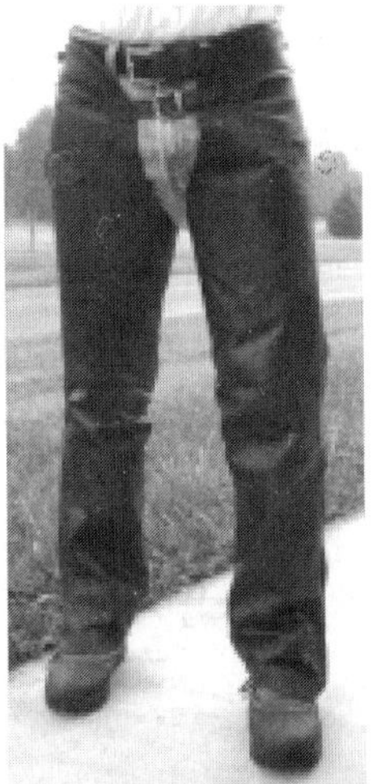

Long chaps

Half chaps

Even though long and half chaps are worn regularly by trainers and trail riders, they are not allowed for showing in most *PFHA* show classes. However, for those classes requiring Western dress, wearing either long or half chaps is required *(PFHA – Constitution and Rule Book, Chapter Two, Section VII, Subsection I, 2)*. On the other hand, riders are not allowed to wear long chaps or half chaps for showing in *CONFEPASO* sanctioned shows of any kind (horses and equitation).

Zamarros (also called "**Colombian chaps**") are wide, long chaps made of cow leather with its original hair. They are traditional and a requirement in Colombia to show Paso Fino horses and the three Colombian diagonal Paso horse breeds. If, however, the rider is female, zamarros are optional.

In the *CONFEPASO* rules, zamarros (dark colored without white spots) are required for the rider showing Colombian diagonal Paso horse breeds and optional for showing Paso Fino (Classic Fino), Paso Performance, Paso Pleasure, Paso Trail, and Paso Versatility horses *(Reglamento de Competencias de Caballos de Paso - CONFEPASO, Chapter 2, Article 4)*. However, riders competing in *CONFEPASO* equitation classes are not allowed to wear zamarros *(Reglamento de Competencias para Amazonas y Jinetes en Equitación – CONFEPASO, Chapter IV, Article 20, Section G)*.

Note: Before showing Paso Fino horses or competing in equitation classes, the rider should verify what tack and attire are required for the specific class, either in *PFHA* or *CONFEPASO* sanctioned shows, by reading the current association/federation rules.

CHAPTER 14

THE BIT – MAGIC OR SCIENCE?

This chapter is based on the author's long experience with Paso horses (Paso Fino and the three Colombian diagonal Paso horse breeds) and the scientific research and thesis written by the author and Sergio Quiroz Ochoa for the *Universidad Nacional de Colombia* entitled, "Estudio de Algunas Variantes que Inciden en el Funcionamiento de las Embocaduras de los Equinos Colombianos" (translated as, "The Study of Some Variants Affecting the Operation of Bits of Colombian Horses"). The photos in this chapter are provided courtesy of the tack store of *Ocala's School of Equestrian Art.*

ORIGINS OF THE BIT

When the horse was domesticated and used to carry products on its back, only a piece of cord wrapped around the horse's neck was used to control the animal. Later, this same cord was wrapped a second time around the horse's nose and jaw (above the muzzle) in order to gain more control of the horse. This double-wrapped cord was the origin of the current halter and jaquima.

Still later, this cord was wrapped a third time in the mouth to gain more control of the "hottest" horses. Once this third wrap proved to provide more control of the horse, single bits made of hard materials, such as bone, were developed. Then, during the age of metals, bits started to be made of different metals and in many designs.

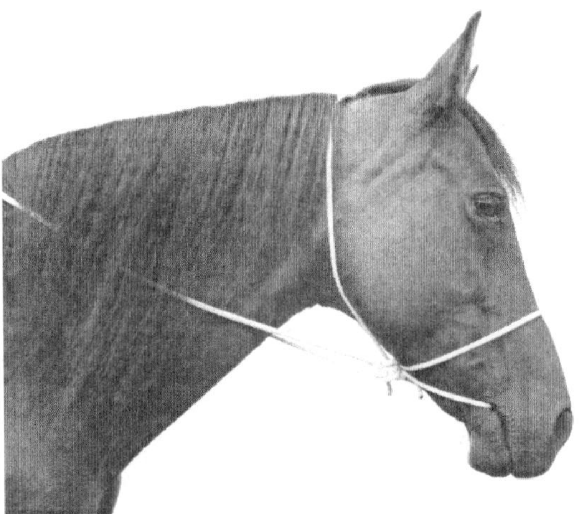

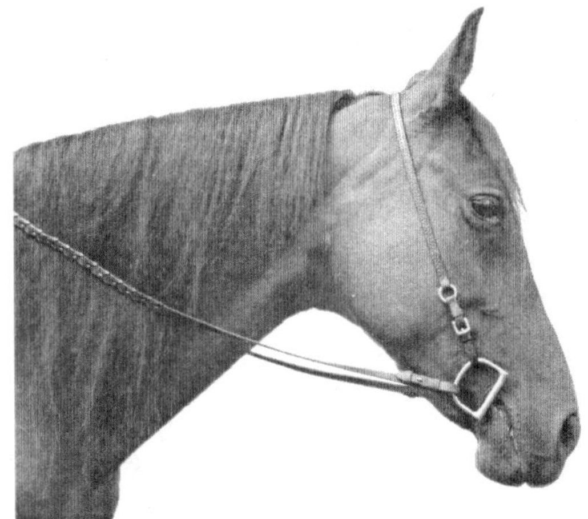

DEFINITION OF BIT

"Bit" is the general term used to define the piece of tack that is put in the horse's mouth, allowing the rider to ′drive′ the horse through the reins. Because the rider is at a remarkable disadvantage compared to a horse in terms of body weight, size, and strength, the bit becomes one of the most important elements that helps the rider control a horse. The reins, attached to the rings on both sides of the bit, let the rider apply pressure in the horse's mouth in order to ′drive′ the animal.

Throughout history, each style of equitation designed specific bits for its own purposes. In general, however, bits may be classified into two types:

- **Snaffle**: This bit consists of a mouthpiece made of two or three small jointed pieces of metal (articulated mouthpiece), with a ring at the end of each side. When the rider applies force on the reins attached to the snaffle rings, it causes pressure in the horse's mouth, but no increase in initial force. The snaffle bit commonly is used for racing, jumping, and dressage. Additionally, a snaffle may be the first bit used on a young Paso Fino horse during training.

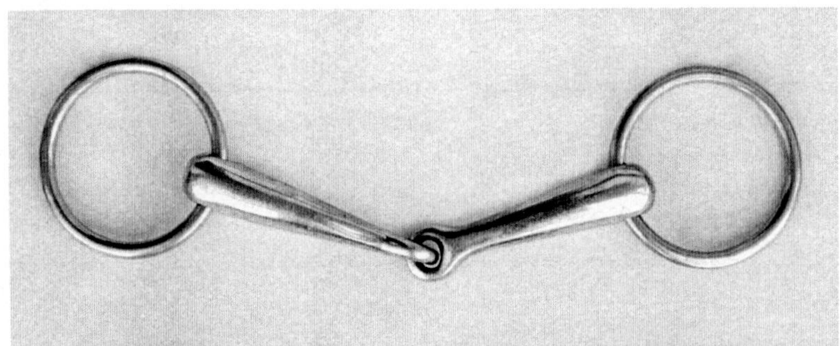

- **Curb**: This consists of a mouthpiece, a shank on each side of the mouthpiece, and a chain (known as "curb-chain"). Because the curb bit provides leverage, force applied on the reins by the rider's hands increases in magnitude and produces more pressure in the horse's mouth. Curb bits are commonly used for gaited horses, among others.

THE PASO CURB BIT

Paso curb bits that are handmade in Colombia, South America, are the most common bits used worldwide to ride Paso Fino horses (and the Colombian diagonal Paso horse breeds). The Paso curb bit is a special kind of bit that evolved from those brought to America by the Spanish Conquistadors during the 15th century. The main difference between the Paso curb bit and the other curbs is the presence of some joints that reduce the bit's severity.

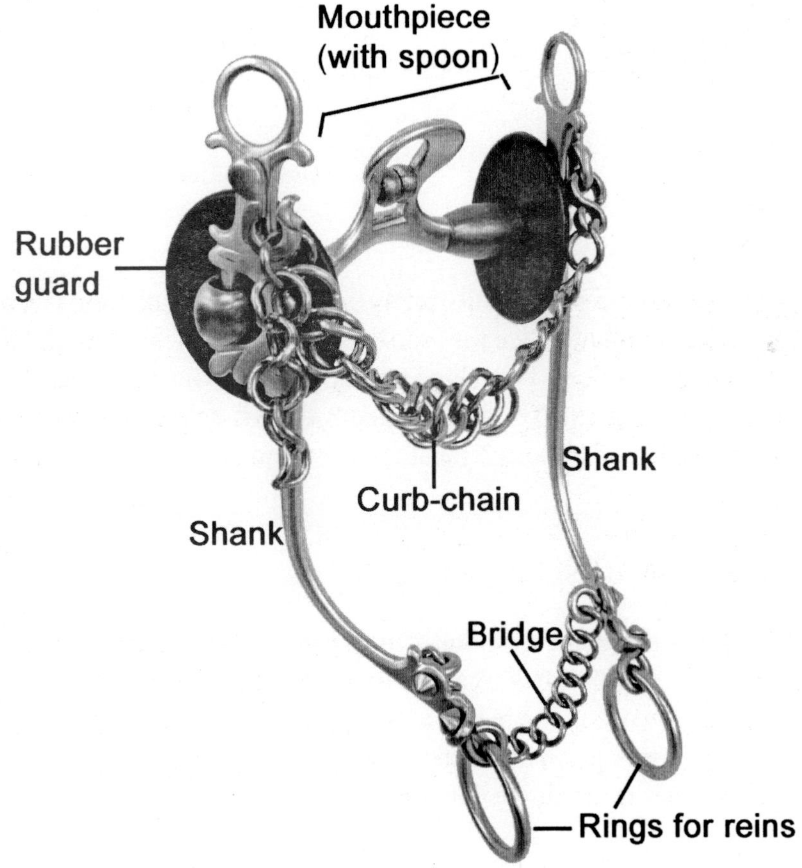

The parts of the Paso curb bit and their different designs and uses are listed below:

- **Mouthpiece**: This part of the curb bit is put into the horse's mouth, just over the tongue and the bars (of the mouth). The function of the mouthpiece is to apply pressure on the mouth's bars in order to keep control of the horse. The mouth's bars are the lower interdental spaces on both sides (of the mouth), between the premolars and canines in males over four years old, and between the premolars and corner incisors in younger males and most mares.

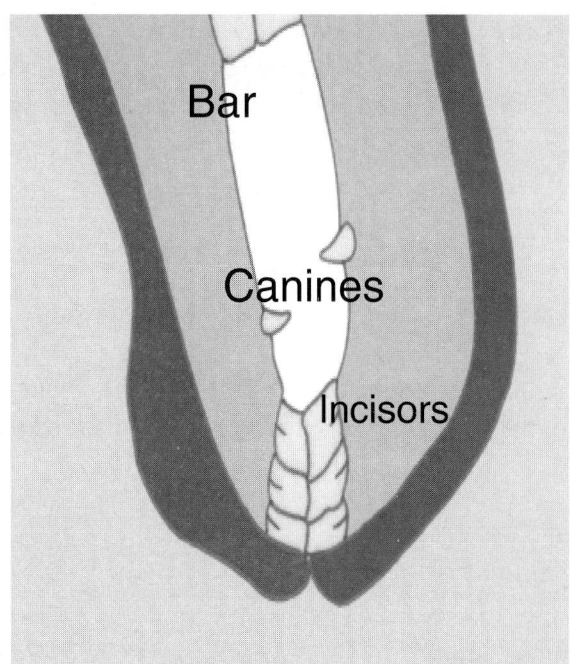

The mouth's bar
(Lateral view)

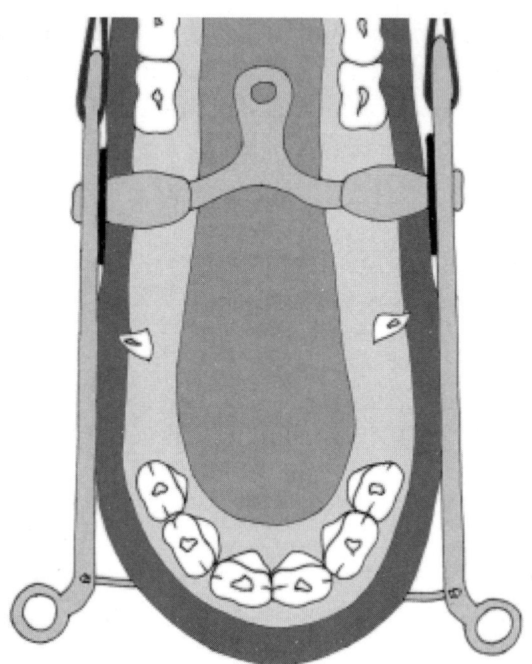

Mouthpiece position in the horse's mouth
(Top view of mandible)

The mouthpiece for Paso Fino horses should fit exactly in the horse's mouth from one corner of the mouth to the other. Thus, the width of mouthpiece for Paso Finos is from 4 inches (about 10.2 cm.) to 5 inches (about 12.7 cm.). The mouthpiece joins both shanks of the Paso curb bit by means of a small ring located at the end of each side. Where each small ring joins a shank, there is a circular rubber guard (usually black-colored) that prevents the corners of the horse's mouth from becoming injured by the joint of the mouthpiece and the shank.

The mouthpiece of a Paso curb bit may have different designs:

- **Three-piece jointed mouthpiece with spoon**: This is a mouthpiece formed by a small central piece of steel projected upwards, which looks like a short spoon that joins a long roller (made of steel or copper) on each side. The two joints on both sides of the spoon give certain mobility to the mouthpiece, which reduces severity. When attached to small shanks, this type of mouthpiece is commonly the first used with young horses during the bitting training period.

  Note: The three-piece jointed mouthpiece (with small shanks) described above is called a "baby bit" for Paso Fino horses.

- **Rubber bar**: This is a slightly curved piece of steel that is covered by the same length of rubber hose. The rubber cover makes this type of mouthpiece relatively soft for the horse's mouth. Thus, rubber bars commonly are used with young horses, as a part of the second curb bit during the bitting training period, when the horse needs to be worked with a more rigid mouthpiece. The diameter of the rubber bar is from 3/4 of an inch (about 1.9 cm) to 7/8 of an inch (about 2.2 cm).

- **Spoon and rollers**: This is a one-piece, straight mouthpiece with a central spoon projected upwards and rollers on both sides of the spoon. The size of the spoon is from 1 to 1 ½ inches wide and 1 ½ to 3 inches long (high), which keeps the horse's tongue under the mouthpiece. The rollers, made of steel or copper, provide softness because of their rotation in the horse's mouth. Some spoons have from one to three bead rollers made of steel or copper for the horse to play with, using its tongue. A complete single roller on each side of the spoon (known as "barrel roller") is softer and more ′comfortable′ for the horse's mouth than a series of bead rollers, which are more severe.

  When attached to small shanks, this kind of mouthpiece may be used for young horses during the bitting training period as a part of the third curb bit. This type of mouthpiece commonly is used for more advanced horses during the collection and finishing training periods, when attached to regular size shanks (see Chapter 15: "Horse psychology and training").

- **Port and Rollers**: This kind of mouthpiece has a central port (like an inverted U) with steel or copper rollers on both sides, either barrel type or beads (more severe). The central port gives the tongue room to be free of pressure under the mouthpiece, and therefore the side rollers are supported on the bars of the horse's mouth. This kind of mouthpiece is recommended during the collection training period for horses with thick tongues. This type of mouthpiece also is useful when riding trained horses that pull strongly against the reins.

  Note: When a central port has bead rollers at the bottom, it may be classified as a spoon because the tongue does not pass free, as it does under a real port. Some ports have a three-piece jointed mouthpiece.

- **Metal bar with rollers**: This is a straight bar of steel with one or more bead rollers in the middle and barrel rollers (steel or copper) at both sides.

  Any mouthpiece with rollers should be reviewed each time it is used in order to assure that the rollers are working (rolling) properly. After a Paso curb bit is used, the mouthpiece should be rinsed with water to remove all particles of food that may later affect rolling. The common diameter of mouthpieces with rollers is from ½ inch (1.2 cm) to ¾ inch (1.9 cm).

  Rollers made of copper (barrel rollers or beads) on any type of mouthpiece increase the production of saliva when in the horse's mouth, which softens the bit action. A mouthpiece made of "sweet iron" (spoon, rollers, etc.) also increases the production of saliva. To make a mouthpiece less severe in the horse's mouth, the mouthpiece may be covered with flexible cohesive bandage, such as Co-Flex or Vet-Wrap.

  Note: Other more severe types of mouthpieces (for instance with chains) are neither recommended nor explained in this book.

  The designs of mouthpieces described above are shown on the following page.

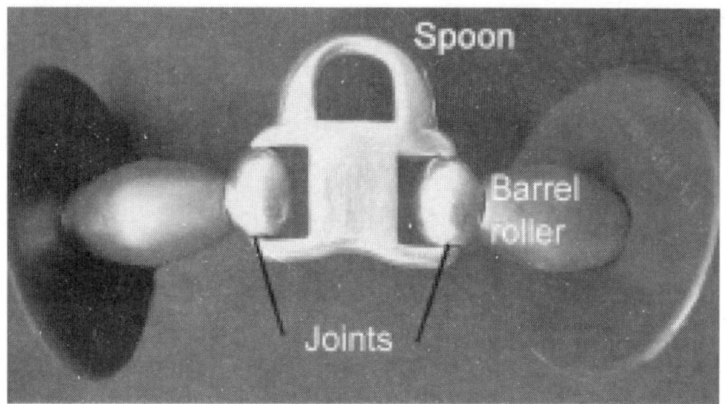

Three-piece jointed mouthpiece

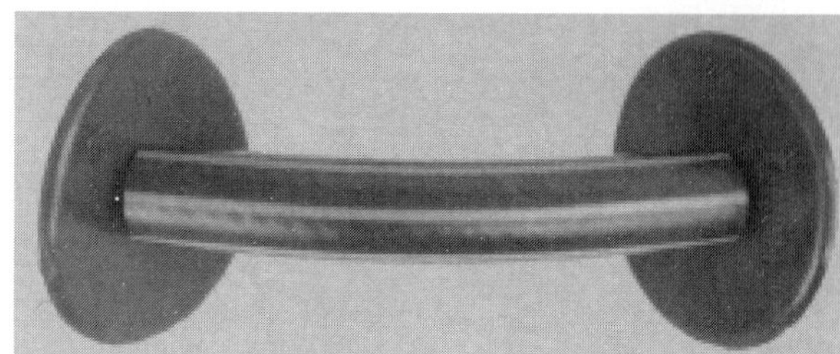
Rubber bar

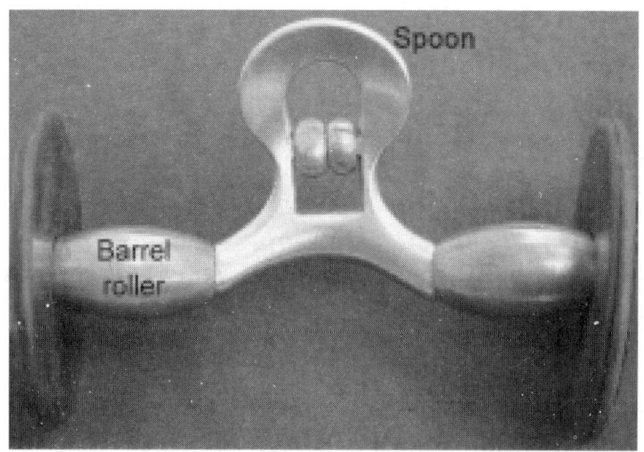

Spoon and barrel rollers

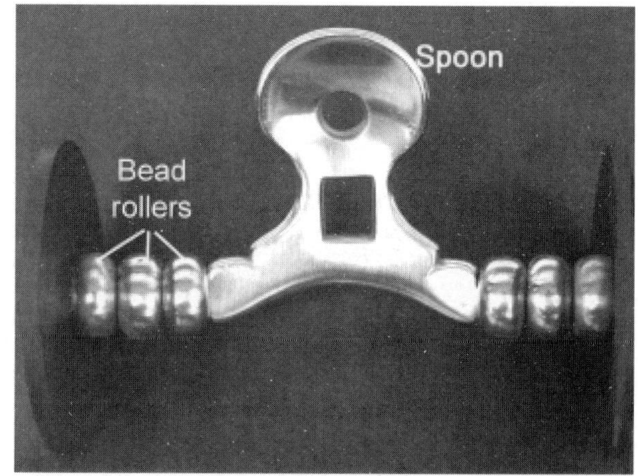

Spoon and bead rollers

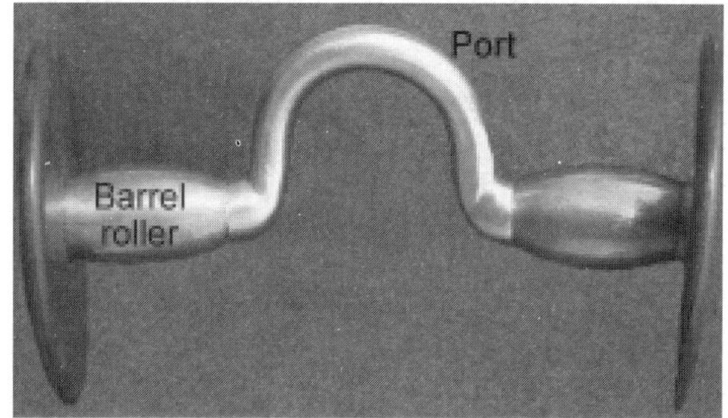

Port and barrel rollers

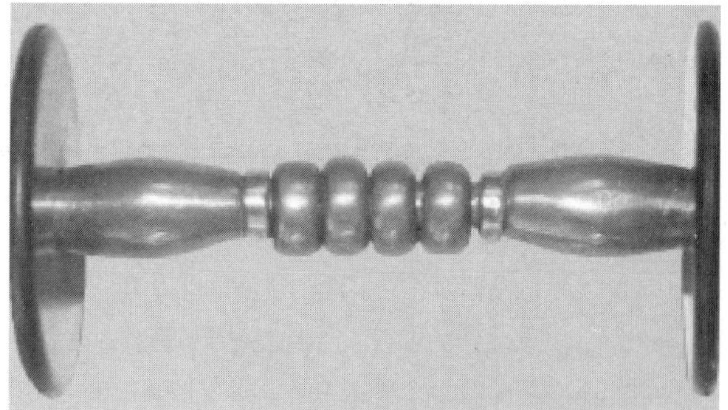
Metal bar with rollers

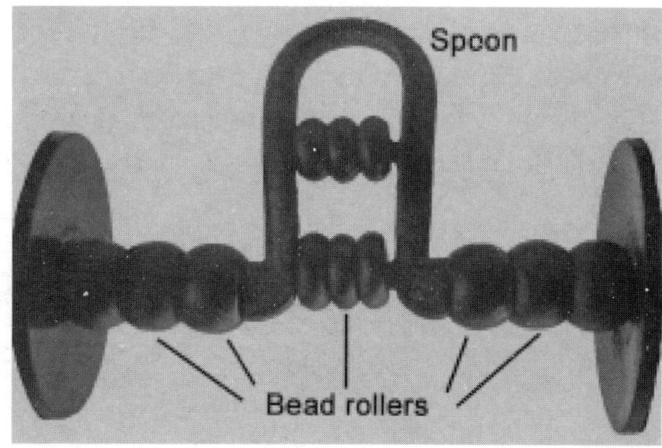

This mouthpiece is made of 'sweet' iron. Although it looks like a port, it is actually a spoon because there is no room for the tongue to be free of pressure.

- **Shanks**: Two shanks, usually made of steel, join each end of the mouthpiece. The upper end of each shank has a slot used to attach the bit-hanger. About 1 inch below this slot, the shank has a small hook to tie the curb-chain. About 1 inch below this hook, there are one or two small vertical slots where the ring at each end of the mouthpiece joins to the shanks.

  The section of shank from the slot that attaches the bit-hanger to the slot (or slots) that joins the mouthpiece is known as the "upper section of the shank." The "lower section of the shank" starts at the slot (or slots) that joins the mouthpiece, projects downward towards the back, and ends where there is a hook that holds a ring to attach one side of the reins. There is a small hook that is part of the bridge (small chain) about 1 inch in front of the hook that holds the ring for the rein.

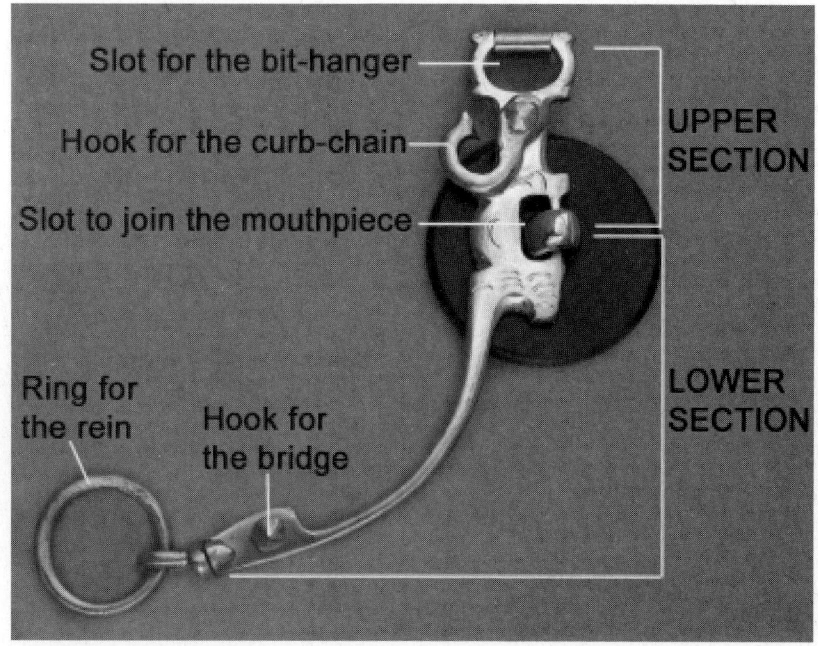

The upper section of the shank cannot exceed 3 inches long in PFHA sanctioned shows *(PFHA – Constitution and Rule Book, Chapter Two, Section VII, Subsection F).*

The distance from the mouthpiece to the lower end of the shank (the lower section of the shank) cannot exceed 6 inches (about 15 cm.). This is applicable for all *Paso Fino Horse Association* sanctioned shows *(PFHA – Constitution and Rule Book, Chapter Two, Section VII, Subsection F)*, and for *all CONFEPASO* sanctioned shows, as well *(Reglamento de Competencias de Caballos de Paso – CONFEPASO, Chapter 2, Article 2, Section 1 "Rienda y Jaquima").*

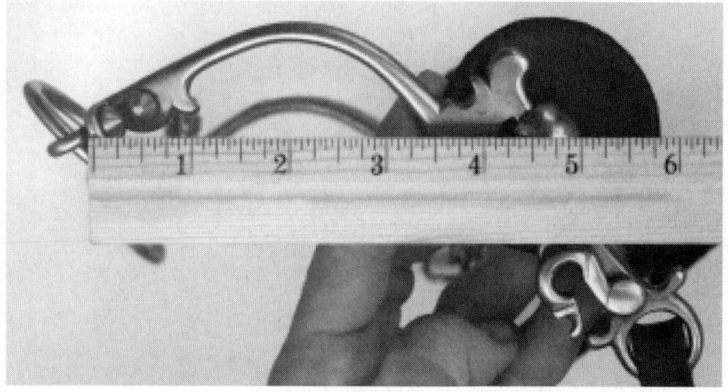

Shanks are named, based on the shape of their lower section:

- **"C"-shaped shank**: This type has one backwards curve.
- **Chair-shaped shank**: This type of shank looks like a chair seen from one side.
- **Wide-angle-shaped shank**: The lower section of the shank projects straight back at an angle of about 130-145 degrees to the upper section of the shank.
- **"S"-shaped shank**: This type of shank forms an "S."
- **Right-angle-shaped shank**: The lower section of the shank projects straight back at an angle of 90 degrees to the upper section of the shank.
- **Straight shank**: The lower section of the shank projects straight down from the upper section of the shank. This kind of shank is rarely used to ride Paso Fino horses because it traditionally has been considered too severe.

The designs of shanks described above are shown below and on the following page.

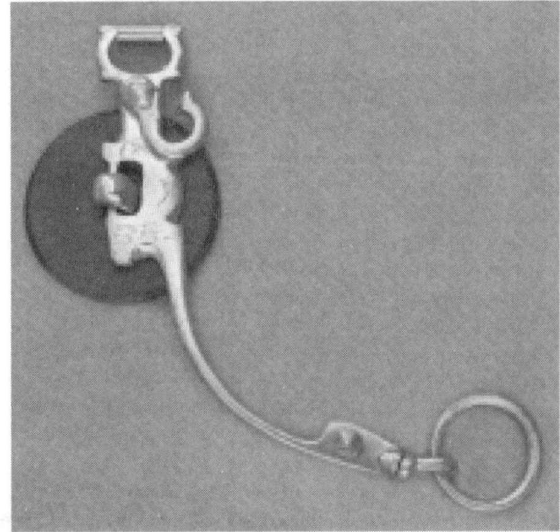

"C"-shaped shank

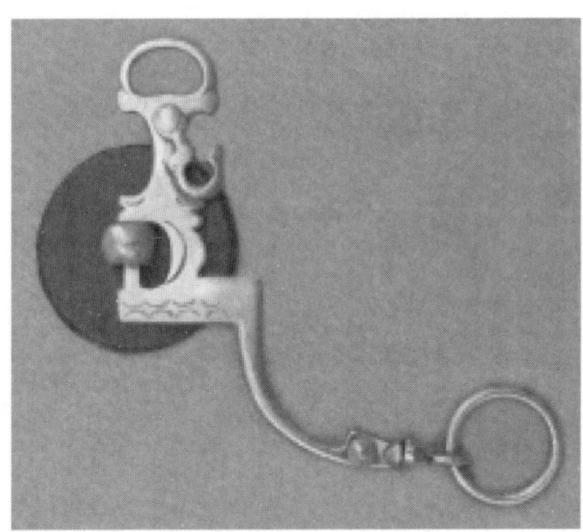

Chair-shaped shank

Wide-angle-shaped shank

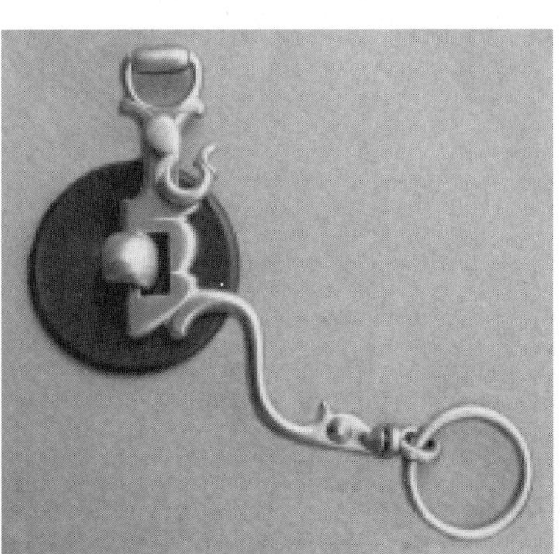

"S"-shaped shank

Right-angle-shaped shank

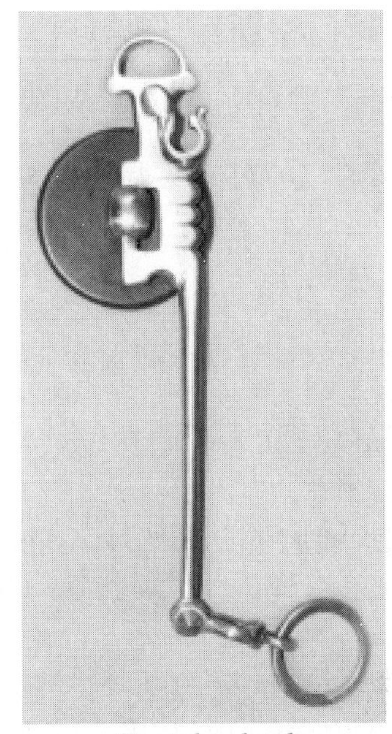

Straight shank

The joints between the two ends of the mouthpiece and each shank allow some movement that helps to adjust the bit properly in the horse's mouth, and reduce the severity of a rider's rough or inexperienced hands. However, because a shank with two slots joining the mouthpiece allows less movement, it is slightly more severe than a shank with only one slot.

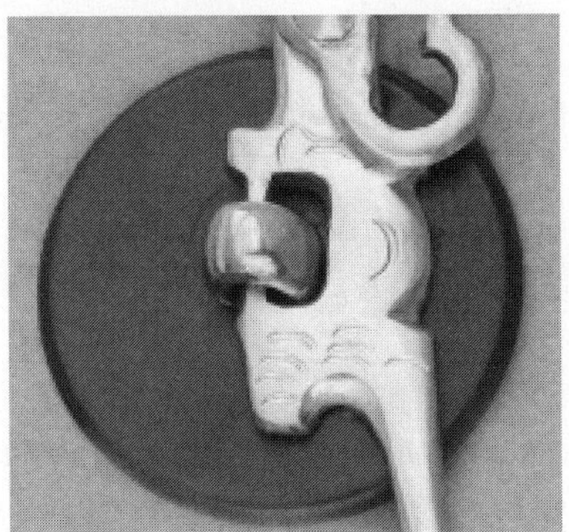

One slot on the shank

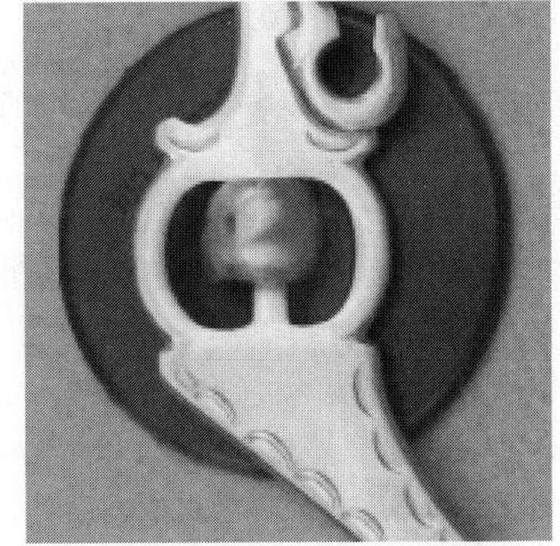

Two slots on the shank

- **Curb-chain**: This is a chain made of either steel or copper, with rings (of about ¾ of an inch in diameter), that are designed to lay flat when the chain is properly twisted. The curb-chain's length is about 6 to 7 inches. One end of the curb-chain is attached to the hook on the right shank. When the bit is on the horse, the free end of the curb-chain is attached to the hook on the left shank using one of the last rings. Once the curb-chain is adjusted properly, it remains next to the horse's lower jaw, just above the chin. If the curb-chain rubs the horse's skin, it may be covered with rubber or soft leather.
- **Bridge** or **small chain**: This is a very thin (metal) chain formed by either small rings or short straight pieces. The bridge connects the lower ends of both shanks, just in front of the rings for the reins. The bridge's function is to keep the shanks parallel when the rider uses the reins. Therefore, the bridge should be the same width as the mouthpiece or be slightly wider.

FACTORS AFFECTING PASO CURB BIT FUNCTIONING

Some important variables of Paso curb bit functioning are described below:

- **Length of the shanks**: Longer curb bit shanks are more severe on the horse's mouth than shorter shanks. Therefore, when longer shanks are used, the rider needs to apply less force on the reins to ´drive´ the horse.

- **Tension of the curb-chain**: When a horse with a bit has the curb chain attached tightly, the rider only needs to apply light force on the reins to ´drive´ the horse. Conversely, if the curb-chain is attached loosely, the rider may need to apply greater force on the reins to ´drive´ the horse.

- **The shank's shape**: The shank's shape ("C"-, chair-, wide-angle-, "S"-shaped shanks) does not have a magic or special effect on the horse's head set.

- **Thickness of the mouthpiece**: A thicker mouthpiece exerts less pressure on the horse's mouth than a thinner mouthpiece. Therefore, the horse with a thinner mouthpiece requires less force on the reins than the horse with a thicker mouthpiece.

- **Position of the rider's hands**: While maintaining contact with the horse's mouth through the reins, the rider can affect the horse's head position depending on the position of his/her hands. Holding the reins higher helps raise the horse's head, and holding the reins lower helps lower the horse's head.

Note: The laws of physics that explain the variables above are explained in Appendix C.

- **Tension of the bit-hanger**: The height of the mouthpiece in the horse's mouth, which depends on the tension of the bit-hanger, may cause some differences in the bit's final effect. The mouthpiece is at the right height in the horse's mouth when the skin of both corners of the mouth (right and left) makes one or two wrinkles. When the bit-hanger is too short and the mouthpiece is higher than explained above, the horse becomes very uncomfortable because the corners of its mouth are over-stretched. Conversely, when the bit-hanger is too long, and there are no wrinkles at the corners of the horse's mouth, as soon as the rider pulls the reins, the mouthpiece rubs or rolls upwards on the mouth's bars producing discomfort, making the bit more severe.

- **The width of the mouthpiece**: The width of the mouthpiece must fit the width of the horse's mouth exactly in order to assure maximum comfort for the horse and to obtain maximum control. If the mouthpiece is narrower than the width of the horse's mouth, the bit is not right for the horse. This may be compared to a person attempting to wear shoes that are too small.

  On the other hand, if the mouthpiece is wider than the width of the horse's mouth, a small portion of the mouthpiece may protrude out of the mouth at either side, which may not provide stability for the horse. The horse may learn how to pull harder on the side of the rein that corresponds to the side of the mouthpiece that is commonly out of its mouth.

- **The length of the spoon**: A small central spoon in the mouthpiece of about 1 ½ inches in length (height) does not really touch the horse's palate (roof of the mouth) when the curb-chain is tightened to act as a **fulcrum** (give support). The main function of the spoon in this case is keeping the horse's tongue under the mouthpiece.

  A longer central spoon in the mouthpiece of about 2 ¼ inches to 3 inches length (height) can actually touch the horse's palate and cause the horse to react unpredictably. The horse's most common reaction, when the spoon touches its palate, is to open its mouth in order to keep the spoon away from the palate. Shortening the barbada of the jaquima is a way to keep the horse from opening its mouth. Some horses pull less against the reins when the spoon touches the palate, and others change their head position, either by raising the face or by pulling the face down below the bit, in an attempt to keep the spoon from touching the palate.

  Mouthpieces with a small central spoon (1 ½ inches long) or a moderately long central spoon (2 inches) are the most common types of mouthpieces for fully trained Paso Fino horses (and Colombian diagonal Paso horses). Using a mouthpiece with a longer spoon requires that the rider carefully observe the horse's reaction and behavior.

- **Anatomy of the horse's mouth**: Three anatomical characteristics of the horse's mouth must be considered when choosing the right mouthpiece: the thickness of the tongue, the roundness and thickness of the mouth's bars, and the height of the palate.

  - When the horse's **tongue is thick**, the bars (of the horse's mouth) are located lower than the level of the tongue. Therefore, if a straight mouthpiece is used, pressure is placed on both the mouth's bars and the tongue, which is not desirable for two reasons: First, the mouthpiece should put pressure on both sides of the mouth's bars evenly to properly ′drive′ the horse, which is not completely possible when part of the pressure is put on the horse's tongue. Second, the pressure made with the mouthpiece on a thick tongue inhibits normal blood circulation throughout the tongue, which is very unhealthy for the horse.

    The horse often will pull against the reins (which is very uncomfortable for the rider) because the horse's tongue gradually looses its sensitivity. Moreover, when a horse with a thick tongue is ridden with a bad quality (even sharp) mouthpiece with a central spoon, the tongue may be severely injured, almost to mutilation. The solution for riding a Paso horse with a thick tongue is to use a mouthpiece with a port.

  - When mouth's bars are inspected, some horses have **rounded and fleshy bars** and others have **sharp bars**. Fleshy and rounded mouth's bars have thicker tissue covering the bones that accept the pressure of the mouthpiece with fewer problems. Sharp mouth's bars have thinner tissue covering the bones, which makes them more sensitive to pressure by the mouthpiece and less accepting of rough or inexperienced use of the reins by the rider. Therefore, a horse with sharp bars (of the mouth) needs a thick mouthpiece.

  - The **height of the palate** is important if the mouthpiece's central spoon or central port can reach the palate and put pressure on it. If the spoon or port touches the horse's palate, the trainer may prefer a bit with a shorter spoon or port. However, if making pressure on the palate is desired, the trainer must pay close attention to the horse's response.

- **Damaged bars of the mouth**: When one or both mouth's bars are injured due to incorrect use of a bit, the horse should not be ridden with a bit, either temporarily while the mouth's bars heal, or permanently if the tissue does not heal well or the effect on the horse's behavior is devastating. The two options for riding horses with injured mouth's bars, or horses that do not accept a bit in their mouths, consist of using either a training jaquima, with the reins attached to the bosal (nose band) or the barbada, or riding the horse with a hackamore. The hackamore has a lever as well as a curb bit, but the mouthpiece of the curb bit is replaced by a nose band made of leather, rope, or metal chain across the horse's nose, instead of in the mouth.

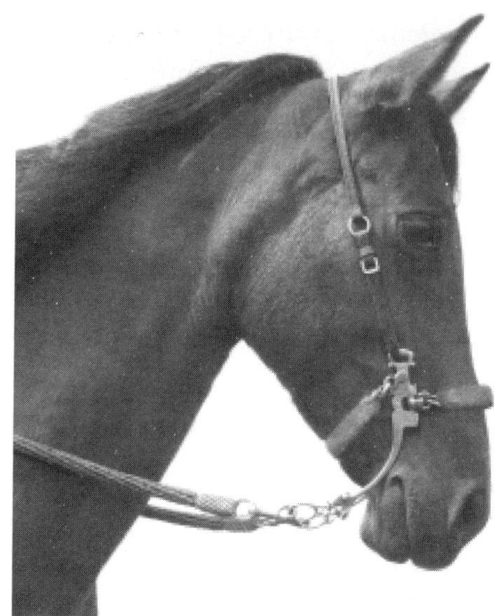

Colombian hackamore (also known as "Patefreno" in Spanish)

SELECTION OF THE PROPER BIT

Although a trial and error method may be used when choosing the proper bit for a horse, the tips listed below can help achieve more successful results.

- Each horse needs to have its own properly selected bit. The mouthpiece should be chosen after inspecting the horse's mouth. The length, type, and thickness of the mouthpiece have to fit the width of the mouth (between both corners of mouth), the thickness of tongue, the thickness of mouth's bars, and the height of the palate. Getting advice from an expert is always a good idea, as the improvement may be significant for a minimal investment in time and money.
- The size of the shanks is chosen according to the horse's level of training and responses, when the rider applies commands via the reins. A horse beginning training with the bit must be ridden with a short shank bit (lower section of shanks no longer than 3 inches). Gradually, the shanks may be changed for longer ones if the horse requires this. Ideally the horse should be ridden with shanks from 3 inches to 4 ½ inches long. It is not recommended that horses be ridden with shanks longer than 6 inches. In fact, this is not allowed in *PFHA* and *CONFEPASO* sanctioned shows.
- Although Paso curb bits are designed specifically for Paso Fino horses and Colombian diagonal Paso horses, any kind of bit is an imposition to the horse, and the trainer/rider should have the goal of helping the horse learn how to work with the bit in as comfortable a manner as possible. In other words, because a horse is not a machine, but a live being that reacts differently to the tack, the rider's commands, and environmental stimulus, finding the proper bit is not as simple as installing a new chip in a computer or replacing a part of a car. The horse must be trained gradually to use the bit. This requires an understanding of biological factors, such as the anatomy and physiology of the mouth, and the psychology of the horse.
- Because the tension of both the bit-hanger and the curb-chain affect the horse's behavior when the horse is ridden with a Paso curb bit, both factors should be taken carefully into account when choosing and adjusting the proper bit.

Note: Although the analysis above is for the Paso curb bit, it also is applicable to other kinds of curb bits.

CHAPTER 15

HORSE PSYCHOLOGY AND TRAINING

Before discussing the training process of a Paso Fino horse, it is important to understand some key points related to the horse's psychology, instincts, and language. This knowledge allows the trainer to evaluate and improve training and riding techniques.

THE HORSE, PART OF AN ECOSYSTEM

In any ecosystem, energy permanently circles and is transformed from one state to another. The "food chain" is one of the ways in which energy is transformed in the ecosystem.

In land ecosystems, plants use nutrients and water from the soil, carbon dioxide from the air, and the energy from the sun's rays to produce biomass (leaves, branches, flowers, seeds, etc). This process is called, "photosynthesis." Plants are the first level of the food chain, also known as the "producers."

Herbivores eat plants (or parts of them) to obtain the nutrients required for their physiological functions. The non-digested material is returned to the soil as excrement, where later it turns into fertilizer for the plants. Herbivores are known as "first order consumers."

Predators eat the meat from herbivore bodies. Therefore, predators control the herbivore populations by hunting the weakest/sick specimens. Predators are known as "second order consumers."

Another more evolved kind of predator called "super predator" not only eats meat from herbivores, but also from other predators. Super predators are known as "third order consumers."

For this chapter, the ecosystem of interest is the one related to horses and humans. Because they are so far apart in the food chain, the horse (herbivore) and the human (super predator) should have a difficult relationship. The horse may be used as a meat source for human consumption as it was thousands of years ago when horses only were considered as prey.

After a long process of evolution over millions of years, the horse and the other equine species have adapted their anatomy and physiology to run faster in order to escape from predators, and also have developed special sensory organs to detect danger. The horse sleeps several short periods of time per day (from 15 to 30 minutes each), usually standing up on three legs (the two forelegs and one of the hind legs), in order to be ready to run when any possible danger is detected or a predator attacks.

This situation has not changed much over time. Although some of the few herds of wild horses spread throughout the world have been pushed to live closer to people, any wild horse prefers to be far away from the presence of humans. Additionally, in normal conditions, horses (wild or domestic) in a pasture do not attack people because they recognize humans as predators. Conversely, horses may keep enough distance from people in order to run away when necessary.

Because horses instinctively know that humans are still potential enemies (super predators), a person must approach a domestic horse, that has been previously handled, at the animal's head (front or side). When approaching the horse, a person should walk slowly, avoiding loud noises. By gently talking to the horse, a person may calm the animal and awaken its curiosity. Once close enough, a person may try to pet the horse's neck and the withers. These tactics help to give the horse time to interpret a person's good intentions.

On the other hand, considering how big, strong, heavy, and fast horses are when compared to people, anyone who is around a horse must take the following precautions in order to reduce the risk of an accident:

- When standing next to a horse, a person should maintain enough distance from the animal to keep from accidentally being hit by the horse's head, legs, or tail. The recommended minimum distance a person should be from a horse is the length of an arm fully extended (2 feet, at a minimum).

  Even though the minimum distance from the horse is maintained, because a horse may move very fast after being spooked by any stimulus from the environment (such as a loud noise, a horsefly, a bird flying around, or the wind blowing), a person must keep an eye on the animal at all times in order to move away from it quickly if this becomes necessary.

- If anything falls down under the horse (such as a brush, a curry comb, a pair of reins, etc.), it never should be picked up directly from where it has fallen. The item should be picked up after it has been kicked away from the horse.

- Leading/holding a horse by the halter with no lead rope is unsafe because, if the animal spooks, wants to run away, or becomes aggressive, the handler is at risk of being hurt or having to release the halter, allowing the horse to run free. Additionally, while leading/holding a horse only by the halter, there is a common tendency to pass one or more fingers through one of the halter rings, which increases the risk of injury.

  Therefore, in order to lead a horse properly, the handler should use a pisador (lead rope) attached to a halter or a jaquima. The handler should hold the pisador with one hand close to the halter/jaquima, straighten the arm in order to keep a safe distance from the horse, and walk parallel to the horse's head. The other hand should hold the remainder of the pisador, properly looped.

Alysa Stephens leading Mistica de El Gaucho (Gaucho de Besilu x Three O'clock Mamacita) at Ocala's School of Equestrian Art.

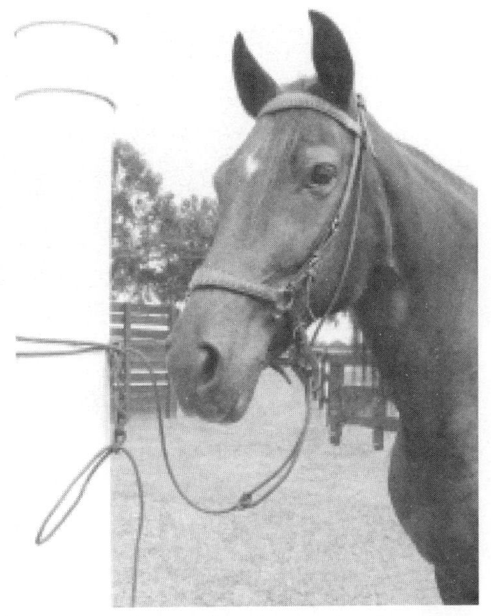

- When tying a horse with the pisador (lead rope) to a pole, the knot must be made so that the horse cannot release it and escape. However, the knot also must be made so that a person is able to release it rapidly and easily in case of emergency. In addition, the knot should be tied on the post at the height of the horse's nostrils, when the head is held at rest. The maximum length of the pisador, from the jaquima to the knot tied to the pole, should never be more than 3 feet.
- It is extremely dangerous to wrap or tie any piece of tack that is put on a horse (such as a lead rope or reins) to any part of a human body or to clothes worn when riding or handling a horse.

SOCIAL BEHAVIOR OF THE HORSE

Horses, either wild or domestic, are herd animals with very well-defined social structures. In a herd of wild horses (or a herd of horses without human intervention), the main stallion has a harem of 5 to 15 mares and a group of young horses. The stallion identifies its mares and the other members of the herd by their fragrance. The stallion tests any spot of urine or pile of manure found on the prairie to determine if it was excreted by one of his mares, or another member of the herd, and also to locate mares in heat. The stallion has several functions in the herd, such as breeding mares in heat, guaranteeing the unity of the group, and protecting both harem and territory from predators and other stallions.

Mares that comprise the harem have a perfect social order from the highest to the lowest status, based on their dominance, proven by several previously held battles. The strongest (most dominant) mare, called the "Alpha mare," leads the herd to a safe place when there is any sign of danger. The stallion, meanwhile, tries to divert the cause of danger from the herd. In the herd's social order, colts and fillies have a lower status than the mares, according to age. Additionally, offspring from the strongest mares have a higher status in the herd than offspring from the weakest mares.

While the stallion is busy breeding one of the mares in heat several times over one or more days, the opportunistic and well-developed young stallions in the herd breed other mares in heat. This behavior ensures that offspring do not always come from the main stallion, which is a natural way for wild horses to reduce close-breeding.

Domestic horses also have a social order, not necessarily established for reproductive reasons. Horses sharing the same pasture, independent of their gender, gain status in the herd after fighting. The strongest horses have the first turn to eat and drink, and also lead the weakest animals. Additionally, alliances may be formed between some members of the herd, which make them much stronger in the group. ´Good friends´ spend some time scratching each other.

Horses kept alone in stalls or pastures, especially stallions, usually are ready to fight with other horses on the farm in order to establish their social order. The same situation may happen when horses from different pastures or farms meet at a show or a parade. Therefore, people who manage these horses have to be careful when handling, tying, or riding horses close to others and must be able to recognize a horse's signals of aggression in order to prevent conflicts.

When any person starts to handle or ride a horse, he/she enters into part of the horse's herd as either a leader (with higher status) or as a subordinate (with lower status), but not with an even status. To be successful, a trainer/rider must develop leadership skills to achieve the role of the Alpha mare, which leads the horse away from danger and saves its life. Once this goal is accomplished, the horse is ready to ´give all´ to that person.

THE HORSE'S LANGUAGE

A horse communicates with other horses using two kinds of language.

- When an audible language is desired, the horse uses the vocal cords located in the larynx to produce a sound called, "whinny." This is especially common between a broodmare and her foal, a stallion seeing mares, a mare in heat looking for a stallion, and a lonely horse looking for the other horses of its group.

- Most of the time, however, horses use a silent but complex system of body language by moving some body parts, such as the ears, mouth, head, neck, tail, and legs. This helps keep predators from locating them as would happen if horses only communicated by whinnying.

Note: Because domestic equines (horses, donkeys, and mules) easily accept people around them as part of their herds, a horse usually attempts to communicate with people by using both whinnying and body language. Therefore, a horseperson should learn to interpret these two languages as much as possible in order to understand any behavior or reaction from the horse.

Some signals of the horse's body language are explained below.

- Signals with the ears are easy to understand:

    - If ears are pointed backwards and flattened against the poll, it is a clear signal that the horse is angry. Any person who is around, or riding the horse, should determine why the animal is angry and try to change the horse's behavior by getting its attention.

    - If both ears are pointed forward, it is a signal that the horse's attention is on the environment at the front, such as an unknown/scary noise, an animal, or an object. When handling or riding a horse, the handler or rider should evaluate what is causing the horse to keep its ears pointed forward, and, if necessary, should get the horse's attention by applying one or more commands.

      Note: The first horse of the group on a trail ride keeps its ears pinned forward, and the horses following the lead horse keep their ears turning back and forth all the time.

    - When ears are pointed one to each side, it is a signal that the horse's attention is on both sides with no specific concern.

    - If both ears turn back and forth, it is a clear signal that the horse is interested in everything around it, including the handler/rider. This sign of alertness is considered very valuable in the Paso Fino breed and is associated with brio.

    - If during a ride the horse's ears are turned back toward the rider, this is a signal that the animal is alert to the rider's commands.

    - If one ear is turned to the front and the other is turned to the back, this means that the horse's attention is divided and that the horse may be confused.

    - When a horse is dozing, its ears are droopy and at rest, with either both ears toward the back or each ear toward the side.

Attention to the front

Attention divided

Signs of aggression with ears and teeth

- Signals a horse makes with its mouth may be easily interpreted:
  - A calm, relaxed horse keeps its lips relaxed.
  - When a young horse approaches an older horse while opening and closing its mouth as if it is attempting to speak, this is a signal of submission, as if the young horse was saying *"I do not want to bother you...do not attack me...I want to be your friend..."*
  - If the horse shows its incisor teeth, this is a clear signal of aggression. This usually is accompanied by ears pointed backwards and flattened against the poll.
  - When a horse sticks its tongue out and also licks its lips during a training session, this is a sign of comfort and submission to the trainer.
- The horse also uses its head-neck set to communicate:
  - When spooked, a horse will suddenly raise its head-neck set and face the object or place from which an unknown noise has come. At this time, the ears point in the same direction. This also makes other horses be alert.
  - When a dominant horse wants other horses to move away from it, it lowers its head-neck set, keeps its ears pointed back and flattened against the poll, and may show its incisors as a signal of aggression.
  - When a horse shakes its head and ears side-to-side, as attempting to keep from being bitten by insects (without having insects around) or saying no, it is a sign of discomfort. This happens, for instance, when a horse does not want to be caught in the pasture.
- The horse uses its tail for several reasons:
  - A horse swishes its tail in order to disperse insects (such as flies) and also to show discomfort. A stallion may swish its tail from side to side while moving toward a mare in heat before breeding.
  - A horse may raise its tail above the level of the croup while running on its own in a pasture/corral in order to show comfort and freedom.
  - If a horse has its tail down and between its hind legs, this is a sign of submission, depression, or disease.

- The horse uses its legs to communicate for these reasons:
  - A stalled horse may paw the ground with one of the forelegs as a sign of boredom, frustration, or anxiety. A horse tied to a pole (or cross-tied) may display the same behavior. However, this also may be a sign of discomfort.
  - If a standing horse raises one of its hind legs, this may be a sign of abdominal pain (colic) or discomfort caused by insects.

BEHAVIOR OF THE HORSE

People sometimes attempt to describe horses as lazy, angry, affectionate, etc. Those adjectives are not always completely objective for two reasons. First, the meaning of these adjectives may be different for each person, depending on what is expected from the animal. Second, a horse may change its behavior depending on the handler's/rider's leadership. For example, a very laid back horse with a timid rider may be very active with a rider who is a leader.

Just as a person has a better relationship with certain kinds of people because of compatible psychologies, the relationship between man and horse needs the same element of compatibility to be successful. Therefore, some Paso Fino trainers specialize in certain bloodlines because they know the usual behaviors and responses of those horses during training and they have learned how to obtain the best results from those horses. This also explains why one trainer may not be successful with a horse, while another trainer obtains very good results with the same horse. This does not mean that the first trainer used the wrong methods, but more likely that his/her psychology did not match with the horse and vice-versa.

Moreover, a horse may try to test its rider/handler as a way to prove dominance. For example, a horse may test its rider/handler by refusing to load in the trailer. The response of the rider/handler will show his/her dominance, or lack thereof. This behavior is natural in horses because they always want to achieve a higher status and dominance in the herd. For instance, a young, strong stallion tests the leader stallion. The young stallion has nothing to lose, except getting kicked and bitten, but if he is lucky and beats the stallion, he will have his own new herd.

DIFFERENCE BETWEEN BRIO, FEAR, AND AGGRESSION

The highly desirable "brio" of the Paso Fino breed and the three Colombian diagonal Paso horse breeds is part of their psychology. This means that horses are either born with brio or not, but it cannot be created. A horse with brio may be touched, petted, tied, etc., without any problem. However, when it is time to work, the horse exhibits all the qualities defined as brio (in Chapter 4: "Unique characteristics of the Paso Fino horse").

Unfortunately brio commonly has been misunderstood and confused with fear and/or aggression. This confusion has affected negatively the genetic selection, training methods, and marketing of the Paso horse breeds.

Fear is when the horse shies from several situations and tries to escape as a response to bad experiences from the past. However, a horse also may be extremely spooky due to a vision or hearing problem or a lack of exposure to the environment.

On the other hand, aggression is the response of some horses when defending themselves from what they consider dangerous. An aggressive horse may attack people or other horses by biting, striking (like boxing), or kicking. Additionally, aggressive horses refuse to submit in any way.

Unfortunately, the Paso Fino market has been affected negatively by this misunderstanding of terms, causing some people new to Paso Finos not to like horses with brio because they confuse it with aggression.

THE HORSE'S LEARNING PROCESS

A trainer must use horse logic instead of human logic. Therefore, some aspects of the horse's learning process must be understood prior to training:

- The horse does not moralize, which means that the horse does not differentiate between good and bad behaviors for itself.
- The horse cannot think like people by relating a series of events to make decisions. The horse instinctively responds to the rider's commands, the stimuli of the environment (such as noises or objects in the way), and conditioned stimuli.
- A conditioned stimulus is the resultant behavior of a horse to a consistent reinforcement, either positive or negative.
- Although it has a good memory, the horse cannot learn many skills in one session. Therefore, the trainer should plan the training sessions to reach specific goals gradually, according to the horse's current training stage. The plan should be flexible so that it may be adapted to any kind of horse's mind.

TRAINING BASICS

The training process of a horse takes time (months or years) for the animal to develop both physical and mental skills. The first step is helping the horse to trust the trainer. Only after this happens, may the horse accept a person's leadership.

The trainer must create a code of commands (including voice commands, if so desired) related to the horse's responses. This is accomplished by giving positive stimuli immediately after the horse performs correctly and giving negative stimuli immediately after the horse performs incorrectly. The horse gradually associates its action with the immediate stimuli of the trainer (either positive or negative). A trainer always must be conscious of what the horse is learning, either good or bad, from any activity.

While training the horse from the ground, the trainer should pet the animal and talk softly and gently as a positive stimulus. Additionally, the trainer should give the horse a food treat, such as a piece of carrot or apple, some sugar or grain, or a commercial horse treat. When riding the horse, the trainer may reduce pressure on the reins or pet the horse and talk gently as a positive stimulus.

Some common methods of correcting a horse are as follows: From the ground, the handler/trainer may correct a horse's misbehavior by checking or shaking the lead line, swinging the end of the lead line, or making the horse walk sideways. When riding, the trainer may stop the horse and back up, flex the horse's neck to both sides, squeeze one or both calves, and/or talk loudly. A whip may be used on the horse's shoulders, or its lower neck, when the horse does not move forward, or when the horse does not want to leave the barn area.

The rider must never correct the horse when the animal is not able to perform an exercise that it has not been taught. This action will teach nothing, but rather make the animal feel like it is being attacked. Additionally, a negative stimulus should never be used as revenge for a mistake made in the past (longer than four seconds before) because the horse cannot associate the two events.

The horse should learn how to perform exercises on both sides evenly. Therefore, the trainer should ask the horse to perform exercises on each side the same number of times. This helps the horse to have balance and collection, while moving both straight ahead and turning toward each side. The training sessions must be done frequently (ideally every day) and consistently to keep the horse from forgetting what it already has learned. Additionally, the horse starts to use the muscles needed to perform the gait and to develop the endurance necessary for work.

THE FOAL'S TRAINING

The first training session of a foal is begun within the first two to three hours after birth (see Chapter 8: "Reproduction" – First attention to the new foal) by the person staying with the newborn and the mare. Once the foal stands to nurse, this person may "imprint" the foal with selected activities, as follows: 1) Each hoof is lifted and its bottom gently tapped two or three times with the wooden handle of a hoof hammer. 2) The foal's head (including mouth and ears), neck, and croup are caressed and petted. 3) The foal's girth area is embraced. 4) Clippers are moved next to the foal's ears and around the muzzle to help the foal get used to their sound and vibration. Because the foal has no real fears right after birth, in theory, the foal accepts all these activities for the rest of its life.

The foal should be handled properly from birth to assure that it continues to have positive memories related to its life's activities. The foal should be taught to be led, tied, brushed, and have its hooves picked up and cleaned. Additionally, the mouth and girth area should be desensitized. These skills help later on during deworming, vaccinating, hoof trimming/shoeing, treating wounds, grooming, tacking up, etc.

Some Paso Fino people incorrectly say that a foal loses its brio when being handled from a tender age. This is not true because brio is natural in a horse. However, handling a foal (or a young horse) excessively may make it confused or lose its respect for the handler and is not recommended.

If the foal did not have the imprinting session after birth and further handling, the trainer must be gentle when catching the foal the first time in order to cause minimum stress. A well-built stall (see Chapter 9: "Facilities for horses") is the best place to catch the foal. If the foal's dam is docile, she may be put with the foal in the stall and used to make the foal stay in one of the stall's corners. Once the foal is in the corner, the trainer should approach it slowly and talk softly. To catch the foal, the trainer should place one arm on the foal's chest and the other arm behind its hindquarters. The foal's neck should be wrapped once with a rope and then a properly sized halter may be put on the foal's head. The halter may be kept on continuously, but changed for a bigger halter as the foal grows.

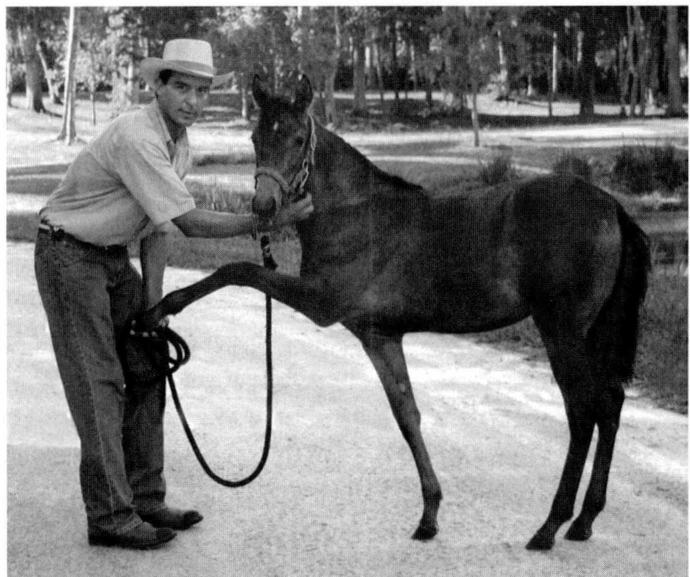

William Arboleda, an expert on handling and training Paso Fino foals, has dedicated years to developing different "imprinting" activities. In the photos William shows some exercises that he does with two of his 'disciples,' at Besilu Collection, Ocala, FL.

Once the halter is on the foal, the trainer may start lead training. Before taking the dam out of the stall, the trainer should attach a lead rope to the halter ring located at the foal's jaw and take the lead rope with one hand, close to the halter. The free end of the rope should be looped and held with the other hand. After the mare is taken out of the stall, the trainer should pet the foal and talk softly in order to give it confidence and get its attention.

The first step in training the foal to be led consists of pulling the lead rope firmly, but gently, to either side in order to make the foal relax its neck (toward each side), lose its balance, and walk one or two steps to the side. When this is achieved, the trainer begins releasing the pulling force on the lead rope and petting the foal. After repeating this exercise several times, the foal learns to walk to one side when the rope is softly pulled. Using the same method, the trainer starts teaching the foal to walk to the other side. Soon, the foal learns to be led to either side when the trainer pulls the rope softly or just walks in that direction. At this point, the foal is accepting the trainer's leadership. Once the training session ends, the foal should be put back with its dam.

During the second session, ideally the following day, the trainer should repeat the same exercises in the stall until the foal walks easily to both sides. After that, the foal should learn how to be led toward the front (ahead). For this, the trainer should walk toward the front until the foal walks one or two steps forward. Immediately thereafter, the trainer should pet the foal as a positive stimulus. Walking to each side, as well as to the front, should be practiced several times.

During the third session, the trainer should practice the exercises done during the prior session and also may try to lead the foal outside the stall. Although the foal may have been out of the stall several times with its dam, it often refuses to be led out because the situation has changed. When this happens, an easy way to lead the foal is by passing the loop of a rope (about 2 ½ feet diameter) behind the hindquarters, and passing the rope's free end through the halter ring at the jaw. To make the foal walk out of the stall, the trainer pulls gently on the lead rope that is attached to the halter, and more forcefully on the rope attached to the loop behind the foal's hindquarters, until the foal starts to walk forward.

Note: Passing the loop of a rope behind the hindquarters, and passing the rope's free end through the halter ring at the jaw, may be used to lead horses of any age when they are difficult to load in a trailer.

After the foal learns how to be led while both walking and performing the gait with only the lead rope attached to the halter, the trainer should then repeat two or three refresher sessions per week on a regular basis. During these sessions of about fifteen minutes each, the foal may be introduced to different places, buildings, objects, pieces of tack, vehicles, etc. on the farm and also to trailer loading. The trainer may improve the foal's confidence by petting, brushing the coat, and picking its hooves up.

When the foal resists approaching any place or obstacle, the trainer should let the foal gain confidence by petting, making the foal walk calmly, and awaking its curiosity of the area being avoided. If the foal fears an object, such as a grooming tool or a piece of tack, the object should be introduced slowly and gently to the foal by allowing the foal to smell, view, and feel the object all over its neck, back, barrel, and legs.

When a foal is tied to a pole for the first time, the trainer should wrap the lead rope, attached to the halter, around the pole without any knot. If the foal is calm, the lead rope may be tied to the pole with a knot that may be released easily and rapidly, if that is necessary. The distance between the pole and the halter should be from 6 to 12 inches. It is recommended that the trainer remains next to the foal during the first two or three times it is being tied. The trainer may then groom and pet the foal in order to keep the foal from spooking. When the foal calmly accepts being tied, the distance from the knot to the halter may be increased to about 2 feet. The trainer may then walk away from the foal, but still keep watching. The halter, rope, and knot must be strong because, if the foal pulls and the rope or halter breaks or the knot becomes untied, the foal will learn that pulling may be a way to escape.

During each session of consistent training, the foal trusts the trainer more and more. As soon as possible, the foal should learn how to come to the trainer in the stall and then in the paddock. Any voice command (such as the name of the foal or whistling in a special way) should be used consistently by the trainer while standing at the door of the stall or the paddock to get the foal's attention. Once the foal comes to the trainer, he/she may provide a treat and pet the animal, as a positive stimulus, and then attach a lead line to the foal's halter. When the foal consistently becomes easy to catch, the halter may be taken off. After that, each time the foal is caught, the trainer should wrap the foal's neck with the lead rope and then persuade the foal to move its muzzle towards the bosal-barbada, while putting the halter on its head. This work with the foal teaches it how to accept the halter and the jaquima, as part of the submissive relationship with the trainer, for the rest of its life.

Although longeing Paso Fino foals is a very common practice, it is not recommended for young horses because the effects are usually more damaging than beneficial. Longeing may cause stress to undeveloped bones, joints, and tendons, and the resulting pain may cause the foal to develop some vices, such as pulling on the rope and swishing the tail. Moreover, longeing a young horse on a concrete floor may have more devastating effects, not only causing severe lesions as a result of hitting the hooves on the hard flooring, but also causing injury to the foal if it were to fall down. Nevertheless, longeing in a proper way is a very good practice for horses 27 months of age or older, and is an important part of formal training (see "Longeing" on page 257).

FORMAL TRAINING

Although unfortunately there is not a standard method to train Paso Fino horses, some suggested methods described below are accepted widely in the Paso Fino world. At 27-29 months of age, the young horse should be started in training with some **GROUND WORK**. Assuming that the horse at this age has been trained properly as a foal, ground work is the first phase of formal training that consists of several stages: desensitization, adapting to the training tack, and longeing.

Note: The pictures in this chapter from this point on were made with the help of *Mr. Gustavo Zúñiga*, a professional Paso Fino trainer, from Ocala, FL.

- **Desensitization**: Before putting tack other than a halter on a young horse, the trainer may use a towel or lightweight saddle pad to touch, rub, and "sack out" the horse's body (including the legs), while the animal stays in a stall, is held by a lead line, or is tied to a post. Once the animal accepts each part of its body being touched, the trainer should provide a positive stimulus to the horse by petting it and speaking softly. Three sessions of desensitization are usually enough, but some horses may need additional sessions to completely become calm.

- **Adapting to the training tack**: After desensitization, each piece of tack that the trainer is going to use during the training process (except the bit) should be introduced to the horse one by one: the breaking halter (or training jaquima, or longeing jaquima), pad, saddle, girth, reins, breast plate, crupper, canastilla, collar, etc. The young horse should smell, view, hear any noise the tack makes, and feel each piece of tack as it is being rubbed all over the horse's neck, shoulders, back, and hips. Finally, the tack should be placed on the horse where it normally will be used.

  After three-to-five sessions of adapting to the training tack, the horse is ready to learn how to have the tack on while moving. For this, the young horse is tacked-up with the essential gear: breaking halter with a lead line attached, pad, saddle, and cinch. As described in Chapter 13, the breaking halter is made of cord, with optional rings to attach to the reins.

  Once the horse is properly tacked-up, the trainer takes the horse on a short lead in the round pen and other places where the animal will work, initially at a walk, and then at a Paso Fino gait. If the animal tries to buck, the trainer handles this by firmly pulling the lead line to either side. Two or three sessions are usually enough to help the young horse feel comfortable with the tack.

- **Longeing**: Proper longeing is a very helpful method for training the young horse before the breaking stage. Initially, the pisador (lead line) is attached to the longeing jaquima's bosal at the center ring. This allows the trainer to keep the horse's neck and back properly bent in the shape of a circle by applying light force on the lead line. Longeing the young horse on a soft ground of sand, clay, or grass, ideally in a 25 to 30 feet radius round pen (without a central pole), teaches the animal to use its hindquarters to propel its body forward, and to use the head, neck, and back to keep its balance. The horse learns to propel its breathing rhythm according to what is needed for work and improves its athletic endurance. Additionally, the horse becomes receptive to the commands applied through the lead line, which enables the horse to learn from the reins more quickly when the work under saddle begins.

  The trainer should longe the young horse in big circles (20 to 25 feet in radius) by holding the lead line with one hand and maintaining flexible contact. The trainer should stay parallel to the horse's flank. The horse should learn how to stop, walk, perform the gait at different speeds, and change direction. For these exercises, the trainer may apply different commands with the lead line (such as holding/pulling the lead line to stop), walk one or two steps toward the front of the horse, or use voice commands. A long whip may be used as an encouraging tool for some horses. Longeing should be practiced for about 15 sessions of 20 to 30 minutes each.

As a complementary exercise to longeing, the trainer should have the horse walk in small circles of about 8 to 10 feet in radius. The exercise consists of asking the horse to bend its back and neck, while using the legs to turn properly (see details below). This exercise should be done an even number of times in each direction. For this exercise, the trainer stays parallel to the horse's flank.

Flexing the horse's neck is another important ground work exercise that should be alternated with the above exercise. The trainer begins flexing the horse's neck to each side. This exercise should be started while standing on one side of the horse and pulling back the rein of the opposite side over the horse's withers. This makes the horse flex the neck, while standing still, until its muzzle touches either at its point of shoulder or at its forearm. As soon as the horse flexes its neck as described, the trainer releases the rein, as a positive stimulus, and then pets the horse.

When the horse accepts flexing its neck easily on both sides, flexing may be done while the trainer stands still at the side of the neck being flexed.

At 28 to 30 months of age, the young horse is started in the second phase of formal training, in which it is ridden **UNDER SADDLE**. This consists of several stages as follows: breaking, schooling, collecting, and finishing.

- **Breaking**: The trainer should teach the young horse how to stand quietly while being mounted. To do this, the horse must be tied to a pole with a cord breaking halter and a lead line, and then properly tacked-up with the pad and the saddle. To mount, the trainer stands on the left side of the horse, places the left foot in the left stirrup, holds on with the hands on the horse's neck and the saddle, and pushes his/her body up in order to stand erect for few seconds. Then, the trainer dismounts. This exercise should be repeated several times until the horse accepts it calmly.

  Afterwards, the trainer may get on the horse, sit on the saddle without using the right side stirrup, and move his/her seat side-to-side slowly in order to teach the horse to accept pressure on its back while the horse is standing still. After mounting and dismounting several times (while the horse stands quietly), the trainer should place his/her right foot in the right stirrup. The next goal is to teach the horse how to stand still while being mounted, without being tied to a post. Once the horse accepts being mounted on its left side, without being tied to a post, the trainer may repeat the same exercises on the horse's right side. Teaching the horse how to stand still for mounting may require several sessions, but should be reinforced every day.

  The round pen is the safest place for the first rides on a young horse. Usually, it is helpful if a very lightweight rider gets on the horse first, while the trainer holds and leads the horse. This is done at a walk in different directions while the lead line is attached to the breaking halter. The rider should use the reins attached to the side rings of the noseband in order to direct the horse the same way it is being led by the trainer. The young horse gradually should be introduced to stopping, turning to each side, longeing, and changing speed from a walk to a Paso Fino gait and vice-versa. Although the horse is still confused, unbalanced, and stiff after several sessions like this, the horse usually starts to trust the rider and learn how to respond to commands from the reins.

For the next sessions, the trainer starts to ride the horse in the round pen. The trainer rides the horse at a walk in different directions (straight and turning), stops, backs up, goes at a faster speed than a walk, and performs circles from 12 to 25 feet in diameter. If the horse tries to pull on the reins with more than a light contact, the trainer needs to stop the horse immediately by pulling the reins back, as a negative stimulus for such behavior.

The trainer begins flexing the horse's neck while sitting on the saddle. At this stage, flexing of the neck should be done until the horse's muzzle reaches its shoulder/forearm, and also until the muzzle reaches the saddle pad behind the trainer's leg. The trainer pulls back one of the reins to make the horse flex its neck. If the horse refuses to flex its neck with him/her on its back, the trainer may do this from the ground (ideally in deep sand), as it was done as ground work. When the horse flexes its neck to both sides from the ground, the trainer re-mounts and does it from the horse's back. For difficult horses, it may help to flex their necks, initially, in the stall instead of the round pen.

If the horse rears up, attempting to keep its neck from being flexed, a collar (see Chapter 13: "Tack and attire") may be put on the horse while it is saddled. Each side of the reins is passed through a ring of the collar that is located at both shoulders and then attached to the jaquima's bosal. The reins passing through the collar help direct the head-neck set for proper flexing.

Flexing the horse's neck without collar

Flexing the horse's neck with collar

During the breaking stage, flexing the horse's neck to the side helps the trainer to have better control of the animal if it misbehaves; for example, by bucking or taking off. Having the head-neck set bent over to one side, causes the horse to be off balance and, therefore, vulnerable.

Moreover, flexing the neck of the horse to each side stretches the muscles of the neck, back, and hindquarters, which gives the horse flexibility. When the horse is flexible on both sides, the trainer is able to keep the horse centered, both while moving forward (at a walk or in gait) and backing up. However, even though this exercise provides important benefits during training, flexing the neck to the side is not a magic solution to all the problems a horse may have during the training process, and therefore, flexing the neck should not be overused.

Another important exercise consists of stretching the muscles of the poll and the neck to make them more flexible. While the horse stands, the trainer holds and pulls evenly and consistently on both sides of the reins. Once the horse slightly relaxes its poll and neck, as if attempting to tuck its face, the rider immediately releases the pressure (as a positive stimulus). Immediately after, the trainer repeats the same exercise, but with the idea of making the horse tuck its face slightly more. This exercise should be repeated many times until the horse tucks its face until its chin almost reaches its chest, with the poll relaxed, and thereafter lowers its head. When this goal is accomplished repetitively, the trainer should make the horse walk while keeping its face vertical and then perform any Paso Fino motion. This prepares the horse to have a proper head-neck set.

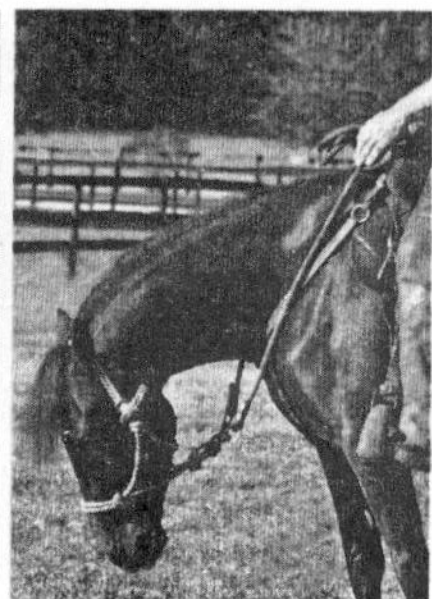

A complementary exercise that gives the horse flexibility at the poll, neck, back, hips, and legs is flexing of the neck while walking in circles. This consists of having the horse walk in circles of about 9 to 12 feet in diameter, while its neck is being flexed. This is done by pulling on the rein (of the side that is turning). The rein should be released as soon as the horse flexes its neck. This exercise should be started on the horse's easier side (to turn), and then on the more difficult side, making sure that it is performed the same number of times on each side. In addition, the trainer should ensure that the horse walks in circles, using the legs to turn properly: that is, 1) crossing the inside hind leg (of the turn) over the outside hind leg, 2) slightly shortening the step of the inside front leg to pivot for the turn, 3) moving the outside shoulder and the outside leg forward more than the inside ones, 4) and crossing the outside front leg over the inside front leg.

The entire breaking stage takes about 12 sessions. The trainer only considers this stage complete when the horse has learned how to move forward (ideally) in gait, stop and flex its neck on each side while standing still, back up several steps, and turn to either side at a walk and at a faster speed (in gait), when the trainer applies gentle commands with the reins.

To teach the horse how to back up, the trainer pulls back on both reins evenly until the horse moves one step back; then, the trainer releases the pressure on the reins and pets the horse's neck as a positive stimulus. Afterwards, the trainer encourages the horse to back up two steps by doing the same activity, and so on for three steps, etc.

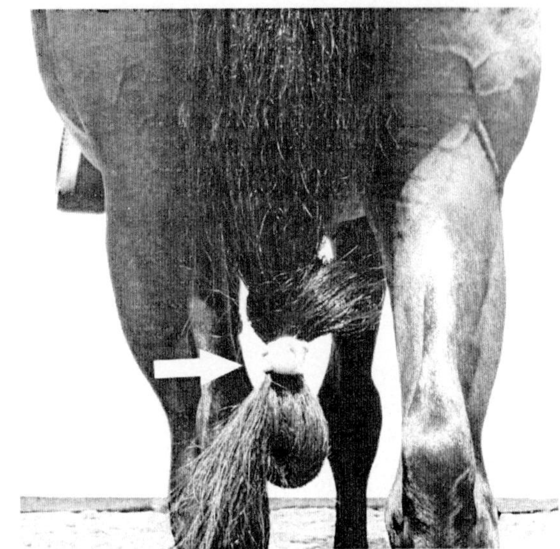

Note: Once backing up is started during training, the horse's tail should be tied to keep the horse from stepping on the tail's skirt and tearing it. A common way to do this consists of tying the end of the tail to one side of the saddle with a cord. Another way is bending the lower end of the tail's skirt and tying it with an elastic band.

- **Schooling**: This stage starts with basic training and ends when the horse accepts the commands applied solely on the bit reins (known as the "bitting" stage).

  - **Basic Training**: For this stage, the cord breaking halter is exchanged for a training jaquima, made of rawhide leather with straps or round pieces no wider/thicker than ¾ inch (except the bosal), and reins attached to the rings on both sides of the bosal. The initial bosal should be a soft type, made of flat leather, about 1 inch wide. The trainer applies commands with the reins, voice commands, seat, legs, and back to make the horse walk, change speed, stop, turn to both sides, and back up.

Although each trainer may develop his/her own code of commands and positive/negative stimuli to train a young horse, some options are explained here. To help the horse begin walking, the trainer, while sitting on the horse, changes the horse's center of gravity. This is done by slightly rocking his/her seat forward or leaning his/her body slightly forward-sideward, while gently pulling back on the rein of the side to which he/she is leaning. To keep the horse walking, the trainer relaxes his/her waist and follows the rhythm of the horse.

To encourage the horse to go faster, the trainer should squeeze both thighs or calves, or use voice commands, such as making a "clicking" or a "kissing" sound. To make the horse turn to either side, the trainer twists his/her trunk at the waist in the same direction of the horse's turn, pulls back the corresponding side rein, and squeezes the thigh slightly backwards on the turning side.

To make the horse stop, the trainer pulls back both reins evenly while pushing down on his/her seat in order to sit deeper. After this is practiced several times, the horse begins to respond to the commands made with the seat, and the reins gradually may be pulled back less.

Eventually, the trainer should flex the horse's neck to the horse's shoulder and also to the saddle pad behind the trainer's leg.

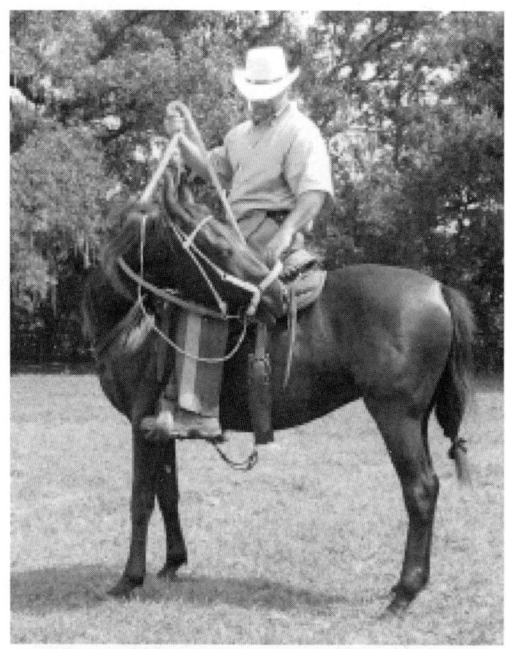

Flexing of the neck, to the saddle pad behind the trainer's leg

Backing up straight is a very important exercise that the horse must learn how to perform consistently (with diagonal pairs of legs). Therefore, this exercise should be practiced often during each training session in order to teach the horse balance and precision.

Working the horse in circles is an important exercise because the animal develops strong leg muscles and tendons, increases balance, improves rhythm, learns how to bend the back and neck for the turn, and uses the legs and shoulders properly.

Once the horse is responsive to these commands, the trainer may start to work outside of the round pen, initially at those places previously introduced to the horse. If the horse is very nervous about obstacles in the environment (vehicles, buildings, trash cans, etc.), leading the horse with the pisador (lead line) may help the horse improve its confidence. Instead of leading the horse on foot, others prefer to use a well-trained adult horse (usually a gelding) to "pony" the young one. At the beginning, the young horse should be led very closely to either the person or the pony horse, but once the horse in training improves its confidence, it gradually may be ridden further away from the guidance of others. The young horse may be ridden alone when it works with no fear.

The trainer should teach the horse how to work without pulling on the reins, but rather by maintaining light and constant contact, while performing the gait. If the horse starts to pull on the reins, the soft bosal of the jaquima should be changed to an intermediate severe type (cord knotted bosal, viril bosal, or leather bosal with covered metal balls). If the horse continues to pull against the reins, the trainer should forcefully pull on the reins to a stop, back up the horse, and flex the horse's neck to each side. Being persistent discourages the horse from pulling on the reins. A horse that continues to pull on the reins may be ridden with a severe bosal (metal bosal, either hinged and curved, or metal flat chain bosal) to make this correction, but once the horse does not pull on the reins, usually after two or three sessions, the bosal should be switched to a soft or intermediate severe type again.

About three weeks after basic training is started, most trainers use a second pair of reins attached to the two "jaw rings" of the jaquima's barbada (the rings are separated from each other by 2 to 3 inches), in addition to the reins attached to the side rings of the bosal. Some trainers use a collar (that works like a martingale), passing one or both pairs of reins through rings placed at the horse's shoulders, in order to improve the head-neck set position and to prevent the horse from rejecting the commands applied through the reins.

Two pairs of reins attached to the jaquima without using a collar

Two pairs of reins attached to the jaquima with a pair of reins passed through the rings of the collar

The basic training period takes about four to five weeks and allows the horse to learn how to respond to commands, improve its desire to work, gain better balance, and perform a more rhythmic gait. After each training session, the trainer should evaluate what proportion of the entire training time the horse worked well and how much improvement was made.

Note: Paso Fino horses are gaited since the day they are born due to genetics. However, because of the extra weight of the rider and the tack carried on their backs, and the confusion of learning to be ridden, a horse in training may lose its balance and, therefore, its gait may not be rhythmic and symmetrical; it may be more lateral (such as a pace) or more diagonal (such as a trot or a "pasi-trocha"). When the horse advances in its training process, it gradually gets its balance back, learns how to respond to the rider's commands, and develops the muscles to perform the Paso Fino gait with collection, perfect rhythm, and symmetry. This maturation process may take from a few weeks to a few years (in extreme cases).

- **Bitting**: The final goal for this stage is helping the horse learn how to respond to the commands applied through the reins that are attached to the bit. The first element in the horse's mouth should be a cord jetera (see chapter 13: "Tack and attire").

Once the jetera is put in the horse's mouth over the tongue, the two ends should wrap under the horse's lower jaw, slightly below the corners of the mouth, and be tied behind the jaw. The use of a jetera, properly tied and with no reins attached to it, teaches the horse how to keep the tongue still, while having an object in its mouth. This also prepares the horse for easier acceptance of a bit. The trainer does not attach any reins to the jetera yet, but continues the same training exercises by using the two pairs of reins attached to the training jaquima, as mentioned above.

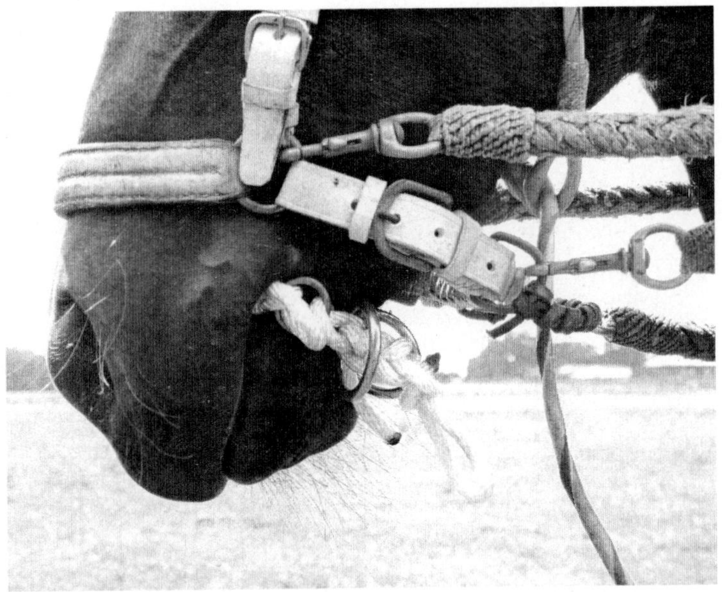

After the horse has been ridden with the jetera in its mouth for about ten training sessions, the trainer should attach a pair of reins to the metal rings of the jetera. The pressure on the reins attached to the jetera should be very light during the first rides. The horse should perform the same exercises as before, mainly with the pair of reins attached to the jaw rings of the barbada.

During the following 15 to 20 sessions, the trainer should work the horse with the same exercises: walking and performing the gait in a straight line and doing turns; flexing the neck to both sides, while the horse stands and while the horse walks in circles; backing up straight and backing up with the neck bent, etc. These exercises are done by using the reins attached to the barbada (jaw rings), and gradually using the reins attached to the jetera at the same time. The horse should learn how to work comfortably with the jetera and be very responsive to the commands applied with both pairs of reins (attached to the jetera and the jaw rings of the barbada).

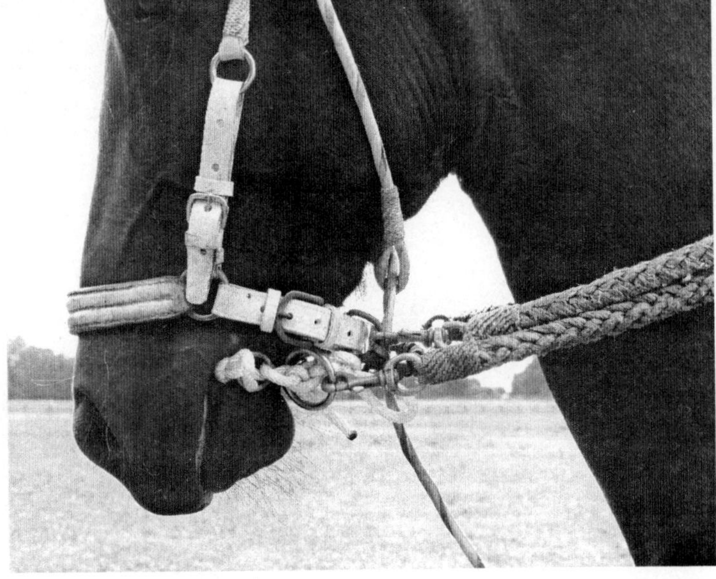

Note: After a few rides with the reins attached to the cord jetera, the trainer may choose another kind of jetera made of a different material (see chapter 13: "Tack and attire").

Because the horse should keep its poll relaxed at this stage, the trainer should flex the horse's poll by using both pairs of reins (one pair attached to the jetera, or to the bit in later stages, and the other pair attached to the jaw rings of a well-tightened, braided training barbada), as was explained previously.

From now on, because the horse's poll is becoming flexible and relaxed, due to the exercises above, the horse should learn to flex its neck from one side to the other side, while maintaining its poll at the same height and its face in a vertical position. For this, after the trainer has flexed the horse's neck to one side and is going to flex it to the other side, he/she should hold the reins steady, or lightly pull on them, to make the horse back up one or two steps, just as the neck and head are close to pointing straight forward. Then, the neck may be flexed to the other side, while keeping the poll at the same level and the face vertical. In addition to obtaining better flexibility, this prepares the horse to have an arched neck and vertical face in the future.

At this time, the horse is ready to use a metal bit. The first bit on a Paso Fino horse is a "baby bit." This is a Paso curb bit with a three-piece jointed mouthpiece attached to small short shanks. Before the bit is put in the horse's mouth, some honey or molasses may be put on the mouthpiece in order to make it tastier and promote acceptance. Doing this every day for several sessions will be very helpful in getting the horse to accept the bit more easily.

The mouthpiece of the bit must be positioned over the tongue, and the bit hanger adjusted, until one or two wrinkles occur at both corners of the mouth. The curb chain should be hooked loosely, and the reins are not attached initially to the bit. The purpose is to give the horse some time to learn how to keep a piece of metal in its mouth.

Note: If the horse starts to object to the mouthpiece of the bit with the tongue, a jetera may be put in its mouth, with the baby bit over it, with reins attached only to the barbada of the jaquima and/or to the side rings of the bosal.

After three sessions of training with the "baby bit" in the horse's mouth, without reins being attached, a pair of reins may be attached. The trainer starts to apply commands with both pairs of reins (barbada and bit), but primarily with the reins from the barbada, while practicing the same exercises (walking and gaiting straight ahead and circling, stopping, etc.). After several sessions, the trainer gradually increases use of the reins from the "baby bit."

From now on, the goal of the training sessions is to gradually make the horse work more using the reins that are attached to the Paso "baby bit." During the last minutes of each ride, the trainer may test the improvement of the horse by increasing use of the reins from the bit to ′drive′ the horse.

Note: When the horse salivates profusely with the bit in its mouth at any stage of the training, this is a sign of acceptance, not only of the bit itself, but also of the rider's commands applied with the hands through the reins. Production of saliva is increased if the mouthpiece or parts of it are made of copper or ′sweet′ iron.

When the horse is responsive to the reins attached to the Paso "baby bit" and to the barbada (about ten sessions), this bit may be changed to a Paso curb bit with a more rigid mouthpiece (such as a rubber bar), attached to short shanks. After 15 to 20 sessions in which the horse is responsive to the reins attached to this bit and to the barbada, a new bit may be used. The third bit should have a mouthpiece with a short central spoon and barrel rollers that are attached to short-to-intermediate shanks (3 to 4 inches long). Although the trainer still uses two pairs of reins, one pair attached to the bit and the other to the barbada, the trainer keeps building responsiveness to the bit, by using the pair of reins attached to it as much as possible.

During this stage, the trainer should flex the horse's neck to each side by using the two pairs of reins (from the bit, but especially from the jaquima's barbada).

As the training process advances, backing up may be an exercise used as a correction of certain undesired behaviors, such as pulling on the reins or breaking gait. When the horse finally is responsive to the reins from the bit, the bitting stage of about 18 to 25 weeks may be considered over. Of course, the young horse is neither collected nor finished, because it needs to improve many skills, including the balance/symmetry of its gait, head-neck set position, collection, and rapid responsiveness to the commands.

Notes:

- Although waiting longer may cost more for the horse's owner, a horse exhibiting excellent show qualities up to this training stage should not be rushed. If the young horse promises great potential, it deserves to have the time to mature in the training process in order to show its maximum splendor later on.
- Usually young stallions are not started in reproduction before the "bitting" stage of the training process has started. If the stallion starts to breed mares before this stage, he may become more difficult for the trainer to collect and finish the stallion's training because the stallion's attention will be on the farm's mares instead of the trainer.
- Unfortunately, when a horse does not seem to have the ability to excel in the show ring, the following stages of training often are barely completed and the horse often is dedicated/sold for trail riding, without fully being trained.

- **Collection**: Because training a Paso Fino horse from this stage on requires more expertise, some professional trainers dedicate their time solely to riding horses at this crucial stage and the next one (finishing). During this stage (collection) of about 12 to 15 weeks, the horse should improve its gait in several aspects: demonstrating a better rhythm and symmetry, performing a greater cadence, and showing consistency of the step extension and the forward speed. In addition, the horse should use the hind legs underneath its body to propel the body forward (known as collection) and demonstrate a proper neck-head set position. To do this, the horse should learn how to round the top of its body (croup, back, and neck).

The horse still should be ridden with both pairs of reins (one pair attached to the jaw rings of the barbada and the other pair to the bit). This does not mean that the horse is not bitted. Even though the trainer primarily uses the bit reins to apply commands, the reins from the barbada help neutralize any severe actions the trainer may need to use while ´pushing´ the horse harder.

At this time, the horse's head-neck set position is very important. The ideal position of the neck is arched, with the poll maintained at its highest point. The ideal head position is with the face vertical or with its nose slightly raised. Maintaining a vertical face (or close to it) is not only a means of aesthetics, but also the best way to make the horse receptive to the commands applied though the reins and, to use its rear legs to propel its body forward with collection.

Flexing of the poll and flexing of the neck to the sides, with the face tucked, provide the foundation of a proper head-neck set position. At this stage, the trainer may employ several exercises/training methods to obtain a consistent, appropriate head-neck set:

- Longeing the horse periodically, for about 20 minutes while tacked to a longeing jaquima (with a long lead line attached to the center ring of the bosal) and a non-severe bit, with side reins attached to it and tied to a surcingle (a wide, long strap that is placed behind the withers and surrounds the horse's barrel). This allows the horse to improve balance of gait and find the right spot to be comfortable with the bit and the head-neck set.

- Riding the horse with the reins (from the barbada and/or the bit) passed through the side rings of a collar put on the horse's shoulders.

- Riding the horse with draw reins. To use these reins, the horse must have a non-severe bit in its mouth. A snaffle or a rubber bar mouthpiece, with small to intermediate long shanks, are good options to use. The draw reins consist of a piece of cord or strap about 11 feet long, with ends that are passed through each rein ring of the bit, and then attached to each side of the cinch.

Horse being ridden with draw reins (passed through the bit's rings) and training reins attached to the jaw rings of the barbada

Even after using these training methods, the anatomy of the horse's neck may affect the neck-head set position: A horse with a swan neck shape may reach the vertical easier. Although the trainer must work longer, a horse with a regular (even) neck shape may also reach the vertical. Conversely, a horse with a "deer" neck shape may rarely reach the vertical.

In order to improve gait collection and promote a rounded croup, back, and neck, a canastilla should be used on the horse's hindquarters, slightly tightened behind the thighs/gaskins (see Chapter 13: "Tack and attire"). The canastilla encourages the horse to propel its body forward with its hind legs under the hips and the abdomen.

- **Finishing**: This is the last period of the formal training of about 12 – 20 weeks. Because there is a code of commands already established between trainer and horse, ideally only one trainer completes the training process to keep the horse from becoming confused or developing vices. The goal is to train the horse to have perfect balance and naturalness of gait, full responsiveness to the commands, and a desire to work. Finally, the trainer finds the most appropriate bit for the horse and uses only one pair of reins attached to the bit.

The trainer asks the horse for more power and alertness when working in circles; going up and down in gait over inclined surfaces; stopping immediately when asked; and backing up straight with precision. Riding the horse (wearing four shoes) over a sounding board or a concrete/pavement surface allows the rider to "calibrate" the rhythm, symmetry, and cadence of the Paso Fino gait. Because the horse should keep the gait over an extended period of time during either a show or a trail ride, the trainer should alternate rides of about one hour with rides of about half hour. During each session, the horse should be asked to walk every once in a while, not only to take "a breather," but also to relax its muscles, recycle lactic acid, and cool its mind and body down.

When the training process is finished, the horse should be ridden regularly with proper and consistent application of commands in order to retain the physical shape and mental capacity needed to achieve perfection. With time and maturation, the horse will respond to very light commands from the rider, such as stopping with seat and thigh pressure, backing up with light contact on the reins and seat/thigh pressure, and turning (while maintaining the gait cadence) by using minimal pressure on the reins and the seat.

Mr. Gustavo Zúñiga, professional Paso Fino trainer, riding his Paso Performance mare, "Mountain Meadow Rosalina" (Capuchino x Guaracha del Conde)

BAD BEHAVIOR

A horse that misbehaves is not safe to ride or be around. Some bad habits may be corrected by using methods that persuade the animal to quit the undesirable behavior:

- **Shying**: This term applies to a horse under saddle that spooks at most noises, at unknown obstacles, or simply resists leaving the place where it feels safe (e.g., barn or farm). The most common cause of shying is lack of exposure to the environment.

  "Ponying" the shy horse with a well-trained adult horse for several sessions usually will decrease the shyness. On the other hand, a rider who is a leader may often help the horse go through scary places just by being calm, confident and applying light and consistent commands. However, vision problems (such as myopia, hypermetropia, double image vision, and inverted image vision) may also cause shying, which obviously cannot be resolved with training.

- **Pulling while tied**: The horse pulls while being tied to a pole as a result of a previous experience in which pulling was a successful way to escape (because the halter/lead rope broke or the horse slipped the halter off). The first step in solving this problem is to tie the horse to a steady and strong pole with a Colombian jaquima, which has a thick and strong pisador made of either rawhide or nylon. The second step consists of standing at the side of the horse's flank and vigorously sacking the horse out, with a towel or a lightweight saddle pad, behind the hind legs (gaskins and cannons) several times when the animal starts pulling back (as a negative stimulus). Once the horse stops pulling and stands balanced, the trainer stops doing it and pets the horse (as a positive stimulus). This should be repeated several times until the horse consistently behaves properly while being tied.

- **Biting**: Some horses (especially males) start to bite people just as play when they are still very young. Because this does not look very dangerous in a young horse (and may even look cute), the horse is not corrected. When the horse matures and turns into an adult still having this vice, the horse becomes difficult to handle and may even cause a serious safety problem. Therefore, biting should ***NEVER*** be tolerated, but immediately corrected by slapping the horse's lips. Additionally, a horse that tries to bite may be led with a lead line, ending in a chain passed over its nose (as done with horses that strike – see below). If the horse tries to bite, the handler should pull the lead rope firmly, as a negative stimulus.

- **Kicking**: This easily may be corrected in young horses by vigorously sacking the horse out, with a lightweight saddle pad on the hind leg, immediately after the horse attempts to kick. If a horse in a stall takes a position to kick, the handler should make the horse turn around and face him/her by swinging a rope or a lightweight saddle pad on the horse's hindquarters.

- **Striking**: Although this is not very common in Paso Finos, some aggressive horses attempt to strike (kick with the front legs) their handlers in order to keep control of the situation. A horse that starts to strike should be led with a lead line with the end attached to the halter, having a chain passed over the horse's nose (see Chapter 10: "Health basics" – Methods of restraint). When the horse tries to strike, the handler should pull the lead line firmly several times to make the horse stop.

- **Refusing to turn to one side**: Horses, just as people, use one side of their body better than the other side. Therefore, the trainer/rider should work the horse on both sides, which gradually helps the horse to use both sides evenly. Sometimes, however, a horse may avoid turning to one side due to the presence of sharp points on its teeth or pain in its back, neck, or leg.

  After resolving these possible causes, the horse may be longed in big circles to each side in order to progressively make the horse work more evenly. The trainer also should work the horse in small circles, as was done during the ground work. For this, the trainer (being on the ground) makes the horse walk in small circles, bend its back and neck, while using the legs to turn properly (as described previously). In addition, while being on the horse, the trainer should flex the horse's neck to each side, while the horse stands and also while the horse performs circles.

- **Swishing the Tail**: A horse under saddle may swish its tail as a response to discomfort caused by ill fitting tack (bit, pad, saddle, etc.), confusing/rough rider's commands, insect/fly bites, pain, poor attitude, fear, or a mixture of these causes. Because this is considered a bad habit in Paso Finos, the rider should identify the cause of the discomfort in order to make an immediate correction, and keep the horse from developing this vice. The use of a canastilla on a young horse in training prevents the animal from starting to swish its tail as a protest when the trainer is asking for a difficult exercise. On the other hand, some horses swish their tails constantly due to a poor attitude when the rider pushes, which is very difficult to solve with training.

Note: Other bad habits, caused by the boredom of confinement, are discussed in Chapter 9: "Facilities for horses."

CHAPTER 16

EQUITATION - NOT JUST SITTING PRETTY

Equitation encompasses all horseback riding activities that are associated with transportation, work, recreation, or the many disciplines/sports, such as dressage, jumping, racing, polo, rodeo, horse-mounted bullfighting, etc. In addition, when equitation is practiced with discipline, it becomes an artistic manifestation and a wonderful sport that raises the spirit, exalts human talent, and allows riders to enjoy the majesty of the horse.

Since the time when riding horses became important to different civilizations, humans have been learning about the relationship between the horse and rider. Over time, scientific research, combined with artistic and cultural factors, prompted many different styles of equitation to develop.

Scientific research about the horse primarily has focused on the following topics:

- Developing new horse breeds for different purposes, such as work, travel, and sport.
- Learning the proper methods for breeding, equine nutrition, facilities, hoof trimming and shoeing, health maintenance, medicine, etc.
- Studying the horse's psychology in its natural habitat in order to develop new horse training techniques.
- Studying the horse's anatomy and physiology to take the most advantage of it.

Other research has been oriented to the horse-rider "duo":

- Identifying the athletic skills the rider needs for better riding.
- Studying the physics of the interaction between horse and rider.
- Designing comfortable tack for the rider.
- Designing proper tack to fit the horse's anatomy.

A wide variety of equitation styles have developed, based on artistic and cultural factors of different civilizations:

- Horses have been an important part of human cultures, and proper riding has always been considered a manifestation of beauty, elegance, and art.
- Many equestrian sports have developed, not only for competition, but also for fun.
- The horse's tack and the rider's attire have been designed not only for comfort, but also for aesthetics.

BENEFITS OF EQUITATION FOR THE RIDER

In whichever discipline it is practiced, and independent of the horse breed, equitation is a wonderful recreational activity that develops the rider's psychological and physical skills. Concentration, self-control and coordination, balance, discipline, and self-motivation are all enhanced by the practice of equitation.

Yuliana Suárez Lebrón riding "Campanera del Conde" (Bolívar de Sol Reye x Artiquera) through an obstacle course at Ocala's School of Equestrian Art. Photo by Jesús A. Soto.

- Concentration: Because the horse is bigger, heavier, stronger, and faster than humans, practicing equitation encourages the rider to pay attention to the horse's body language, its reactions to the environment, the gait, and the horse's responses to commands. This lets the rider adjust and implement proper commands to obtain the best results from the horse.

- Self-control and coordination: While on a horse, the rider must learn how to control emotions (such as fear, panic, anger, and frustration) and reactions (such as screaming and releasing the reins), as well as coordinate movements in order to avoid a lack of communication with the horse and possibly undesired consequences. Self-control and coordination allow the rider to maintain the status of leader and be able to apply proper commands in all situations.

An example of loss of self-control and coordination occurs when a beginning rider is afraid. The most common unconscious reactions are instinctively adopting a fetal position (which consists of leaning/bending the body forward), squeezing the calves and feet against the horse, and holding onto the saddle. This lack of self-control causes several problems to occur. The rider's fetal position may actually make the situation worse because the rider is off balance. The rider's calves and/or feet squeezing the horse could encourage the horse to move faster. Although the rider may keep holding onto both reins, control of the horse through the reins will be poor if the rider's main concern is holding onto the saddle. Additionally, because of the poor control of the reins, the horse may change direction freely.

- Balance: At a minimum, balance on a horse requires four skills:
  - Equilibrium to stay on the horse.
  - Using the seat as the center of gravity.
  - Using both sides of the body evenly, including arms, hands, and legs, to apply commands.
  - Adapting to the horse's movements.

- Discipline: As with any other sport, equitation should be practiced with discipline, which encourages the rider continuously to improve riding skills. Moreover, discipline learned from equitation positively impacts most of the rider's other activities.

- Self-motivation: When riders see improvement in their equitation skills, they are motivated to keep growing, not only as riders, but also as leaders. Therefore, throughout history, equitation has been seen as a sport for powerful/privileged people (royalty, the military, politicians, and their respective families) to develop their leadership skills.

  Practicing equitation, however, is not always easy and rewarding for the rider when a horse does not cooperate due to a lack of training, vices, or a dominant temperament. Although these situations may cause the rider to feel frustrated, this feeling should never stop the desire to improve. Rather, it is an opportunity to solve a new problem, improve skills, and plan new strategies with the horse.

THERAPEUTIC HORSEBACK RIDING

Therapeutic horseback riding consists of using the horse as a therapeutic tool for people of any age who are challenged with mental, emotional, and/or physical disabilities. Persons with multiple sclerosis, muscular dystrophy, spinal cord injury, blindness, stroke, Down's syndrome, autism, mental retardation, emotional disabilities, learning disabilities, etc., may take advantage of therapy with horses.

The psychological, emotional, and physical benefits for individuals who participate in therapeutic horseback riding have been proven and are widely documented, not only in Canada and the United States by the *North American Riding for Handicapped Association (NARHA)*, but in many centers around the world, using different breeds of horses.

Although trotting horse breeds (Quarter horses, Thoroughbreds, and Percherons) and trotting pony breeds (Shetland and Welsh ponies) are the most common types of mounts used for therapeutic horseback riding, some riders benefit from riding smoothly gaited horses, especially those riders who have problems with balance or cannot ride on trotting horses. For example, Paso Fino horses (and the three Colombian diagonal Paso horse breeds) successfully are used in Medellín, Colombia, South America in *ACEPASO - Academia de Equitación del Caballo de Paso* (one of the three Paso riding schools founded by the author in Colombia) for its therapeutic horseback riding program.

The horse is an excellent therapeutic tool for several reasons:

- Being around and/or in contact with a horse stimulates the human senses because of the animal's large size, unique fragrance, and fascinating shape, combined with the sounds it makes while walking/gaiting, eating, and whinnying.
- Because the horse's temperature is higher than a human's, and also increases when the animal is working, a rider with rigid muscles and joints may accomplish some muscle and joint relaxation during a riding session after the first 20 minutes.
- The horse's walking motions make the rider stretch and relax several muscle groups in the lower back, buttocks, and legs, which help develop stronger muscles and improve balance and coordination.
- When riding a horse, a person improves several important skills, such as independence, balance, flexibility, coordination, and self-confidence.

Additionally, equitation of the Paso Fino horse is an excellent option for thousands of riders around the world, either disabled or not, to enhance personal skills, whether equitation is practiced for competition or not.

EQUITATION OF THE PASO FINO HORSE

The equitation of the Paso Fino horse requires the rider to maintain proper posture and apply the correct commands to obtain the smoothest, evenly alternated, four-beat gait from the horse (Classic Fino, Paso Corto, or Paso Largo), as well as its maximum responsiveness, elegance, and brio.

The expression *"equitation of the Paso horses"* may be used broadly because it makes reference not only the equitation of the Paso Fino horse, but also the three Colombian diagonal Paso horse breeds (Colombian Collected Trote and Galope, Colombian Pure Trocha, and Colombian Trocha and Collected Galope). Practicing this unique equitation is more than riding a beautiful and well-gaited horse. When riding any Paso horse either for pleasure or competition, the rider may be compared to a musician who plays an instrument with perfect rhythm, melody, harmony, and cadence.

The sport of Paso horse competitions has two disciplines:

- Judging the horse, in which only the animal is evaluated (see Chapter 4: "Unique characteristics of the Paso Fino horse" and Chapter 18: "Other Paso horses"): These competitions do not take into consideration the equitation of the rider.
- Judging the rider, in which equitation is evaluated: In these competitions, the quality of the horse is not evaluated, but rather the way the rider applies the commands, maintains good posture, and takes advantage of the horse's potential.

PREPARATION AND TRAINING OF THE PASO FINO RIDER

The Paso Fino rider of any age, over time, should achieve skills and knowledge to ride horses properly.

- **General knowledge about horses**: The rider should dedicate time to learn about horses, such as their habits, psychology, anatomy, physiology, and handling.
- **The horse's body language**: In addition to the whinny, the horse communicates with other horses (and people) through a complex body language. Therefore, it is highly recommended that a rider learns the signs of the horse's body language, mainly those made with the ears, head, mouth, and tail.
- **General knowledge about Paso Finos**: The rider should know about the Paso Fino gait, standards of the breed, style of equitation, proper commands, training basics, and tack.
- **Physical preparation**: Before mounting, the rider carefully should stretch several groups of muscles in the neck, back, shoulders, arms, wrists, fingers, waist, and legs to avoid becoming sore after riding. A second stretching session is needed after dismounting. The rider should train these groups of muscles to channel their strength while riding. Practicing disciplines such as Pilates, martial arts, and yoga, among others, help the rider improve proprioception (ability to feel and control all the voluntary parts of the body) and, consequently, lead to better posture and more efficient control when riding.
- **Development of balance**: To achieve the four elements of balance (maintaining equilibrium, using the seat as the center of gravity, applying commands evenly on both sides, and adapting to the horse's movements), the rider should have several riding sessions, under proper instruction, without using stirrups.

Students from Ocala's School of Equestrian Art develop their balance riding on pads with no stirrups: Left, Grant Varney riding La Sombra Ideal (Photo by Robin Varney). Right, Mrs. Diana Venegas riding Aparecida de MED (Photo by Beth Nabors).

- **Practice**: Paso Fino riders should continue to improve their riding skills with hours of practice. This allows the rider to achieve maximum comfort, efficiency, and elegance, while obtaining the best performance from the horse. Having a plan of action, well-defined objectives, and proper riding instruction and supervision, assure continuous improvement. Using large mirrors, strategically located in the working arena, may improve equitation skills further by allowing the rider to watch himself/herself during practice sessions.

  Just as the rider needs to practice frequently, the horse also needs regular training sessions in order to maintain maximum athletic/physical condition. Additionally, prior to any form of competition, the horse and rider should train together in order to understand each other during the performance and become a harmonious pair.

- **Leadership**: A rider should develop his/her own leadership with a horse, and no one else can do it for him/her. It is common to see that, once a trainer has established a leading relationship with a horse, he/she will ride the horse very easily. But, when a less experienced rider is on the same horse, he/she is often not as successful. Only when the less experienced rider establishes his/her own leading relationship with the horse, will he/she be able to obtain similar results with the horse.

Note: Children (12 years of age or under) and any new rider (no matter the age) should wear a safety helmet to protect the head from accidentally hitting the ground.

BASICS ABOUT EQUITATION

Some fundamental tips about Paso Fino equitation are listed below.

- **Mounting and dismounting**: To mount, the rider stands on the left side of the horse, slightly diagonal, and able to look at the horse's head. The rider holds both reins evenly with the left hand, and with light contact on the horse's mouth, makes sure the animal is standing quietly. Still holding the reins, the rider places the left hand on the horse's neck about 3 inches in front of the withers. With the right hand, the rider turns the left stirrup in order to place the left foot in it. Then, while placing the right hand either on the saddle's cantle or on the right side of the saddle's pommel, the rider pushes his/her body upward until both legs are straight, supporting the main weight of the body on the left stirrup. The rider swings the right leg straight over the horse's croup and then to the horse's right side, in order to sit in the saddle. Finally, the rider places the right foot in the right stirrup without looking down at it (see photos on the next page).

  To dismount, the rider should reverse this process. However, instead of keeping the left foot in the stirrup, to support the body weight until the right foot reaches the ground, many riders take the left foot out of the stirrup and slowly slide down, until both feet touch the ground simultaneously (see photos on page 280). It is safer to dismount this way in case the horse moves.

Mrs. Debbie Kolody, a student of Ocala's School of Equestrian Art, showing the appropriate way to mount a horse.

Mrs. Debbie Kolody showing the appropriate way to dismount.

Two important aspects of mounting and dismounting are related below:

- **Mounting and dismounting on the horse's left side**: From anatomical and physiological points of view, neither the rider nor the horse has a preferable side for mounting and dismounting. However, as a general rule in equitation, mounting and dismounting from the left side of the horse is the correct way. This tradition originates from the time when warriors, armed with swords, went into battles riding horses. Because most warriors were right handed, they kept their swords tied at their waists on their left sides, making it easier to take the sword out when needed (with the right hand). In these circumstances, an armed rider (with the sword hanging at the waist's left side) could mount and dismount easier from the horse's left side.

- **Emergency dismounting**: The rider needs to know how to dismount quickly and safely from a horse during an emergency. In very dangerous situations, such as when a horse is out of control or is falling (having tripped), the rider has just a few seconds to get off the horse safely.

  Developing this ability does not mean that the rider needs to do a fast dismount for all difficult situations. If faced with a difficult situation on a horse, the rider must first take his/her feet out of the stirrups and try to solve the problem by using proper commands to maintain control. After that, the rider has the option to do a fast dismount, if necessary, or to put his/her feet back in the stirrups after the problem is resolved.

- **Riding commands**: All commands used to ride a horse must be discreet and well-planned, with the goal of helping the horse to use its body optimally and find its own balance. The rider must know what command is necessary to obtain a specific response from the horse; however, if a command is not working, the rider should know how to change it for another. The rider of a Paso Fino horse may also apply most of the commands used in other styles of equitation:

  - **Pressure in the horse's mouth through the bit and the reins**: Reins, commonly attached to the bit on trained horses, are one of the most important commands used to ′drive′ a horse either in desired direction (turns), change forward speed, stop, or back up. The rider's hands should have constant contact (pressure) with the horse's mouth through the bit and the reins. Contact is variable, from very light (just holding the reins in place) to intermediate, depending on the horse, the bit used, the way the horse has been trained, and other commands given.

    Contact should never be a pulling battle between the horse's mouth and the rider's hands, but a way the rider communicates with the horse. For example, when the rider has the horse moving forward (either walking or in gait) and increases contact by pulling back on the reins, it is interpreted by the horse as a request to reduce the forward speed or to stop. If the horse is standing still and the rider pulls the reins back, it is interpreted by the horse as a request to back up.

    Reins also may be used to make the horse turn and perform circles. Softly pulling back the rein, inside the planned turn in place, makes the horse move in that direction. Additionally, the rider may hold the rein outside the turn to keep the size of the circle consistent. The more the rein outside the turn is held back, the bigger the circle.

    There are three different ways to hold the reins on a fully bitted horse:

    - o Each rein is held in one hand beneath the little finger (pinky) and extending upward until the rein leaves the hand over the forefinger. The thumb presses the rein against the forefinger to keep it from slipping. Excess reins should hang on the horse's right side.

- Each rein is held in one hand between the ring and little (pinky) fingers, extending upward, until the rein leaves the hand over the forefinger. The thumb is placed on the rein to press it against the forefinger, which keeps the rein from slipping. Excess reins should hang on the horse's right side.

Note: These two methods of holding reins are valid for *PFHA* equitation show classes, with either flat or round reins *(PFHA – Constitution and Rule Book, Chapter Three, Section I, Subsection B, 2, b, (1) and (2)),* and for *CONFEPASO* equitation show classes, with either flat or round reins *(Reglamento de Competencias para Amazonas y Jinetes en Equitación – CONFEPASO, Chapter VI, Article 31, Section C, subsections 1 and 2).*

- Most professional Paso riders hold reins in a third way. Both reins are held in one hand. The other hand holds the rein on the same side as that hand (e.g., the left hand holds the left rein), slightly below the first hand that holds both reins. Excess reins should hang on the horse's right side.

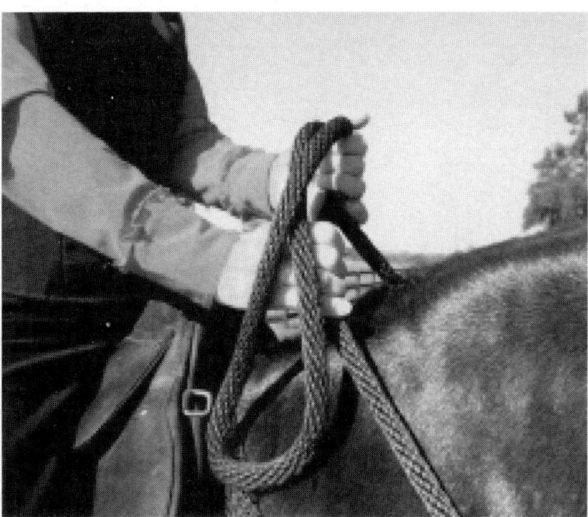

Note: This method of holding the reins is preferred in *CONFEPASO* equitation show classes for riders 12 years old and over, with either flat or round reins *(Reglamento de Competencias para Amazonas y Jinetes en Equitación – CONFEPASO, Chapter VI, Article 31, Section C, subsection 3).*

Paso Fino horses in training are ridden with two pairs of reins (see Chapter 15: "Horse psychology and training"). The trainer holds the two reins of each side with the respective side hand, either both reins being held below the pinky or keeping the reins apart (e.g., one rein held below the pinky and the other between the ring and middle fingers).

- **The rider's seat and waist**: The rider also may use the seat and the waist to turn the horse. Twisting the trunk at the waist makes the seat bone that is inside the turn put more pressure on the horse's back, which encourages the horse to turn in that direction. In addition, riders may use their seat and waist as a command to stop a horse. This is accomplished by lowering the back, which makes the buttocks and seat bones sit deeper in the saddle, and causes more pressure on the horse's back.

- **Pressure with the legs**: By putting pressure with one or both calves on the horse's barrel, or tapping (slightly "kicking") the horse with one or both heels, the rider will encourage the horse to perform either a higher cadence of gait or a faster speed.

  Riders may use their legs for other purposes. When one calf is squeezed against the horse's barrel about 6 inches behind the cinch, the horse's hindquarters are moved to the opposite side of the pressure. This may be applied during several exercises, such as side-passing, making the horse move straight in one track when it has been moving its legs asymmetrically in two tracks, and ending a circle next to a fence to continue moving straight ahead.

  Note: A horse moves in one track when both hooves on each side hit the ground in the same line, either curved (as in a circle) or straight ahead. A horse moves in two tracks when the hooves on the same side move asymmetrically rather than in the same line.

- **Voice commands**: After applying positive stimuli repetitively, a horse may be trained to respond to some voice commands, such as changing gait (e.g., from Paso Corto to Paso Largo), turning to either side, stopping, and backing up. The rider also may make a variety of noises (such as whistling, clicking, and kissing) to encourage the horse to stay alert and to increase either the cadence of the gait or the forward speed. Likewise, the horse may be taught to come to the trainer/owner in the pasture just with a voice command.

- **Whip and spurs**: Some horses may require that the rider uses tools, such as a whip and/or spurs, in order to make the horse more responsive. These tools and voice commands should be used correctly, and alternated with other commands, in order to keep the horse from becoming too familiar with them and causing the element of surprise to be lost.

Note: Riders must understand that horses usually do what is asked by the application of commands. However, when a rider expects the horse to perform something but applies the wrong commands, the communication with the horse is confusing, which may cause loss of control.

- **The rider's field of vision**: The entire field of vision of a person is about 180° when looking toward the front, thanks to the peripheral vision that lets a person perceive what is happening on both sides of the face. This wide field of vision allows a rider to see simultaneously between the horse's ears and to each side.

  The rider should be watching between the horse's ears in order to see the direction and the obstacles in front, as well as where the animal's attention is placed. For example, one or both ears, that keep turning back and forth, mean that the horse's attention is placed on the rider and the environment at the same time. This is very desirable in the Paso Fino breed because it is a sign of alertness. If both ears of the horse are pointing forward, this means the animal is more interested in the forward environment (noises, other horses, unknown objects, the barn, etc.) than in the rider. When this occurs, the rider must try to get the horse's attention in order to maintain control.

- **The horse's head set**: The proper head position (head set) for the Paso Fino horse is when the face is either vertical (perpendicular to the ground level) or slightly above:

  - With the head in this position, the horse looks very elegant.
  - The rider has more control of the horse's mouth, poll, and hind legs to optimize the gait (collection, smoothness, and harmony).
  - The horse has balance, which makes it more receptive to the rider's commands.

  Once its poll becomes relaxed after proper training, the horse may keep its face vertical (or slightly above), while the neck, back, and croup become rounded, and the hind legs are maintained underneath, in order to propel the body forward; thus, enhancing collection.

  When a Paso Fino horse has its poll stiff, the animal avoids the pressure made by a rider through the reins by trying to raise its face as far above the vertical as possible. In addition, the horse avoids rounding its neck, back, and croup, which causes the hind legs not to be flexible underneath. Conversely, some horses with stiff polls keep their faces below the vertical and pull down against the reins to keep the riders from controlling and driving them.

  In some cases, the horse's neck has been excessively flexed during the training process, causing the neck's muscles to lose tone; therefore, these horses keep their faces completely tucked down while putting no pressure against the reins. In addition, these horses do not use their hind legs properly and are absolutely off balance. This shows the importance of gradually teaching the horse to have a proper head-neck set in connection with the rear legs, and not one imposed on the horse by forcing the head-neck set or over-flexing the neck.

- **The horse's center of gravity**: As with any other living creature, the horse's body has a center of gravity, that may be described as the place where its own balance is located. When the horse is seen from one side, its **center of gravity** (**G**) is at the point where horizontal and vertical lines meet, as follows:
    - A horizontal line may be made by drawing a line from the point **M1** (which is the middle of the straight line drawn from the horse's withers and point of shoulder) to the point **M2** (which is the middle of the straight line drawn from the hip bone and the buttock or the bone below the tail).
    - A vertical line may be made by drawing a perpendicular line from the horse's back to the ground that crosses the rear end of the sternum (on the barrel's bottom), as shown in the picture below:

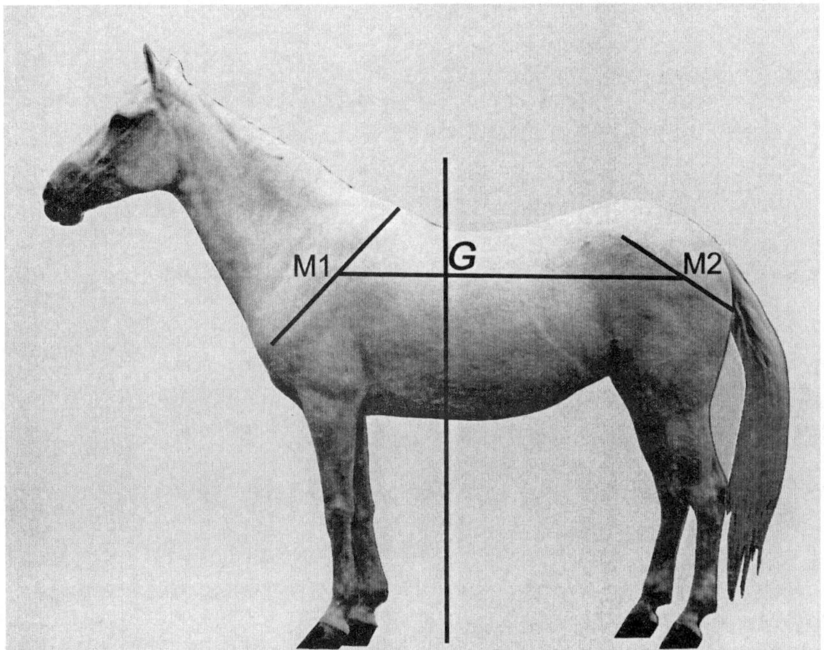

Knowing about the horse's center of gravity is important to properly place weight on the horse's back (saddle and rider, for instance), and before the horse is going to pull anything (carriage, plow, logs, etc). Any piece of tack and/or weight must be placed, or attached, as closely as possible to the horse's center of gravity in order to help the horse work comfortably and efficiently.

The comfort a horse feels when it carries a weight, properly placed close to its center of gravity, is similar to what a hiker feels when carrying a backpack. A backpack that is out of place will cause great discomfort. However, when the same backpack is placed properly, close to the hiker's center of gravity, it is comfortable to carry even when very heavy.

A saddle is placed properly on the horse's back when the front edge of the pommel is approximately on top of the withers and the front edge of the saddle panel is placed behind the top of the horse's shoulder (so that the saddle panels do not interfere with the movement of the horse's shoulders). Then, when a rider gets on the horse, its balance is less affected because the weight of the saddle and the rider are placed close to the horse's center of gravity.

POSTURE OF THE PASO FINO RIDER

Although a rider may think that the riding position is not important, it actually affects the horse's performance in many ways. For example, if the rider's trunk is inclined backward on a moving horse, the horse usually tries to raise its face and move forward faster in order to compensate for the lack of balance caused by the rider. A rider will lean his/her trunk back for several reasons, such as placing the feet too far forward, having stirrups longer than needed, placing hands too high, holding the reins too long, or sitting on the tail bone instead of the seat bones.

At all times, a rider must have (and look in) perfect control of the Paso Fino horse and maintain proper posture on the animal, both when the horse stands and when it is in gait. Having good posture on a horse allows the animal to stay balanced, which makes both rider and horse become a pair.

The correct posture of the Paso Fino rider is explained below:

- From the side, the rider should be seen as follows:
  - The rider's neck should be straight and elegant, but not stiff. Eyes should look forward between the horse's ears.
  - The rider's shoulders should be relaxed, and the back should be straight and perpendicular, but not tense.
  - The rider's arms should hang relaxed from the shoulders and vertical, with elbows pointing slightly down and held next to the side ribs (but not squeezed against the side ribs). Elbows should never be placed behind the back.
  - The forearms should be as aligned as much as possible with the reins, but this depends on the horse's head set. For example, if the horse tends to have its face too high, the rider should move his/her hands lower, and vice-versa.
  - The little (pinky) fingers should be more relaxed than the forefingers, which makes the hands look inclined forward (not vertical). Hands should be located above the horse's neck and slightly in front of the saddle pommel. Hands should be held slightly separated, but no further apart than the size of an apple. Hands should be held steady with the fingers flexible to make adjustments to the reins in order to communicate better with the horse.
  - The rider should sit with the seat bones placed in the deepest part of the saddle seat. The buttocks should be distributed evenly on both sides of the saddle and maintain contact with the saddle while the horse performs any motion of the Paso Fino gait (or any gait performed by the Colombian diagonal Paso horse breeds, such as Trote, Trocha, or Galope).
  - The waist should be flexible to neutralize any movement of the horse that affects the rider's balance.
  - The rider's legs should rest in a natural position, with the inside thighs in contact with the saddle skirts and flaps. Thighs should be extended down and inclined slightly forward with the knee-caps pointing forward.
  - Feet should be parallel to the horse's body with the balls of the feet resting on the stirrups. Heels should be about 1 inch lower than the toes. Toes should not pass forward beyond a vertical line from the knee caps; thus, the rear of the heels become aligned perpendicularly with the hips, elbows, shoulders, and head.

- From the front and the rear, the rider should be seen as follows:
  - Trunk should be straight and perpendicular to the horse.
  - Shoulders should be apart, straight, and level, but not tense.
  - Elbows should be naturally placed next to the side ribs (but not squeezed against the side ribs).
  - Hands should never be crossed over the horse's neck.
  - Calves should appear perpendicular to the ground.
  - Feet should point forward while the balls of the feet rest evenly on the stirrup bottoms.
  - Stirrups should be even (in length).

Jessica Varney on "Intimidator de MED" (Arlequin Tres x Jibarita de La Victoria, and owned by Mildred Arent), shows the proper posture when riding a Paso Fino. Photos courtesy of Ocala's School of Equestrian Art.

Note: The posture of the rider explained above demonstrates what is required for *Paso Fino Horse Association* equitation show classes *(PFHA – Constitution and Rule Book, Chapter Three, Section I, Subsection B, 2, from a to f)* and for *CONFEPASO* equitation show classes *(Reglamento de Competencias para Amazonas y Jinetes en Equitación – CONFEPASO, Chapter VI, Article 31).*

SOME TIPS BEFORE RIDING

Before riding, a rider should pay attention to several details that help make a comfortable and safe ride or training session.

- After eating a full meal with grain, a horse needs to rest one hour, at a minimum, before intense physical activity.
- The horse should be groomed before the ride for beauty, comfort, and health. Additionally, this time shared with the horse improves the relationship between horse and rider.
- During grooming, the rider should inspect the horse's body in order to ensure that there are no injuries, inflamed areas, or sore points. The rider also should check to see if the horse exhibits signs of dehydration (see Chapter 10: "Health basics").
- The horse's mouth area should be inspected to verify that there are no cuts on the corners of the mouth, tongue, gums, palate, and mouth's bars (the lower spaces on both sides of the mouth, between the incisors and the premolars).
- Hooves should be cleaned to determine if there are wall cracks, infected areas with a bad smell (thrush), or any incrusted element that may cause trauma. Additionally, this is the opportunity to check the horseshoes (wear and attachment to the hooves).
- The condition of the jaquima (headgear), the bit hanger (or the bridle if that is the case), and the reins should be reviewed before riding to prevent accidents that may occur if one of these pieces of tack has broken.
- The bit should be chosen according to the anatomy of the horse's mouth and the horse's training level. Once the bit is on the horse, the tension of the bit hanger that positions the bit in the mouth, should be adjusted until one or two wrinkles of skin are seen on the corners of the mouth. Additionally, the tension of the curb-chain should be adjusted according to both the way the horse has been trained and the force that a rider needs to apply to the reins to ′drive′ the horse (see Chapter 14: "The bit: magic or science?").
- All the tack on both sides of the horse should be reviewed before the rider mounts in order to ensure that everything is properly placed and tight. Special attention should be paid to the girth, because it usually needs to be tightened a second time before mounting (many horses bloat their barrels when the girth initially is tightened; thus, it is often necessary to tighten the girth a second time).

SOME SAFE TRAIL RIDING TIPS

A horse used for trail rides should have one or two identification tags attached to the jaquima and/or the saddle. This helps locate the horse in case it is lost on the trail, after the rider either dismounts or falls off. Information contained on the tag should include the horse's name, horse owner's name, telephone numbers, and address.

When riding in a group, riders must keep a minimum distance of 8 feet between horses (approximately the length of a Paso Fino horse). This keeps the rider and the horse from being kicked/bitten by any aggressive horse in close proximity. Additionally, a rider may stop the horse, if needed, to avoid running into a horse/rider in front.

A group of trail riders should have a signal or sound code to advise the others about danger and any change of speed, direction, or inclination of the ground. Each rider must pay attention to the signals made by the rider in front, and immediately repeat them for the riders behind.

During windy days, horses are more alert and tend to be spookier to any noise or sudden movement in the environment, such as tree branches or bushes shaking, a blowing tarp or plastic bag, a piece of metal roof shaking, or just the wind blowing into the horse's ears. Therefore, the rider must pay more attention to everything in the environment in order to anticipate the horse's reactions and help the animal trust his/her commands.

JUDGING EQUITATION

Riders in *PFHA* and *CONFEPASO* equitation sanctioned shows are judged, based on the proper application of commands to obtain the best gait and control of the horse, and on the rider's body posture as explained above.

- ***PFHA* equitation classes**: Because in equitation classes riders are required to ride the horses in Paso Corto and Paso Largo motions, riders should compete on a Paso Performance or a Paso Pleasure horse *(PFHA – Constitution and Rule book, Chapter Three, Section I, Subsection B, 2, g (4) and (5), and h).*

  The equitation categories (only for youth riders), as well as any other youth class (except Gold or Silver Medal Advanced Equitation), offered in a show may include:

  - First option.
    - o Open youth: Riders (both genders) from 7 to 17 years old.
  - Second option.
    - o Sub-junior youth: Riders (both genders) from 7 to 12 years old.
    - o Junior youth: Riders (both genders) from 13 to 17 years old.
  - Third option.
    - o Sub-junior youth - level I: Riders (both genders) from 7 to 9 years old.
    - o Sub-junior youth - level II: Riders (both genders) from 10 to 12 years old.
    - o Junior youth – level I: Riders (both genders) from 13 to 15 years old.
    - o Junior youth – level II: Riders (both genders) from 16 to 17 years old.

  (PFHA – Constitution and Rule book, Chapter Three, Section I, Subsection A, 7, a).

  The attire for riders is the official Paso Fino show costume *(PFHA – Constitution and Rule book, Chapter Three, Section I, Subsection B, 2, i)*. This attire consists of a bolero type jacket with long sleeves, a shirt or blouse, and full length riding pants or jumpsuit, that covers the boots, all in a conservative color. A matching or contrasting cummerbund is optional. Male riders wear an unadorned tie. This attire is completed with a Spanish type hat (made of felt, leather or suede) with a flat and round crown and a flat or slightly rolled brim. The hat must have a matching or contrasting hatband *(PFHA – Constitution and Rule book, Chapter Two, Section VII, Subsection I, 1)*. However, riders 12 years of age and under must wear safety headgear (helmet) *(PFHA – Constitution and Rule book, Chapter Two, Section VII, Subsection I, 3)*. Wearing chaps and half chaps is not allowed.

Once the contestant duos (a duo is a rider and a horse) pass the entry gate of the show ring at a Paso Corto gait, they turn to the right and keep working next to the rail, one behind the other, with the rail at their right side (counterclockwise manner). They change direction (by a reverse toward the center of the ring) or gait only when they are asked. The sequence of gait is Paso Corto, Paso Largo, Walk, Reverse, and repeat. One halt, at a minimum, will be asked during Paso Corto motion. In addition, for safety, any rider who is unable to control his/her horse will be excused *(PFHA – Constitution and Rule book, Chapter Three, Section I, Subsection B, 2, h).*

Judges may ask the riders to perform two or more additional tests, individually, in order to compare their riding skills. The tests available are listed below *(PFHA – Constitution and Rule book, Chapter Three, Section I, Subsection B, 2, g and h)*:

- Riding without stirrups at Paso Corto, while maintaining proper body posture. If desired, the rider may cross the stirrups over the saddle pommel.
- Backing up the horse smoothly and under control. The horse must keep its mouth closed, and head quiet, while backing up.
- Dismounting and mounting properly. Before mounting, the rider must check and adjust (if necessary) the bit's curb chain and girth.
- Performing one figure eight at Paso Corto.
- Making a transition from Paso Largo to Walk on a quiet rein.
- Answering some questions about the parts of the horse and tack, according to the names given in the *PFHA - Constitution and Rule book.*

Junior youth riders (from 13 to 17 years old) may be asked to perform any of these tests. However, sub-junior youth riders (from 7 to 12 years old) may be asked to perform tests only from the following list: backing up, making a transition from Paso Largo to Walk on a quiet rein, and answering questions about the parts of the horse and tack *(PFHA – Constitution and Rule book, Chapter Three, Section I, Subsection B, 2, g and h, (1)).*

Based on the skills of the riders, each judge fills out the judging charts for the class. Thereafter, the speaker announces the numbers and names of the riders placed, while they are awarded their respective ribbons.

The ribbons given to riders who place in the class are as follows:

- First place: Blue ribbon.
- Second place: Red ribbon.
- Third place: Yellow ribbon.
- Fourth place: White ribbon.
- Fifth place: Pink ribbon.
- Sixth place: Green ribbon.

Above, Jessica Varney, a student of Ocala's School of Equestrian Art, riding her Paso Performance mare, "India de Calidad" (Ponderosa Coloso x Katiuskita de Calidad).
Photo donated by WNC Photography.
In her short show career, Jessica has received numerous awards by ***PFHA.*** *In* ***2005****: National Champion Horsemanship and Reserve National Champion Equitation Sub-Jr. Youth Level I. Hi-point Youth and Sub-Jr. Youth of the Year. Hi-point Sub-Jr. of the National Show. Hi-point Classic Fino, Performance, Equitation, and Horsemanship Sub-Jr. Youth of the Year. Hi-point Equitation and Horsemanship Sub-Jr. Youth Level I of the Year.*
In ***2006****: Reserve National Champion Horsemanship Sub-Jr. Youth Level II. Hi-point Youth and Sub-Jr. Youth of the Year. Hi-point Classic Fino, Performance, Pleasure, Equitation, and Horsemanship Sub-Jr. Youth of the Year. Hi-point Equitation and Horsemanship Sub-Jr. Youth Level II of the Year.*

Right, Lysandra Venegas-Singer, a student of Ocala's School of Equestrian Art, riding the Paso Performance mare, "La Biblia de la Esperanza" (Capuchino x Amarrosa de Vuelta Grande), owned by Diana Venegas and Lysandra Venegas-Singer.
Photo donated by WNC Photography.
In ***2006****, her first show year, Lysandra was awarded by* ***PFHA*** *Hi-point Equitation Jr. Youth and Hi-point Horsemanship Jr. Youth of the Year.*

- ***CONFEPASO* equitation shows**: Riders may compete on any Paso horse breed: Paso Fino, Colombian Pure Trocha, Colombian Collected Trote and Galope, or Colombian Trocha and Collected Galope. The horse should have the tack required by *CONFEPASO (Reglamento de Competencias para Amazonas y Jinetes en Equitación – CONFEPASO, Chapter IV, Article 28).*

Note: The tack required for showing in *PFHA* and *CONFEPASO* sanctioned shows is described in Chapter 13: "Tack and attire."

There are 12 different equitation show categories according to the age and gender of the riders as follows:

- Category 1: Girls from 4 to under 6 years old.
- Category 2: Boys from 4 to under 6 years old.
- Category 3: Girls from 6 to 8 years old.
- Category 4: Boys from 6 to 8 years old.
- Category 5: Girls from 9 to 11 years old.
- Category 6: Boys from 9 to 11 years old.
- Category 7: Girls from 12 to 14 years old.
- Category 8: Boys from 12 to 14 years old.
- Category 9: Girls from 15 to 17 years old.
- Category 10: Boys from 15 to 17 years old.
- Category 11: Women from 18 to 24 years old.
- Category 12: Men from 18 to 24 years old.

(Reglamento de Competencias para Amazonas y Jinetes en Equitación – CONFEPASO, Chapter V, Article 29).

The attire for the riders includes dark color leather boots, black or dark blue pants, and a white shirt with a collar and long sleeves. Wearing a black or dark blue vest, a short jacket (also called bolero jacket), or a full length jacket is optional. All riders under 12 years of age must wear safety headgear (helmet). Riders 12 years of age or older wear a white or beige straw hat with a black or white hatband. Wearing zamarros (Colombian chaps) is not allowed *(Reglamento de Competencias para Amazonas y Jinetes en Equitación – CONFEPASO, Chapter IV, Article 20, from A to G)*. Wearing chaps, half chaps, or zamarros (Colombian chaps) is not allowed because they obscure the rider's legs.

Contestants over 12 years of age must complete a written theoretical test prior to the competition. This test is designed and reviewed by the judges, based on the rules *(Reglamento de Competencias para Amazonas y Jinetes en Equitación – CONFEPASO, Chapter V, Article 30 "Pruebas Obligatorias," Section 1)*. Failing the test causes a contestant to be eliminated *(Reglamento de Competencias para Amazonas y Jinetes en Equitación – CONFEPASO, Chapter VI, Article 39, Section H)*.

Each contestant duo (rider and horse) must perform an individual presentation of up to three minutes *(Reglamento de Competencias para Amazonas y Jinetes en Equitación – CONFEPASO, Chapter VI, Article 35)*. The other contestants wait for their turn. The exercises of the individual presentation are as follows:

- **Figure Eight**: For this exercise, the show ring has two cylindrical posts (10 cm. = 4 inches of diameter and 2 m. = 6 ½ feet height) distanced 3 m. (about 10 feet), one from the other. The contestant duo must perform three full figure eights as follows:

  The duo enters the posts from the center of the show ring (facing the rail) and performs two full figure eights; thereafter, the duo turns by circling the post furthest from the last turn, changes direction by going from one post to the other, performs one more figure eight (by entering the posts from the rail side), and stops in the middle of the posts, while facing the center of the show ring *(Reglamento de Competencias para Amazonas y Jinetes en Equitación – CONFEPASO, Chapter V, Article 30 "Pruebas Obligatorias," Section 2)*. If the rider is competing either on a Colombian Collected Trote and Galope or a Colombian Trocha and Collected Galope horse, the third figure eight (which comes after changing direction) must be performed in Galope.

- **Back up**: After stopping in the middle of the posts, the contestant duo must back up straight for four to six steps (at the rider's discretion). The contestant will be penalized if, while backing up, the horse does not perform a straight line, moves its head excessively or opens its mouth. Likewise, the contestant will be penalized if the horse does not back up with diagonal movement of the legs or if the hooves are not raised from the ground and placed back again *(Reglamento de Competencias para Amazonas y Jinetes en Equitación – CONFEPASO, Chapter V, Article 30 "Pruebas Obligatorias," Section 3)*.

- **Serpentine**: For this exercise, the show ring has two parallel lines with three to four marks (such as cones) at each line. All the cones are evenly distanced 3 m. (about 10 feet). The contestant duo must go between the cones by combining straight lines (while moving from one line of cones to the other) and semi-circles around each cone (while changing direction to move toward the opposite line of cones). The contestant duo must perform the full serpentine in both directions. However, if the rider is competing either on a Colombian Collected Trote and Galope or a Colombian Trocha and Collected Galope horse, the second serpentine (in a reverse direction of the first serpentine) must be performed in Galope *(Reglamento de Competencias para Amazonas y Jinetes en Equitación – CONFEPASO, Chapter V, Article 30 "Pruebas Obligatorias," Section 4)*. See drawing below.

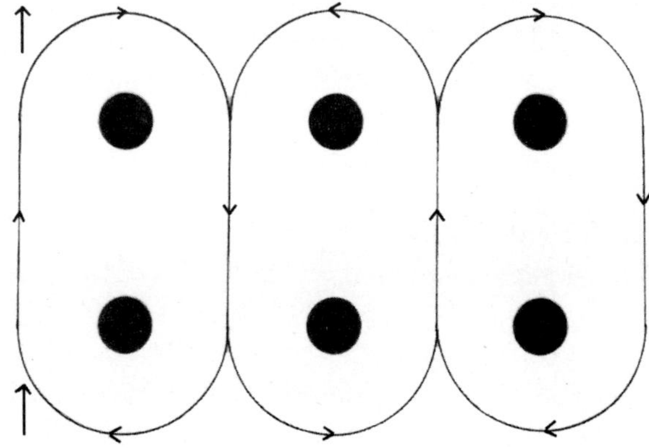

- **Sounding board**: For this exercise, the show ring has a board made of wood planks (or slats) from 15 m. (about 49 feet) to 20 m. (about 65 feet) long and 2 m. (about 6 ½ feet) wide. The contestant duo must pass over the sounding board straight, centered, and in gait in one direction, reverse in a circle outside of the sounding board, and pass over the sounding board in the opposite direction. If the rider is competing either on a Colombian Collected Trote and Galope or a Colombian Trocha and Collected Galope horse, the second time passing over the sounding board must be performed in Galope. The sounding board lets judges listen to the sound made by the horse's hooves to confirm the rhythm of the horse's gait *(Reglamento de Competencias para Amazonas y Jinetes en Equitación – CONFEPASO, Chapter V, Article 30 "Pruebas Obligatorias," Section 5).*

  While each contestant duo performs the figure eight during the individual presentation, the announcer states the rider's name and age, information related to the school, city or country that the contestant duo is representing, and some information about the horse (name, color, gait, and owner).

After all contestant duos have performed the individual presentation, judges may ask contestants with tie scores to perform one or more tests from the following list:

- Halting the horse properly and gently, and restarting in gait when the judges indicate. This is commonly done on the sounding board.
- Switching horses with another contestant.
- Turning around ("reverse") toward the center of the show ring.
- Working on circles (3 m. = 10 feet diameter at a minimum) in each direction.
- Dismounting and mounting.
- Un-tacking and tacking up the horse.

(Reglamento de Competencias para Amazonas y Jinetes en Equitación – CONFEPASO, Chapter V, Article 30 "Pruebas Opcionales o de Dificultad").

Based on the rider's skills, each judge fills out the judging chart for the class and takes it to the computation table, where the average is calculated. Based on the final results, one judge explains the class and places the riders. While the riders receive their medals and/or ribbons, the announcer repeats the names and other important information of the riders and horses placed in the class.

The awards given to the riders who placed in the class are as follows:

- Champion: Gold medal and tricolor ribbon.
- First place: Silver medal and blue ribbon.
- Second place: Bronze medal and red ribbon.
- Third place: Yellow ribbon.
- Fourth place: Pink ribbon.
- Fifth place: White ribbon.
- Honorable mention to all other contestants.

(Reglamento de Competencias para Amazonas y Jinetes en Equitación – CONFEPASO, Chapter VIII, Articles 49 and 51).

Note: There is a Paso Youth Equitation World Championship (also known as *CONFEPASO* Youth "Mundial") every other year, held in a different country by one of the associations/federations affiliated with *CONFEPASO*.

CHAPTER 17

PURCHASING A PASO FINO HORSE

These days, millions of people worldwide enjoy many different breeds of horses and a wide variety of equestrian activities. The Paso Fino breed is rapidly becoming popular in many countries where, every day, more enthusiasts want to enjoy the amazingly smooth gait, brio, beauty, and gentle temperament of these horses.

Before purchasing a Paso Fino horse, the prospective owner should pay attention to several factors, related not only to the horse itself, but also to personal and economic needs. This chapter provides some guidelines for buying a horse that meets each reader's expectations.

LEARNING ABOUT THE PASO FINO BREED

At this point, the reader may have a general idea about Paso Fino horses, their special characteristics, and the amazing passion people feel for them. It is recommended that potential buyers dedicate some time for thorough research before purchasing a Paso Fino. That research may include the following:

- Attending several Paso Fino shows as a spectator.
- Taking Paso Fino riding lessons in order to learn about proper equitation, gait, tack, and characteristics of the breed.
- Visiting farms that offer Paso Fino horses for sale.
- Reading other printed material, such as the *Paso Fino Horse Association, Inc. - Constitution and Rule Book*; the *CONFEPASO - Rule Books* (for horses and/or equitation); and magazines dedicated to the Paso breeds. Some recommended magazines, among others, are listed bellow:
  - ***Paso Fino Horse World*** (English)
  - ***Paso Fino Report*** (English/Spanish)
  - ***Show Time Paso Fino - Equestrian Magazine*** (English/Spanish)
  - ***Conquistador*** (English)
  - ***Fedequinas*** (mainly Spanish)
  - ***Confepaso*** (mainly Spanish)

- Visiting the web-sites of farms and associations offering Paso Fino horses, services, forums, and products:
  www.pfha.org
  www.pasopedigree.com
  www.americanpasofinos.com
  www.pasofino.org
  www.pasoregistry.com
  www.ocalapasofino.com

THE IDEAL HORSE FOR THE PURPOSE

Depending on how a Paso Fino horse is going to be used, it must have a series of characteristics related to gait, conformation, beauty, temperament, and brio described as follows:

- **For show**: The *Paso Fino Horse Association, Inc. (PFHA)* and *CONFEPASO* include many show categories for Paso Fino horses of both sexes (including geldings) as follows: Classic Fino, Paso Performance, Paso Pleasure, Bellas Formas (Conformation), Paso Versatility, Paso Western Pleasure, and Paso Trail (see Chapter 4: "Unique characteristics of the Paso Fino horse"). In most categories, the horse may be shown either by an amateur owner, professional or youth rider.

  When purchasing a Paso Fino horse for show, the customer must first define what type of horse is desired by answering, at a minimum, the following questions:

  - For what show division (e.g., Classic Fino, Paso Performance, Paso Pleasure) will the horse be competitive?
  - What age and gender are preferred?
  - Who is going to ride in the show: the owner, a youth, or a professional rider?

  The Paso Fino show horse should have brio and the appropriate gait for the category in which it is going to compete (see The Paso Fino gait and Paso Fino show categories in Chapter 4: "Unique characteristics of the Paso Fino horse") and be very well-trained. The show horse should also be beautiful, healthy, with no defects, and have a good temperament.

  If the horse is going to be shown in the United States, it must have a valid Certificate of Registration issued by the *PFHA*. To compete in a *CONFEPASO* sanctioned show in the United States or any other country, the horse must be registered in an association/federation affiliated with *CONFEPASO*, including the *PFHA*.

- **For reproduction**: In general, most show horses may be used for reproduction (except geldings, of course). Additionally, some horses unable to compete due to injuries or chronic diseases (not genetically transmittable) may also be used for reproduction.

  Moreover, for the permanent improvement of the Paso Fino breed, ideally only outstanding Paso Finos having the best characteristics should reproduce. Such characteristics include excellent gait, powerful rear legs, brio, proper conformation, beauty, and good temperament.

Additionally, the horse must have a Certificate of Registration with good bloodlines (also called pedigree). Having outstanding Paso Finos in the horse's bloodlines (confirmed by genetic testing and parentage verification) is considered a sign of genetic potential to produce excellent offspring. Stallions and broodmares with previous offspring may be evaluated, in terms of genetic value, based on the characteristics transmitted to their offspring. The greater percentage of outstanding offspring, the higher the genetic value.

Note: Before purchasing, the horse's reproductive ability should be verified by a veterinarian.

- **For trail rides**: Paso Finos are wonderful and special horses for riders of all ages to enjoy on the trail. By reviewing their origins, it is easy to understand why Paso Fino horses are able to keep their smooth gait for long rides, even when the topography is mountainous. Most trail riders prefer mares and geldings over stallions. This is because mares and geldings usually keep their attention on both the rider and the trail instead of on the other horses, as some stallions do.

  The ideal Paso Fino horse used for trail riding must be smoothly gaited, firm stepping on any ground, docile, kind, well-trained, responsive to the rider's commands, and developed for endurance. Such characteristics make trail riding enjoyable and easy for the rider. Bad habits, such as aggressiveness (biting/kicking people or other horses), spooking, refusing, bucking, and rearing up are never acceptable for a trail riding horse. Neither having a Certificate of Registration, nor good pedigree, is important for trail horses.

- **For carriage driving**: The horse for carriage driving, either for recreation or competition, must have certain special characteristics:
  - Emotional stability: Horses that spook, or are impatient or "hot," cannot be used because they are not safe.
  - Docility: Aggressive horses that kick or want to fight with other horses are not appropriate.
  - Work disposition: Horses without spirit will not provide an enjoyable ride.
  - Although its gait does not need to be very smooth, the horse's legs must be sound and well-balanced.

Mr. Ronald Kilburn driving his Paso Fino, "Maximiliano El Sombra." Photo by Bravo Equine Enterprises.

Paso Finos may be shown in Paso Pleasure Driving classes of *PFHA* shows when offered. They are judged based on Paso Corto (30%), Paso Largo (30%), Walk (10%), appearance (15%), and manners (15%) *(PFHA – Constitution and Rule Book, Chapter Three, Section VI, Subsection F).*

- **As a companion**: A Paso Fino horse is ideal to keep as a pet if it is curious, friendly, and smart, so the owner may enjoy its companionship. For aesthetic purposes, the Paso Fino horse should have both beautiful conformation and color. The Paso Fino breed has a wide variety of colors from which to choose: black, seal bay, bay, buckskin, dun, blue dun, chestnut, chestnut with flaxen mane-tail, palomino, grey, roan, flea bitten, white, pinto, cremello, and perlino (see Chapter 5: "Colors of Paso Fino horses").

  The horse kept as a pet or for beauty does not need to be trained under saddle nor be well-gaited, but must have excellent ground manners. In addition, the horse does not require a Certificate of Registration.

Once clear about the type of horse to purchase, the Paso Fino enthusiast must decide on the amount of money to pay for this investment. At this point, the guidelines about pricing presented below may be helpful.

FACTORS IN PASO FINO HORSE PRICING

Three main factors are involved in pricing a Paso Fino horse: related to the horse; the market laws; and human emotions.

- There are many factors **related to the horse** itself:
  - The motions of Paso Fino that the horse is able to perform and/or the division the horse will be shown: "Classic Fino" horses have the highest prices, followed by "Paso Performance" horses. "Paso Pleasure" horses are less expensive than "Paso Performance" horses. "Trail" horses, that are not shown, are the least expensive.
  - The prizes (ribbons, points, championships, and special titles) already obtained in different regional, national, and international shows. A brilliant show career increases the horse's value.
  - Already proven genetic and reproductive qualities for producing high quality offspring: The best stallions and broodmares of the Paso Fino breed are highly valued. This information is based, for example, on the annual "Top Ten Sire" and "Top Ten Dam" awards given by the *PFHA*, and more recently "The Colombian Paso Fino Sire of the Year" ("El Reproductor del año de Paso Fino Colombiano") award given by *FEDEQUINAS* in Colombia.

    Thus, a horse whose pedigree includes outstanding, well-known ancestors commonly commands a higher price than one whose relatives are not famous.
  - The horse's sex (gender): When high quality Paso Fino show horses are compared in terms of price, stallions are generally more valued than mares and mares more valued than geldings. The outstanding "Classic Fino" stallions dominate the prices due to the many mares they breed to every season and the money they produce from stud fees. The price of outstanding "Classic Fino" mares, however, has increased over the last five years, because they are able to produce several foals every season by using embryo transfer technology.

    When the prices of "Pleasure" quality horses are compared, mares are usually more valued than stallions and geldings. The same is true for "trail" quality horses.

- Horses with good natural abilities, such as gait, brio, and temperament (kindness, fast learning, and work disposition) are highly valued.
- Well-trained horses have additional value, not only because they show their best qualities, but also because reaching such a level of training requires an investment of time and money.
- Beauty in terms of good conformation, proper size, attractive color, and grace usually gives the horse extra value. Show horses, and those dedicated to reproduction, must have natural beauty.
- Paso Fino horses over 13 years old tend to bring lower prices, except for outstanding horses in competition, or those being used for reproduction of high quality offspring.

  Some new Paso Fino enthusiasts think about buying young/green horses (between one and three years of age) in order to pay lower prices and learn from them. However, young horses usually are not fully trained (if already started in training), which means that there is still uncertainty about the horse's final abilities. In addition, with some exceptions, young horses usually need to be "finished" in training by professional trainers, which not only may increase their final costs, but often take longer for owners to ride them. Therefore, if the main idea is to ride the horse for fun, a fully trained horse, even one considered mature, may be the best option.

- Because Paso Fino horses are considered goods and investments, their prices are affected by the **market laws** of "supply" and "demand" as follows:
  - Horse prices drop when the supply is high (many Paso Finos for sale in the market at the same time) and the demand is low (very few customers buying horses).
  - Horse prices rise when there is a low supply (very few Paso Finos for sale in the market) and their demand is high (many customers buying horses).
  - Horse prices are steady when supply (horses for sale) and demand (customers buying horses) are even.
- Paso Fino horses are more than goods for many people; they also affect complex **human emotions** which, in turn, affect horse pricing. A happy owner may place a high price on a horse due to the positive things it has brought to his/her life. For example, the owner may be very proud of the many prizes the horse has obtained, feel rewarded about the good times the horse has provided, or may just feel "love" for the horse. These, and many other human emotions, encourage an owner either to refuse to sell the horse or to raise the price. On the other hand, an enthusiast may agree to pay any price for a Paso Fino horse simply because he/she has fallen in love with that horse and can afford it.

ONGOING HORSE NEEDS AND EXPENSES

Purchasing a Paso Fino horse is certainly a great experience for a person who wants to enjoy such a wonderful breed. Any horse, however, has some regular needs, and corresponding expenses, that should be considered prior to purchase.

A horse needs a place to live (stall, pasture, or corral) and someone who feeds, grooms, and takes care of it everyday. Does the new horse's owner have a farm? Is the owner going to take care of the horse? If not, is the owner paying somebody else to do it or paying for boarding the horse?

A horse needs everyday supplies, such as feed (hay, grain, minerals, vitamins, salt), bedding material (if in a stall), etc., and some periodic supplies, such as grooming implements, dewormers, vaccines, and drugs. Additionally, the horse needs proper tack for both daily handling and riding.

A veterinarian must be contacted for assistance, related to both the horse's health care program and any possible sickness. A farrier should be contacted to take care of the horse's hooves, by either trimming or shoeing them. An equine dentist (who may also be a veterinarian) should assure that the horse's teeth and bite are in good condition and are well-aligned. In addition, if the horse requires training/exercising, and the owner is not able to do this regularly, the horse may require the services of a professional trainer.

PREVIOUS INSPECTION AND TESTS REQUIRED

When the right Paso Fino horse is found, and price and payment are agreed upon, the prospective owner should arrange for a health inspection, by a veterinarian, usually contacted directly by the customer. The veterinary inspection must verify the following:

- Normal conformation, including observing that both sides of the horse are even.
- Sound legs, including bones, tendons, joints, and hooves. In addition, leg balance should be verified while the horse stands, walks, and performs the Paso Fino gait (in one or more motions).
- The absence of any physical defect, or if there is a defect, that the defect does not affect the purpose of purchasing the horse.
- Normal vital signs (cardiac and respiratory rates) at rest and after being exercised.
- Normal specialized sense organs (vision, hearing, and touch, at a minimum).
- Inspection of the mouth, ensuring that the tongue, bars, and gums are healthy and pink-colored.
- Good teeth, assuring that the six upper incisors fit perfectly with the lower incisors, and that they are not worn abnormally. The premolar and molar teeth should also be checked to look for sharp points that may require floating. In addition, the presence of wolf teeth or cavities should be noted.
- Possible bad habits, such as walking in the stall/weaving, cribbing, wood chewing, (see Chapter 9: "Facilities for horses") that affect the horse's health and/or the condition of the facility.

The veterinarian should ask the horse's seller and/or his/her veterinarian for the horse's health records. These records should include vaccines and dewormers given and the last Coggins test result. Although the Coggins is considered valid for one year, it is recommended that a new Coggins be drawn before the purchase. When collecting a blood sample for the Coggins, the veterinarian may take an additional blood sample for a complete blood analysis (see Chapter 10: "Health basics"). In addition, if the horse is highly priced, the veterinarian should take X-rays of its legs. Many veterinarians also like to make a gastric inspection with an endoscope.

When buying a stallion for reproduction, the veterinarian should make a complete inspection of its reproductive organs (external and internal), verify its libido, and provide a semen test that includes volume, concentration of spermatozoa, progressive motile spermatozoa, normal spermatozoa, and the semen's viability after being frozen. If the stallion bred mares during the last season, the veterinarian could verify its fertility.

When buying a broodmare for reproduction, the veterinarian should make a complete inspection of its external reproductive organs and its internal reproductive tract by using ultrasound. Additionally, obtaining reproduction records, and seeing live offspring, will give the buyer a better idea of the mare's potential as a broodmare.

OTHER RECOMMENDATIONS

- To guarantee the best quality when purchasing a Paso Fino horse, the new enthusiast should look for good advice either from an expert or, at least, from somebody with good knowledge and greater experience with this breed.
- Never purchase a Paso Fino horse with quality that is lower than desired, neither for its bloodlines nor for its low price. Often, the owner will not feel rewarded enough with the horse to justify the monthly expenses.
- The customer should always ride the horse (if the horse is already trained) he/she wants to buy to feel both the gait and the horse's responsiveness. The horse should behave while being ridden by itself, and with other horses next to, behind, and in front of it.
- The customer should visit the prospective horse more than once, if possible; two visits will help the buyer gain a better perspective of the positive and negative aspects of the horse.
- Bad behaviors, such as shying, pulling while tied, biting, kicking, striking, refusing to turn to one side, and swishing the tail (see Chapter 15: "Horse psychology and training") should be discovered if it all possible prior to purchase. If the horse has one or more of these undesired behaviors, the customer should evaluate whether he/she can accept this, before making a final decision.
- A good quality Paso Fino horse is much more than great joy; it is a financial investment that may increase in value in the market, either as a show winner and/or by producing valuable, high quality offspring. The horse's owner may, therefore, wish to purchase a horse mortality/theft insurance policy in order to protect his/her investment.

Note: Except for the show classes, the same criteria should be used for purchasing a Colombian diagonal Paso horse (Collected Trote and Galope, Pure Trocha, or Trocha and Collected Galope).

CHAPTER 18

OTHER PASO HORSES

The expression "Paso horses" includes not only Paso Finos, but other gaited horses that share many common elements, such as origin, brio, smoothness, training techniques, and equitation. These include the three Colombian diagonal Paso horse breeds: Collected Trote and Galope, Pure Trocha, and Trocha and Collected Galope. Like Paso Finos, each one of these breeds has a completely natural and smooth gait from the day the horse is born.

Also like the Paso Fino breed, *CONFEPASO* (*Confederación Internacional de Caballos de Paso*) promotes, protects, and sets rules for the three Colombian diagonal Paso horse breeds and has show categories for each breed. The sport of Paso horses has two disciplines in the show ring; judging the horse and judging the equitation of the rider.

Even though the diagonal Paso horse breeds were developed in Colombia, South America, where they are amazingly popular for both showing and riding for pure pleasure, their popularity rapidly is increasing in other countries with associations/federations affiliated with *CONFEPASO*. Fortunately for the development of these breeds, most of these horses remained in Colombia for many decades, except for a few animals exported mainly to Venezuela. This favored the concentration of genes in each breed and prevented the loss of genetic material during that time, which made purification easier.

The Colombian diagonal Paso horse breeds were not very well known in countries outside of Colombia and Venezuela until *CONFEPASO* began celebrating a Paso breed's world championship every year in different affiliated countries, alternating a biannual Paso horse World Cup with a biannual Paso (youth) equitation World Championship. For example, in 2002 the 4th Paso (youth) equitation World Championship took place in Medellín, Colombia. In 2003 the 6th Paso horse World Cup took place in Medellín, Colombia. In 2004 the 5th Paso (youth) equitation World Championship took place in Caguas, Puerto

Rico. In 2005 the 7th Paso horse World Cup took place in San Juan, Puerto Rico. In 2006 the 6th Paso (youth) equitation World Championship took place in Kissimmee, Florida – United States. Others are coming up every year.

The general public of the United States saw the three Colombian diagonal Paso horse breeds shown during the 4th Paso horse World Cup - *CONFEPASO* (1999), which took place in Tampa, Florida. After that event, some of these horses were imported, although initially they could neither be registered nor shown in the United States, due to the absence of an association for that purpose.

This situation changed after the *American Trote and Trocha Association, Inc.* (*ATTA*) was founded in 2001 to promote the Colombian diagonal Paso horse breeds throughout the United States by registering, exhibiting, educating, and sponsoring several annual shows and clinics judged with the *CONFEPASO* international rules. The *ATTA* now offers support for the enthusiasts who want to be involved in the exciting sport of the Colombian diagonal Paso horse breeds in the United States.

ORIGIN

Although most current breeds of horses in the Americas were developed from the initial Barb breed, their differences throughout the American continents are caused by many factors, such as geographic isolation, variation of topography and living conditions, crosses made with other breeds, human selection for different purposes (such as developing new gaits), and different training techniques.

The three Colombian diagonal Paso horse breeds had the same ancestors and a similar developmental process as Paso Finos. Their ancestors were the several groups of horses taken to Colombia by the Spanish conquerors, during the first three decades of the sixteenth century, in order to expand their territory to South America. These horses were descendants of the Barb breed horses, brought to the Americas by the Spanish Conquistadors at the end of the fifteenth century. The initial Barb horses taken to Colombia were not kept a pure breed, but were crossed with other horse breeds, such as the Andalusian.

Although Colombian horses initially were developed for work, and as a means of transportation, some became very smooth and sometimes multi-gaited. Over time, the current four distinct Colombian gaits (Paso Fino and the three diagonal Paso gaits) began developing. Once outstanding specimens started to appear, their owners began to exhibit them in Colombian towns, in front of friends and horse enthusiasts, and during livestock shows. This was the small beginning of the horse shows in Colombia during the 1930's. These events, and the surging passion for well-gaited horses, became the foundation of many Paso horse breeder associations. *ASDEPASO* was the first Paso horse association in Colombia, founded in Bogotá in 1946. Currently, 25 associations of Paso horse breeders are affiliated with *FEDEQUINAS (Federación Colombiana de Asociaciones Equinas)*, the federation of equine associations in Colombia. In addition to work/means of transportation, and show, due to their versatility, these breeds may be used for many other purposes, such as trail riding, endurance competition, therapeutic horseback riding, cutting and team penning, carriage driving, dressage, and also for company.

"Electron de La Divisa" is a 14 year old Trote and Galope stallion, trained in Portuguese High Schooling (dressage) by William Sanders, the rider. In the photo, Electron is performing a "passage," which shows the versatility of this breed. Photo courtesy of William and Lynda Sanders (owners), from Norco, CA. Photo by Lynda Sanders.

In horse gaits, the word "diagonal" refers to the specific mechanics of moving the legs, in which each pair of opposite front and hind legs move in unison, or in a close sequence. Although most horse breeds in the world perform the "trot" (with diagonal mechanics), the Colombian diagonal Paso horse breeds perform the smoothest diagonal gaits. Their natural smoothness is due to the following:

- Many crosses of horse breeds over centuries.
- Hard work on the very diverse Colombian terrains, especially in mountainous areas.
- A long, strict, selection process oriented to produce very smooth horses to ride for long journeys, while performing beautiful and demanding gaits.
- Special training techniques that optimize the horse's performance.

BREED CLASSIFICATION OF THE COLOMBIAN DIAGONAL PASO HORSES

Although the Collected Trote and Galope, Pure Trocha, and Trocha and Collected Galope breeds look smaller than other well-known light horse breeds, they are not pony-type horses. Actually, along with Paso Finos, the three Colombian diagonal Paso horse breeds are also classified among the light horse breeds (see Chapter 4: "Unique characteristics of the Paso Fino horse").

Note: The light horse breeds have a height from 13 hands and 2 inches (137 cm.) to 18 hands (182cm.) and a body weight from 666 lbs. (300 kg.) to 1,666 lbs. (750 kg.). Their conformation includes a slightly narrow, intermediate to long body in proportion to their size and thin, aerodynamic leg bones. They are used for riding under saddle in all equestrian sports, traveling, cattle herding, and driving small and intermediate size carriages.

The three Colombian diagonal Paso horse breeds are smooth and very enjoyable gaited horses for their riders. For showing, a Colombian diagonal Paso horse must exhibit one of the coat colors allowed in the *CONFEPASO* rules: solid colors (black, seal bay, bay, buckskin, dun, blue dun, chestnut, palomino, and chestnut with flaxen mane and tail), grey/white, flea-bitten, and roan colors. Horses with white markings on these colors may have some restrictions in competition, as well as horses with eyes of different colors (see Chapter 5: "Colors of Paso Fino horses").

As with Paso Finos, the Colombian diagonal Paso horses in gait, either under saddle or not, should have their tail extended back, arched down, and kept steady with beautiful long hair hanging down. Additionally, when in gait, they should not swish their tails in any direction.

THE COLOMBIAN COLLECTED TROTE AND GALOPE HORSE

- **Standard**: The average height of adult Collected Trote and Galope horses (at five years of age or older) is 14 hands and 1 inch (about 144.7 cm.).

  The minimum height for showing Trote and Galope horses in *CONFEPASO* sanctioned shows is 138 cm. (13 hands, 2 and 5/16 inches) for adult mares (five years or older) and 140 cm. (13 hands, 3 and 1/8 inches) for adult males *(Reglamento de Competencias de Caballos de Paso - CONFEPASO, Chapter 4, Article 7, Section 3 "Alzadas Mínimas," Subsection A).*

  Note: 1 hand = 4 inches; 1 inch = 2.54 cm; 1 hand = 10.16 cm.

  The average weight of adult Collected Trote and Galope horses is 890 lbs. (400.5 kg.), but ranges from 730 lbs. (328.5 kg.) to 1,060 lbs. (477 kg.).

  The Collected Trote and Galope horses are slightly bigger (taller and wider) and more muscular than Paso Finos. Their heads are refined and moderately small, but slightly wider and more rectangular than a Paso Fino's. Their necks are preferably arched, very muscular (thick), and generally "swan" shaped (crest is longer than the lower edge) or "even" shaped (similar length of crest and lower edge).

  Although the Colombian Collected Trote and Galope horses may have luxurious and long manes, it is common to cut them ("roached mane") for show, pleasure, and work. This look makes them appear to have even wider necks. However, it is not a rule, and these horses may keep their long manes while competing.

The chest should be slightly wider than a Paso Fino's. The hips should be slightly longer, wider, and more rounded, but also well-proportioned. The stifle appears to be located slightly higher and more forward than a Paso Fino's, which makes the gaskin (portion of leg above the hocks) look more arched at the rear, when seen from the side.

The cannon and pastern bones are thin to provide an aerodynamic design for the gaits. The joints (carpus, hock, and fetlock) are very noticeable but firm. However, due to a slightly heavier body, the Collected Trote and Galope horses may have leg bones slightly thicker than Paso Fino horses, and hocks that are bigger.

- **Gaits**: These horses must perform both gaits, Collected Trote and also Collected Galope, depending on the rider's commands:

  - **Collected Trote**: Although the word, "trote" (pronounced /troh-tay/), may be translated into English as "trot," because of its unique smoothness and collection, this breed preserves its name in Spanish to differentiate it from other trotters.

    When any horse breed (such as Andalusian, Thoroughbred, Hanoverian, Quarter Horse) performs a trot, each foreleg hits the ground at the same time as its opposite hind leg (this is a diagonal) to produce a two-beat gait with a suspension in the air after each beat. This suspension between beats pushes the rider up, which encourages "posting" in order to have a more comfortable ride. Therefore, this kind of trot is known as a "thrown trot."

    A Trote performed by these Colombian horses is also an evenly alternated, two-beat diagonal gait (like a trot). One diagonal beat occurs when a foreleg hits the ground at the same time as its opposite hind leg, but there is no suspension in the air (or very little) after each beat. This means that there is always a diagonal pair of hooves on the ground, which makes Trote seem like a smooth, elegant march, and full of energy as the horse pounds the ground. A horse in Trote lets the rider enjoy a comfortable ride, seated on the saddle without "posting."

    The sequence of footfalls in Trote is as follows: right fore and left rear hooves are moved together (first beat), and then left fore and right rear hooves are moved together (second beat). For instructional purposes, the sound produced by the two beats may be described as "TAS - TAS," respectively (see diagram on page 308).

    Trote must be performed with rhythm, symmetry, energy, smoothness, and collection. Both diagonal hooves (front and rear) should be intermediately-to- highly elevated. The hocks should move back and forth with energy and elasticity. When the horse performing Trote is viewed from the front or the rear, it is easy to see the diagonal of each beat. A horse in Trote exhibits a cadence from slow to moderate, an extension of steps from short to moderate, and a forward speed from slow to moderate (see table on page 314). Although some horses may perform Trote with a quick cadence, and for a decade (from approximately 1992 to 2002) this was very popular and successful in the show ring, currently, the ideal Trote is not performed whith a quick cadence.

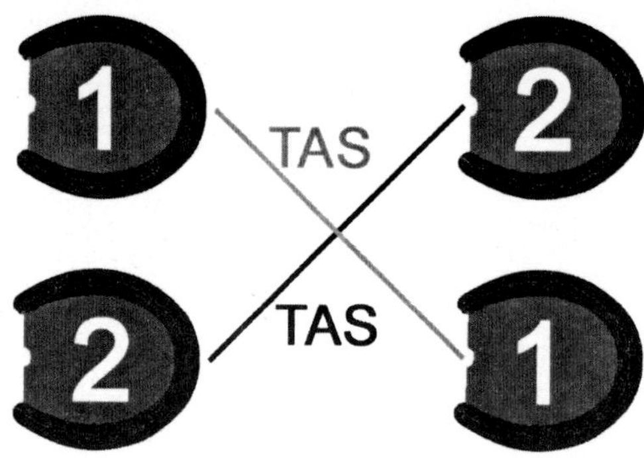

Sequence of footfalls in Trote

- **Collected Galope**: The word "galope" (pronounced /gah-low-pay/) may be translated into English as "canter," which is a smooth, three-beat gait that is very enjoyable for the rider. However, it should never be confused with "gallop," which is a faster, four-beat gait, performed by a horse when running.

  In Galope, a series of footfalls starts with one of the hind legs (first beat), followed by the other hind leg and simultaneously its opposite foreleg (second beat), and finishing with the other foreleg opposite to the first hind leg (third beat). For instructional purposes, the sound produced by the three beats may be described as "TA - **CÁ** - TA," respectively (see diagram below).

  Note: The sounds TA – **CÁ** –TA of a Galope gait are referred to in Spanish as CA – **TOR** – CE sounds.

  When a horse performs circles in Galope, its outside hind leg should start the mechanics of the gait, and the inside foreleg should end it, in order to lead the horse in towards the circle. If the horse, for instance, performs Galope turning to the right side (clockwise), the three beats should be as follows: left hind leg, right hind leg/left foreleg (together), and right foreleg. This is a natural ability that any horse does when it is free in a pasture/corral, which is practiced and improved during training in Galope. When the horse performs Galope in a straight direction, it will lead with either foreleg.

  Galope should be performed with rhythm, smoothness, and collection. The cadence is moderate, the extension of steps is moderate, and the forward speed is moderate (see table on page 314). *FEDEQUINAS* (in Colombia) has over 30,500 registered Colombian Collected Trote and Galope horses.

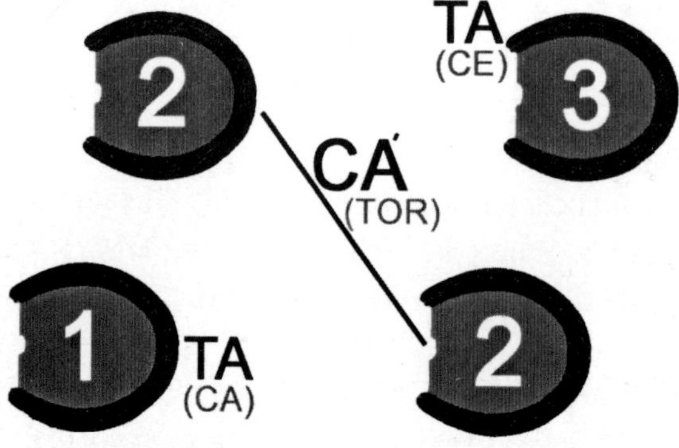

Sequence of footfalls in Galope

REPRESENTATIVE STANDARD OF COLOMBIAN COLLECTED TROTE AND GALOPE STALLION

Don Pepe *performing Trote.*
Rider: Ramón Elías Vargas.
Photo by Ada Barandica C.

Don Pepe *performing Galope.*
Rider: Mario Franco.
Photo by Ulises Muñoz

DON PEPE

** Multi-champion Trote - Galope stallion in Colombia (15 times Grand Champion) and in the United States.*
Registration number: 202,279 D (ASDESILLA)
Foaling date: 07/29/1998
Color: Bay
Sire: Monarca (Cónsul II x Cantinera)
Dam: Coqueta (Capricho x Copetona)
Breeder: Jesús Palacio (Colombia)
Owners: Aida Robles and John Jairo Galvis
Farm: Las Jotas Paso Fino Farm, Miami, FL
Courtesy of Las Jotas Paso Fino Farm

Above, "Emperador," a beautiful Trote-Galope stallion owned by Dr. Robert Anderson, posing for the photographer. Photos courtesy of Criadero Hidalgo, LLC. Jay, FL. Photos by Olga García.

Below, Olga García (the Author's wife) riding "Aliada de la Luisa" (Poema de La Luisa x Ansiedad de La Luisa), a Trote-Galope mare owned by Mildred Arent and Diego Bravo. Left, performing Trote; right, performing Galope. Photos by Bravo Equine Enterprises.

THE COLOMBIAN PURE TROCHA HORSE

- **Standard**: The average height of adult Pure Trocha horses (at five years of age or older) is 14 hands (142 cm.).

  The minimum height for showing adult Pure Trocha mares (five years or older) in *CONFEPASO* sanctioned shows is 136 cm. (13 hands, 1 and 9/16 inches) and 138 cm. (13 hands, 2 and 5/16 inches) for adult Pure Trocha males *(Reglamento de Competencias de Caballos de Paso - CONFEPASO, Chapter 4, Article 7, Section 3 "Alzadas Mínimas," Subsection B).*

  The average weight of adult Pure Trocha horses is 870 lbs. (391.5 kg.), but ranges from 720 lbs. (324 kg.) to 1,000 lbs. (450 kg.).

  Pure Trocha horses are as big and refined as Paso Finos. They also have plenty of grace, beauty, vivacity, and brio. Their heads are very refined and moderately small with a medium-length neck, ideally "swan" or "even" shaped. The facial profile should be straight. The mane has luxurious and long hair, which should be kept long. Short ears are considered better looking than long ears.

  The rib cage should be cylindrical. The hips should be muscular, rounded, very well-proportioned, but not very wide from one hip bone to the other. The stifle appears to be located higher and more forward than a Paso Fino's, as in Collected Trote and Galope horses, but the gaskin should be slightly more arched at the rear, when seen from the side.

  For aerodynamics, the leg bones should be as thin as a Paso Fino's or even slightly thinner.

- **Gait**: The Pure Trocha horses only perform the Trocha gait. The word "trocha" may be translated into English as "trail" or "path." This name was given because this gait was developed on the mountain trails of Colombia.

  Trocha is a four-beat diagonal gait, in which the four hooves move unevenly alternated (non-isochronic) as follows: a diagonal pair of legs move, starting with the front leg (first beat) and followed almost immediately after (1/30 of a second) by its opposite hind leg (second beat); about 1/10 of a second after this first diagonal pair of hooves hits the ground, the other diagonal pair of legs move, starting with the front leg (third beat) and followed almost immediately after (about 1/30 of a second) by the opposite hind leg (fourth beat).

  Due to the amazing quickness (cadence) of hoof beats when a Trocha horse performs the gait, at normal speed the human eye may only detect the movement of each diagonal pair of hooves hitting the ground. However, when a video of the horse is viewed in slow motion, it is easy to see the non-isochronic, four diagonal beats. The sound produced by the sequence of Trocha beats is best described as "TRAH – TRAH," each TRAH representing the sound made by each diagonal pair of hooves (front and opposite rear) hitting the ground (see diagram on page 313).

  Trocha must be performed with symmetry, rhythm, energy, and collection. In addition, the hooves must be highly elevated when moving. A horse in Trocha should exhibit a cadence from moderately to extremely quick, an extension of steps from short to moderate, and a forward speed from very slow to moderate (see table on page 314). A rider is smoothly carried by the Pure Trocha horse, without any side-to-side movement, providing a very comfortable and powerful ride in the saddle.

REPRESENTATIVE STANDARD OF COLOMBIAN PURE TROCHA STALLION

CONDE DEL VIENTO

** Sire of multi-champion Pure Trocha horses.*
Registration number: 141,930 D (ASDESILLA)
Foaling date: 05/16/1992
Color: Bay
Sire: Pregón de Pahuana (Fedayin de Pahuana x Veruska)
Dam: Chispa del Viento (Conde de Barro Blanco x Corbata)
Breeder: Hacienda El Viento
Owner: Carlos Agudelo
Farm: Hacienda El Viento
La Ceja, Antioquia (Colombia)
Rider: Walter Echeverry
Courtesy of Criadero El Viento
Photo by Ulises Muñoz

Note: The "representative standard" horses of the Colombian diagonal Paso breeds were selected by the author for their outstanding characteristics, including gait, conformation, bloodlines, genetic value, and show records.

This unique gait originated due to a combination of the following:

- A long history of crossing Paso Finos with trotting horses (such as Trote and Galope) in order to produce smooth, fast, firm, endurance horses to travel up and down the mountain trails of Colombia, especially from the coffee producing areas.
- Trocha became the resting gait of some Paso Finos when their riders asked them to go faster though the mountains, especially going down hill.
- After outstanding Trocha specimens appeared (such as *Petrarca*, *Candelazo*, *Rebelde*, *Arco* and *Tupac Amarú*, among others), breeders carefully began selecting and crossing specimens that only performed Trocha, which included the practice of inbreeding.

Currently, Pure Trocha is one of the fastest growing categories in the horse shows (exposiciones equinas) in Colombia, which is seen by the large number of excellent horses in the show classes and the many enthusiasts (several thousand) that attend the shows. *FEDEQUINAS* (in Colombia) has over 45,000 registered Colombian Pure Trocha horses.

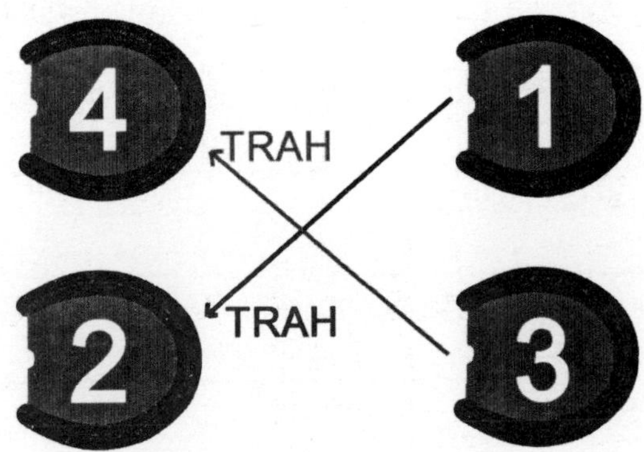

Sequence of footfalls in Pure Trocha

THE COLOMBIAN TROCHA AND COLLECTED GALOPE HORSE

- **Standard**: The average height of adult Trocha and Collected Galope horses (at five years of age or older) is 14 hands and 1 inch (144.7 cm.).

The minimum height for showing Trocha and Galope horses in *CONFEPASO* sanctioned shows is 138 cm. (13 hands, 2 and 5/16 inches) for adult mares and 140 cm. (13 hands, 3 and 1/8 inches) for adult males *(Reglamento de Competencias de Caballos de Paso - CONFEPASO, Chapter 4, Article 7, Section 3 "Alzadas Mínimas," Subsection A)*.

The average weight of adult Trocha and Collected Galope horses is 890 lbs. (400.5 kg.), but ranges from 730 lbs. (328.5 kg.) to 1,060 lbs. (477 kg.).

These horses must perform both Trocha and also Collected Galope gaits, depending on the rider's commands. However, the Trocha gait performed by a Trocha and Collected Galope horse may have a slightly slower cadence than the gait a Pure Trocha horse performs, probably due to their slightly bigger size.

The Trocha and Collected Galope horses have a very similar conformation, height, and weight to the Collected Trote and Galope horses. In addition, although Trocha and Collected Galope horses may keep their manes long and luxurious, they commonly have them cut ("roached mane") for show, pleasure, and work, as is done on Collected Trote and Galope horses.

The Trocha and Collected Galope horse is the newest breed of the Colombian diagonal horses because, for a long time, it was believed that the Trocha gait might be ruined when the horse performed the Collected Galope. However, *Don Danilo* (born in 1954, son of *Danesa*), one of the most famous and important stallions in Colombian horse history, was able to perform all the Colombian gaits (Paso Fino, Trocha, Collected Trote, and Collected Galope), and excelled when performing Trocha and Collected Galope, which led to the popular approval of Trocha and Collected Galope as a breed. After time, *Don Danilo* received the Trocha and Collected Galope "Fuera de Concurso" ("Outstanding in Contest") title. Currently, *FEDEQUINAS* has over 4,500 registered Colombian Trocha and Collected Galope horses.

CADENCE, EXTENSION OF STEPS, AND FORWARD SPEED

For better understanding, the gaits above are compared in the following table:

DIAGONAL GAIT	*CADENCE*	*EXTENSION OF EACH STEP*	*FORWARD SPEED*
COLLECTED TROTE	From slow to moderate	From short to moderate	From very slow to moderate
TROCHA	From moderate to extremely quick	From short to moderate	From very slow to moderate
COLLECTED GALOPE	Moderate	Moderate	Moderate

Notes:

- Cadence: The quickness with which the hooves move and hit the ground.
- Extension of the steps: The distance of ground covered by each hoof's movement.
- The forward speed: The speed at which the horse travels in a consistent gait.

JUDGING THE COLOMBIAN DIAGONAL PASO HORSES – *CONFEPASO*

Among other classes, *CONFEPASO* has different show classes for the three Colombian diagonal Paso horse breeds, and the Paso Fino, according to sex and age. The "lead-line" classes are for young horses (colts and fillies separated) from 18 to 24 months of age and from 25 to 30 months of age. Horses 31 months of age and older are shown under saddle (stallions and mares separated) as follows: Schooling horses from 31 to 36 months old and fully trained horses from 37 to 48 months old, 49 to 60 months old, 61 to 77 months old, and over 77 months old. Additionally, geldings under saddle of any age have separate classes according to gait: Bellas Formas Paso Fino (Conformation), Paso Fino (Classic Fino), Pure Trocha, Trocha and Collected Galope, Collected Trote and Galope, and Paso Performance *(Reglamento de Competencias de Caballos de Paso - CONFEPASO, Chapter 3, Article 2).*

Before each horse enters the show ring, a licensed veterinarian conducts a pre-entry exam to determine the horse's good health, ground manners, and the accomplishment of some standard parameters, such as a minimum height *(Reglamento de Competencias de Caballos de Paso - CONFEPASO, Chapter 4, Article 7)*. Issues detected during the pre-entry exam that prevent the horse from competing are listed below:

- When a horse refuses either to be examined or tacked up.
- Height at the withers is under the minimum standard for the category, according to the gender and breed for different ages (18 to 24 months, 24 to 30 months, 30 to 36 months, 36 to 48 months, 48 to 60 months, and over 60 months).
- Hooves that are sensitive to pressure made with a hoof tester on the soles, hooves bigger than allowed (see Chapter 7: "Hoof trimming and shoeing"), abnormal stepping, wearing pads inside the shoes, wearing therapeutic shoes, absence of one or more shoes (except for the young horses in the lead-line classes, which are accepted either wearing four shoes or completely unshod).
- Over-bite or "parrot mouth" (upper incisors more forward than lower incisors) and under-bite or "sow mouth" (lower incisors more forward than upper incisors).
- Bleeding from the mouth or any open wound.
- Missing two or more permanent teeth, except if those teeth were lost as a result of an accident. In that case, the horse is evaluated by the technical committee of the association/federation affiliated with *CONFEPASO* to determine if the horse is able to compete.
- Bighead disease (see Chapter 10: "Health basics").
- Blindness in one or both eyes.
- Deafness.
- Any deformation or defect of the ears.
- Bursitis (hard or soft enlargement) on the poll area.
- Sway back appearance.
- Genital abnormalities (both genders).
- Abnormal udder (in mares).
- Uneven or knocked-down hips.
- Any bone fracture or muscle atrophy.
- Tailless, dead tail syndrome, injected tail, foreign materials introduced into the tail, the use of rubber bands or other elements to pressure the tail to avoid swishing, tail with recent surgery that exhibits bleeding, recent scars or swelling.
- Swollen/enlarged areas on the legs, lameness, over-worn hooves, muscle cramping, Stringhalt syndrome, stepping on the toe of one or more hooves, severe leg imbalance.
- Two different colored eyes.
- Unacceptable white markings: pink skin (pinto, perlino or cremello coats); solid-colored, grey or roan horses with big white markings on the face and/or legs, as prohibited in the rules (see Chapter 5: "Colors of Paso Fino horses").
- Dyed coat, skin, mane, tail, or hooves.

JUDGING PROCEDURES

A warming up stage occurs at the beginning of each show class for horses under saddle, during which all the contestants work in the ring (in gait), one behind the other in a counterclockwise direction for two rounds; thereafter, they change direction (reverse) toward the center of the ring in a circle of 3 meters (about 10 feet) or less. Then, they perform two more rounds in the ring in the clockwise direction, and finally they pass over the sounding board *(Reglamento de Competencias de Caballos de Paso - CONFEPASO, Chapter 5, Article 3, Section B and Section K, Subsection 3, a).*

Horse breeds that perform two gaits (Colombian Collected Trote and Galope and Colombian Trocha and Collected Galope) must perform this sequence, alternating both gaits. During this stage, judges usually meet and talk with each other. They disqualify those horses that exhibit lameness or any other health issue, do not perform the gait being judged, or have any problem that makes them unable to compete *(Reglamento de Competencias de Caballos de Paso - CONFEPASO, Chapter 5, Article 3, Section B and Section K, Subsection 3, a).*

Then, judges separate and do not talk with each other in order to judge every horse performing individually, while the other contestants wait for their turns. The individual presentation consists of the following exercises in strict sequence: figure eight (three times – two figure eights in one direction and one figure eight in the other direction), stop, straight backing up (from four to six steps), serpentine (in both directions), and passing over the sounding board (in both directions) *(Reglamento de Competencias de Caballos de Paso - CONFEPASO, Chapter 5, Article 3, Section C and Section K, Subsection 3, b).*

If the individual presentation is not performed in the correct sequence, the rider forgets to perform one exercise, or the exercise is not complete, the horse will be penalized eight points and, in addition, the horse must perform the missing/incomplete exercise *(Reglamento de Competencias de Caballos de Paso - CONFEPASO, Chapter 5, Article 3, Section C and Section K, Subsection 3, b).*

While each horse performs the gait over the sounding board, the rider, judges, and audience will hear the symmetry, rhythm, and cadence of the gait. In order to assure that the audience easily hears the horse's gait over the sounding board, several microphones often are installed underneath the board.

The Pure Trocha horses and the Paso Fino horses perform all the exercises (except backing up) only in one gait, either Trocha or Paso Fino, respectively. The Collected Trote and Galope and the Trocha and Collected Galope horses must perform all the exercises in both gaits, either Trote and Galope or Trocha and Galope, depending on the case *(Reglamento de Competencias de Caballos de Paso - CONFEPASO, Chapter 5, Article 3, Sections D, E, F, G).* When each contestant is performing individually, the announcer provides some information about the horse (name, registration, age, color, sire, and dam), the name of the breeder, current owner, and rider.

After every horse has performed individually, each judge selects up to six horses (up to seven for Schooling horses and geldings). Those horses not selected by any judge are excused and retired from the show ring, after the announcer thanks their owners and riders for participating. Thereafter, the judges compare the group of horses selected with at least two tests, from seven optional tests, in order to make a better evaluation. The optional tests include comparing two or more horses performing gait one next to the other (parallel), stopping and restarting gait, performing reverse, performing figure eight, performing circles around a post, comparing conformation according to the standard of the breed (after the tack is taken off), and, as the last choice, the judges may ride the horses *(Reglamento de Competencias de Caballos de Paso - CONFEPASO, Chapter 5, Article 3, Section I and Section K, Subsection 3, b).*

Horses are judged for rhythm, cadence, and smoothness of their gait (24 points), brio and temperament (8 points), rear legs (6 points), front legs (6 points), and hip steadiness (6 points), all of which total is 50 points = 50%. They also are judged for training, responsiveness to the reins, and head-neck set (8 points), consistency of the gait (8 points) and harmony of the gait (8 points), all of which total is 24 points = 24%. Other qualities judged are phenotype (conformation) of the head, neck, chest, rib cage, back, croup, and height according to the gait/breed (14 points), leg balance (8 points), color (2 points), and tail (2 points), all of which total is 26 points = 26%. Total 100 points = 100% *(Reglamento de Competencias de Caballos de Paso - CONFEPASO, Chapter 5, Article 3, Section J).*

After the pre-selected horses are compared with the optional tests, each judge takes his/her individual results of the class to the computation table, where the average is calculated. Then, based on the final results, one of the judges explains the class and announces the judges' decisions *(Reglamento de Competencias de Caballos de Paso - CONFEPASO, Chapter 5, Article 3, Section K, Subsection 5).* After the judge's explanations, and while the horses are awarded their respective ribbons, the announcer repeats their names, other important information, and the places obtained in the class.

Drug testing and/or physical/rectal examination is conducted by a licensed veterinarian on all the under-saddle horses that are awarded first and second place in all classes, as well as horses randomly selected by the veterinarian, the show director, or the judges. The sample (blood and/or urine and/or saliva) and/or the examination is taken/conducted immediately after the horse leaves the show ring in order to detect prohibited substances used to enhance normal performance *(Reglamento de Competencias de Caballos de Paso - CONFEPASO, Chapter 6, Article 2, Section B, 1 and Section I, 1).*

The lead-line championship of the breed/gait for each sex (colts or fillies) is determined by comparing the two horses awarded first place (blue ribbon) in the regular classes (18 to 24 months old and 25 to 30 months old). The reserve championship is determined by comparing the first-place horse (blue ribbon) that did not win the championship and the horse that was awarded second place (red ribbon) in the class where the champion lead-line horse was awarded first place *(Reglamento de Competencias de Caballos de Paso - CONFEPASO, Chapter 4, Article 6, Sections A and B).*

The under-saddle championship of the breed/gait for each sex (mares or stallions) is determined by comparing the horses awarded first place (blue ribbon) and second place (red ribbon) in all the regular classes: 31 to 36 months old (optional, but the horse's owner previously should have notified the organization if his/her horse is participating or not), 37 to 48 months old, 49 to 60 months old, 61 to 77 months old, and over 77 months old *(Reglamento de Competencias de Caballos de Paso - CONFEPASO, Chapter 4, Article 6, Section C).*

The rider is required to wear zamarros for showing Colombian diagonal Paso horses; this is optional for showing Classic Fino and Paso Performance horses (see Chapter 13: "Tack and attire").

Note: For more information about the *American Trote And Trocha Association, Inc.* and the Colombian diagonal Paso horse breeds, visit the web site at *www.usatta.com*

APPENDICES

A. MINERALS AND VITAMINS: The following tables summarize information regarding minerals and vitamins, including their function in the body, common sources, signs of deficiency, and signs of excess.

- **MACRO MINERALS**:

These minerals should be part of the horse's diet everyday because they are needed in relatively great amounts. If they are not present in the proper amounts in forage and concentrate (feed), macro minerals should be added to the diet as supplements.

MACRO MINERAL	*FUNCTION*	*SOURCES*	*SIGNS OF DEFICIENCY*	*SIGNS OF EXCESS*
CALCIUM	An important component of the skeleton (35%) and teeth, thus highly needed for growth Required in muscle contraction Intervenes in blood clotting	Mare's milk Some green or dry forage (such as Alfalfa) Well-balanced concentrates (feed) Mineral supplements	Weak/deformed bones in young horses Slow growth rate Involuntary stiffness of muscles in lactating mares	Brittle bones Interferes with the absorption of other minerals (such as phosphorus and magnesium)
PHOSPHORUS	A component of the skeleton (14% - 17%), thus highly needed for growth Part of some metabolic compounds, such as *ATP*	Some green or dry forage Grains and concentrates (feed) Mineral supplements	Lack of energy Weak/deformed bones in young horses Weak bones in mature horses Reproductive problems in the mare	Nutritional secondary hyperparathyroidism
MAGNESIUM	A component of the skeleton and teeth Important for production of energy in the body	Forages Mineral supplements	Stiffness of muscles Intestinal spasm Irritability Sweating without reason	*Not reported in horses*
POTASSIUM	Electrolyte that helps regulate liquids in the body Maintains the acid-base balance	Forages Cane molasses Mineral supplements	Reduced intake of water and, therefore, reduced appetite Weight loss and weakness	Magnesium deficiency
SODIUM CHLORIDE (SALT) ***Note***: Horses should have free access to a salt block/brick (supplemented with minerals, or not).	Both sodium and chloride are electrolytes that help regulate liquids in the body Maintains the acid-base balance Chloride also is a part of the bile salts Sweat has a high content of sodium chloride diluted in it	Salt (iodized salt, sea salt, mineral salt, salt blocks, salt bricks)	Dehydration Reduced appetite Weight loss Weakness Low growth rate Low milk production	The horse rejects very salty food If the horse ingests an excess of salt, the water intake is increased If water is not present, after having an excess of salt, the horse may suffer a severe electrolyte-fluid imbalance that causes diarrhea and abnormal frequent urination, followed by weakness and death

- **TRACE MINERALS**:
These minerals do not need to be added to the horse's diet because the small daily amounts required are usually present in forage and feed.

TRACE MINERAL	*FUNCTION*	*SOURCES*	*SIGNS OF DEFICIENCY*	*SIGNS OF EXCESS*
COPPER	Involved in synthesis of melanin Helps utilize stored iron Helps formation of cartilage and bone	Forages and grains Cane molasses Mineral supplements	Contributes to the development of anemia Weak and thin bones	*Not reported in horses*
IODINE	Required for synthesizing thyroxine	Forages Iodized salt Mineral supplements	Abnormal reproductive cycle of the mare Hypothyroidism (goiter)	The same as deficiency
IRON	Takes part of hemoglobin (found in the red blood cells) that transports oxygen in the circulatory system	Forages Mineral supplements	Contributes to anemia after a severe loss of blood (due to hemorrhage or a large infestation of internal or external parasites)	May cause weakness of the muscle where injected in excess
MANGANESE	Necessary for the metabolism of carbohydrates and fats Leads to formation of cartilage in foals	Forages and grains (except corn)	Big joints and deformed bones in young horses	*Not reported in horses*
SELENIUM	A part of some enzymes Its function is associated with vitamin E	Forages Grains Mineral supplements	Muscular stiffness and dystrophy (white muscular disease) in newborn and nursing foals when the mares' diet is deficient in selenium during pregnancy and/or lactation	Cracking of the coronary band in the hoof Hair loss Blindness Death caused by respiratory failure and heart attack
SULFUR	A part of some amino acids Improves the coat condition when added to the diet in the proper amount	Feed high in protein Mineral supplements	Coat in bad condition	Lethargy Colic and convulsions Difficult breathing Death
ZINC	A part of many enzymes	Forages Mineral supplements	Slow growth rate Alopecia (a skin problem)	Copper deficiency Lameness

- **FAT SOLUBLE VITAMINS**

Although horses may obtain these vitamins from forages, young, growing horses, pregnant and/or lactating mares, horses in training, and horses of any age kept in stressful situations need the addition of vitamins to the diet, when they are not fed concentrates (feed) containing them.

FAT-SOLUBLE VITAMINS	*FUNCTION*	*SOURCES*	*SIGNS OF DEFICIENCY*	*SIGNS OF EXCESS*
VITAMIN A	Important for vision, growth, reproduction, and immune cells	Green plants contain carotene, the precursor of vitamin A	Reduced appetite Excess tearing Blindness at night Reproductive problems Low growth rate Low resistance to infections Dry/rough coat	Muscular weakness Depression Hair loss in large amounts and shedding of skin
VITAMIN D	Promotes absorption of calcium and phosphorus in order to build bones	Hay cured in sunshine Horses exposed to sunlight are able to synthesize Vitamin D	Low growth rate Rickets	Calcification of vital organs (e.g., heart) Weight loss Bone abnormalities Death
VITAMIN E	Required for developing immune cells	Green forages Grains (before being rolled) and plant seeds	Muscular stiffness and dystrophy (white muscular disease)	Toxicity has not been reported in horses Supplementation of Vitamin E works as a natural calming agent
VITAMIN K	Required for blood clotting	Produced by intestinal bacteria	Susceptibility to hemorrhage	Hematuria and renal failure

- **WATER SOLUBLE VITAMINS**

These vitamins do not need to be supplemented in the horse's diet because they are produced by the intestinal bacteria.

WATER-SOLUBLE VITAMINS	***FUNCTION***	***SOURCES***	***SIGNS OF DEFICIENCY***	***SIGNS OF EXCESS***
VITAMIN B1 (THIAMIN)	Important part of energetic metabolism	Produced by intestinal bacteria	Reduced appetite Poor coordination of hind legs Weight loss Weakness	*Not reported in horses*
VITAMIN B2 (RIBOFLAVIN)	Important part of energetic metabolism	Produced by intestinal bacteria	*Not reported in horses*	*Not reported in horses*
VITAMIN B12	Important part of energetic metabolism	Produced by intestinal bacteria	Although deficiency is not reported, weak and anemic horses often improve their condition after injections of Vitamin B12	*Not reported in horses*
BIOTIN	Improves quality of hooves and skin	Produced by intestinal bacteria Grains (especially corn) also contain biotin	*Not reported in horses*	*Not reported in horses*

B. RECORDING CHARTS: Following are examples of six recording charts.

CRIADERO CASA BRAVA – Ocala, FL (USA)
STALLION BREEDING RECORDS OF ______________________

Breeding date	Mare's name	Color	Mare's owner's name	Contact information	Breeding of method pregnancy	Veterinarian	Date to check pregnancy	Pregnancy diagnosis date	Pregnant (+) or Empty (-)	Next service date (if empty)	Second verification	Date of birth	Foal sex	Foal color	Length of gestation (days)

CRIADERO CASA BRAVA – Ocala, FL (USA)
SEMEN COLLECTION OF ______________________

Semen collection date	Temperature of artificial vagina	Volume of semen collected	Concentration of spermatozoa	% of normal, progressive motile spermatozoa	Number of doses split	Used fresh or way of preservation (fresh/cooled)	Veterinarian

CRIADERO CASA BRAVA – Ocala, FL (USA)
MARE BREEDING RECORDS OF ______________________

Breeding Date	Stallion's Name	Color	Stallion's owner's Name	Contact information	Breeding Method	Veterinarian	Date to check pregnancy	Pregnancy diagnosis date	Pregnant (+) or Empty (-)	Next service date (if empty)	Second verification pregnancy	Date of birth	Foal sex	Foal color	Length of gestation (days)

CRIADERO CASA BRAVA – Ocala, FL (USA)
HOOF CARE

Date	Horse's name	Work done on left foreleg	Work done on right foreleg	Work done on left hind leg	Work done on right hind leg	Farrier	Veterinarian	Trainer	Special notes	Next appointment date

CRIADERO CASA BRAVA – Ocala, FL (USA)
VACCINES

Date	Horses vaccinated	Product	Serial number of product	Laboratory	Diseases prevented	Dosage	Method of administration	Special reactions	Veterinarian	Next vaccination date

CRIADERO CASA BRAVA – Ocala, FL (USA)
INTERNAL PARASITE CONTROL

Date	Horses dewormed	Product	Laboratory	Active agent	Dosage	Method of administration	Special reactions	Veterinarian/ technician	Next deworming date	Next product to use

C. THE PHYSICS OF THE PASO CURB BIT

The laws of physics that explain the variables affecting the functioning of Paso curb bit are as follows:

- **The length of shanks**: Longer curb bit shanks are more severe on the horse's mouth than shorter shanks. Therefore, when longer shanks are used, the rider needs to apply less **force** on the reins to ´drive´ the horse.

A Paso curb bit acts as a **second degree lever** because the **resistance (R)** of the bars of the horse's mouth (the lower spaces on both sides of the mouth, between the incisors and the premolars) against the mouthpiece is located between the **force (F)** made by the rider's hands on the reins and the **fulcrum (f)** or support given by the curb-chain on the horse's lower jaw.

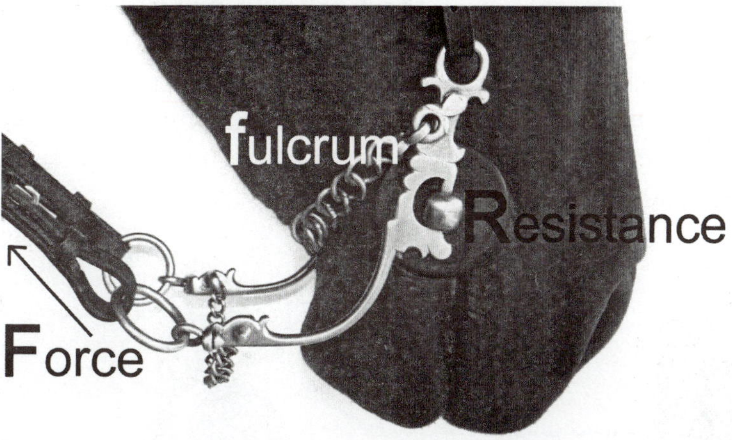

Once a Paso curb bit is in a horse's mouth and is activated by the force of the rider's hands on the reins, this force has the tendency to rotate the horse's jaw. The force's tendency to rotate the horse's jaw around the mouthpiece (which acts as the axis of rotation) is known as the "**moment of the force**" or "**moment**."

In Physics: **moment (M) = force (F) x distance (D)**

In the curb bit, the **force (F)** is made by the rider's hands on the reins, and the perpendicular **distance (D)** is measured from the mouthpiece (axis of rotation) and the line of action of the rider's **force (F)** upon the reins. The resultant **moment (M)** may vary by changing one or both variables (**distance** and/or **force**).

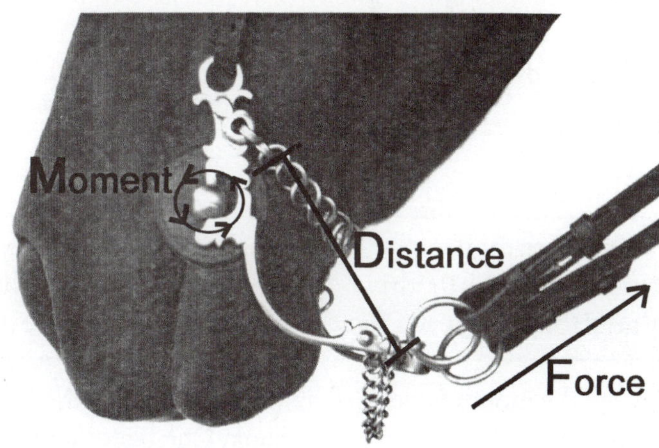

This concept is important in a study of the Paso curb bit because the magnitude of the **moment** becomes the magnitude of the force that the mouthpiece, ultimately, makes on the bars of the horse's mouth to cause pressure on them. Therefore, the higher the **moment** around the mouthpiece, the greater the pressure made on the mouth's bars.

In order to prove the effect of changing **distance** by varying the length of the shank's lower section, eight Paso curb bits were used in the research. Two bits represented each of the following four different types of shanks: "C-," "S-," wide-angle-, and chair-shaped shanks. The two bits that represented each type of shank had similar characteristics, such as weight, material, type of mouthpiece, curb-chain design and tension on the horse's jaw, but one bit had a longer lower section of shank than the other.

The results of the research were consistent. When bits with longer shanks (the lower section) were used on the horses in the study, the animals pulled the reins less compared to those times when they were ridden with shorter shanks. This may be explained with the formula **M** = **F** x **D**. The longer **distance (D)** provided by the longer shanks increased the magnitude of the **moment (M)** that made the mouthpiece cause greater pressure on the mouth's bars and, therefore, the horses reduced the resistance against the reins.

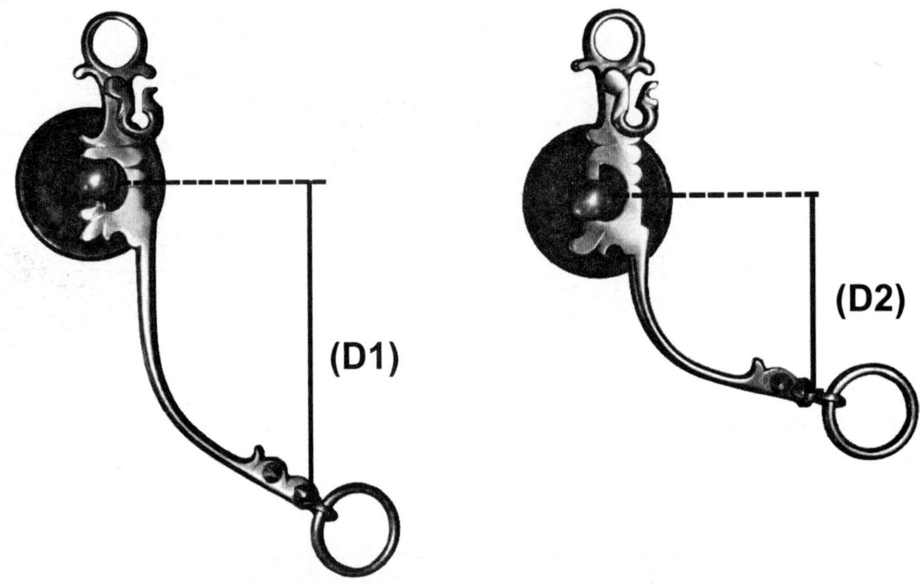

A longer shank (picture on left) gives a longer ***distance (D1)*** *that produces a higher* ***moment of force*** *(and ultimately greater pressure on the bars of the horse's mouth) than a shorter shank (picture on right) that provides a shorter* ***distance (D2)****.*

- **Tension of the curb-chain**: When the horse with a bit has the curb chain tightly attached, the rider only needs to apply light force on the reins to ´drive´ the horse. Conversely, if the curb-chain is loosely attached, the rider may need to apply greater force on the reins to ´drive´ the horse.

The **distance (D)** between the mouthpiece and the line of action of the **force (F)** on the reins is not necessarily the same length as the lower section of shank. One factor that may affect the final useable

distance (D) of the lever is the tension of the curb-chain. This may be seen by using the same bit on a horse, but adjusting the curb-chain with two different levels of tension. The horse pulls more against the reins when there is lower tension (when the curb-chain is attached more loosely) than when there is higher tension on the curb-chain (when the curb-chain is attached more tightly).

The explanation is simple. When the curb-chain is less taut at the horse's jaw and the rider pulls the reins back, the bit rotates back on the mouthpiece (the axis) until the curb-chain finally acts as a **fulcrum** (gives support). This causes the potential effect of the shank's **distance** to be lost, and therefore the horse is able to pull more against the reins. Conversely, when the curb-chain is more taut and the rider pulls the reins, the bit rotates back less (or not at all) on the mouthpiece because the curb-chain acts as a **fulcrum** more quickly, which keeps the bit from losing the effective **distance** of the shank, and therefore the horse is able to pull less against the reins.

This explains why the curb-chain should be tighter when a child (whose hands and arms are not strong) rides a horse than when the same horse is ridden by an adult with the same curb bit. This strategy compensates for the child's lack of strength by taking advantage of the full **distance** of the shank.

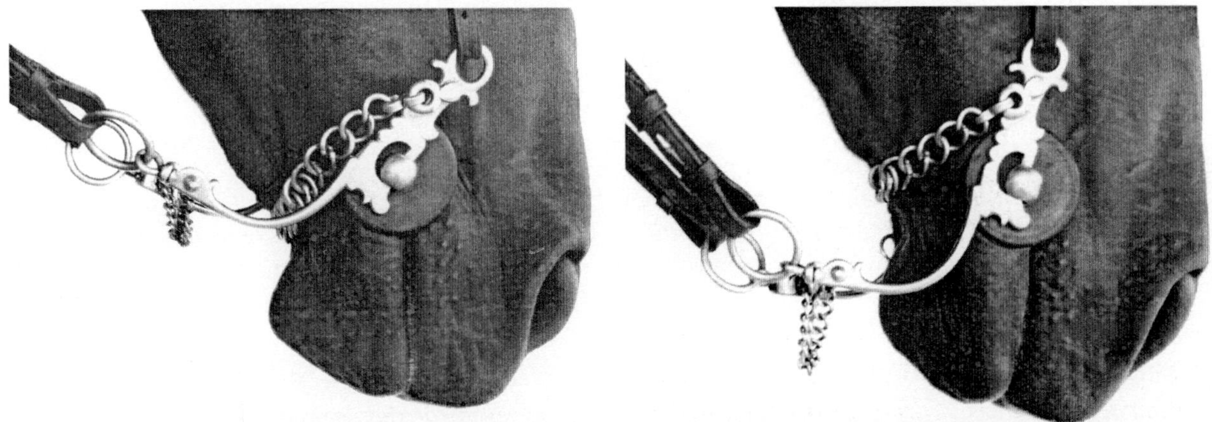

The tension of the curb-chain changes the potential effect of the shank's ***Distance****. When a Paso curb bit has a loose curb-chain (picture on left), this provides less effective* ***Distance,*** *and the horse is able to pull more on the reins. When the curb-chain is tighter (picture on right), this provides a higher effective* ***Distance,*** *and the horse pulls less on the reins.*

- **The shank's shape**: The shank's shape ("C," chair, "S," etc.) does not have a "magic" effect on obtaining a specific head set during the ride.

This theory was proven by using four bits with similar characteristics, such as weight, material, type of mouthpiece, length of shanks, and curb-chain design and tension. The distance from the mouthpiece to the rein's ring was exactly the same and so was the distance from the mouthpiece to the curb chain's hook. The only difference was the shape of the shanks: "C"-shaped shank, chair-shaped shank, wide-angle-shaped shank, and "S"-shaped shank.

No statistical differences were found in the horse's head position or pulling against the reins when each study animal was ridden with each bit. Based on physics, the effect on the horse's mouth is not caused by whether the shank is curved or straight, but rather by the magnitude of the **force** the rider applies on the reins and the **distance** (and location) between points of physical action (**resistance**, **force**, and **fulcrum**).

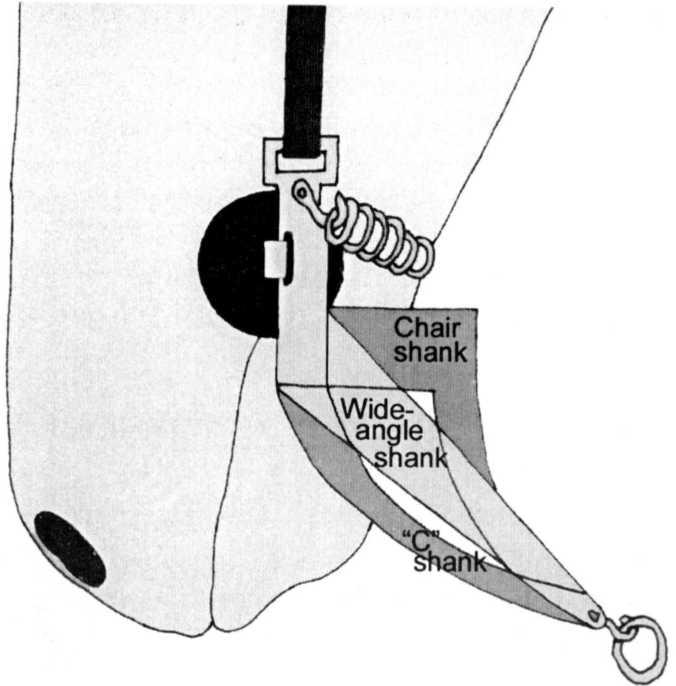

The shank's shape itself does not affect the horse's behavior in any special way. The three shanks in the drawing ("C-," wide-angle-, and chair-shaped shanks) provide similar pressure on the horse's mouth and head-set position, if the same force is applied on the reins, because they share the same points of physical action.

- **Thickness of the mouthpiece**: A thicker mouthpiece exerts less **pressure** on the horse's mouth than a thinner mouthpiece. Therefore, the horse with a thinner mouthpiece requires less **force** on the reins than the horse with a thicker mouthpiece.

The **pressure** on the bars of the horse's mouth, among other variables, depends on the mouthpiece's thickness. The formula in Physics that calculates pressure is shown below:

$$\textbf{pressure (P)} = \frac{\textbf{force (F)}}{\textbf{area (A)}}$$

In the Paso curb bit, the **force (F)** applied on the bars of the horse's mouth is the magnitude of the **moment of force (M)** made by the mouthpiece (explained above in "**The length of shanks**"). The **area (A)** is determined by the mouthpiece's thickness that is placed on the mouth's bars. The **pressure (P)** is the final effect of the curb bit, caused by the mouthpiece on the bars of the horse's mouth.

When comparing two similar bits that differ only in the thickness of the mouthpiece, the bit with a thinner mouthpiece exerts the magnitude of the **moment of force** on a smaller area of the bars of the horse's mouth than the bit with a thicker mouthpiece. Therefore, for the same **moment**, a thinner mouthpiece causes greater pressure on the horse's mouth than the thicker mouthpiece. In practical terms, the rider must be more careful and gentle with the force applied on the reins when the horse has a thinner mouthpiece in its mouth.

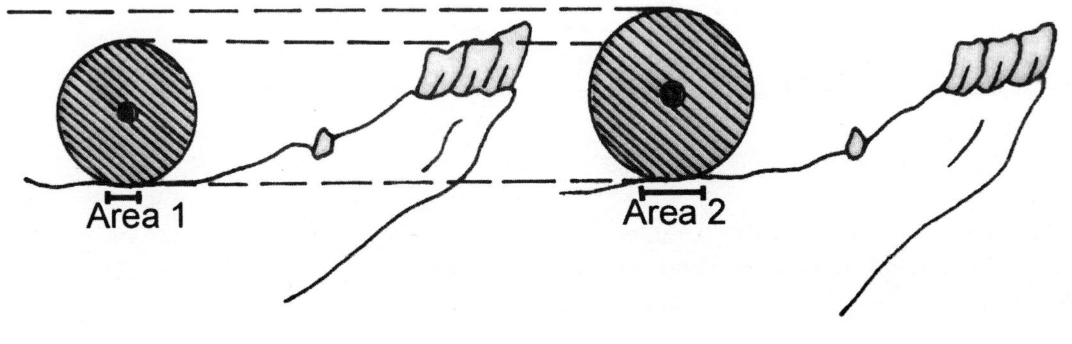

If:

$$\textbf{P1} = \frac{\textbf{moment of force} \text{ (constant)}}{\textbf{area 1} \text{ (of a thin mouthpiece)}} \qquad \textbf{P2} = \frac{\textbf{moment of force} \text{ (constant)}}{\textbf{area 2} \text{ (of a thick mouthpiece)}}$$

and **Area 1 < Area 2**, then **P1 > P2**

*A thinner mouthpiece distributes (divides) the magnitude of the **moment** onto a smaller surface of the bars of the horse's mouth (**area 1**), causing greater final pressure (**pressure 1**) than the final pressure (**pressure 2**) obtained when the **moment** is distributed (divided) onto a larger surface of the bars of the horse's mouth (**area 2**) made by a thicker mouthpiece.*

- **Position of the rider's hands**: While maintaining contact with the horse's mouth through the reins, the rider is able to affect the horse's head position depending on the position of his/her hands. Holding the reins higher helps raise the horse's head, and holding the reins lower helps lower the horse's head.

When the rider pulls the reins to keep contact with the horse's mouth, the **force** applied has a particular magnitude (measurement) and a direction. The **direction** of the **force** coincides with the reins' direction from the bit toward the rider's hands.

In Physics, the **direction** of a **force** may be split into two components as follows: the force's horizontal component (called "**Fx**") and the force's vertical component (called "**Fy**"). Depending on the **direction** of the **force**, either component **Fx** (horizontal) or **Fy** (vertical) may have a greater proportion of the entire magnitude of **force**. If the **direction** of the **force** is 45 degrees over the ground's level, **Fx** and **Fy** share even proportions of the magnitude of **force**. If the angle of the **force** is inclined less than 45 degrees over the ground's level, **Fx** has a greater proportional magnitude than **Fy**, and vice-versa. In addition, as the angle of **force** gets closer to zero degrees over the ground's level, **Fx** is increased.

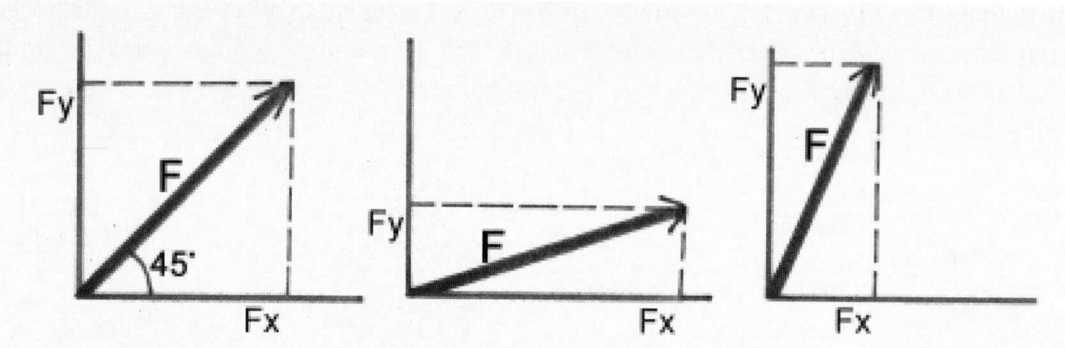

Therefore, if the rider lowers his/her hands while holding the reins, **Fx** has a higher proportional magnitude than **Fy**, which makes the horse's head set tend to be lower. Conversely, when the rider raises his/her hands while holding the reins, **Fx** is reduced and **Fy** is increased, which makes the horse's head set tend to be higher.

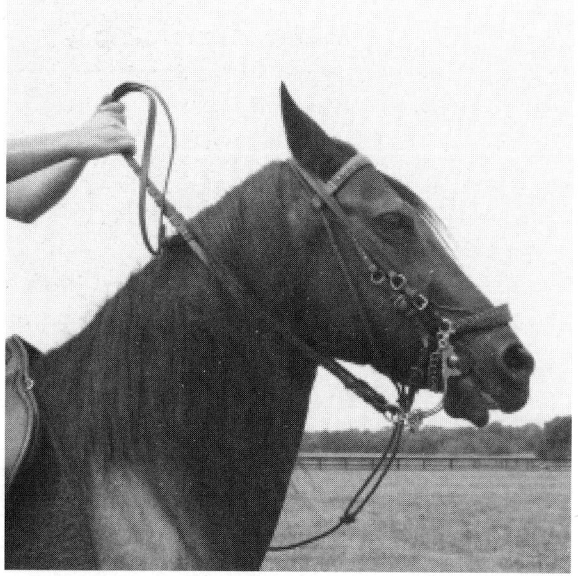

Holding the reins higher helps raise the horse's head

Holding the reins lower helps lower the horse's head

Notes:

1. The analysis through "Physics of the Paso Curb Bit" presented above is most applicable for riders with gentle hands who are able to apply proper commands through the reins to accomplish goals planned for the horse. Additionally, a good, lasting, and well-planned training process for the horse, as explained in Chapter 15. "Horse psychology and training," is needed to obtain the best results from the horse by using a bit.

2. Although the analysis is for the Paso curb bit, it also may be applicable to other kinds of curb bits.

THE HORSES ON THE FRONT COVER AND THE BACK COVER

Front Cover:

AMADEUS DE RESORTE CUARTO

** Multi-champion Classic Fino stallion, "Fuera de Concurso" ("Outstanding in Contest") in Colombia, sire and grandsire of outstanding Paso Fino horses in numerous countries.*

Registration number: 19,476 (PFHA).
Foaling date: 08/08/1983 (Colombia).
Sire: Resorte Cuarto (Resorte III x Cascanueces).
Dam: María Centeno (Mañanero x Pólvora).
Breeder: Agudelo y Vélez.
Owner: Silvana Cárdenas.
Courtesy of Criadero Agualinda
Rionegro, Antioquia, Colombia.

Photo by Alba Regina López "AlGalope."

Back Cover:

PROFETA SEGUNDO DE BESILU

** 2005 **PFHA** Piedmont Classic (Asheville, NC) Champion (1st place) Classic Fino stallion, 2006 **PFHA** Miami International Show (Miami, FL) Champion (1st place) Classic Fino stallion and Grand Champion Classic Fino stallion/colt.*

Registration number: 39,489 (PFHA).
Foaling date: 05/13/2000 (USA)
Sire: Profeta de Besilu (Nevado x Profetiza)
Dam: Manuela del Conde (Capuchino x Zaemis)
Breeder: Besilu Collection
Owner: Benjamín León, Jr.
Farm: Besilu Collection
Ocala, FL, USA.
Courtesy of Besilu Collection (breeder of two Classic Fino stallion World Champions). Excellence and Tradition is the Besilu Collection's motto.
This photo, and the photo on the back cover, with the author riding Profeta Segundo de Besilu were taken by Olga García.

SPECIAL THANKS

To my dear friend MILLIE (MILDRED) ARENT, who made it possible for me to move to the United States, a great nation, and encouraged me to write this book.

To JENNIFER MOORE and JANIS PAUSHTER, two friends who joined me during the process of writing this book as the editors, and worked with me to assure that the book was written in proper English. Thanks for the hundreds of hard working hours that you put into this book.

To my friends GLENNA STRUTHERS and SANFORD L. BRYGIDER, who offered valuable editorial and technical comments.

To my brother FABIO BRAVO, for his advice during the process of writing this book, and to my sister CECILIA BRAVO, for finalizing the drawings in the book.

To Dr. TIFFANY ATTEBERRY (D.V.M. – Practice limited to equines), for her advice on chapter 8: "Reproduction."

To Dr. THEODORE E. SPECHT (D.V.M – Practice limited to equines), for his advice on chapter 10: "Health basics."

To my supporters and sponsors:
CARLOS AGUDELO - Hacienda El Viento (La Ceja, Antioquia, Colombia)
ROBERT and REBECCA V. ANDERSON - Criadero Hidalgo, LLC (Jay, FL, USA)
JULIO and MARTHA ANZOLA (Ocala, FL, USA)
MILDRED ARENT - Ocala's School Of Equestrian Art
and Criadero Aristocratica (Ocala, FL, USA)
SILVANA CÁRDENAS and CRIADERO AGUALINDA (Rionegro, Antioquia, Colombia)
ALAN and LINDA CARRUS (Ocala, FL, USA)
ALLEN and JUDY BRICK FREEDMAN - Charlotte Valley Farms (Anthony, FL, USA)
JOHN J. GALVIS and AIDA T. ROBLES - Las Jotas Paso Fino Farm (Miami, FL, USA)
KATREENA HALEY (Gainesville, GA, USA)
MICHAEL HINGLE (Slidell, LA, USA)
JERRY and DEBORAH JACOBS - Ticker Time Paso Fino Farms (Auburn, IN, USA)
KERTRIN KOHLER – El Río del Zorro (Osteen, FL, USA)
BENJAMIN LEON, Jr. - Besilu Collection (Ocala, FL, USA)
DAVIS LOVE, III - Sinclair Farms (Sea Island, GA, USA)
JORGE MONTENEGRO - Galaraga Ranch (Dade City, FL, USA)
EDGAR and ALEI ORTIZ - United Paso Fino Show Horses (Summerfield, FL, USA)
JULIO and LORI PEREZ – Caribe Paso Fino Farm (Ocala, FL, USA)
JORGE and ANGELA REDONDO - Hacienda Los Angeles (Anthony, FL, USA)
KAY REEVES - Rosa Salvaje Farm (Troy, AL, USA)
VICENTE RODRÍGUEZ - Hacienda Culminante (Ocala, FL, USA)
WILLIAM and LYNDA SANDERS (Norco, CA, USA)
RUBEN SIERRA – Hacienda La Sierra (Summerfield, FL, USA)

ALLEN and GLENNA STRUTHERS – Pasos del Cielo Ranch (Anthony, FL, USA)
JORGE and MICHELLE SUÁREZ – Criadero 4Js (Summerfield, FL, USA)
RICHARD THOMPSON - Thompson Trails Farm (Reddick, FL, USA)
MIKE and TINA TRIPOLI - Adam's Grove Paso Fino Farm (Drewryville, VA, USA)
DIANA VENEGAS and LYSANDRA VENEGAS-SINGER – Royal Eagle Farm (Belleair, FL, USA)
MAURICIO VILLA - KUDA Store (Windermere, FL, USA)
LEE and MARGARET VULGARIS – Grassland Farm (Marion, MA, USA)
RANDY and DONNA WILKERSON - Wild Magnolia Ranch, LLC (Bonita Springs, FL, USA)
DALE and MARY YOUNCE - Brio Farm (Magnolia Springs, AL, USA)

To the PRESIDENTIAL PRESS SECRETARY OF COLOMBIA, for providing me with the photo of Mr. Alvaro Uribe Vélez, President of Colombia.

To C.J. MARCELLO, Jr., Executive Director of PASO FINO HORSE ASSOCIATION, Inc.

To ANA SALGADO, President of CONFEPASO.

To BEATRIZ SALGADO, Executive Director of FEDEQUINAS.

To BERNARDO VASQUEZ, President of FEDEQUINAS and Ex-president of CONFEPASO.

To SYLVIA DEAN and CARLOS ISAZA, for their patience and help during our long sessions of photographing horses.

This book was printed by INVest Impresiones, in March 2007.
Medellín, Colombia, South America
E-mail: investimpresiones@gmail.com
PBX: 238 63 11